THE ONE YEAR® CLASSIC FAMILY DEVOTIONS

THE ONE YEAR® CLASSIC *family* DEVOTIONS

INCLUDES WEEKLY ACTIVITIES FOR THE WHOLE FAMILY!

TYNDALE HOUSE PUBLISHERS, INC., CAROL STREAM, ILLINOIS

Visit Tyndale's website for kids at www.tyndale.com/kids.

The One Year Classic Family Devotions

The devotions in this book are taken from *The One Year Book of Family Devotions, Volume 2* by Tyndale House Publishers, ISBN 978-0-8423-2510-3, and *The One Year Book of Family Devotions, Volume 3* by Tyndale House Publishers, ISBN 978-0-8423-2617-9.

Designed by Dean H. Renninger

For manufacturing information regarding this product, please call 1-800-323-9400.

ISBN 978-1-4964-0255-4

Printed in the United States of America

21
7 6 5 4 3

January 1
GETTING FIT

Read 1 Timothy 4:6-13.

Ryan came inside after jogging a few miles. His face was covered with sweat. "Wash up, Ryan. Dinner is ready," Dad said.

After supper Ryan announced his plans for the evening—more running. Dad frowned. "You've been spending more than enough time training for the track meet," he said. "As a matter of fact, Son, you've been neglecting your other responsibilities."

"Yes," added Mom. "I'm concerned about your devotional life. Weren't you going to spend more time reading the Bible this year?"

Ryan looked down at the floor. "There's nothing wrong with wanting to have a strong body, is there?" he asked quietly.

"Not at all," Dad replied. "But a healthy body is only part of a complete person. In the Bible Paul wrote often of running races and training our bodies."

"He did?" Ryan looked up, his eyes wide with interest.

"Yes. He wrote to Timothy that physical exercise is important but that spiritual exercise is the most important," replied Dad. "Just as you work hard to get physically fit and build up your muscles, so you must work at living God's way to build up your Christian life. You need to practice such things as reading the Bible, praying, and telling others about Jesus. It takes hard work."

GET SPIRITUAL EXERCISE.

Ryan thought about his dad's words. Then he nodded and smiled. "Okay, Dad," he said. "I'll try to balance my devotions, chores, homework, and track."

HOW ABOUT YOU?

Is there a special activity that takes too much of your time? Perhaps you play sports, watch TV, or have a pet with which you spend your free time. Maybe you spend a lot of time with your best friend. Whatever you do, be sure you don't neglect your time with God.

TO MEMORIZE:

Physical exercise has some value, but spiritual exercise is much more important, for it promises a reward in both this life and the next.

1 TIMOTHY 4:8

BY LYNN STAMM-REX

January 2
STILL THE SAME

Read Psalm 119:89-91.

Dad just walked out on us. No reasons, no apologies, Andy thought. *I wonder why.* His mom tried to help him understand, but he knew she didn't really understand it herself.

One day Mom said, "Our house costs too much, Andy. We're going to move into an apartment. It will be a big change, but we'll get used to it."

Moving was not something Andy had planned on. As long as he could stay in the same neighborhood and go to the same school, he could pretend things were still the same. But now—a new school and all new kids?

Moving day came, and with it all the changes Andy dreaded. The only thing that didn't change was their church, but even there people acted differently.

In Sunday school one day, Mr. Robinson called on Andy to recite the memory verse. "I am the Lord, and I do not change," Andy quoted. "Malachi 3:6."

GOD NEVER CHANGES.

Mr. Robinson nodded. "Even if the whole world seems upside down, God is always the same," he said. "God loves us and will be with us, just as He was with Abraham in his journeys, with Daniel in the lions' den, and with Jonah in the big fish." As Andy listened to Mr. Robinson, he realized that God had been with all of His people throughout the changes they experienced.

Andy breathed a quiet prayer, just between himself and God. *Thank You for staying with Mom and me. I'm glad You're just the same as when Dad was with us. Please help me remember that even though things change, You will never change or go away.*

HOW ABOUT YOU?

Are you discouraged when changes come? The Bible gives many examples of people who had to learn about God's care during changing times. God promises to care for you in difficult times just as He cared for them.

TO MEMORIZE:

I am the Lord, and I do not change.

MALACHI 3:6

BY PHYLLIS I. KLOMPARENS

A SPECIAL GIFT

Read Psalm 122:1-9.

"I told you to get up long ago, Matt. Now hurry!" Matt's mother spoke from the doorway of his room. "We'll be leaving for church soon!"

Matt sleepily opened his eyes. It was so hard to get up in the morning!

The next time Mom checked on him, he was fast asleep.

"You're going to have to get to bed earlier," said Mom with a sigh.

The following day was Matt's birthday, and as soon as he heard his dad and mom get up, he jumped out of bed too. He threw on his clothes and ran downstairs.

"Hmmm," Mom said. "Strange how easy it was for our sleepyhead to get out of bed this morning."

"Today's a special day, Mom!" said Matt, eyeing the big box on the table. "Can I open my present now?"

Dad picked up the box. "I don't know, Matt. You don't seem to like gifts very much. You seemed to ignore one you got yesterday."

"*What?*" exclaimed Matt. "You had a gift for me yesterday? You never gave it to me!"

SUNDAY IS A SPECIAL DAY.

"Oh, it was given to you—you just didn't open it. And it wasn't from us. It was from God."

Sundays are a gift from God. He sets Sunday apart for us to meet with other believers and learn more about Him. But, just like any other gift, you're not going to get anything out of it unless you *open* it. You can only get the gift of a new day by opening your heart—and getting out of bed in the morning.

Matt smiled as Dad handed him his present. "I guess I'll have lots more gifts to look forward to after this one, huh?"

HOW ABOUT YOU?

Do you have trouble getting up for church on Sundays? Church is a gift, but it's one you have to *open*. Treat Sunday as a special day and be ready to see what gifts God has in store for you.

TO MEMORIZE:

This is the day the LORD has made. We will rejoice and be glad in it.

PSALM 118:24

BY LENORA MCWHORTEN

January 4

THE OLD MANSION

Read 1 Samuel 16:6-12.

"I can hardly wait to see the old mansion!" exclaimed Ashley. She and her family were on their way to visit Grandma and Grandpa, who had recently become caretakers of a large estate. As they drove, Ashley talked about her day. "There's a new girl in my class—her name is Addie—and her clothes are totally not with it!" declared Ashley.

"What does it matter if she doesn't wear the latest fashions?" her brother Aiden asked. "What she's like is more important than what she wears."

"Oh, you just—" began Ashley, but Mom cut her off.

"Aiden is right, Ashley," said Mom.

Several hours later, Dad turned down an overgrown lane that led to a large old house. Ashley frowned. "This can't be the right place!" she exclaimed. "This looks more like a dump than a mansion!" But when her grandparents welcomed them inside, Ashley could hardly believe her eyes. The floors glistened, and carpeted steps curved up to the second floor. "Oh, wow!" she exclaimed. "I can't believe how nice this is! The outside looks so run down."

DON'T JUDGE BY APPEARANCE.

"Yes," said Grandpa. "The place is being restored, but the firm that was hired for the outside work can't begin until next month." He smiled. "This house is a good example of why we shouldn't judge by appearance."

"We talked about that on our way over here," said Mom. "We sometimes forget that God says the heart of a person is much more important than how they look or dress."

Ashley looked around at the beautiful house and then out the window to the overgrown front yard. *Mom's right,* she admitted to herself. *I did judge Addie by the way she looks on the outside, and that was wrong. When I get back to school, I'll try to find out what she's really like.*

HOW ABOUT YOU?

Do you reject people because of the way they look? Remember, God says it's the inside that counts. Think about someone you know who's left out because of their appearance. Will you be a friend to that person? Do it for Jesus.

TO MEMORIZE:

Stop judging by mere appearances, but instead judge correctly.

JOHN 7:24, NIV

BY LENORA MCWHORTEN

January 5

GROWING TWO WAYS

Read Colossians 1:10-12.

It was time to measure again. José was eager to see how much he'd grown. For four years now, Dad had marked the new height on his closet door.

"When Aunt Carmen comes home from the mission field," José said, "she'll be surprised by how much I've grown!"

"Four years make quite a difference," his dad agreed.

José remembered the day Aunt Carmen had left for the mission field. He had just asked Jesus to be his Savior. Aunt Carmen had been so pleased. She'd hugged him when they saw her off at the airport. "You'll be practically grown by the time I come home," she had said. "I'll pray you grow to be more like Jesus, too!"

And now Aunt Carmen was due to return. José knew she would notice his physical growth. But would she see spiritual growth as well? He decided to ask Dad about it.

Dad smiled. "That's a good question," he said. "Now, let's see—I know that you used to have a terrible temper. Do you think you're controlling it better now?"

"I yelled at Nathan last week," José confessed. "But I apologized later."

GROW SPIRITUALLY.

Dad nodded. "I'd say that's progress. And what about those boys you've been inviting to church? I think you've made progress in helping others learn about Jesus. What about Bible knowledge? Do you know more about God than you did when Aunt Carmen left?"

José nodded. "Yeah. I've learned a lot in Sunday school."

"Then Aunt Carmen ought to be pleased—like I am," said Dad.

HOW ABOUT YOU?

Have you taken inventory to see if you've grown spiritually? Are you more friendly, kind, and loving than you used to be?

TO MEMORIZE:

Grow in the grace and knowledge of our Lord and Savior Jesus Christ.

2 PETER 3:18

BY RUTH I. JAY

January 6

DON'T HARVEST THE EDGES

Read Leviticus 19:9-13; 23:22.

Tony liked to hang around his father's repair shop and watch as Dad worked. One Saturday Dad was fiddling with a broken toaster. Finally he set the toaster down. "All finished," he said. On a card he wrote, "Labor, one hour—$10.00." Then he cleaned the toaster.

Tony frowned. "Dad, you counted wrong," he said. "I know you worked on that thing for over an hour, besides the time you spent cleaning it." When his father just smiled, Tony continued. "Whenever you round off the amount somebody owes you, I know you always make it lower, not higher. How are you ever going to make money that way?"

"Oh, I'm managing," Dad replied cheerfully. "I believe that if I give my customers good service and don't charge any more than I have to, they'll keep coming back. Besides, the Bible teaches that we shouldn't 'harvest the edges.'"

Tony looked confused. "Huh? I don't get it."

BE GENEROUS, NOT GREEDY.

"Well, in Leviticus God told farmers to leave some of their crop behind when they harvested it, so that poor people could take what they needed. I figure that the principle applies to my business, too. It means I shouldn't try to squeeze every nickel I can out of my customers."

"If the farmer did all the work, he should keep all the harvest," objected Tony.

"But it's God who gives us the strength to work, and He blesses our efforts," Dad reminded Tony. "You've got a good head for business, Son, but you need to learn to be more generous. Even if nobody else notices, God will!"

HOW ABOUT YOU?

Do you cheat others in little ways—skipping chores when you think Mom won't notice, doing a sloppy job on your schoolwork? Begin making an effort to do a little more than what is required.

TO MEMORIZE:

Some who are poor pretend to be rich; others who are rich pretend to be poor.

PROVERBS 13:7

BY SHERRY L. KUYT

January 7

DOGS OR CATS?

Read Psalm 104:24-31.

"Which do you like best, Grandma?" asked April. "Your dog or your cat?"

Grandma put Ashes, the cat, on her lap, but Ashes jumped right down. "Well, Ashes can be quite aloof. Dusty, on the other hand, always accepts my attention."

"I think I'd rather have a dog like Dusty," April announced.

"Both animals can teach us lessons about God," Grandma continued. She picked up a ball and threw it. "Fetch, Dusty," she said. Dusty chased after the ball, brought it back, and wagged his tail, waiting for the ball to be thrown again. "He wants to do what pleases me."

"And we should want to please God, right?" asked April, as Ashes rubbed against her leg. "What do you learn from your cat, Grandma?"

Suddenly a ball of gray fur landed on Grandma's lap. Grandma stroked the cat's head. "When Ashes does jump on my lap, it's special, because it's her choice to come to me," said Grandma. "Do you remember the robots we saw at the science fair that did whatever they were commanded to do? Would you like a hug from a robot?"

EVEN ANIMALS CAN TEACH.

"No," giggled April. "That wouldn't mean much."

"We aren't robots either," said Grandma. "God created us with a free will. He is pleased when we choose to come to Him."

"So your dog shows us we should want to please God by doing what He wants," April said. "And your cat shows us that God wants us to willingly give Him our love. But which do you like best?"

"I like them both," Grandma said with a smile.

HOW ABOUT YOU?

Do you like animals? God often teaches lessons through them. Treat all animals with kindness and watch their behavior. Maybe the Lord will use an animal to teach you an important lesson.

TO MEMORIZE:

All the animals of the forest are mine,
and I own the cattle on a thousand hills.

PSALM 50:10

BY V. LOUISE CUNNINGHAM

A New Start

For God loved the world that He gave His only begotten Son, that whoever believes in Him should not perish but have everlasting life. For God did not send His Son into the world to condemn the world, but that the world through Him might be saved.

JOHN 3:16-17, NKJV

The beginning of a new year is a good time to think about new beginnings and a fresh start. Jesus came to this world to give us a new start. We ask for His forgiveness of our sins. We invite Him into our hearts. And He offers us salvation and a new beginning. As you think about the new year this week, thank God for sending His Son. Thank Him for saving you and the world through this great love. Use John 3:16-17 to solve the crossword puzzle.

ACROSS

2. One who saves; a redeemer
5. The new beginning offered in Christ
6. We ask for God's __________ of our sins.
8. The opposite of death

DOWN

1. Forever or without end
3. Jesus died on the _____ for our sins.
4. Belief and trust in God
5. An act of breaking the law of God
7. Our world

ANSWER KEY

ACROSS: 2. savior; 5. salvation; 6. forgiveness; 8. life

DOWN: 1. everlasting; 3. cross; 4. faith; 5. sin; 7. earth

January 8

FOOD FOR THOUGHT

Read Psalm 139:1-5, 23-24.

"Mom, can we buy this cereal?" Stephanie asked, giggling at her mother's raised eyebrow. "Just kidding, Mom," she said. "I know this one has a ton of sugar." She replaced it with a different kind. Then, with a grin, she parroted Mom's often repeated words, "You are what you eat." Mom smiled.

When they arrived home, Stephanie flipped on the radio and began humming the melody of a popular song. But Mom turned off the radio. "The words of that song encourage a life that isn't pleasing to God," she said.

"But it has a nice tune," Stephanie protested.

"Listening to that kind of music is like eating food that isn't good for us. Our minds eat up the words whether we pay attention to them or not," Mom said.

As Stephanie helped her mom put away the groceries, she thought about how she often listened to the radio at Cheri's house. She and Cheri were usually doing something else while they listened, but she could still sing all the words to the songs they heard.

"We are what we think about," said Mom. "We need to fill our minds with thoughts that are pleasing to God so we'll grow spiritually."

FEED YOUR MIND GOOD THOUGHTS.

Stephanie put the box of cereal she had chosen in the cupboard. "From now on I'll choose music like I choose cereal," she decided.

HOW ABOUT YOU?

Do you listen to certain kinds of music or do anything else that encourages an unchristian way of life? What you hear or look at gets into your mind whether you are aware of it or not. God is pleased when you focus on things that help you grow spiritually.

TO MEMORIZE:

Then the Spirit of the LORD came upon me, and he told me to say, "This is what the LORD says to the people of Israel: . . . I know every thought that comes into your minds."

EZEKIEL 11:5

BY KATHERINE R. ADAMS

January 9
A SURE GUIDE

Read Psalm 18:24-33.

The Johnsons—Heather, Brad, Mom, and Dad—had spent the past few days with Grandpa and Grandma. Mom had driven the family car while Dad drove a truck they'd borrowed so they could take along some items to store in the grandparents' attic.

The family treasured the long talks, funny jokes, and delicious food. It was hard to say good-bye, because it would be four years before the Johnsons would come back from Peru, where they were going as missionaries. As they prepared to go home, fog settled in. "Oh, dear," moaned Mom. "John, how will I ever see the way home?"

"The fog lights on this truck will pierce through the mist, so I'll lead the way," said Dad. "Just follow me and keep your eyes on my taillights."

Mom nervously gripped the steering wheel, but as the children prayed and sang, she gradually relaxed. When they safely reached home, they all thanked God.

"As I was driving, I couldn't help but think that God was using this fog to prepare us for Peru," said Dad. "Because we're going to an unfamiliar country, the future seems foggy to us. The people, customs, and language are relatively unknown to us, so we don't know exactly what's ahead. But God knows all about it. He'll take care of us."

JESUS WILL GUIDE YOU.

"That's right," agreed Mom. "I had your taillights to guide me, and we all have the Lord to guide us as we go to Peru. We can trust Him."

HOW ABOUT YOU?

Do you worry about a different school, an unfamiliar town, a new family or step-parent, or a new challenge? God knows your fear and your future. Read His Word for instruction and encouragement. Then ask God to guide you—He will!

TO MEMORIZE:

For that is what God is like. He is our God forever and ever, and he will guide us until we die.
PSALM 48:14

BY JAN L. HANSEN

January 10

A FINE-FREE DAY

Read Romans 6:18-23.

"Oh boy! This is my lucky day," Steve shouted. "Listen to this, Mom." From the newspaper he read, "Wednesday has been declared Fine-Free Day at the local library. All overdue books may be returned without paying a fine."

Mom smiled. "The librarian will be sorry when she sees you coming!"

Soon Steve was on his way to return his overdue books. As Steve pedaled toward the library, his neighbor, Mr. Burns, staggered out of his house. *Drunk again!* Steve thought.

"Hi ya, Steve," Mr. Burns slurred. "Where ya goin'?"

"To the library to return overdue books." Steve stopped his bike. "Today is Fine-Free Day."

"Sure wish they'd have Fine-Free Day at city hall." Mr. Burns's blurry eyes stared at the boy. "Hey, yer a Christian. Ya suppose God has a Fine-Free Day?"

Steve blinked, then replied, "Sure He does, Mr. Burns. Today is Fine-Free Day with God, too. Jesus paid our fine at Calvary. If you'll turn your life over to Him, He'll forgive you!"

JESUS PAID YOUR FINE.

Mr. Burns shook his head. "Ya only have a few sins. I've got a pack of 'em."

Steve pointed at his backpack, crammed with books. "It makes no difference to the librarian if I have one overdue book or ten. I don't have to pay a fine today. And it makes no difference to God if I have a few sins or a whole pack."

"Ya really think so, son?" Mr. Burns asked. "I'll have to think that over."

HOW ABOUT YOU?

Are you carrying sins for which you need to repent? Whether they're a few little sins or a lot of big ones, they must be paid for. To find out more, talk to a trusted Christian friend or adult.

TO MEMORIZE:

For God says, "At just the right time, I heard you. On the day of salvation, I helped you." Indeed, the "right time" is now. Today is the day of salvation.

2 CORINTHIANS 6:2

BY BARBARA J. WESTBERG

January 11

STRONG AS AN EAGLE

Read Psalm 28:1-3, 6-9.

Kevin and Jessica were having a great time on a weeklong visit to their grandparents' home. The ground was covered with snow, and they would stay outside for hours, building snow forts and walking on the ice-covered lake. Then they would come in and sip hot chocolate in front of the fire.

One afternoon they persuaded Grandpa to go for a walk with them. They took off down the road, laughing and talking and occasionally throwing a snowball at each other. Suddenly Grandpa whispered, "Hey, kids! Don't move. Look over there!" Kevin and Jessica looked where Grandpa was pointing. A huge bird sat on the branch of a tree. "It's an eagle," whispered Grandpa. Suddenly, with a powerful flap of its wings, the eagle took off over the treetops.

"Wow!" Kevin said. "That's one strong bird!"

"You're right," agreed Grandpa. "You can be strong like that too," he added.

"How?" Kevin asked.

GOD GIVES STRENGTH.

"Those who trust in the Lord will find new strength. They will soar high on wings like eagles," replied Grandpa. "That's in Isaiah 40."

"I've heard that verse, Grandpa," said Jessica. "But I never thought about what it meant before."

"It's a picture," said Grandpa, "a magnificent picture of the strength we have when we put our trust in the Lord."

HOW ABOUT YOU?

Do you have problems at school? Do you live in a tough home situation? Is it hard for you to make friends? Trust Jesus to help you. He doesn't promise to take problems away, but He does promise to give you the strength needed to handle them. The next time you see a picture of an eagle, think of God's promise.

TO MEMORIZE:

I can do everything through Christ, who gives me strength.

PHILIPPIANS 4:13

BY LENORA MCWHORTEN

January 12

THE CORNERSTONE

Read Ephesians 2:19-22.

Jeremy and Samuel watched as the construction workers built a new apartment complex on the corner of their street. "It sure is tall," commented Jeremy. "I wonder how they get a tall building so straight."

"Let's go to the mall and ask Mr. Cohen," said Samuel. "He knows a lot about buildings."

The boys raced down the street to the mall. "So you want to know about buildings," said Mr. Cohen, who was their Sunday school teacher. "Tell me, do you know what a cornerstone is?"

"No," Jeremy replied. Samuel shrugged his shoulders.

"The cornerstone is a special stone or brick," said Mr. Cohen. "Accurate instruments are used to lay the cornerstone. All the other bricks in the building are lined up with it. If the cornerstone is laid straight, the rest of the building will be straight because the other bricks are laid one by one, using the cornerstone as a guide."

"Hey, that's cool!" said Samuel.

LIVE AS JESUS WOULD.

Mr. Cohen smiled. "The Bible tells us that Jesus is our cornerstone."

The boys looked surprised. "We aren't buildings," laughed Samuel.

"No, but the Bible uses the word *building* or *house* when referring to the church—that is, all the people who have trusted Jesus as their Savior," answered Mr. Cohen. "It says that Jesus is the cornerstone of His church. Our actions and attitudes must line up with His."

"So if we act and think like Jesus, we help to build His church the way He wants it, right?" Jeremy asked.

"Right!" replied Mr. Cohen. "Always let Jesus be your guide."

HOW ABOUT YOU?

Do you look to Jesus as your example when you are deciding how to act or think? If you line your actions up with Jesus, you'll be helping to build God's church His way.

TO MEMORIZE:

We are his house, built on the foundation of the apostles and the prophets. And the cornerstone is Christ Jesus himself.

EPHESIANS 2:20

BY DEANA ROGERS

January 13

SURPRISE DESSERT

Read Revelation 21:3, 18, 21-23.

Zach took a bite of his meatloaf. "We learned about heaven in Sunday school today," he said. "I know heaven is supposed to be wonderful, but won't it be boring, just walking around singing hymns?"

"I'm sure we'll be doing more than that," Dad said with a smile.

"Yeah, well . . . that's what Mr. Davis said too," admitted Zach. "The Bible doesn't tell us a lot about it, though, does it?"

"No," replied Dad, "but we do know that it's a wonderful place. And the best part will be finally being with Jesus."

Zach ate his last bite. "Why didn't God tell us more about heaven?"

"Well, it would be impossible to understand all the good things He has planned for us," said Dad. He looked over at four-year-old Bobby. "Finish your carrots, Bobby," he said. "We're almost ready for dessert."

"What is it?" Bobby asked.

HEAVEN WILL BE WONDERFUL.

"It's a surprise," Mom said. "I promise you'll like it."

"Can I have mine now, Mom?" asked Zach.

"Let's wait till Bobby's ready," Mom said. "If he sees it, he'll get so excited that he won't want to finish his carrots."

Soon they were all enjoying strawberry shortcake. "I just thought of another reason God didn't tell us exactly what heaven will be like," Zach announced. "If we knew, we'd probably get so excited we wouldn't be able to focus on what God wants us to do on earth now.

Mom smiled. "Right—like Bobby wouldn't have been able to finish his carrots if he knew what dessert was coming. We just need to obey God and trust that His 'dessert' will be just right!"

HOW ABOUT YOU?

Do you ever wonder what heaven will be like? The Bible tells some things about it, but you won't really know what God has in store for you until you get there. In the meantime, keep busy doing God's will on earth and telling others about Jesus so they can go to heaven too!

TO MEMORIZE:

You will show me the way of life, granting me the joy of your presence and the pleasures of living with you forever.

PSALM 16:11

BY SHERRY L. KUYT

January 14

THE EMPTY COCOON

Read 1 Corinthians 15:35-38, 40, 42-44.

"What's that?" cried Lisa when her brother showed her a pale green object dangling from a branch.

"Isn't it cool?" replied Nick. "It's called a chrysalis, and there's a caterpillar inside. Or at least, he used to be a caterpillar."

Lisa frowned. "I don't like caterpillars." As she went into the house, she saw her mother wiping tears from her eyes. "What's the matter?" Lisa asked.

"I just got a phone call," Mom said softly. "Grandma Carter died."

"Oh no!" wailed Lisa. "I don't want her to die!"

"I know, honey, but Grandma is happy now. She's in heaven."

Lisa and Nick were a little nervous when they went to the funeral home and walked up to the casket where Grandma lay. "She looks like she's asleep," said Lisa.

The next day, they attended the funeral, and after the service, they all went to the cemetery where Grandma was to be buried.

CHRISTIANS WILL HAVE NEW BODIES.

Lisa was quiet as they sat on the patio that evening. "I thought Grandma was in heaven, but they put her in the ground," she said at last. As she spoke, Nick came over, carrying the branch with the chrysalis dangling from it. He held it up.

"The caterpillar spun a chrysalis around itself. After a while, it burst open and a butterfly came out," Mom said.

"I love butterflies!" said Lisa. "They're prettier than caterpillars."

"That's like what has happened to Grandma Carter," said Dad. "She has left her old shell—her earthly body—and now it's like an empty chrysalis. The real Grandma has gone to be with Jesus." He smiled. "God will give her a beautiful new body, too."

Just then a butterfly fluttered past Lisa's nose. "Look!" she squealed. "A caterpillar in its new body."

HOW ABOUT YOU?

Has someone you love died and gone to heaven? The Bible teaches that those who love the Lord go to be with Him when they die. Though their bodies were buried, they're not in them anymore. God will give them wonderful new bodies someday.

TO MEMORIZE:

Our bodies are buried in brokenness, but they will be raised in glory.

1 CORINTHIANS 15:43

BY BARBARA J. WESTBERG

You Just Wait

Those who trust in the LORD will find new strength. They will soar high on wings like eagles. They will run and not grow weary. They will walk and not faint.

ISAIAH 40:31

Waiting upon the Lord is a way to show patience. As we wait, our faith grows stronger. Do you remember when you learned to read? You had to build reading strength. First, you learned each letter and its sounds. You had to be patient as you practiced. You had to wait until you were able to go to the next step. In time, however, you figured out how to read words, sentences, and paragraphs. As we pray and learn to be thankful, we are waiting upon the Lord. This builds our spiritual strength. In time, we will find strength we never imagined.

Help the runner get through the maze and reach the finish line.

SEE ANSWER IN BACK

January 15

NO DIFFERENCE

Read Romans 3:10-12.

At a special service at Jenny's church, Derek, one of the roughest boys at school, surprised everyone by becoming a Christian.

After church, Jenny walked home with her friend Brittany, who had only recently started coming to their church. Jenny was surprised to hear her new friend's comments. "Maybe Derek's behavior will improve now that he's a Christian," said Brittany. "His family is very poor, you know, and his dad drinks. I'm glad I don't have a family like that. I'm glad I was born a Christian."

"Nobody is born a Christian," objected Jenny.

Brittany shrugged. "Oh, I know some people think that, but I don't agree."

The next week the circus came to their city. Brittany invited Jenny to go with her. The girls arrived just in time. "Oh no!" groaned Brittany as the gatekeeper waited for their tickets. "I forgot the tickets!" She explained the situation to the gatekeeper, asking if they could please go on in and bring the tickets later. As he shook his head, Brittany squared her shoulders and looked him straight in the eye. "Do you know who I am?" she asked haughtily. "I'm the mayor's daughter!"

YOU ARE A SINNER.

"Well, Miss Mayor's Daughter, show me your ticket, and you can get in."

After walking away in silence, Jenny glanced at Brittany. "It didn't matter who you were, did it?" she asked quietly. "If the gatekeeper wouldn't let you into the circus even though you were the mayor's daughter, what makes you think God will let you into heaven just because you come from a Christian family?"

HOW ABOUT YOU?

Do you think you were born a Christian? You weren't. The Bible says it makes no difference who you are. Whether you're from the best home in town or the worst, you need to accept Jesus into your heart.

TO MEMORIZE:

Everyone has sinned; we all fall short of God's glorious standard.

ROMANS 3:23

BY HAZEL W. MARETT

January 16

A HEAVY BURDEN

Read Philippians 4:6-7.

"Mom, I wish Dad still lived here," said Kyle as he finished getting ready for school. "If I had just behaved better, maybe he wouldn't have left."

"Honey, Dad's leaving had nothing to do with you. He loves you as much as ever," Mom said patiently, putting an arm around Kyle. She and Dad had told Kyle this many times. He wanted to believe them, but he just couldn't.

Thoughts of his dad often popped up at school between the sentences Kyle was reading. He finally got his mind off his problems when his teacher showed the class an interesting book on space travel. And he was thrilled when she said he could take it home for the evening.

Kyle tucked the heavy book under his arm and began walking home. As he walked, the book seemed to grow heavier and heavier. By the time he reached home, his arm ached.

Mom met him at the end of the driveway. "That book looks heavy," she said. "Let me help you." She reached down and took it. "Guilty feelings can also be heavy to carry," she continued. "The feeling that Dad left because of you is a burden too heavy for you to carry."

GIVE YOUR BURDENS TO JESUS.

"I wish I didn't have that feeling," Kyle said. "It hurts."

"Yes, just like your arm hurts from carrying the book. Wouldn't you like Jesus to carry the burden for you?" Kyle nodded, and together they asked Jesus to carry Kyle's heavy burden.

HOW ABOUT YOU?

Do you have a burden too heavy for you? If your parents are separated or divorced, do you wonder if it's your fault? Or perhaps secret worries about school or friends constantly fill your mind. It's important to talk about heavy burdens to an adult who can help you turn them over to Jesus.

TO MEMORIZE:

Give all your worries and cares to God, for he cares about you.

1 PETER 5:7

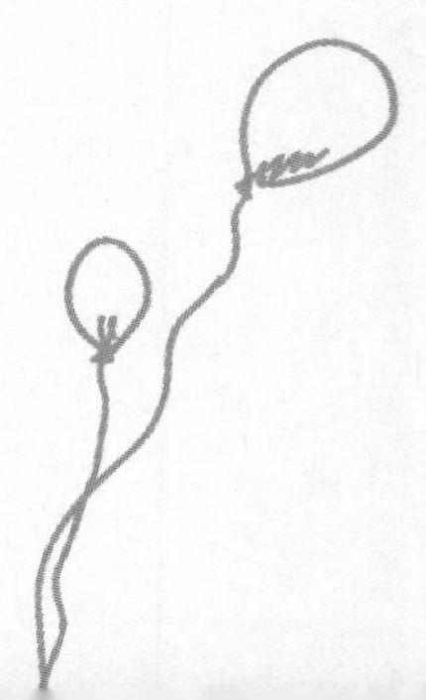

BY KATHERINE R. ADAMS

January 17

PATTERN FOR LIFE

Read Ephesians 2:2-7, 10.

Mandy curled up on the sofa to read a book. Her mother knelt on the floor, surrounded by colorful fabric, pattern pieces, scissors, and pins. Mandy looked up from her book. "What are you doing, Mom?" she asked.

"I'm making a shirt for myself," replied Mom as she pinned a pattern piece onto the fabric.

"I don't see how you can make all those pieces come together and look like the picture on the pattern envelope!" Mandy said.

Mom smiled. "You could do this too, if you wanted to," she said. "If I just follow the directions, my shirt will turn out like the one in the picture."

As Mandy watched her mother stitch pieces together on the sewing machine, she asked, "Mom, do you think God has patterns for our lives?"

"Patterns?" asked Mom. "What do you mean?"

"Well, in Sunday school, Mrs. Crane said that God has a plan for each of us," explained Mandy. "She also said we should do what God tells us in the Bible so we can become what God wants us to be. That might be like following the instruction sheet that comes with your pattern."

FOLLOW GOD'S INSTRUCTIONS.

"That's a good illustration!" said Mom. "Yes, God is making each of us into something special, Mandy. Even when things look confusing or impossible—like these shirt pieces did to you—we have to keep following God's instructions. Then He'll make us into beautiful finished products." Mom smiled at Mandy. "You're a smart girl. I know you could learn to sew if you put your mind to it."

Mandy grinned. "Next time you go to the fabric store, maybe I can come along," she said. "It might be fun."

HOW ABOUT YOU?

Do you know that God has a pattern for your life? Instructions are found in the Bible. As you learn and obey what God tells you through His Word, you will become more like Jesus, and the pattern, or plan, He has for you will become evident in your life.

TO MEMORIZE:

We are God's masterpiece. He has created us anew in Christ Jesus, so we can do the good things he planned for us long ago.

EPHESIANS 2:10

BY JUDITH K. BOOGAART

January 18

THE ACTIVITY BOX

Read Matthew 11:28-30.

"We have a lot to do today," said Mom as she put bread in the toaster.

"We always have lots of work on Saturday," complained Jessica.

"Yeah," murmured Justin. "Saturdays are no fun anymore!"

Dad poured a cup of coffee. "I don't like them, either—not because of the work, but because they're days of whining and grumbling," he said. "I'm sure the Lord is not pleased with that. Maybe we can find a way to make our work more interesting."

Justin scowled. "I don't see how," he said.

"Please find me a shoe box, Justin," said Dad a few minutes later. "Jessica, you can bring me some paper and a pencil." When the children returned with the items, Dad said, "Let's write everything we have to do today on slips of paper and put them in this box."

"Change sheets, vacuum, clean bathrooms." Mom quickly named several tasks.

"Wash the car, wash the dishes, water the plants," suggested Justin.

WORK CHEERFULLY.

"Now," Dad said, "we'll take turns drawing out a slip and doing whatever is written on it."

"Then let's pack lunch and go to the park when the box is empty," said Mom.

"All right!" Jessica and Justin cheered. Jessica reached for the box.

Dad held up his hand. "We forgot something," he said. "We need to give the Lord some time too."

"Read a chapter in your Bible," Jessica wrote on a slip of paper.

"Thank God for our family," wrote Justin.

"Call Uncle John and invite him to church," said Dad.

Then Dad held the box out to Jessica. "This is going to be the best Saturday we've had in a long time," she said as she drew out a slip and looked at it. Then she groaned. "Even if I do have to clean the bathrooms!"

HOW ABOUT YOU?

Have your tasks become boring? Make your own activity box, and do your tasks cheerfully! You may be surprised by how enjoyable a work day can be.

TO MEMORIZE:

Work willingly at whatever you do, as though you were working for the Lord rather than for people.

COLOSSIANS 3:23

BY BARBARA J. WESTBERG

January 19
GOD'S PLAN

Read Romans 11:33-36.

Brent never forgot the day his new baby sister, Emily, came home from the hospital. Dad and Mom had told him that her spinal cord was damaged before she was born and she would never be able to walk.

Brent couldn't quite believe it. *Maybe if we all take really good care of Emily, her legs will become well,* he thought. When Brent mentioned this to his mother, she shook her head sadly. "No, the doctor said that her legs will never work. Instead of thinking about that, let's remember that this is God's plan for Emily and our family."

"How can it be God's plan?" Brent asked.

Mom sat down next to Brent. "Emily is going to need special care because her legs have no feeling," she said. "She will not know if they are hot or cold or if they have been bruised. That's where you and I fit into God's plan for her," said Mom. "It will take time and love to protect her and to help her learn about her disability."

"Oh," murmured Brent.

"Will you help Emily?" Brent's mother asked.

ACCEPT GOD'S PLAN.

Brent was quiet for a while. Then he said, "I wish Emily could learn to walk. But since she can't, I want to help her."

"Great!" said Mom, squeezing his shoulder. "God knew Emily would need a big brother like you."

HOW ABOUT YOU?

Do you have a brother, sister, or friend with a disability? God has placed that person in your life as part of His plan for you. As you love and encourage your sibling or friend, God will use you to be a blessing. Or perhaps you have a disability yourself. God wants to use you to be a blessing too.

TO MEMORIZE:

Encourage those who are timid. Take tender care of those who are weak. Be patient with everyone.

1 THESSALONIANS 5:14

BY JORLYN A. GRASSER

January 20

CURIOSITY'S CAPTIVE

Read Luke 5:27-31.

"Uncle Jerry makes me so mad!" said Jana as she slammed down the telephone. "That was Cheri, and she was crying. The electric company will turn off their electricity if they don't pay their bill by tomorrow. Uncle Jerry's out drinking with his buddies again."

Dad looked over the edge of the newspaper. "I feel sorry for Jerry," he said.

Jana huffed. "I feel sorry for his *family*! Uncle Jerry is selfish and mean!"

"We need to pray for him. He's in bondage to alcohol," Dad reminded her.

"He could get loose if he wanted to! He just—" Jana was interrupted by a banging sound from the garage. "What's that?"

"I don't know," Mom said, concerned. "We had better find out." When they opened the door, they saw their dog with a plastic pitcher over his head, bumping into everything.

Mom gathered the frightened dog in her arms. Dad got out his pocketknife and carefully cut the pitcher from the dog's neck.

CARE FOR OTHERS.

"Rudy must have stuck his nose in the pitcher, then pushed it up against something as he pushed his head farther inside," said Jana.

Dad nodded. "Scolding him and telling him how foolish he was wouldn't have helped him at all," he observed. "He was caught and couldn't do anything to help himself. He needed us to help him. You know, Uncle Jerry is like Rudy. He is caught in a trap so powerful he cannot break loose. God can deliver him. And if God wants to use us to help, He will show us how."

HOW ABOUT YOU?

Do you know people who are caught in the trap of sin? It might be alcohol or drugs or other things. Ask God to give you compassion for them, and pray for them.

TO MEMORIZE:

Finally, all of you should be of one mind. Sympathize with each other. Love each other as brothers and sisters. Be tenderhearted, and keep a humble attitude.

1 PETER 3:8

BY BARBARA J. WESTBERG

January 21
HURTFUL WORDS

Read James 3:8-17.

"Am I doing this right, Grandma?"

Grandma examined the crocheted scarf Amanda handed her. "Looks good to me," she said.

"What do I do next?" asked Amanda.

"Make the next row exactly like this one," Grandma replied. "By next week when I go to stay with your aunt Denise and Darci, you should be able to follow the pattern by yourself."

"We wish you could stay with us all the time, don't we, Mittens?" Amanda brushed her bare toes over the fur of the cat at her feet. "Darci is so stuck up. In fact, Darci is nothing but a spoiled brat. She—"

"That's enough, Amanda!" Grandma said sternly. "Remember, Darci is my granddaughter, and I love her as much as I love you."

"But you don't know what she did—" began Amanda.

BUILD UP OTHERS.

"Dinner is ready!" Mom's call from the kitchen interrupted Amanda.

After dinner, Amanda and Grandma returned to the family room. "I'm going to work on my—oh no! Look, Grandma!" Amanda pointed at the cat, who was playing with a mass of tangled thread. "Mittens unraveled all my hard work!"

Grandma smiled sympathetically. "It takes time and careful thought to crochet a scarf, but anyone—even a cat—can unravel one."

"That's for sure," said Amanda, picking up the mess.

"It's like that with everything," Grandma continued. "It always takes more effort to build up than to tear down. It's easy to be hurtful and find fault with people, but God wants us to help build people up."

Amanda sighed. "I'll try to do better, Grandma. Now, back to my scarf."

HOW ABOUT YOU?

Do you say hurtful things about others? This would be a good day to start building people up rather than tearing them down.

TO MEMORIZE:

Encourage each other and build each other up, just as you are already doing.
1 THESSALONIANS 5:11

BY BARBARA J. WESTBERG

Have No Doubt

If you need wisdom, ask our generous God, and he will give it to you. He will not rebuke you for asking. But when you ask him, be sure that your faith is in God alone.

JAMES 1: 5-6

What if, every time you have a problem, you ask God for His wisdom about it? He doesn't want to "reproach" or punish you when you need answers. He wants to share His wisdom when you ask for it. Be still in your mind and heart when you pray. Don't think about what you *want* the answer to be. Don't think about the many answers there *might* be. Just ask in faith, and God will give you *His* wisdom.

Write about a problem that you haven't taken to God for answers.

____

____

____

____

____

List any doubts you have about how to solve this problem.

____

____

____

____

____

Now cross out all your doubts.

What if you did this with every problem? It's what God wants you to do when you ask for His wisdom. Erase the doubts in your mind and heart. Then just ask Him for help.

January 22
T-SHIRT DAY

Read Matthew 26:69-75.

Karin and her family spent a week at Mountain View Bible Camp, and Karin had a wonderful time. "Can I please buy a camp T-shirt?" she begged one day. "Everyone else has one." Mom agreed, and Karin promptly put the shirt on. On the front was a picture of the chapel with the words "Proclaiming His Word to the World." On the back it said, "Mountain View Bible Camp." Karin wore the shirt almost every day that week, proud to be a part of the group.

Back home, Karin stuffed the shirt in a drawer and forgot about it. Mom didn't forget, though. From time to time she suggested that Karin wear it, but Karin always refused. "I like it," she insisted, "but it just wouldn't look right."

One Friday was declared T-shirt Day at school. Again Karin begged for a new shirt. "Not this time," Mom replied. "Wear your camp shirt. It's almost new."

"I can't wear that," protested Karin. "It wouldn't look right at school. Everyone else will wear shirts with cool sayings on them or they'll be from exciting vacation places like Yellowstone."

DON'T BE ASHAMED OF JESUS.

"Wasn't camp exciting?" asked Mom. "You loved your shirt before."

Karin bit her lip. "It was different at camp," she said.

"Yes, it was," Mom said. "It was comfortable to be identified as a Christian then, because others shared your faith."

Karin bristled. "Are you saying I'm ashamed to let others see that I'm a Christian?"

"Are you?" asked Mom softly.

Karin thought about it. "I guess maybe I have been," she confessed.

HOW ABOUT YOU?

Do your friends and teachers know you're a Christian? Do you pray before you eat, witness when you can, and speak up for your faith in the classroom? Don't be ashamed of Jesus. Others need to know Him too.

TO MEMORIZE:

Never be ashamed to tell others about our Lord.

2 TIMOTHY 1:8

BY JAN L. HANSEN

January 23

ALL-THE-TIME FRIEND

Read 1 Thessalonians 5:16-19.

"You've spent a lot of time texting your friends tonight," observed Mom as Emily put down her phone.

"We don't know what to do about Sierra," Emily explained. "She's being a . . . a *sometimes* friend. She wants to be friends when she needs help with homework, but she ignores us the rest of the time."

"I'm sorry to hear that," said Mom. "But no more texting tonight. It's almost bedtime. Have you had your quiet time with the Lord yet?"

Emily yawned. "I'm too tired tonight," she said. "I'll read my Bible and pray in the morning." She turned to go. "'Night, Mom. 'Night, Dad."

As Emily hurried downstairs the next morning, she tripped. "Mom!" she wailed. "My ankle!" Mom hurried to help. *Dear God,* prayed Emily silently while her mother wrapped her ankle, *this hurts so bad! Please take this pain away and make my ankle better.*

Unable to walk, Emily stayed home from school. "Emily," said Mom after making her comfortable on the couch, "you told me about how it bugs you when Sierra wants to be friends only when she needs you for something, remember?"

PRAY ALWAYS.

Emily nodded. "Friends should be friends all the time."

"I agree with you, and I thought about that last night," said Mom. "Remember how you spent so much time texting your friends, but you were too tired to talk to God?"

"Well, I prayed this morning," Emily defended herself.

"Did you?" asked Mom. "About what?"

"My ankle," said Emily quickly. Then she blushed.

"So you prayed when you needed *help*. Does that remind you of someone?" Mom raised her brows. "God is an 'all-the-time' friend," she added. "Don't you think it hurts Him when we're only 'sometimes' friends with Him? When we talk with Him only when we need help?" Thoughtfully, Emily nodded.

HOW ABOUT YOU?

Do you talk to God as you do to a friend, or do you pray only when you have a need? Take time to thank Him and praise Him for being your Lord. Treat Him like a good friend *all* the time.

TO MEMORIZE:

Never stop praying.

1 THESSALONIANS 5:17

BY NANCE E. KEYES

January 24

THE WRONG BOOK

Read Genesis 1:1-3, 6, 9, 14, 20, 24, 26, 31.

Getting out his science book, Scott sat down at the kitchen table to do some homework. *Wow!* he thought to himself after reading a few pages. *This sure doesn't sound like what it says in the Bible.* Feeling confused, he went to talk to his dad, who was replacing some spark plugs in the car. "Dad, my science book doesn't teach Creation like the Bible does," said Scott. "According to my book, many scientists believe that the earth and people and everything just 'happened' to come into existence."

"Well, Son," said Dad, "you might as well know right now that some books are wrong. People have written them, and people can sometimes make mistakes. But the Bible has no errors."

"Is that because the Bible was inspired by God?" Scott asked.

"That's right," Dad replied. "That's why we call it the Word of God—and it tells us that God created everything. In addition to that, our common sense tells us that people couldn't have just 'happened.' What if I told you this car just 'happened'—that nobody put the engine, the body, the seats, the wheels, and all the other parts of this car together, but they just all came together by themselves?"

GOD MADE EVERYTHING.

Scott laughed. "I'd tell you that was crazy," he said.

"You'd be absolutely right," Dad replied. "And the human body is far more complicated than this car. We're not accidents. We are part of God's plan and creation."

HOW ABOUT YOU?

Have you heard people talk about evolution as if it were fact? Don't believe it! God made the whole world and everything in it. He made you, He loves you, and He has a wonderful plan and purpose for your life.

TO MEMORIZE:

In the beginning God created the heavens and the earth.
GENESIS 1:1

BY CHARLES VANDERMEER

JOY IN THE MORNING

Read 1 Corinthians 15:51-57.

"Dad!" cried Sara as she and her mom entered his hospital room. She ran to the bed and flung her arms around her father's frail shoulders. "How are you feeling?" she asked.

Dad hugged her close. "I'm afraid the news isn't good," he said.

A lump jumped to Sara's throat. "I'll pray for you to get better, Dad." Dad smiled and squeezed her hand.

A few weeks later, Sara woke up to see Mom sitting on the edge of her bed. "Mom! You're here! How's Dad?"

"Oh, Sara," said Mom with a sob. "Dad is with Jesus now."

Tears flooded Sara's eyes. "What? No! I prayed that God would heal him, that he wouldn't be sick anymore!"

"And he's not sick anymore," said Mom as she pulled Sara into her arms.

"But I don't understand!" cried Sara. "How could God let Dad die?"

AFTER DEATH, JOY AWAITS CHRISTIANS.

"I don't know, honey," said Mom. "Sometimes God allows things to happen that we can't understand." She brushed the hair out of Sara's eyes. "But think of how Dad must have felt when he opened his eyes and saw Jesus. There's a Bible verse that says, 'Joy comes with the morning,' and today that came true for Dad. He woke up to find himself in the presence of Jesus, free of sickness and pain."

"I'm glad he's not sick anymore," said Sara. "But I miss him so much already!"

"So do I," said Mom, her eyes brimming with tears. "But someday we'll wake up to find ourselves in the presence of Jesus, and when we do, Dad will be there too."

HOW ABOUT YOU?

Have you experienced the death of a family member or friend? It's natural to feel sad and even wonder how God could allow it to happen. But remember that for a Christian, death is passing from this life on earth to a life in heaven with Jesus. Ask God to give you comfort and peace, and remember that one day, He will wipe away all your tears.

TO MEMORIZE:

Weeping may last through the night, but joy comes with the morning.

PSALM 30:5

BY PHYLLIS I. KLOMPARENS

January 26

CAN RIGHT BE WRONG?

Read 1 Corinthians 8:8-13.

Darrell burst into the room. "Mom, guess what happened at Bible club!" he exclaimed. "Troy accepted Jesus as his Savior!"

"How wonderful!" Darrell's mother responded. "I'm happy Troy's a Christian, but I'm afraid he won't get much encouragement at home."

"I'll help Troy," Darrell said eagerly.

A few weeks later, Darrell wasn't so sure about that. "I asked Troy to go with me to Don's house to play pool," he grumbled, "but you know what he said? He said, 'Darrell, I thought you were a Christian!' Then he walked away! What's wrong with playing pool?"

Darrell's mother was thoughtful. "Maybe Troy's father plays a lot of pool in the bars, so Troy associates playing pool with drinking, wasting money, and being away from home too much—things his dad does. Troy probably doesn't understand that a quiet game of pool in somebody's basement can be okay. Darrell, I think you ought to stay away from playing pool so you're not a stumbling block to Troy."

DON'T BE A STUMBLING BLOCK.

"I don't see why I shouldn't play," objected Darrell.

His mother thought for a moment. "Troy's a baby Christian. Seeing you do something he considers wrong might hurt him spiritually. Joining you might lead him to play pool in the wrong place. As he grows in his Christian life, he'll learn how to handle his actions. But right now, pool playing is a problem for him."

Darrell nodded thoughtfully. "Okay, Mom. I'll try."

HOW ABOUT YOU?

Are there things you think are okay to do but which bother other people? Remember, a Christian's actions influence others. Do your activities draw people to Christ or turn them away? Refuse to be a "stumbling block."

TO MEMORIZE:

You must be careful so that your freedom does not cause others with a weaker conscience to stumble.

1 CORINTHIANS 8:9

BY JAN L. HANSEN

January 27

DREW'S MOUSE

Read James 2:14-20.

School began in the usual boring way for Drew. *We need some action around here,* Drew thought. He peeked into his desk to check on the little mouse he had in a small box.

A few minutes later Mrs. Madden had to go to the office. She appointed Jennifer to be class monitor. Quietly Drew took the mouse from his desk and released it.

"There's a mouse!" Many of the kids screamed and jumped up on their chairs.

"Take your seats," Jennifer instructed. "It won't hurt you." The mouse ran right over Jennifer's shoe. "Ahhhh!" she shrieked. She climbed onto her chair.

"Everyone sit down," Jennifer ordered. "There's nothing to worry about." But she remained standing on her chair.

Just then Mrs. Madden returned to the chaos. She dismissed the class for an early lunch so that a janitor could remove the mouse.

After school Drew told his mom about Jennifer and the mouse. He told her everything except how the mouse got there. "It was pretty funny," he said. "Jennifer told the class to sit down because there was nothing to worry about, but she stayed standing on her chair."

LIVE WHAT YOU BELIEVE.

"That's a good example of what we discussed in my Bible study this morning," said Mom. "Just as Jennifer's actions didn't match her words, Christians' actions don't always match what they say they believe."

Drew felt guilty. He knew that Jennifer wasn't the only one whose actions didn't match her words. He would need to talk to his mother and his teacher.

HOW ABOUT YOU?

Do you say you believe in Jesus but carelessly lie, cheat, or treat others unkindly? Or do you act out your faith by living a godly life? Ask God to help you act according to your faith.

TO MEMORIZE:

So you see, faith by itself isn't enough. Unless it produces good deeds, it is dead and useless.

JAMES 2:17

BY NANCE E. KEYES

January 28
TRUE FREEDOM

Read Proverbs 6:20-23.

Christina ran into her bedroom and slammed the door. How unreasonable could her mom be? Christina wanted to go to the slumber party at Sarah's house, but her mom wouldn't let her go. "You know the girls are much older than you are and rather wild," Mom had said.

But Christina yelled, "You never give me any freedom!"

She was still sniffling when she heard a sound at her window. Looking up, she saw a bird beating its wings against the glass. It seemed to be trying to get inside. As she watched, her mom knocked on the door. "I have some clean laundry, Christina."

As Mom set the clothes on the dresser, she saw the bird beating on the glass. "Christina," Mom said softly, "open the window and let the poor bird in. It's cruel to keep him out when he desperately wants to get in."

"Mom, he wouldn't know what to do once he got inside. He'd be trapped and scared and wouldn't know how to get out again! He might get hurt."

TRUE FREEDOM INCLUDES RULES.

"But don't you want him to have his freedom?" Mom asked.

"He's got more space and freedom outside," Christina said grumpily.

Mom smiled and nodded. "So by saying no, you're really giving him freedom and protecting him," she said. "That's what I'm trying to do for you."

HOW ABOUT YOU?

Do you feel that your parents are restricting your freedom by giving you rules and expecting you to obey? In love, they are actually protecting you from situations or things that could harm you. Trust their judgment and obey their decisions. True freedom includes living within bounds set up by God.

TO MEMORIZE:

Their command is a lamp and their instruction a light;
their corrective discipline is the way to life.
PROVERBS 6:23

BY JAN L. HANSEN

God Has Prepared

No eye has seen, no ear has heard, and no mind has imagined what God has prepared for those who love him.

1 CORINTHIANS 2:9

Perhaps you want to be accepted by a certain group, such as a sports team or club. But it doesn't happen. Maybe you'd like to live in or travel to a certain place, but you can't. When you are disappointed, remember that God has His own plan for you. You can't imagine it—nobody can. When you are discouraged, just focus on your love of God. He has prepared things for you. His plan for you is unfolding.

Circle the words that mean "plan."

K	A	N	C	D	X	O	A	Y	J	G	T	Q	P	T
A	S	A	K	A	Q	O	N	X	D	N	W	C	D	K
G	T	R	L	K	L	R	W	E	O	T	V	A	M	L
R	M	R	Y	G	Y	C	D	J	S	W	Y	Z	V	E
M	Y	A	Q	Z	V	K	U	U	T	D	O	I	A	R
P	G	N	L	C	X	K	Y	L	R	U	Q	I	S	S
O	F	G	L	Y	G	A	R	Q	A	F	B	N	C	S
R	V	E	A	C	M	E	V	D	T	T	R	J	H	H
G	B	S	T	C	R	V	M	W	E	C	E	A	E	N
A	U	K	B	N	H	S	F	Y	G	Z	U	D	M	P
N	T	K	Z	H	K	A	X	B	I	Z	A	E	E	E
I	P	P	R	E	P	A	R	E	Z	T	J	S	K	A
Z	D	M	F	J	M	P	G	T	E	B	U	I	B	M
E	S	S	H	A	P	E	Y	R	I	K	P	G	D	X
J	I	F	L	H	P	M	B	O	N	X	M	N	K	D

arrange
calculate
chart
design
frame

organize
prepare
scheme
shape
strategize

SEE ANSWER IN BACK

January 29

THE BEST HAMBURGER!

Read 1 Corinthians 13:1-3.

"Dad sure looks tired lately," said Bonita to her brother, Stephano. It was Saturday morning, and the two children were playing catch in the front yard. Just a few minutes earlier, they had watched their dad slowly walk down the road to the bus stop. Even though it was Saturday, he had to go to the office.

"Dad's tired because of that big report he's writing for the convention next month," Stephano said.

"Mom's been busy too," Bonita added. "It's not easy teaching full time and keeping the house straight. I wish we could help them."

"Well, we already helped Mom clean the house," said Stephano, "but there are some jobs kids just can't do!"

They threw the ball back and forth for a while, then Bonita spoke excitedly. "Stephano, how much money do you have?"

"I'm rich!" Stephano said, smiling. "All last week I helped Mr. Gonzales clean out the back room at his grocery store, remember?"

SHOW LOVE FOR PARENTS.

"I've got babysitting money saved up," said Bonita. "I thought we could take Dad and Mom out for dinner. It would let them know we appreciate them."

And that's just what Bonita and Stephano did. Their parents were very surprised.

"You know," said Dad as they were eating, "this is the best hamburger I've ever tasted!"

"I agree," Mom said with a smile. "It's terrific to know that our children care about us!"

HOW ABOUT YOU?

When was the last time you did something special for your dad and mom or told them how much you appreciate the hard work they do? Dads and moms sometimes become very busy and therefore very tired. Read 1 Corinthians 13, a chapter in which the apostle Paul talks about love. Then show that kind of love to your parents.

TO MEMORIZE:

"Honor your father and mother." This is the first commandment with a promise.

EPHESIANS 6:2

BY LENORA MCWHORTEN

January 30

HER OWN DECISION

Read James 1:5-6.

"Come on, Sue," Erika called. "It's time for choir."

Sue put her books in her locker and shut the door. "I decided not to go, Erika. It's such a nuisance having to stay after school twice a week."

"But, Sue, we planned on it," Erika said, glancing at her watch.

"Erika, let's forget choir this year," urged Sue. "Let's go to my house and play my new video game instead."

Erika hesitated. She wanted to stay, but she didn't want to go to choir alone. She knew Sue wouldn't change her mind, either. "Well, okay," she agreed slowly.

That night Erika's mom asked how choir was. "Sue and I decided not to join this year," Erika explained.

"Was that really your choice or Sue's?" Mom asked.

Erika looked down.

"You have a talent, Erika, and you've always said you wanted to use it for the Lord. The training you get at school will help you develop your talent, and besides, you had a lot of fun singing at the concerts last year. The main person you're hurting by not joining is yourself."

DECIDE WITH GOD'S HELP.

Erika thought about her mother's words. This wasn't the first time Sue had discouraged her from doing something she wanted to do.

"Mom, I'll join the choir next week," she said firmly. "I'm not going to let Sue talk me out of doing things anymore! I'll ask the Lord to help me make my own decisions."

HOW ABOUT YOU?

Do you let others tell you what you should or shouldn't do? Sometimes friends can sound pretty convincing, and if you're not careful, they'll make your decisions for you. God wants you to make your own decisions. Ask Him to help you have wisdom.

TO MEMORIZE:

I can do everything through Christ, who gives me strength.

PHILIPPIANS 4:13

BY LENORA MCWHORTEN

January 31

HE KNOWS HIS OWN

Read John 10:1-5, 11-14.

Gary settled back in his seat as his science teacher began showing a movie about Adélie penguins.

Gary watched the penguins swim toward the coast in the spring. They slid and waddled across the icy land, searching for a nesting place. How funny they looked! Soon they stopped at a rocky place, which was called a rookery. Large numbers of penguins would lay eggs and raise their young there. A million penguins could live in a single rookery, but each penguin family had its own nest.

When the lights came on, Gary had some questions. "If thousands of penguins live in one spot, how can a penguin tell which babies are hers?" he asked. "They all looked dressed alike to me." The class laughed.

"That's a good question, Gary," his teacher said. "Each penguin has a different voice. The parents can pick out their own children from thousands of other penguins just by the sound of their voices."

GOD KNOWS HIS OWN.

That evening Gary told his parents about the penguins. Dad smiled and nodded. "You know, God does the same thing for us," he said. "There are millions of people all over the world, but God knows those who belong to Him. If they stray away from Him, God calls them back to Himself by His Word. He knows His own children, and He takes care of them."

"I'm glad I belong to Jesus," Gary said.

HOW ABOUT YOU?

Do you wonder if God cares about you or your circumstances? If you've trusted Christ as your Savior, you belong to God. He knows you by name. He cares about every detail of your life. He has promised to care for you. Trust Him.

TO MEMORIZE:

But God's truth stands firm like a foundation stone with this inscription: "The LORD knows those who are his," and "All who belong to the LORD must turn away from evil."

2 TIMOTHY 2:19

BY JAN L. HANSEN

February 1

GRANDPA FORGETS (PART 1)

Read Isaiah 44:21; Luke 12:6-7.

"Hi, Grandpa!" exclaimed McKenna. McKenna had come to the supermarket with her father, who was picking up a cake to celebrate her eighth birthday the next day. *Why is Grandpa staring at me as if he doesn't know me?* she wondered. McKenna noticed that Grandpa had been acting strange lately. Mom said he'd recently been diagnosed with Alzheimer's disease, and that was what caused him to forget a lot of things. But she certainly didn't expect him to forget her!

Just then, Grandma appeared. "Robert, I told you to wait by the magazines," she scolded gently. Seeing McKenna, she gave her a quick kiss. "Are you all ready for your birthday party?" she asked.

"Party?" asked Grandpa. "Who's having a party?"

"McKenna is. We talked about it at breakfast," said Grandma patiently. She took his arm. "Let's go buy a birthday present for a certain little girl, shall we?"

That night as Mom tucked her into bed, McKenna told her about Grandpa's strange behavior. Mom sighed. "Grandpa isn't well," she said. "The disease he has causes him to forget things—sometimes even people he loves."

GOD NEVER FORGETS YOU.

McKenna swallowed hard. "But Grandpa and I are friends. He said so himself . . . and friends aren't supposed to forget each other."

"I know, honey," said Mom, giving McKenna a hug, "but earthly friends do sometimes forget—especially if they have certain diseases. But you can thank God for always being there for both you and Grandpa. Jesus is a friend who sticks 'closer than a brother'—or even closer than a grandfather."

As McKenna snuggled into bed, she thought about her mother's words. She thanked God that He would never leave her. And she prayed for her grandpa and thanked God for him as well.

HOW ABOUT YOU?

Are you sad because someone seems to have forgotten you? Perhaps a friend moved away or a grandparent doesn't seem to remember you anymore. Stop for a moment and thank God that He never forgets His own! Then pray for the person you miss. He or she may be feeling lonely too.

TO MEMORIZE:

A real friend sticks closer than a brother.

PROVERBS 18:24

BY CAROL J. BROOKMAN

February 2

GRANDPA FORGETS (PART 2)

Read Psalm 121:1-8.

Pink and yellow balloons hung around the living room. A big sign reading "Happy 8th Birthday, McKenna" was hanging over the sofa. Many of McKenna's aunts, uncles, and cousins were already there when Grandpa and Grandma arrived. Grandma hugged and kissed everyone. But Grandpa stood by the door, a confused expression on his face. "Who are these people?" he asked.

"They're your children and grandchildren, dear," said Grandma.

McKenna noticed that Grandma sounded like she was talking to a small child. *I guess that's because Grandpa forgets a lot of things,* she thought. McKenna walked over to her grandpa and slipped her hand into his. "I'm glad you came to my party," she said.

Grandpa looked down at McKenna, and a soft smile spread over his face. He patted her head, and for a minute she thought he was going to be like he'd always been. But then he said, "Is this your house, little girl?"

KEEP TRUSTING GOD. 

"Of course, Grandpa," McKenna replied. "You've been here lots of times."

When McKenna and her dad helped clean the kitchen after the party, McKenna closed the dishwasher door with a bang. "Why does Grandpa have to have Alzheimer's?" she muttered. "It's a horrible disease, and I can't think of a single reason why God would let it happen."

"Neither can I," said Dad, and McKenna's eyes widened. "That surprises you, doesn't it?" Dad asked. McKenna nodded. "Grandpa's disease is sad," continued Dad, "and we sometimes can't understand why such sad things happen in life. God doesn't ask us to understand, but He does ask us to trust Him. He promises to be with us in difficult times. He's there to strengthen and comfort us when we're hurting."

"So . . . I guess I have to keep trusting Jesus even when I feel like crying," said McKenna soberly. "I'm glad He'll help me through it."

HOW ABOUT YOU?

Are you wondering why God is allowing something difficult to happen in your life? He doesn't always reveal *why* things happen, but He wants you to trust Him and to give you comfort and help.

TO MEMORIZE:

My grace is all you need. My power works best in weakness.

2 CORINTHIANS 12:9

BY CAROL J. BROOKMAN

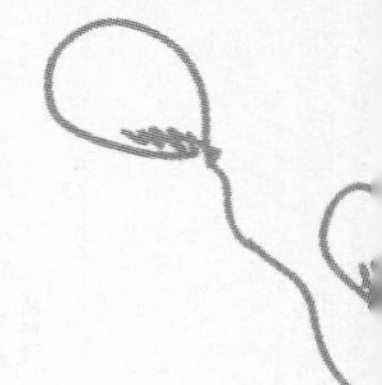

February 3
OPEN WIDE

Read Psalm 81:10-16.

Doug was delighted when robins built a nest on a high ledge of the front porch. When the mother bird began sitting on it, he was sure there were eggs in it.

Doug waited eagerly for the eggs to hatch. Then one day he heard peeping sounds and saw the robins bringing worms to the nest. The baby birds had hatched! He was so excited that he called Grandpa to tell him about it.

"I'll be over to see the little family soon," Grandpa said.

A few days after the birds had hatched, Doug saw three bald little heads bob up every time a worm was brought to the nest. The babies were getting stronger. Soon he heard louder cheeps, and the little heads shot up with beaks wide open.

When Grandpa came over, Doug showed him the hungry little birds with their wide-open beaks just showing above the nest. "They've been getting stronger," Doug said.

"What do you think would happen if they wouldn't open those mouths for food?" asked Grandpa.

HAVE DAILY DEVOTIONS.

"Well, I guess they'd never get strong enough to fly," said Doug.

"Smart boy." Grandpa smiled. "Now, what do you think happens when Christians don't open up to take in God's Word—the spiritual food He gives to make us stronger Christians?"

Doug grinned. "Smart, Grandpa," he teased, then added, "I'm going to start 'opening wide' today by reading my Bible and praying."

HOW ABOUT YOU?

Are you "opening wide" to take in the spiritual food God wants to give you? Spend time with God daily and grow strong in your Christian life.

TO MEMORIZE:

It was I, the LORD *your God, who rescued you from the land of Egypt. Open your mouth wide, and I will fill it with good things.*

PSALM 81:10

BY CAROLYN E. YOST

February 4

THE MISSING PIECE

Read Psalm 130:1–131:2.

Karen hung up the phone and walked over to her parents, who were assembling a jigsaw puzzle. "Cindy Lawson got the summer babysitting job at the Tylers' house," she announced. "Isn't that awful?"

Mom looked puzzled. "That's a nice opportunity for Cindy."

"But I wanted the job," grumbled Karen.

"You should be glad for your friend," said Dad. "Besides, you'll find other things to do this summer."

"No, I won't," Karen pouted. Then her face brightened. "Maybe if I call Cindy back and tell her how much I wanted the job, she'll let me have it."

"I think you should let the matter drop," said Mom.

"But I'm sure God wants *me* to have this job," whined Karen. Then she glanced at her father curiously. He had picked up a puzzle piece and had gotten out a pair of scissors. He seemed to be considering cutting the puzzle piece. "Dad, what are you doing?"

DON'T INSIST ON YOUR OWN WAY.

"I'm trying to fit this piece into this empty spot," explained Dad. "If I cut off this bump here and glue it onto the other side, I can make it fit."

"You know that won't work," scolded Karen. "Besides, you'll need that piece somewhere else."

Karen's mom laughed. "I think I know what your father is trying to say, Karen. That puzzle piece represents you."

"Right," said Dad. "Trying to jam that piece into a place where it doesn't fit is like you trying to get your way about that job. Even if you succeeded, you would miss out on whatever God really wanted you to do."

HOW ABOUT YOU?

Do you get upset when things don't go the way you want? Remember that God is in control, and He knows what's best for you. Let Him put you in the right place at the right time.

TO MEMORIZE:

I long for the Lord more than sentries long for the dawn,
yes, more than sentries long for the dawn.

PSALM 130:6

BY SHERRY L. KUYT

Use Your Words

If I could speak all the languages of earth and of angels, but didn't love others, I would only be a noisy gong or a clanging cymbal.
1 CORINTHIANS 13:1

God wants us to say things with love. When people don't speak with love, their voices sound like metal banging or jangling. Think of the last time you spoke in anger or jealousy or impatience. What did you sound like? Did the way you spoke help or hurt understanding? No matter what language we use, if we speak with love, we will be following God's will. And it will help us to be understood.

Use this code to decipher the missing words below.

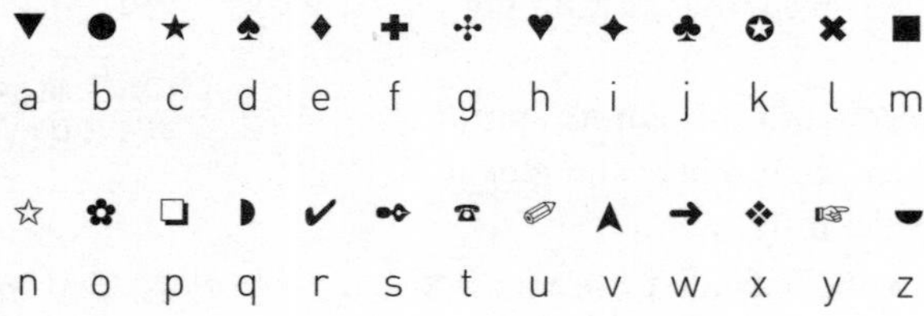

Three things will last forever—faith, hope, and love—

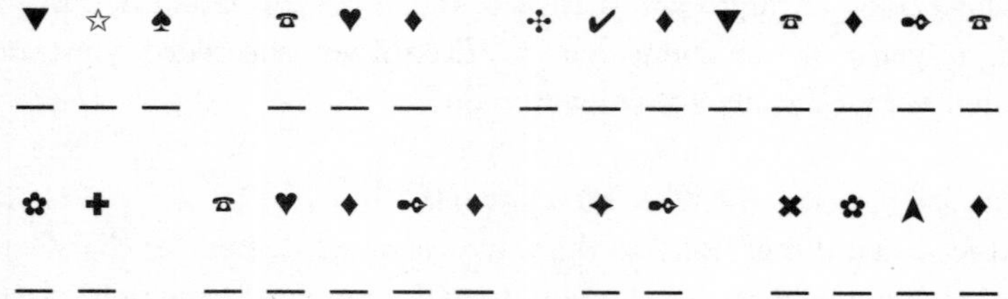

ANSWER KEY
And the greatest of these is love. (1 Corinthians 13:13)

February 5
LIFEPRINTS

Read Colossians 3:8-9, 12-14.

When the morning school bell rang, Tyson pushed past several children and hurried to the drinking fountain. He edged in at the front of the long line. "No cuts!" called several children, but Tyson ignored their complaints and took a long drink. When he went to hang up his coat, he found a coat on the hook nearest the door—his favorite spot. So he moved the coat to a place down the line and put his own coat on the hook instead.

In class, Tyson spent a lot of time daydreaming instead of studying. At lunchtime, he tried to be the first one out the door and the last one back in. "No fair," he grumbled when he had to stay inside for recess to finish the homework he hadn't completed.

After school Tyson invited Jerry over to play. "I got a new detective set," he said. "Let's see if we can lift fingerprints."

The boys played until Tyson's dad came home from work. After Jerry left, Tyson told Dad about the "detective work" they had been doing. "You leave prints on everything you touch, you know," said Tyson.

WITNESS THROUGH ACTIONS.

"I know, Son," said Dad. "What kind of prints have you been leaving all day?"

Tyson squinted at his dad. "The same kind as always, of course," he said. "Your fingerprints don't change."

"True," agreed Dad, "but wherever you go, you leave other prints too. Let's call them 'lifeprints.' Everything you do makes an impression—or a lifeprint—on other people. What kind of prints do you think you made today on your teacher and on the kids at school?"

HOW ABOUT YOU?

What kind of lifeprints are you making? Do others see selfishness and laziness in your prints, or do they see kindness, courtesy, faithfulness, and friendliness?

TO MEMORIZE:

Since God chose you to be the holy people he loves,
you must clothe yourselves with tenderhearted mercy,
kindness, humility, gentleness, and patience.
COLOSSIANS 3:12

BY HAZEL W. MARETT

February 6

JUST A PEEK

Read James 4:6-10.

Coming into the kitchen, Tara spied a plate with an assortment of candies on the counter. *Maybe Mom would let me have a piece!* she thought. But Mom was upstairs. *Oh, well,* thought Tara, *I'm sure she'd say no anyway, but . . .* She walked closer and looked at the candy again. Then she reached out and picked up a piece. She broke off a tiny corner and tasted it. It was as good as it looked.

Soon the whole thing was gone. *I've gotta try a little piece of fudge, too,* she decided. It was delicious, and when that was gone, Tara tried some peanut brittle. She moved the remaining candies around a little so the plate wouldn't look so empty. Then she went to her room.

When Tara came to the kitchen for dinner, the candy plate wasn't in sight. After everyone had eaten, Mom smiled and said, "Wait till you see what Mrs. Anders made for us." She brought out the plate of candies. "I thought this plate was fuller, but isn't it lovely?" She handed it to Dad. "You can each choose a couple of pieces for dessert."

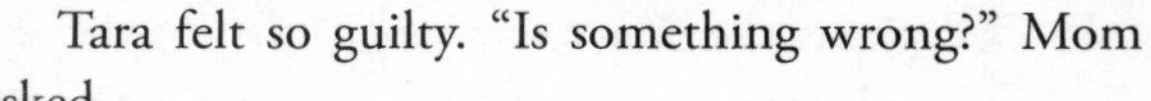

RESIST TEMPTATION.

Tara felt so guilty. "Is something wrong?" Mom asked.

"I ate some of the candy!" Tara blurted out. Tears filled her eyes, and the story spilled out. "I'm sorry," Tara said when she finished.

Mom nodded. "Tara, do you see how you gave in to temptation little by little—how looking led to handling and tasting and eating?" she asked. "That's how Satan works. He gets you to give in just a little at a time so it doesn't seem so bad. He does that with other things that tempt us too—not just with candy. We need to resist Satan, and the best way to do that is to refuse to take even one small peek."

Drying her eyes, Tara nodded.

HOW ABOUT YOU?

Are there things you think you'd like to try that you know you shouldn't? Be very careful! Satan wants you to try just a little. He knows you might try a little more the next time. Follow God's advice. Resist Satan. Say no right from the start.

TO MEMORIZE:

Resist the devil, and he will flee from you.

JAMES 4:7

BY HAZEL W. MARETT

February 7
THE RIGHT KEY

Read Acts 16:25-31.

"Sure you don't want to come along to pick up Grandma?" asked Riley's grandpa.

Riley shook his head. "Okay," said Grandpa, holding out a key chain. "The silver key with the round top is the house key. Grandma and I will be back soon."

Riley took the keys and went up the walk. *None of these keys look like the one Grandpa described,* he thought. He tried each one in the front door. None worked.

After what seemed like forever, his grandparents arrived. "Hey, there," Grandpa greeted him. "I didn't expect to see you sitting outside!"

"I couldn't get in," Riley explained.

Grandpa was surprised. "Oh, no! Now I remember! I took the key off the ring to have a duplicate made. I must have forgotten to put it back. I'm sorry, Riley."

"Well, I have a key that will work," said Grandma. She smiled, handing it to Riley.

A moment later Riley had the door open. "Whew!" he exclaimed. "There's nothing worse than being locked out of the house when all you want is a glass of milk and one of Grandma's cookies!"

BELIEVE IN JESUS.

"Actually, there is something worse," said Grandpa. "It's worse to expect to get into heaven but find out too late that you have the wrong key."

"What do you mean?" asked Riley. "You don't get into heaven with keys."

"No, not actual keys," agreed Grandpa, "but many people think being in a Christian family or living a good life is the key to getting in to heaven. That doesn't work, though. Jesus said, 'No one comes to the Father except through Me.' Only those who believe in the Lord Jesus Christ have the right key." Grandpa paused. "How do you expect to get in to heaven?" he asked. "What key do you have, Riley?"

Riley smiled. "I have the right one!" he exclaimed. "I believe in Jesus, and I trust Him to save me."

HOW ABOUT YOU?

What key are you counting on for entering heaven? Good works? A Christian family? These are useless in opening heaven's door. Jesus is the Door to heaven. Believing in Him as your Savior is the only key.

TO MEMORIZE:

Believe in the Lord Jesus and you will be saved,
along with everyone in your household.
ACTS 16:31

BY MARY ROSE PEARSON

February 8

SMART MOVE

Read Romans 12:9-17.

"Got caught peeking during a spelling test, didn't you?" Peter accused his sister Abby as they played checkers. "I heard the kids in your class talking about it."

"Yeah," Abby admitted. She studied the board game. "I'll never do that again."

"Gotcha!" Peter yelled triumphantly. "Your bad move gives me three pieces."

Abby looked up as her mother and little sister Cindi came into the room. "Which color are you, Abby?" asked Cindi.

"Red. Can't you tell?" Abby teased as she moved a black checker.

"Are not," protested Cindi. "You moved a black piece."

"It's easy for Cindi to see which side you're really on in spite of what you said," commented Mom. "She just had to see your moves." She paused for a moment. "Your friend Jasmine was watching your moves today too."

Abby stared at her mother. "What?"

"Jasmine called and said to tell you that she's not interested in going to church with someone who cheats on a spelling test," Mom said. Abby blushed.

WITNESS BY THE WAY YOU LIVE.

"I was pleased when you invited Jasmine to come to church," Mom said, "but she saw the move you made at school. I'm afraid she won't believe anything you say now about how good God is. That is a big deal."

"Oh-h-h! I . . . I'm sorry," Abby said. "I'm a Christian, and I want Jasmine to become one too."

"Then she needs to see that Jesus makes a difference in your life," said Mom. "Obviously, she couldn't tell today. Actions spoke more loudly than words."

"What should I do?" Abby asked.

"It's your move," Mom replied. "What do you think you should do?"

"I need to apologize to Jasmine," Abby admitted, "and to God, too."

"Congratulations," said Peter. "That would be a smart move!"

HOW ABOUT YOU?

When people see your actions, will they believe you're on the Lord's side? Actions speak louder than words. Let your actions say that you belong to Jesus.

TO MEMORIZE:

Live in harmony with each other. Don't be too proud to enjoy the company of ordinary people. And don't think you know it all!

ROMANS 12:16

BY HAZEL W. MARETT

February 9

THE RED CELLOPHANE

Read Romans 5:6-11.

"What's that, Grandpa?" Sam pointed to some small cards and pieces of shiny red paper on the kitchen table.

Grandpa smiled. "Grandma found these when she was cleaning the attic the other day," he replied. "When I was a boy, we used to get these as prizes in cereal boxes—they're something like your baseball cards."

"Wow! What are all the shiny red papers for?"

"That's what makes these cards interesting, Sam," replied Grandpa. "Here—look at this one. It has a picture of Babe Ruth on the front." Grandpa showed Sam the picture of a famous baseball player, then turned the card over. "Now . . . see this question on the back of the card? It says, 'What was Babe Ruth's real name?' To find the answer, we put this special paper right over the question, like this. Now what do you see?"

"George Herman Ruth," Sam read. "The question disappeared, and the answer showed up! Cool!"

JESUS' BLOOD COVERS SIN.

"Right," said Grandpa, picking up the cellophane. "This paper taught me a great lesson."

"You mean because you learned that guy's real name?" Sam asked.

Grandpa laughed. "Something more important," he said. "When I was young, I knew I was a sinner—I was the church troublemaker. I'd often heard that we need to have our sin covered by the blood of Jesus, but I never understood it until my Sunday school teacher brought this very same card to class one day. 'I want one of you to read the question on the back,' he said as he turned it over. But he had put the red paper over the question, so we told him we could see only the answer. He nodded. 'When you trust Jesus as Savior, your sin is covered by the blood of Jesus. Then God can't see your sin anymore. Instead, He sees the answer to your sin-problem. He sees Christ living in you.' I've never forgotten that."

Sam nodded thoughtfully. "I'm going to remember it too," he said.

HOW ABOUT YOU?

What does God see when He looks at you? Does He see your sins, or are they covered by Jesus' blood so that He sees Christ in you?

TO MEMORIZE:

It is no longer I who live, but Christ lives in me.

GALATIANS 2:20

BY PHYLLIS M. ROBINSON

February 10

BLOOMS OUT OF DARKNESS

Read James 1:2-5, 12.

Tessa loved to visit Grandpa Nelson's greenhouse. She loved working with Grandpa among the flowers and plants, learning to care for them and keep them healthy. But today she was confused. Grandpa had sent her into the storage room to get some potting soil. There, on a shelf, she saw some beautiful green plants. Grandpa had taught her that plants need light and water to grow, but these were being kept completely in the dark, and the soil in the pot was bone dry.

"Grandpa, those plants in the back room are going to die. Why did you put them there?" Tessa asked as she returned.

"Those are Easter cactus plants," Grandpa replied. "If you keep the plants in the dark for a month, they begin to bloom when you bring them out into the light. So we can have them bloom when we want them to."

"How strange," murmured Tessa.

"Yes, it is," agreed Grandpa. He put down his trowel and smiled. "You know, I think God sometimes puts us in the dark so we can bloom too."

GOD WORKS THROUGH PROBLEMS.

"You mean like when you were in the hospital?" Tessa asked.

Grandpa was glad Tessa understood. "At first I couldn't figure out why I had to be so sick," he told her. "But as I spent time praying and reading God's Word, I learned to relax and wait for God. The Lord showed me that, while I was in the dark, He was giving me the bloom of patience."

HOW ABOUT YOU?

Have you ever wondered why you had to be in the dark? Why you had to be sick, or face a death or divorce in your family, or struggle with school problems? Sometimes the Lord allows problems in order to bring the bloom of patience or prayer into your life.

TO MEMORIZE:

When your faith is tested, your endurance has a chance to grow.

JAMES 1:3

BY RAELENE E. PHILLIPS

February 11

THE LIVING GOD

Read Luke 24:1-9.

Karla stared at the screen as the missionary pictures were being shown. She saw people dressed like those in her own church. There were businessmen and housewives, schoolchildren and toddlers, all kneeling before a strange idol! They were praying. Karla knew that in some countries people worshiped wooden and stone gods, but these people were in a civilized area, a big city.

That evening she talked with her parents about it. "How do you know when you've got the right god?" she asked bluntly.

"What do you mean?" Karla's mom asked. "There is only one true God."

"Sure," Karla replied, "but all those people I saw in the pictures—they think they've got the right god too."

"Yes," Dad said, "but the Bible tells us there is only one God. He is the Creator of the earth. He made everything in it, including people."

Karla was quiet for a long time. Finally she spoke. "So that's why we believe in Him? Because He's so great?"

GOD IS ALIVE.

Dad shook his head. "Partly, but more than that."

Karla was thinking. "Is it because He sent His Son, Jesus, to die?" she suggested.

"There's still more," Dad told her. "Jesus—who is God—did more than die for us, as wonderful as that was! He also rose from the dead. And no other religion in the world has a living Savior."

Karla thought about that for a minute. There were wooden gods, stone gods, golden gods, and probably every other kind. But her God was different. He was alive! Only He could hear and answer her prayers.

HOW ABOUT YOU?

Imagine what it would be like to pray to a stone or a piece of wood or to a person who is dead. If you are a Christian, give thanks for your risen, living Savior. Then tell others about Him too.

TO MEMORIZE:

He isn't here! He is risen from the dead!

LUKE 24:6

BY RUTH I. JAY

Think Love First

Do everything with love.
1 CORINTHIANS 16:14

Your dog ate your homework. Your best friend stopped spending time with you. Your sibling lost your favorite hat at last night's game. When things like this happen, first think "love." When you focus on love, it helps you avoid disappointment. Love makes forgiveness easier. Love makes starting over easier. Whenever you take your next action based on love, life is easier.

Draw lines to match the opposites that show what love is and isn't according to 1 Corinthians 13:4-7.

LOVE IS	LOVE ISN'T
patient	boastful
kind	distrustful
modest	faithless
polite	hopeless
faithful	impatient
hopeful	rude
trusting	unkind

ANSWER KEY
patient/impatient; kind/unkind; modest/boastful; polite/rude; faithful/faithless; hopeful/hopeless; trusting/distrustful

February 12

GOOD-FOR-NOTHING JACOB

Read Matthew 5:13-16.

In the express lane at the store, Jacob stood on one foot and then the other. He had promised Mrs. Moore he'd bring her some brown sugar.

The conversation of the two men in front of him caught his attention. "I'm telling you," complained one, "my grandson is good for nothin'. His folks hire someone to mow the lawn while that kid sits by his computer."

"Yep," the other agreed, "the younger generation is spoiled rotten." Jacob fumed.

When Jacob handed Mrs. Moore her brown sugar and change, she tried to return the change to him. "No thanks," said Jacob.

Mom was just getting her coat on when Jacob arrived home. "Jacob, watch Emily for me, please," she said. "I need to run a few errands." Jacob nodded. Then he watched Emily play on the swing set while he trimmed a hedge.

At the dinner table that evening, Jacob repeated the conversation he had heard at the supermarket. "Well, they did have a point," said Dad.

DO GOOD—FOR NOTHING.

Mother looked up. "Don, are you saying that Jacob is good for nothing?"

"Well," said Dad, "today he ran an errand for Mrs. Moore. What did you get paid for that, Son?"

Jacob shrugged. "Nothing."

"And then you babysat Emily for your mother, and it looks like you trimmed the hedge for me. What did you get paid for those jobs?"

"Well, nothing," Jacob responded.

"Then I guess you're good for nothing, Jacob." Dad laughed. "And I reckon there are a lot more kids out there who are just as good for nothing as you are."

HOW ABOUT YOU?

Do you expect to be paid for everything you do? Start doing at least one good deed a day for nothing. In heaven you will be rewarded for the things done for nothing.

TO MEMORIZE:

Store your treasures in heaven, where moths and rust cannot destroy, and thieves do not break in and steal.

MATTHEW 6:20

BY BARBARA J. WESTBERG

February 13

JUST OUTSIDE JILL'S WINDOW

Read Psalm 91:1-2, 4-5, 9-12, 14.

The Marris family lived in a two-story house surrounded by big trees. Jill especially liked the maple tree outside her bedroom window. She enjoyed the sound of the leaves gently brushing against the glass.

One spring day Jill looked out the window and noticed a wren surveying the crook of a branch. Soon a second wren flew up. Jill stood still so she wouldn't frighten the birds. As she watched, they began to build a nest. The wrens made many trips, gathering twigs and bits of leaves. Jill had to laugh when she saw one of the wrens use a piece of hair ribbon that she had lost in the snow during the winter.

When the nest was finished, Jill checked each day to see if there was anything in it. One morning she saw small eggs in the straw. Soon there were baby wrens too. The parents kept busy feeding the babies!

But one day there was a terrible thunderstorm. The branch swayed back and forth, and the nest swayed with it.

GOD CARES FOR YOU.

"How are the wrens, Jill?" asked Dad, as he was passing her room.

"The branch is swaying in the wind, but the mother wren is covering the babies," Jill answered. "It's great that God created her so she knows how to protect her babies."

"I'll tell you another great thing," said Dad, coming in to take a look. "God uses that very picture—a mother bird spreading her wings to protect the babies—as an example of how He cares for us, His children."

HOW ABOUT YOU?

Have you ever seen a mother bird protect her young? The Bible often uses "word pictures" to illustrate God's love. Remember a mother bird's care for her babies, and you'll know how carefully God protects you.

TO MEMORIZE:

He will cover you with his feathers. He will shelter you with his wings. His faithful promises are your armor and protection.

PSALM 91:4

BY LENORA MCWHORTEN

February 14
VALENTINES

Read Romans 13:8-10.

Jasmine and Brooke giggled as Jasmine slipped an envelope into the valentine mailbox their teacher had set up. "I've never seen such an ugly valentine," said Jasmine. "I can hardly wait to see Erin's face when she opens it."

When Jasmine arrived home that afternoon, her mother asked to see her valentines. "Oh, my! This is a pretty one," said Mom, picking one up. "It even has a chocolate heart on it! I'll bet this is your favorite. Who is it from?" She turned it over. "Oh, from Erin."

To her mother's surprise, Jasmine burst into tears. "Oh, Mom," she sobbed, "I've been so mean to Erin lately. I gave her an ugly valentine, and she gave me such a pretty one. She was nice to me today, even after she got my valentine."

Mom put her arm around Jasmine. "Are you sorry for the way you've been acting?" she asked.

Jasmine nodded and wiped her eyes. "I need to apologize. But what can I say?"

When Mom called Jasmine to set the table for supper, Jasmine bounced into the kitchen. "You seem happier now," observed Mom.

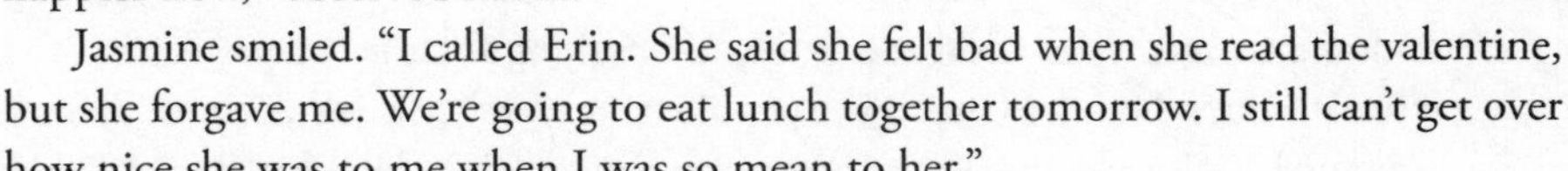

Jasmine smiled. "I called Erin. She said she felt bad when she read the valentine, but she forgave me. We're going to eat lunch together tomorrow. I still can't get over how nice she was to me when I was so mean to her."

"You know," said Mom, "Erin reminds me of Jesus. He loved us even when we were sinners."

HOW ABOUT YOU?

Is it hard to admit you're a sinner? God says you are, but He loves you anyway. Confess your sin and receive His forgiveness.

TO MEMORIZE:

But God showed his great love for us by sending Christ to die for us while we were still sinners.

ROMANS 5:8

BY HAZEL W. MARETT

February 15
THE LITTLEST MEMBER

Read 1 Corinthians 12:12, 18-25.

Brandon stretched, yawned, and turned off the alarm. For several minutes he argued with himself. One voice said, "Get up. It's time for Sunday school." Another voice said, "Why? Your folks don't go." In the end the wrong voice won. "No one will miss me," Brandon mumbled, pulling the pillow over his head.

Later that week Brandon tripped over a tree stump and broke a toe. How it hurt! When the doorbell rang on Saturday, he hobbled to the door. "Oh, hi, Mr. Newman," he said, greeting his Sunday school teacher. "Come in."

Mr. Newman said, "I see you're limping, Brandon. Did you hurt your foot? Is that why you missed Sunday school?" Mr. Newman asked.

"I broke my little toe on Tuesday," Brandon answered. "I didn't come Sunday because . . . well . . . I just figured no one would miss me."

Mr. Newman shook his head. "Oh, Brandon, you *were* missed. You're important to the Lord, to our church, and to me. When you're absent, there's a big gap in our class." He pointed to Brandon's foot and asked, "When you broke your little toe, how did it affect the rest of your body?"

EACH MEMBER IS IMPORTANT.

Brandon grimaced. "I couldn't do much of anything for a few days."

"So it is with the body of Christ, the people in church," Mr. Newman explained. "Every member is important, even those who think they're the 'little toe.' When one member hurts, we all hurt." He stood to leave. "You are important to our class, Brandon. Don't ever forget that."

HOW ABOUT YOU?

Do you feel unimportant? Or do you know someone else who feels that way? If you're a Christian, you're a member of the body of Christ. You're not only important, you're needed!

TO MEMORIZE:

The human body has many parts, but the many parts make up one whole body. So it is with the body of Christ.

1 CORINTHIANS 12:12

BY BARBARA J. WESTBERG

February 16
A WAY TO SERVE

Read 1 Samuel 2:18-19, 26.

It was Saturday, and Melinda lay across her bed as she read an exciting missionary story. *Wow,* she thought. *I wish I could serve God, but I'm only a kid.*

"Melinda, come here, please," Mom called from the kitchen. "Mrs. Rodrigues is sick, and I want you to take this stew over there." Melinda sighed but did as her mom asked.

When she arrived, Melinda noticed that the breakfast and lunch dishes were still on the table. She loaded them into the dishwasher and set the table for dinner.

When Melinda got home, Mom asked her to run some magazines over to Mrs. Wilson. "You're a sweet girl, Melinda," Mrs. Wilson said.

When Melinda arrived home once again, she was singing. "Well, you seem to be in a good mood," Mom remarked. "Would you feed Robbie?"

"Sure," said Melinda.

At dinner Melinda's mood became heavy. "I wish I could grow up fast so I could serve the Lord," she said, "like the missionary I've been reading about."

SERVE GOD BY SERVING OTHERS.

Mom looked up in amazement. "Why, Melinda, you've been doing things for the Lord all afternoon."

"I have?" Melinda asked.

"You helped Mrs. Rodrigues," Mom pointed out. "You visited with Mrs. Wilson. You—"

"But, Mom, that was for *people*," sighed Melinda.

"How do you think missionaries serve the Lord?" asked Mom. "They do it by doing things for people. Everyone can serve God by serving others."

HOW ABOUT YOU?

What have you done to serve God lately? You serve Him by serving others. Make a list of two or three things you can do today to help others.

TO MEMORIZE:

Worship the LORD with gladness. Come before him, singing with joy.
PSALM 100:2

BY BARBARA J. WESTBERG

February 17

A BIG MISTAKE

Read Matthew 14:24-33.

I'd like to do that, thought Melissa when Miss Baker asked for a volunteer to memorize Psalm 100 and recite it for chapel the next week. *But if I made a mistake in front of all those people, I'd just die.* Some of the other girls in Melissa's class expressed the same fear, and no one volunteered.

A little later Miss Baker told the Bible story of Peter walking on the water. She was such a good storyteller that Melissa could almost feel the water beneath her feet. The entire class seemed to relax when Peter and Jesus were finally in the boat with the other disciples and the sea was calm. "Who in this story made the biggest mistake?" asked Miss Baker.

"Peter," was Dawn's quick reply.

"Why do you think it was Peter?" Miss Baker asked.

"He was afraid," suggested Lucy.

"And he didn't trust Jesus," added Melissa.

DARE TO TRY.

Miss Baker shook her head. "Actually, Peter was the only one who *did* trust Jesus. He got out of the boat while the others sat and watched. The ones who made the biggest mistake were the eleven disciples who didn't have faith to do it. We're a lot like them. One of the worst mistakes we make is to allow fear to keep us from trying."

Melissa quickly raised her hand. "Miss Baker, I'll memorize Psalm 100 for chapel," she volunteered.

Miss Baker smiled. "Thank you, Melissa."

HOW ABOUT YOU?

Is there something you want to do for the Lord, but you're afraid to try? Remember Peter. He tried, and when he began to sink, Jesus was there to lift him up. Trying and failing isn't a mistake, but it's a big mistake to fail to try.

TO MEMORIZE:

Do not gloat over me, my enemies! For though I fall, I will rise again. Though I sit in darkness, the LORD will be my light.

MICAH 7:8

BY BARBARA J. WESTBERG

February 18

A SAFE PLACE

Read Isaiah 49:13-16.

"What do you need, Mom?" asked Kayla. She was going to the store for her mother.

"A gallon of milk, a loaf of bread, and cheese slices," Mom replied. "Can you remember that?" She glanced at her daughter. "What are you doing?"

Kayla lifted her head and grinned at her mom. She turned her hand to show her mother what she had done. "I wrote the list on my hand with this pen," she said. "That way I'll be able to remember what you need."

"That's a unique idea, but you could have used a piece of paper," suggested Mom.

Kayla shook her head. "This is better. I might lose paper, but I can't lose my hand."

Mom laughed and gave Kayla a hug. "You're right," she agreed. "Wait a minute. I want to show you an interesting verse in the Bible." Walking over to her desk, Mom picked up her Bible and opened it to Isaiah 49. "Read this," she said.

Kayla read a verse aloud. "I have written your name on the palms of my hands." She looked up at her mother. "Hey, that's neat! God writes on His hands too."

ACCEPT JESUS AS SAVIOR.

Mom nodded. "God said Israel's name was written on His hands, and I believe we can apply that to Christians, too. And God's writing will never come off."

Kayla looked down at the black writing on her hand. "That makes me feel good," she said. She closed her hand over the writing. "In God's hands—that's a safe place to be, isn't it?"

HOW ABOUT YOU?

Have you ever written on your hand to remember a school assignment or someone's phone number? Your hand is a safe place for such things, isn't it? Is your name written on God's hand? God's hands are the safest place to be.

TO MEMORIZE:

See, I have written your name on the palms of my hands.

ISAIAH 49:16

BY LYNN STAMM-REX

Don't Be a Hater

If someone says, "I love God," but hates a fellow believer, that person is a liar; for if we don't love people we can see, how can we love God, whom we cannot see?

1 JOHN 4:20

What if you discovered that choosing the right word about your feelings might help you get closer to God? You don't *hate* Aunt Helen. But you *really* don't like the way she pinches your cheeks. You don't *hate* the whiny second grader next door. But you *really* find whining annoying. So catch yourself the next time you use the word *hate*. What if you looked deeper at what *you* mean?

Below, write the names of three people about whom you've used the word *hate*.

____

____

____

Now, in the lines below, write *exactly* what it is about each person that *really* bothers you.

____

____

____

____

____

The word *hate* is almost never about who a person really *is*. It's almost always about the way someone *acts*. Help people see how their behavior makes you feel. Talking about it can lead to change in actions. And this can help keep the idea of "hate" out of your heart. What if everyone on earth did this?

February 19

AN INHERITANCE (PART 1)

Read 1 Peter 1:3-5.

Kyle liked to visit his great-uncle's dairy farm. He liked to throw down feed from the silo. He liked to swing on ropes in the hayloft. He liked to ride on the tractor. But most of all, he liked to work with Uncle Hank on the old Model T car in the shed behind the tractor barn.

Uncle Hank was working to restore the car to its original condition. It had been taken apart piece by piece, then each part had been cleaned. Worn parts had been repaired or replaced. The old paint had been stripped off the body, the rust removed, and a new coat of paint had been applied. Now the work was nearly done. Kyle would polish the car until it shone as Uncle Hank put the engine back together.

As they were working on the car one day, Uncle Hank turned to Kyle and asked, "How would you like to have this car?" Kyle grinned, and his eyes lit up. Uncle Hank smiled. "Someday it will be yours," he said. "It's going to be your inheritance from me."

That evening Kyle excitedly told his parents about Uncle Hank's decision. Mom smiled. "What a nice thing for Great-Uncle Hank to do," she said.

RECEIVE GOD'S INHERITANCE.

Dad nodded. "It certainly is," he said. After a moment he added, "You know, this reminds me of what God has done for us. He has promised that whoever trusts in His Son, Jesus Christ, will someday enjoy all the blessings of heaven, just as you'll someday enjoy owning that car. Aren't you glad you belong to Him?"

HOW ABOUT YOU?

Is there an inheritance waiting in heaven for you? There is if you've asked Jesus Christ to be your Savior. Want to know more? Ask a trusted friend or adult.

TO MEMORIZE:

It is by his great mercy that we have been born again, because God raised Jesus Christ from the dead. Now we live with great expectation, and we have a priceless inheritance.

1 PETER 1:3-4, NLT

BY TOM VANDENBERG

February 20

AN INHERITANCE (PART 2)

Read Ephesians 1:11-14.

As soon as he could, Kyle visited Great-Uncle Hank and helped him work on the Model T again. After a while, Uncle Hank stuck his head out from under the hood and looked at Kyle. "I want you to know my will states that you will inherit this car," he said. "I'd like you to have a set of keys for it now."

"Wow!" Kyle's eyes glistened as he thanked his uncle.

That night Kyle showed his parents the keys. "So you're really going to own that car," said Dad with a smile.

Kyle nodded, but he had a question. "You said Christians will receive the blessings of heaven as an inheritance from God. How can we be sure of that?"

"Well," replied Dad, "how can you be sure Uncle Hank will give you the car?"

Kyle answered, "I trust him because I've never heard him lie. He even gave me keys to prove that he intends to give me the car."

"That's right," answered Dad, "and we can trust God to do what He said, too, because He has never lied. He also sends the Holy Spirit to live in us to prove that we really belong to Him."

CHRISTIANS HAVE THE HOLY SPIRIT.

"How can we know the Holy Spirit is living in us?" asked Kyle.

Dad answered, "Galatians 5:22-23 says the proof or fruit of the Spirit is love, joy, peace, patience, kindness, goodness, faithfulness, gentleness, and self-control."

Mom nodded. "I also know I'm God's child because the Holy Spirit causes me to be interested in the things of God. And He gives me peace in my heart."

HOW ABOUT YOU?

Has the Holy Spirit given you assurance that you are a child of God? Is He changing your life? Is there evidence of His presence in your life?

TO MEMORIZE:

His Spirit joins with our spirit to affirm that we are God's children.
ROMANS 8:16

BY TOM VANDEN BERG

February 21

THE RIGHT EQUIPMENT

Read 2 Timothy 3:14-17.

"Where's your Bible, Jeff?" asked Jenny as they climbed into the car one Sunday morning.

"I dunno," mumbled Jeff. "I can't find it."

"How about your memory verse?" continued Jenny. "Do you know it?"

"Nah." Jeff shook his head. "I was too busy this week."

"That's enough," said Dad sternly as Jenny started to speak again. He looked at Jeff. "I'm afraid you have been neglecting important things lately, Son." Jeff just shrugged.

The next evening, Jeff and his dad decided to play a round of golf. Dad had just started backing out of the driveway when Jeff noticed the golf bag standing at the side of the garage door. "Hold it!" called Jeff, and Dad stopped the car. "You forgot your golfing equipment!" Jeff said with a laugh. He jumped out and ran to get the golf bag.

"Thanks," said Dad as Jeff put the bag in the back seat. "It sure would be easier not to carry all that stuff along, but it would be pretty hard to play golf without it."

"Yeah," said Jeff with a grin. "You gotta be properly equipped."

BE PREPARED TO SERVE GOD.

"That's true." Dad glanced at Jeff. "Did you know that you have to be properly equipped to be a good servant for the Lord, too? That's one reason why it's important to read the Bible and memorize verses and pray. It helps equip you to serve God."

"Well," murmured Jeff weakly, "I . . . I guess so."

"I'm not properly equipped for the game of golf without my clubs and golf balls. And we're not properly equipped to serve God without a knowledge of His Word." Dad grinned at Jeff. "Tell you what," said Dad. "Take your Sunday school book along, and we'll both learn your memory verse while we drive to the golf course. Okay?" Jeff nodded and ran into the house for his book.

HOW ABOUT YOU?

Are you properly equipped as a Christian? Do you read and memorize God's Word so you can share His love with others? Don't try to play the game—to live a Christian life—without the right equipment.

TO MEMORIZE:

God uses [Scripture] to prepare and equip his people to do every good work.

2 TIMOTHY 3:17

BY LENORA MCWHORTEN

SIN BUGS

Read Matthew 25:41-45.

As Hannah turned a rock over in the backyard, she jumped back. "Yuck, Mom! Look at all these icky bugs hiding under this rock!"

Mom watched the bugs scurry around. "Those are pill bugs," she said.

"They don't seem to like the sun. I think they're looking for a dark place to hide," observed Hannah.

"They're a little like us then, aren't they?" Mom said thoughtfully.

Hannah glanced at her mother in surprise. "Huh?"

"Well, just as these bugs are scrambling for hiding places, we sometimes scramble to find hiding places for the sin in our hearts," explained Mom. "We try to keep it in the dark, but God sees it."

"My Sunday school teacher was talking about sin last week. She says there are two kinds, sins of commission and sins of omission."

"And do you know what that means?" asked Mom, smiling.

DO WHAT YOU SHOULD.

"The sins of commission are the bad things we think or do," answered Hannah. "It's a sin to lie or say something to hurt somebody."

"That's right," said Mom, nodding. "And what are the sins of omission?"

"That's when we don't do things we should do," answered Hannah, "like not calling a friend when we know she's sad."

"Good for you!" said Mom. "You remembered that lesson very well. It's even more important to remember that God sees every sin."

Hannah nodded as she watched the last of the insects disappear. "I'll think of these as sin bugs from now on." She shuddered. "They'll be a reminder that I don't want sin in my heart."

HOW ABOUT YOU?

Are *sins of commission* and *sins of omission* new terms to you? It's sometimes easy to recognize the things we do wrong, but it's harder to realize that not doing something may be a sin too.

TO MEMORIZE:

Remember, it is sin to know what you ought to do and then not do it.
JAMES 4:17

BY V. LOUISE CUNNINGHAM

February 23

NEVER IS A LONG TIME

Read Colossians 3:8-13.

"I'm never going to speak to Michelle again!" yelled Tonya, slamming the door behind her.

Her mother frowned. "Never is a long time."

"I don't care how long it is," Tonya snapped. Tonya's words faded as she ran down the hall to her room.

"Tonya!" Mom called after her. "Let's go visit Aunt Margaret!"

A short trip across town brought Tonya and her mother to the Colonial Plaza Nursing Home. As Tonya walked beside her mom down the hall, her mind was still churning with angry thoughts about Michelle.

"Aunt Margaret, what's the matter?" Mom's startled cry brought Tonya back to reality. Mom knelt beside the old lady's wheelchair.

In Aunt Margaret's hand was a crumpled letter. Tears were streaming down her cheeks. "Oh, Brenda," she sobbed. "I've been so stubborn."

"Stubborn about what?" Mom questioned.

"Too stubborn to say, 'I'm sorry.'" Aunt Margaret's voice quivered as she spoke.

FORGIVE OTHERS.

After listening to a long-winded story, Tonya and her mother finally understood why she was so upset. When they finally left, Tonya was wiping her eyes. In the car she turned to her mother. "You mean Aunt Margaret and Aunt Sarah had not spoken to each other for twenty years?"

Mom nodded. "Yes, and now Aunt Sarah has asked Aunt Margaret to forgive her. They can't even remember why they were fighting. I'm glad they finally decided to forgive each other. Unforgiveness is a heavy burden to carry for all those years."

Tonya gulped. "When we get home, I'd better call Michelle. Never is a long time—too long."

HOW ABOUT YOU?

Do you sometimes say things you don't really mean? Is there someone to whom you need to apologize? Do that now before it's too late.

TO MEMORIZE:

Make allowance for each other's faults, and forgive anyone who offends you.

COLOSSIANS 3:13

BY BARBARA J. WESTBERG

February 24

THE BLANK PIECE OF PAPER

Read Romans 8:12-18.

"I want a volunteer to sign this paper." Miss Rito showed her Sunday school class a blank sheet. "When you sign it, you will be agreeing to obey whatever I write on the paper. I could ask you to mow my lawn or to give me your allowance next week. I can write anything I want on this paper." There were no volunteers. "Don't you trust me?"

Finally Gia raised her hand. "I'll sign it."

After Gia signed her name, Miss Rito took the paper again and began writing. Everyone waited breathlessly. She gave the paper back to Gia. "Read it out loud," she instructed.

"Go to the table," Gia read. "Pick up the Bible, and keep whatever you find under it." Quickly, Gia obeyed. "Ooh," she squealed as she lifted the Bible. On the table was a five-dollar bill!

"Thank you, Gia, for trusting me," Miss Rito replied.

TRUST AND OBEY.

Then Miss Rito told the class, "When we give our lives to Jesus, it's like signing a blank sheet of paper. We say, 'Lord, I am surrendering my life to You. You write in the orders.' Before Gia could receive her prize, what did she have to do?"

"She had to sign the paper," said Lena.

"And she had to do what it said," Brent added.

"Right." Miss Rito nodded. "She had to trust me, and she had to obey me. So we must trust God and obey Him, handing our lives over to Him. He has many rewards for those who do."

HOW ABOUT YOU?

Are you afraid to yield your life to God? Don't worry. Surrender your life to Him. You'll be surprised by all the good things He has in store for you.

TO MEMORIZE:

How great is the goodness you have stored up for those who fear you.

PSALM 31:19

BY BARBARA J. WESTBERG

February 25

THE HOSE WITH HOLES (PART 1)

Read 2 Corinthians 5:14-19.

"I'll hook up the hose to rinse off the car," said Philip. He screwed the end of a hose onto the faucet. "All set," he called.

"Turn it on harder," instructed his father. "I'm not getting much water."

"But it's on all the way," objected Philip.

Dad looked up and laughed. "Look at all the leaks—they look like tiny fountains!" he said.

"Maybe we can fix the hose," suggested Philip. He ran into the house and returned carrying a roll of tape. Leaving the water on so he could see the leaks, he wrapped tape around one of the biggest holes. But that just made the other "fountains" jump higher!

"That's not going to work," Dad said, smiling. "By the time you fix the last leak, the first one will be leaking again." Then he added, "This reminds me of you, Philip. You've been getting into a lot of trouble lately. Although you're always sorry, you're soon in some other trouble."

LET JESUS REMOVE YOUR SIN.

Philip sighed. "What's the leaky hose got to do with that?"

"Trying to be good—to get rid of your sins through your own efforts—is like trying to plug up all these holes with tape," explained Dad. "It won't work! We need a new hose. And what you need is a new heart. I'm not talking about a flesh-and-blood heart. I mean a new spiritual heart—a new nature that helps you want to obey God. Only Jesus can give it to you."

HOW ABOUT YOU?

Have you been trying to get rid of sin through your own efforts? It will never work. Come to Jesus just as you are. Let Him cleanse you and give you a new heart.

TO MEMORIZE:

Anyone who belongs to Christ has become a new person.
The old life is gone; a new life has begun!
2 CORINTHIANS 5:17

BY SHERRY L. KUYT

As He Loves

Now I am giving you a new commandment: Love each other.
Just as I have loved you, you should love each other.
JOHN 13:34

Jesus felt strongly about this teaching—so strongly that He called it a commandment. Remember this commandment in your relationships with others. Sometimes you might want to slam your bedroom door. Before you do, think about who's on the other side. Sometimes you might want to yell at someone. Before you do, think about who will hear your words. Try to love as Jesus loves. It's a command!

Unscramble the words that help describe feelings of love.

noiffeact ______________________

grader ______________________

votedoni ______________________

nonsedfs ______________________

grinca ______________________

hayempt ______________________

chattenamt ______________________

ANSWER KEY
affection; regard; devotion; fondness; caring; empathy; attachment

February 26

THE HOSE WITH HOLES (PART 2)

Read Romans 7:15-19, 23-25.

One evening after Philip had accepted Jesus as Savior, his dad found him on the couch in the living room, frowning. "What's wrong?" asked Dad.

Philip looked up and sighed. "Well, I thought that after I accepted Jesus, I would have a new nature," he explained. "But I still do wrong things. Why do I still sin?"

Dad thought for a moment. "I have to wash the car again. We can talk while we work." Once outside Dad said, "Here," handing Philip the hose. "Hook it up."

When Philip turned the water on he yelled, "Dad, this is the same old hose! Did you think it was the new one?"

Dad smiled. "Not exactly," he admitted, watching the familiar fountain display of the leaky old hose. "I want you to understand why a Christian can still sin. Even though we bought a new hose, it's still possible to try using the old one. In the same way it's possible for a Christian to turn back to his old sin nature. When that happens, we need to admit our sin to God and turn from it. We'll have to fight our old nature until we get to heaven."

TURN AWAY FROM SIN.

Philip sighed. "It sounds like a lot of work to me."

Dad nodded. "Sometimes it is," he agreed, "but we can ask the Lord to help us daily. And just as I'm going to get rid of this hose, someday we'll get rid of our old sinful natures—for good!"

HOW ABOUT YOU?

Do you wonder why you still have a problem with sin even though you're a Christian? It's because your old nature still wants to be in control. Trust Jesus daily to help you live for Him.

TO MEMORIZE:

Our old sinful selves were crucified with Christ so that sin might lose its power in our lives. We are no longer slaves to sin.

ROMANS 6:6

BY SHERRY L. KUYT

February 27
JUST IN TIME

Read Ecclesiastes 12:1-5.

Gavin pulled a brightly colored paper from his pocket. *What's this?* he wondered. It was a coupon for a free candy bar. He had cut it out of the newspaper and then forgotten about it. Eager to get the candy, he hurried to the store, picked up the candy bar, and handed the coupon to the sales clerk.

The clerk smiled at Gavin and looked at the coupon. "Oh, you made it just in time," she said. "It expires tomorrow." Gavin was relieved.

On the way home, Gavin decided to stop at his aunt Carrie's house. He told her about the almost-expired coupon.

"Why don't you sit down and have some lemonade with me?" As she handed him a glass, she said, "Your experience reminds me of something else that we can have for free, but it also has an expiration date."

"What's that?" asked Gavin.

"Salvation," Aunt Carrie answered. "God's gift of eternal life is free to those who accept it, because Jesus paid the price by dying for our sins."

ACCEPT CHRIST.

"I know that," answered Gavin. "But what about the expiration date? I never heard about that before."

"It's the day your life on earth ends," said Aunt Carrie. "God gives us a whole lifetime to accept Jesus as our Lord and Savior. But once this earthly life is over, the free offer of eternal life expires."

"I'm glad I have already accepted God's free gift of salvation," said Gavin with a smile.

"Me too," said Aunt Carrie. "It's good to become a Christian when you're young."

HOW ABOUT YOU?

Have you accepted Christ as your Lord and Savior? If not, talk to a trusted Christian friend or adult who can help answer questions you might have about becoming a Christian.

TO MEMORIZE:

The Father who sent me has commanded me what to say and how to say it. And I know his commands lead to eternal life.

JOHN 12:49-50

BY CAROLYN E. YOST

February 28

THE LOST BATTLE

Read 1 John 1:4-10.

"You're quiet this evening, Madeleine. Is something bothering you?" Dad asked.

Madeleine cried, "I can't do it. I've tried!"

"Tried what?" Dad asked.

"Tried acting like a Christian," Madeleine said. "I told a lie today. Christians don't tell lies. Last week I lost my temper. Christians don't lose their tempers. I might as well give up!"

"Madeleine," said Dad, "sometimes you do things you shouldn't do. But you're still a Christian because you have been born again."

"Then why can't I act like a Christian?" Madeleine asked.

"Living the Christian life is a growing process," Dad explained. "Sometimes we lose a battle, but we have to keep fighting."

"Well, I'm tired of trying to be something I'm not. I'm just a big flop!"

After Mom gave thanks for the food, Madeleine watched her father heap his plate full. "Dad! I thought you were on a diet." Madeleine had been so proud of her father as he had lost pound after pound.

KEEP FIGHTING SIN.

"I was," Dad responded, "but today I ate a piece of cake. I cheated on my diet. It's too hard! I just can't do it! I'm tired of dieting."

"But you look so good," Madeleine said.

Dad shook his head. "I'm tired of trying. I'm just a big flop."

"No, you're not. You . . ." Madeleine smiled. "Oh. You're not a flop because you cheated on your diet, and I'm not a flop because I told a lie. We both lost a battle, but we haven't lost the war."

HOW ABOUT YOU?

Have you ever been tempted to quit living for Jesus because you sinned? Maybe you've decided that being a Christian is too hard. Don't be discouraged if you lose a battle with sin occasionally. Confess your sin. God will forgive you. Victory is sure in Jesus!

TO MEMORIZE:

If we confess our sins to him, he is faithful and just to forgive us our sins and to cleanse us from all wickedness.

1 JOHN 1:9

BY BARBARA J. WESTBERG

March 1

WATER RESCUE

Read 2 Timothy 1:6-11.

Jase ran into the garage where his older brother was working on his car. "Cole! Come quick! Brody fell into Mrs. Scott's pool! She can't get him out!"

Cole grabbed a broom from the corner and shot out of the garage to help their small neighbor boy. Jase ran after him and watched as his brother jumped into the pool and swam to where Brody was thrashing around. Cole had Brody grab the end of the broom and pulled him to the side of the pool, where Jase and Mrs. Scott lifted him out. Brody was exhausted, but he had swallowed only a little water and would be fine.

That evening, Jase couldn't stop asking Cole about his daring rescue.

"I should teach you some livesaving techniques," said Cole. "Too many people think they can just jump in the water and swim to someone who's drowning, but that's the worst thing you can do. The person will just climb on you and pull you under. First you should see if there's a way to pull them in without getting in the water yourself, and only jump in as a last resort, but *never* without something for them to grab on to."

TELL SOMEONE ABOUT JESUS.

"Like a broom!" said Jase. "I wonder if any of the neighbors laughed when they saw you sprinting down the street holding a broom."

"They can laugh all they want," said Cole. "I grabbed the first thing I saw that would help me do what I had to do to save Brody."

"You know," said Jase, "this reminds me of something my teacher said last Sunday—that people are 'drowning in sin.' Sometimes I don't tell my friends about Jesus because I'm afraid they'll laugh at me. But you didn't care what anyone might think when you grabbed that broom. If you had stopped to think about that, Brody might have drowned."

Cole smiled. "Yes, but I struggle with the same thing you do sometimes—I'm afraid my college friends will laugh if I talk to them about Jesus. Maybe I should put that broom in my dorm room to remind me that they need to be rescued too!"

HOW ABOUT YOU?

If you could save someone from drowning, would you? Telling people about Jesus and praying for them is another way to help those who are drowning in their sins. If you are not sure how to do this, ask a Christian friend or trusted adult to help you.

TO MEMORIZE:

Go and make disciples of all the nations.

MATTHEW 28:19

BY VICKI L. REINHARDT

March 2

STILL MORE SANDING

Read Psalm 66:8-12.

Greg watched as his father began refinishing the old table. Dad put a new piece of sandpaper in his electric sander and began to work.

"You're spoiling it," Greg said when Dad finally stopped the sander. "You're making it look like it has all kinds of scratches."

"I'm not done with it yet," Dad answered, turning on the sander once more.

Greg watched for a long time. His father finally stopped sanding and began applying stain. When he had finished staining the wood, the table did look pretty. But the next day he put a new piece of sandpaper in the sander and once again began sanding the tabletop.

"Dad," Greg called out, "you've already put the stain on."

Dad turned off the machine and began to explain. "It still has some flaws in it," he said, taking Greg's hand and rubbing it over the tabletop so he could feel the rough spots. "I'll just keep sanding until it's perfect."

When the table was finished, Greg admired the final product. But he was surprised to hear Dad say, "We're a lot like this table."

LET GOD SMOOTH YOU OUT.

Greg laughed. "I sure hope you're not planning to use the sander on me!"

Dad smiled. "God sometimes uses difficult situations to smooth out our rough places," he explained.

Greg nodded. He thought of the time he broke his arm. He had learned patience as he had to learn to write with his left hand. He would ask God to help him grow and become a better Christian through whatever circumstances came into his life.

HOW ABOUT YOU?

Have you had difficult experiences? Perhaps there has been a death or a divorce in your family. Maybe you or someone you love is sick. Whatever your experience, let God use it to help you grow.

TO MEMORIZE:

When he tests me, I will come out as pure as gold.

JOB 23:10

BY RUTH I. JAY

March 3

BE SHARP

Read Psalm 119:97-104.

Maria climbed slowly into the car. "Hi, honey," said her dad. "It sure was a beautiful day for your picnic."

"Yeah," mumbled Maria.

"Did you have a good time?" Dad asked.

"Oh, sure," she answered after a moment of silence.

Dad glanced at her curiously. "You don't sound very happy. What's wrong?"

"Oh, Dad," moaned Maria, "I blew it! While we were on the swing, Jenna asked me about being a Christian, and I couldn't answer her questions very well."

"I see," Dad said thoughtfully. As they pulled in to the driveway, he spoke again. "I've got something in the garage I want to show you."

"All right," Maria agreed glumly.

Dad walked to his workbench and handed Maria a knife and a piece of wood. "Here," he said. "This is one of my wood-carving knives. Would you cut this stick in half for me, please?"

BE READY TO WITNESS.

Maria tried to do as he directed. "I can't," she complained. "It's dull!"

"You're right," agreed Dad. "It's been away from the sharpener a long time. This knife has to be sharpened often to be of much use. And if we want God to be able to use us, we have to be 'sharpened' by spending time with Him."

Maria looked from her dad to the knife. "You gave me a dull knife on purpose, didn't you, Dad?" she asked. "You wanted me to see that I'm like this knife—I'm dull! You're right, too. I haven't been reading my Bible very often or even praying for my friends. I hope I'll be sharper the next time Jenna asks questions."

HOW ABOUT YOU?

Are you faithful in spending time with the Lord and studying His Word? Are you ready to answer when someone asks you questions about God? If not, it's time to sharpen up.

TO MEMORIZE:

If someone asks about your hope as a believer, always be ready to explain it.

1 PETER 3:15

BY SARA L. NELSON

March 4

JUST THE SHELL

Read 2 Corinthians 5:1-2, 6-8.

David always liked going to the beach with his family. He had been able to get a good-sized collection of shells from their trips. And now, here they were again, he and his father, walking up and down the sandy beach, looking for more shells. Suddenly he stopped and called, "Dad, come here! I found something, but I don't know what it is."

Dad soon joined David, who pointed at a strange-looking sea creature. At least that is what David thought it was. Dad knelt down and looked carefully at David's find. As he did so, David begged him to be careful. He didn't want his father to be bitten. "This one will never bite," Dad said. "There's no life in it."

"How come?" David asked.

David's father picked it up. "Because this is just a shell," he explained, turning it over so David could see what it looked like. "It's a lobster shell. There comes a time in the lobster's life when he squeezes out and leaves his shell."

YOUR BODY IS YOUR SHELL.

Before David could ask any more questions, his father asked if he remembered when Grandpa Jones died. "Do you remember how I explained that Grandpa had gone to heaven?" Dad asked.

David nodded. "But I didn't understand how he could be in the casket and be in heaven, too," David replied.

"It's very much like this shell that you just found. The lobster is gone," Dad said. "This is just his shell. In the same way, when Grandpa died, he left his body and went to live with Jesus because he was a Christian."

HOW ABOUT YOU?

Do you have a Christian relative or friend who has died recently? If so, that Christian has simply left his body and has gone to be with Jesus. Your body is just the house in which your soul lives.

TO MEMORIZE:

Yes, we are fully confident, and we would rather be away from these earthly bodies, for then we will be at home with the Lord.

2 CORINTHIANS 5:8

BY RUTH I. JAY

No Worries

Be strong and courageous, all you who put your hope in the LORD!
PSALM 31:24

It's the day of a big test, and you aren't sure you studied enough. Or it's the night before your big game, and you're afraid you won't play well enough to help your team win. When worries like these come, remember that God can strengthen your heart. Take a moment to think about God's promise in Psalm 31. Put your hope in the Lord. He will give you courage and make your heart strong.

These people risked scorn, embarrassment, or their future by doing the right thing. Now that's courage!

ACROSS

3. He obeyed God, and the walls of Jericho came down.
4. God protected this man from being eaten in a lions' den.
5. He showed courage to be a good neighbor to a dying man.
6. She bravely followed her mother-in-law to a new land.
7. She stood up to a sneaky bully and saved her people.

DOWN

1. With Meshach and Abednego, he would not bow before a false god.
2. This brave little man paid back those he cheated.
4. He defeated a giant using river stones and a slingshot.

ANSWER KEY
ACROSS: 3. Joshua; 4. Daniel; 5. Samaritan; 6. Ruth; 7. Esther
DOWN: 1. Shadrach; 2. Zacchaeus; 4. David

March 5

ONCE IS TOO OFTEN

Read Proverbs 1:20-28.

"Uncle Randy was in a motorcycle accident," said Mom as she hung up the phone. "He had apparently been taking drugs." Lisa and Kristen didn't know what to say. After a moment Mom continued. "You know, the first time Uncle Randy took drugs he said he just wanted to get high once, but he never quit." Mom turned to leave the room. "I'd like some time alone."

"Sure, Mom," the girls answered.

After a few moments Mom heard a crash. She went to investigate and saw pieces of china dolls on the floor. "Girls, you know you're not to handle those dolls. They're antique and very fragile."

"Lisa said it wouldn't hurt to play with them just once," murmured Kristen.

Lisa picked up the pieces. "Can't we fix them?" she asked.

"We'll try," said Mom, "but they'll never be the same. And it won't change your punishment for disobeying."

Mom got the glue, and they went to work. "The cracks still show," observed Lisa.

DON'T TRY DRUGS.

"They look like scars," Kristen added.

"I'm doing my best," Mom answered. "You know, girls, as I try to repair these, I keep thinking of Uncle Randy. His life is full of scars because of drugs. He never finished school, he lost several jobs, and he had this accident." As she set one doll down to dry, she said to her daughters, "When you look at these dolls, I hope you'll think about the results of doing wrong—even one time."

HOW ABOUT YOU?

Have you been tempted to try drugs just once to see what it's like? Once is too much. Doing drugs for pleasure is wrong in God's sight. It's destructive to the body, and taking them once could hurt you for life.

TO MEMORIZE:

For God bought you with a high price. So you must honor God with your body.
1 CORINTHIANS 6:20

BY SARA L. NELSON

March 6

FLYING HIGH

Read Psalm 37:1-8.

Tyler watched the red kite soaring in the bright sky. His brother Mike grinned. "Looks like fun, huh, Tyler? Would you like to be able to fly high like that?"

"Sure would!" Tyler said, grinning back. "But if I were that kite, I'd want to break loose and fly away, high into the sky."

Mike laughed. "But if you broke loose, you'd crash to the ground instead of flying away," he said.

Tyler turned to his father. "Would I, Dad?"

"Yep." Dad nodded. "The kite flies only because the wind pushes it against the resistance of the string. Without that string, it would soon fall."

"Oh." Tyler held the spool of string even more tightly.

"You know," Dad mused, "in a way, we're something like that kite. The string guides the kite, and God guides us. Sometimes it's hard to act the way He wants us to, and we pull against the discipline that He uses to direct us. We try to break loose and fly our own way. But if God ever let us go, we would plunge right down, like a kite whose string has broken."

SUBMIT TO GOD'S CONTROL.

"That's pretty serious," said Mike.

"Would God ever let us go, Dad?" asked Tyler.

"No, Tyler. If you trust Jesus as your Lord and Savior, He'll never let you go," Dad assured him. "But it's important to submit ourselves to God's control."

HOW ABOUT YOU?

Do you sometimes resent the strings you feel God has put on your life? Do you feel you'd like to be free to go wherever you want, to choose your own friends, or to pick your own TV programs? Everyone feels like that sometimes. But God has a reason for everything He allows to happen in your life.

TO MEMORIZE:

Commit everything you do to the LORD. Trust him, and he will help you.

PSALM 37:5

BY JUDITH K. BOOGAART

March 7

A FISH OUT OF WATER

Read 1 Corinthians 12:4-10, 13.

As the small rowboat rocked with the gentle motion of the water, Nicholas watched his father cast his fishing line. "Dad," said Nicholas, "I don't want to go to the new church tomorrow."

"Really?" asked Dad. "Why not?"

"All my friends are back at our old church," replied Nicholas.

Nicholas's dad slowly reeled in his line a little. "I know we're going to miss everybody," he said, "but we had to move, and we still need to go to church."

"Can't we just have church at home?" asked Nicholas. "We could sing and read from the Bible."

"I've got a bite," said Dad. In a few moments he held up a small fish. "What would happen if we threw this fish in the boat and left it there?"

"It would die," said Nicholas.

"And if we throw it back?" asked Dad as he threw the fish into the lake.

"Well, now it will live."

WORSHIP GOD WITH OTHERS.

"What if we took the fish to another lake?" Dad asked next. "Would it be able to live there?"

Nicholas thought a moment. "I think so," he said.

"Well," said Dad, "our family is a little like a fish that's been taken from one lake and put into another. We're in a new place where we have everything we need to go on living—food, clothes, a home." He paused. "But as Christians, we also need to be around other Christians. If we don't go to church, we can begin to die spiritually—like a fish out of water. Besides, we please God when we're part of a church family that cares for one another."

HOW ABOUT YOU?

Have you felt out of place when you had to change churches? Remember, meeting with other Christians is an important part of worshiping God.

TO MEMORIZE:

Yes, the body has many different parts, not just one part.

1 CORINTHIANS 12:14

BY DANIEL A. BURNS

March 8

NO MORE DOUBTS

Read John 20:24-30.

I wish this feeling would never end, Juliana thought as she sat under the stars with her youth group friends. As she and her Christian friends sang God's praises, she felt closer to Him than ever before. But she'd been to retreats before, and she knew that on Monday morning she wouldn't feel the same. *If I don't feel close to God on Monday, maybe He isn't real at all.* Juliana tried to forget these ideas, but she couldn't.

When Juliana arrived home the next day, Mom was busy with dinner preparations. "My cousin, Pauline, is coming for dinner," Mom explained.

"I didn't know you had a cousin," said Juliana as she began to help.

Pauline entertained the family all during dinner with funny stories about Mom's childhood. "I'm glad I got to know you," Juliana told her. "And just think, a few hours ago I didn't know you existed."

"Shame on your mom for not mentioning me," Pauline said with a wink. "But I've been here all along."

TRUST GOD'S WORD, NOT YOUR FEELINGS.

The words stuck with Juliana. Cousin Pauline's existence wasn't dependent on Juliana knowing about her or feeling her presence. It was the same with God. Juliana had doubted God was real because she didn't always feel His presence.

"Tell us about the retreat," suggested Mom.

"It was great," Juliana said. "Really great."

HOW ABOUT YOU?

Have you ever felt God to be especially close, only to be doubtful of His presence when you no longer felt that way? It's nice to feel God's presence, but it's important to know He is there whether you have the feeling or not.

TO MEMORIZE:

Then Jesus told him, "You believe because you have seen me. Blessed are those who believe without seeing me."

JOHN 20:29

BY KATHERINE R. ADAMS

March 9

OUT OF TUNE

Read Philippians 2:1-5.

"Where's my guitar pick?" demanded James. "You've been in my room again, haven't you, Mandy? I left my pick on my dresser, and now it's gone."

"I didn't take it," said Mandy. "And I don't go in your room."

"Well, someone took it!" James stomped down the hall and slammed his bedroom door. Mandy's brother had been acting like this often in recent weeks.

Later that evening James sat at the piano, tuning his guitar. "Where did you find your pick?" asked Mom. "Mandy told me you thought she had taken it."

"It was in my pocket," James muttered. He struck a piano key with one finger. *Plunk! Plunk!* Then he plucked a guitar string. *Ping! Ping! Plunk!* After a few more twists and turns his guitar was in tune.

"You're getting pretty good, Son," said Dad.

"Why do you always listen to the piano and the guitar together?" asked Mandy.

"If all the strings aren't in tune with the piano, they don't sound good with each other, either," explained James.

GET IN TUNE WITH GOD. 

Mom looked at James. "Just like each of your guitar strings has to be in tune with the piano, so every member of the family needs to be in harmony with God. Otherwise, they are out of tune with each other," she said thoughtfully.

Dad nodded. "I've been hearing angry words around here. Could it be someone is out of tune?"

James sighed. "All right—I know it's me," he admitted. "I'm sorry."

HOW ABOUT YOU?

Are you out of tune with God? Do you have trouble getting along with your family and friends? Now's the time to have a little prayer meeting all by yourself, and let God get you back in tune.

TO MEMORIZE:

How wonderful and pleasant it is when brothers live together in harmony!

PSALM 133:1

BY BARBARA J. WESTBERG

March 10

THE EMPTY ROLL

Read Galatians 2:16-20.

"Your hot dog's almost done, Ellis," Aaron told his little brother. Aaron twirled the long fork once more before withdrawing it from the fire. He placed the hot dog on a bun and handed it to Ellis. Then he began to roast one for himself.

"Know what, Dad?" Aaron said to his father, who was roasting two hot dogs at a time. "I think Devon, the new boy at school, is a Christian. I know he goes to church, and he never swears or gets mad. He's not like most of the guys."

"Well, that sounds promising," replied Dad, who moved to the picnic table and handed one of the hot dogs to Mom.

Aaron followed. "Ellis, you're not eating the hot dog I roasted for you," he complained, looking at the untouched meat on Ellis's plate.

"Am too. See?" Ellis held up a half-eaten hot dog bun, thickly spread with ketchup. "I like hot dogs."

"That's just bread," said Aaron. "It's not a hot dog unless the meat's in it."

A CHRISTIAN HAS CHRIST.

"Aaron's right," said Dad. "And here's something else to remember—just as a hot dog roll without the meat isn't a hot dog, a person isn't a Christian without Christ. He's like that empty roll. Take your friend Devon, for instance. I'm glad he's such a nice young man, Aaron, but none of the things you mentioned make him a Christian. He is a Christian only if he's accepted Christ into his life."

HOW ABOUT YOU?

Have you asked Jesus Christ to come into your life? You may be a very nice person—but a very nice person without Christ is not a Christian. Don't be like an empty roll.

TO MEMORIZE:

My old self has been crucified with Christ. It is no longer I who live, but Christ lives in me. So I live in this earthly body by trusting in the Son of God, who loved me and gave himself for me.

GALATIANS 2:20

BY HAZEL W. MARETT

March 11

CHRISTIAN SAYS

Read 1 John 3:16-18, 23-24.

"I'm Simon—and remember, you must always do what Simon *says*," Miss Elrojo, Anthony's teacher, said.

The children straightened their posture, preparing for the competition.

"Simon says, 'Thumbs up,'" said Miss Elrojo. So Anthony turned his thumbs up. "Simon says, 'Step forward,'" Miss Elrojo instructed as she stepped forward. All the children followed her example. "Simon says, 'Snap your fingers.'" But Miss Elrojo clapped her hands instead, and before Anthony could stop himself, he clapped his hands too.

After supper that night Anthony's family learned a Bible verse during evening devotions. "We'll learn 1 John 3:18," said Dad. "Dear children, let's not merely say that we love each other; let us show the truth by our actions." They repeated it together, and Dad explained it. "Our actions should match our words," he said.

"Hey," laughed Anthony, "Simon should learn this verse."

DON'T JUST SAY—BUT DO.

"Simon?" asked Mom. "What do you mean?" So Anthony explained the trouble he'd had when "Simon" said one thing but did another.

"That brings up a good point," observed Dad. "As Christians, we sometimes act like we're playing a game. Maybe it could be called Christian Says. Sometimes Christians say one thing and do another. Can you think of examples?"

"Christians say, 'Read your Bible,' and then they only open it on Sunday," suggested Mom.

"Christians say, 'Go to church,' and then they stay home to watch a game on TV," said Anthony's brother.

"Christians say, 'Be helpful,' and then they don't do chores," added Anthony.

"You've got the idea," said Dad.

HOW ABOUT YOU?

Do you play Christian Says? Remember that people will often follow what you do rather than what you say. Listen to what God says, and love others in deed, not just in word.

TO MEMORIZE:

Dear children, let's not merely say that we love each other; let us show the truth by our actions.

1 JOHN 3:18

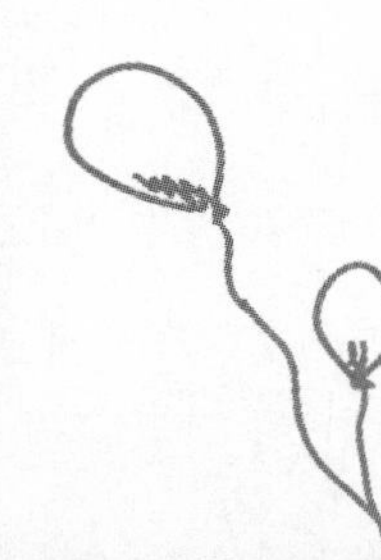

BY HAZEL W. MARETT

Faith in Action: My Devotional Journey

Because of his glory and excellence, he has given us great and precious promises. These are the promises that enable you to share his divine nature and escape the world's corruption caused by human desires.

2 PETER 1:4

This spring, keep a record when you witness your faith in action. Specifically focus on God's promises as they relate to the themes for this season (courage, trust, and witness). Or make a note when you apply your devotional studies in everyday life. This way, you can see your faith in action!

God's promises were revealed to me . . .

MARCH: COURAGE

WHEN ____

____

WHERE ____

____

HOW ____

____

MORE ____

____

____

APRIL: TRUST

WHEN ______________________________

____

WHERE ______________________________

____

HOW ______________________________

____

MORE ______________________________

____

____

MAY: WITNESS

WHEN ______________________________

____

WHERE ______________________________

____

HOW ______________________________

____

MORE ______________________________

____

____

FISHING FOR PEOPLE

Read Matthew 4:18-22.

Grandpa stretched out lazily on the creek bank. Tamara shifted restlessly. "The fish aren't biting here. Let's try another spot, Grandpa," she suggested.

"This is the third spot we've tried," Grandpa reminded her. "Relax."

Tamara sighed. As her cork rocked on the gentle waves, she sighed again.

"Something bothering you?" asked Grandpa.

"Yeah," said Tamara. "I've invited six girls to church this week, and not one is going to come. I think I'll quit inviting anybody to church." Grandpa wrinkled his brow as he looked at Tamara. Then he sat up and started reeling in his line. Tamara jumped up. "You got a bite?" she asked excitedly.

Grandpa shook his head. "No. I'm quittin'."

"But Grandpa, we've got all afternoon," Tamara argued.

"Yeah, but we've been here long enough, and we haven't caught one fish. I'm giving up fishing for good." He stood up. "Pull in your line."

KEEP WITNESSING.

"Please, let's wait a little longer," Tamara pleaded.

As Grandpa checked his bait, he gave his granddaughter a crooked grin. "Well, if you're sure. I just thought you were ready to quit. If you give up that easy fishing for people, I reckoned you would soon tire of fishing for fish, too."

Tamara smiled. "I get the message, Grandpa. When we get home, I'll call Louisa and invite her to church."

Grandpa tossed his line back into the water. "That's more like it," he said. "Just because the fish aren't biting today, it doesn't mean we give up fishing."

HOW ABOUT YOU?

Does it seem like you're wasting your time inviting your friends to church or witnessing in other ways? Don't be discouraged. Sooner or later someone will take the bait. Just keep on fishing.

TO MEMORIZE:

Jesus called out to them, "Come, follow me, and I will show you how to fish for people!"

MARK 1:17

BY BARBARA J. WESTBERG

March 13

A SICK FRIEND

Read Romans 8:18-23.

Sam sat on the porch steps, his chin propped up in his hand. There was a baseball game on TV, but he didn't even care. All he could think about was Roberto! Just the week before, the boys had taken a hike around the park. Now Roberto was in the hospital, seriously sick. When Sam's mom had talked to Roberto's mom that morning, Mrs. Joakim said the doctors had told them Roberto might not get well. That was scary! Sam sat and thought about his friend.

The screen door opened behind him, and Sam's mother brought out a glass of lemonade. "I thought you might be thirsty," she said.

Sam drank the lemonade without even noticing how good it tasted. "Mom, why did Roberto get sick?"

"Well," replied Mom, "all the bad things that happen to us are a result of sin entering the world. It's because of sin that the world is out of balance. Death will come to all of us sooner or later—through sickness, through car accidents, or through other ways. The important thing is that God cares about us, and he cares about Roberto. He is there to give comfort to the Joakim family. He is there to help Roberto face the situation. We should pray that Roberto senses the comfort that the Lord can provide."

GOD GIVES COMFORT.

"Mom, could we pray right now?" Sam asked.

So Mom sat on the step next to Sam, and together they prayed for Roberto.

HOW ABOUT YOU?

Has there been a time when one of your friends or a relative was very sick? Sickness and death are a result of sin entering the world. But God gives comfort to Christians! He promises them an eternal home in heaven. Through Him you can have peace, even in the most difficult times.

TO MEMORIZE:

Yet what we suffer now is nothing compared to
the glory he will reveal to us later.
ROMANS 8:18

BY LENORA MCWHORTEN

March 14

NO ROOM

Read Matthew 7:21-27.

"Are we almost there? It's been such a long ride!" exclaimed Jessica. She and her sister, Kelley, could hardly wait to get to Sea World and the hotel.

"Two whole days in a hotel with a pool!" Kelley giggled.

"We're here, girls," announced Dad. He turned the car toward the hotel.

Inside, Dad approached the desk. "My last name is Gardiner," he said. "We have reservations."

The receptionist checked the computer. "I'm sorry," she said uncertainly. "I can't find your name here."

"Please look again," Dad said. After another search, the receptionist shook her head slowly. "Well, do you have a room with two double beds?" asked Dad.

"No, I don't. I'm really sorry," the lady replied. "There's a convention in town, and all the hotels are full."

"It would be awful to go back home now," wailed Jessica.

BE REGISTERED IN HEAVEN.

Dad nodded. "There's been a mistake," he said, "but don't fret. Let's go have some ice cream while we think about what to do next."

Seated in the restaurant, Dad said, "If this seems bad, think how it would be if we should arrive in heaven someday and discover that our names have never been registered there."

"But, Dad," Jessica said thoughtfully, "that won't happen. The Bible says Jesus has gone ahead of us and has already written the names of those who love Him."

"You're absolutely right," said Dad with a smile.

HOW ABOUT YOU?

Is your name registered in heaven? If not, talk to a trusted Christian friend or adult to find out what you need to do.

TO MEMORIZE:

I saw the dead, both great and small, standing before God's throne. And the books were opened, including the Book of Life. And the dead were judged according to what they had done, as recorded in the books.

REVELATION 20:12

BY PHYLLIS I. KLOMPARENS

March 15
MODEL BUILDING

Read Psalm 32:7-11.

"Mom, why do we have to go to church every Sunday?" Chad asked at breakfast. "Some of my friends don't go."

"Well, we do," his mother answered. "We go to be instructed from God's Word, so please get ready." When Chad was younger, he loved to go to church. But as he grew older, he didn't want to go.

That afternoon the subject came up again. "My friends are playing basketball tonight," said Chad. "May I go?"

"Chad, we're going to church," Dad answered.

"I don't see why we can't just read the Bible at home," Chad grumbled.

After supper the next day Chad covered a table with newspapers. "I'm going to work on my new model car. Just look at all those pieces!" he exclaimed. He began to work but soon asked, "Can you help me with this, Dad?"

Dad shrugged. "I don't think you need me," he said. "Just put the pieces together. It should turn out just fine."

GO TO CHURCH.

"How would I know where the pieces go when I can't understand it?"

Dad walked over to the table. "Chad," he said, "trying to put this model together without my help is like trying to live your Christian life without help from God's people. Lately you've not wanted to go to church, yet our pastor and Sunday school teachers help us understand how God wants us to live."

"I hadn't thought about it that way," said Chad. "I guess you're right."

HOW ABOUT YOU?

Do you think you don't need to go to church? It's great to read the Bible, and you should do that. But God has also provided godly men and women in your church and Sunday school who can help you understand His Word. Learn from them.

TO MEMORIZE:

Teach me how to live, O LORD. Lead me along the right path, for my enemies are waiting for me.

PSALM 27:11

BY DEAN KELLEY

March 16

FOLLOW THE MANUAL

Read Psalm 119:9-18.

Dylan excitedly helped Dad unpack the big box. The small, old TV had given out completely. Dylan looked forward to watching his favorite team on a large screen. "I know how to hook up this baby," he told his father. "I helped Tony get his TV hooked up last Christmas." Dad smiled and let Dylan work.

After connecting the cable box, he plugged the TV cord into the wall socket. He waited for the picture to come into view. When it did, it was blurred. "I know what's wrong," he said, adjusting a few buttons on the set. But still the picture was out of focus.

"Are you sure you've got it hooked up right?" his father asked, offering to check it out.

Dylan pushed his father's hand away. "Sure," he said. "This TV is practically the same as Tony's, and we got it together okay. There's got to be something wrong with this one."

FOLLOW GOD'S BOOK.

"Read the instruction sheet," Dad suggested. "This set could be different from Tony's."

Dylan picked up the instructions that had come with the TV and began to read them. Then he went back to the TV and fixed it.

Dylan was embarrassed. "If all else fails," he said, "read the instructions."

"Better yet," said Dad, "read the instructions *first.* That principle is true in our Christian lives too. The Bible is God's instruction book. It not only tells us how to receive Jesus as our Savior, it also tells us how to live the Christian life. But we won't know unless we read it."

HOW ABOUT YOU?

Are you a Christian? Then the Bible should be your guide, your instruction book. It explains what a Christian should do about sin. It commands every believer to love, to give, to witness, and many other things. God's book is very important.

TO MEMORIZE:

You made me; you created me. Now give me
the sense to follow your commands.
PSALM 119:73

BY RUTH I. JAY

March 17

NEEDED: A LIGHT (PART 1)

Read Psalm 119:105-112.

"It's so dark out!" said Kathy as she and her brother, Josh, stumbled along the path toward their campsite. They had been visiting some friends.

"Yeah," agreed Josh, "but we're almost—" His words were cut off as he caught his toe on a tree root and fell.

Kathy reached down to help him up. "Are you okay?"

"Yes," said Josh, brushing himself off, "but we'd better not go quite so fast." Kathy agreed, and the two of them moved slowly and carefully along until they reached the camp where their parents were waiting.

"We could hear you two coming," Mom greeted them. "Did someone fall?"

"Josh did," replied Kathy, "but he's not hurt. It was so dark we couldn't see."

"Why didn't you use your flashlight?" asked Dad.

"Flashlight?" Kathy and Josh looked at each other. "Oh, our flashlight!" They began to laugh.

"Real smart, Josh," teased Kathy. "You've got the flashlight, you know. You stuck it in your sweater pocket."

USE YOUR BIBLE DAILY.

"I forgot I had it," admitted Josh.

"You two remind me of a lot of people," observed Dad. "They have a light for their path, but they either forget to use it, or they just don't bother."

"Like who?" Kathy wanted to know.

"Like all the Christians who don't read their Bibles," replied Dad, picking up his own. "God says His Word is a light to our path, but it doesn't do any good if we don't use it."

HOW ABOUT YOU?

Do you read your Bible regularly? It contains many principles to help you in your daily life. It has a lot of practical advice. It offers comfort when you hurt. But unless you use it, it can't help you.

TO MEMORIZE:

Your word is a lamp to guide my feet and a light for my path.

PSALM 119:105

BY HAZEL W. MARETT

March 18

NEEDED: A LIGHT (PART 2)

Read Psalm 119:105-112.

"Why don't you sleep at our camp tonight?" Josh asked his friend Kendall. "My mom said it was okay with her."

"Can I, Mom?" Kendall looked over at his mother.

Kendall's mother laughed. "Take your sleeping bag and run along," she agreed.

Soon the boys were on their way. Josh snapped on his flashlight. "Last night I left this thing in my pocket all the way home. I'm not going to make the same mistake twice!" he said as he led the way. He turned back to flash the light on Kendall's path. He continued to leave the beam of light on the path behind him, making sure Kendall could see. "Last night I fell over a tree roo—" Down went Josh.

"Are you okay?" asked Kendall.

Josh got up and retrieved his flashlight. "Yeah," he mumbled. "Walk up here with me so we can both see where we're going."

When they arrived at Josh's campsite, his family was waiting. "We saw your light, and heard a crash," said Mom. "What happened?"

APPLY GOD'S WORD TO YOURSELF.

"Fell again, didn't you?" said Kathy with a smirk.

"Do you know who you remind me of tonight?" Dad asked.

Josh shook his head. "I was using my flashlight."

Dad nodded. "Yep, and you were pointing it on somebody else's path. You remind me of people who hear God's Word preached, and they think, *I hope so-and-so is listening. He really needs this.* Or maybe they read something from God's Word and apply it to somebody else's life. They fail to see that they need it themselves."

HOW ABOUT YOU?

Did you notice that today's Scripture reading is the same as yesterday's passage? Read it again, and emphasize the words *I*, *my*, and *me*. Then when you read other passages in the Bible, such as "Be kind to each other," think of what you should do.

TO MEMORIZE:

I am determined to keep your decrees to the very end.

PSALM 119:112

BY HAZEL W. MARETT

New Places

The Lord is faithful; he will strengthen you
and guard you from the evil one.
2 THESSALONIANS 3:3

If you have to move to a new neighborhood or a new school, remember that God promises His protection. Just think of Abraham. He was old when God told him to leave his home. "Go to a new place," God said, "and I will bless you." So Abraham and his wife, Sarah, obeyed God and left their home. God took care of them as they traveled wherever He told them to go. And God kept His promise by blessing them with a son in their old age.

Help the children find their way to their new school.

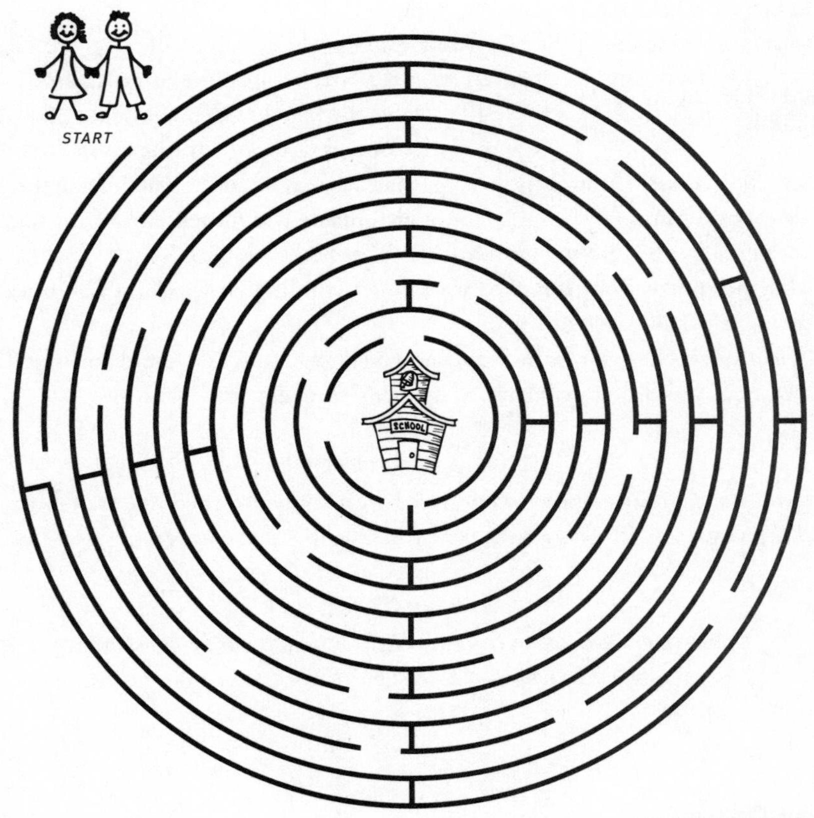

SEE ANSWER IN BACK

March 19

THE TICKING WATCH

Read 1 Corinthians 15:42-45, 51.

Marina screamed and sat up in bed. She began to cry. Her parents quickly came to her bedside, and her mother held her tightly. "Won't it ever stop?" asked Marina between sobs. "I had another nightmare about the accident when Aunt Karen died. I keep seeing the car wreck."

"Try to remember your aunt the way she used to be—lively, loving, and beautiful," Marina's father suggested.

"I try," said Marina, "but I can't seem to remember her that way."

"Honey, you know that Aunt Karen was a Christian," Mom reminded her, "so she's alive in heaven. Can you picture her there?"

Marina shook her head. "I can't see her that way either," she said.

"I want to show you something," said Dad. He left the room, returning soon with a watch, which he placed in Marina's hand.

Marina shuddered. "Oh, take Aunt Karen's watch away," she begged. "It's all broken from the wreck—just like Aunt Karen."

THE REAL PERSON NEVER DIES.

Father took the watch. "Yes," he said, "like Aunt Karen. The case is scratched, and the crystal's broken. But let's look inside." After some prying, Marina's dad lifted the watch from the case. "Look. It's still running," he said. "Only the outside was ruined. And Aunt Karen is still living. Only the case she lived in here—her body—is dead."

After a moment Marina looked up with a trembling smile. "Aunt Karen truly is still alive, isn't she?" she said.

"I'll get a new case for this watch, and you may have it as a reminder," said Dad. "Remember, Aunt Karen will have a new body someday too."

HOW ABOUT YOU?

Has death taken away someone you love? If you and your loved one are Christians, you'll meet again at Christ's return, and you'll be together forever.

TO MEMORIZE:

Dear friends, we are already God's children, but he has not yet shown us what we will be like when Christ appears.

1 JOHN 3:2

BY MARY ROSE PEARSON

March 20

THE RAFT RESCUE

Read John 5:20-24.

"Help! Save me!" Todd screamed as his homemade raft rushed toward the falls. Because the current was rough, he had tied the raft to a tree on the riverbank. However, the once-thick rope had become frayed. When he'd jumped onto the raft, the rope had snapped, sending the raft downstream.

Oh no! Todd thought. *What now? I can't swim well enough to reach the shore. Two miles downstream, the river plunges fifty feet over Drop-Off Point!* The river ran right next to the road, so he waved his arms and yelled.

Todd's father was driving home from work when he looked out at the river. Upstream he could see the raft spinning around—and someone was on it! Quickly stopping the car, he kicked off his shoes and jumped into the river. Being a strong swimmer, he headed toward the middle of the river and waited for the raft to reach him. How surprised he was to see his own son on it! He called out, "Todd, jump! I'll save you!"

LET JESUS SAVE YOU.

Todd looked at the sturdy raft, then at his father in the swirling waters. He wasn't sure he wanted to leave the raft, but he knew it would mean death if he didn't. As he leaped into the surging water, his father caught him. Todd's father slowly made it back to the shore, with Todd in tow.

Back home, Dad said, "What I did for you today is sort of like what Jesus did for us. We couldn't save ourselves from our sins. Just like you had to trust me to save you when you jumped, we need to be willing to trust the Lord."

HOW ABOUT YOU?

Have you put your faith in Jesus Christ? If not, talk to a trusted Christian friend or adult to find out more.

TO MEMORIZE:

The wages of sin is death, but the free gift of God is eternal life through Christ Jesus our Lord.

ROMANS 6:23

BY CHARLES VANDER MEER

March 21

NO REJECTS

Read Psalm 139:14-18.

"Mom, you should have seen the new kid at our youth group last night!" said Tom as he reached for a freshly baked chocolate chip cookie.

"What about him?" asked Mom as she pulled another batch from the oven.

"He's really weird!" exclaimed Tom.

"Oh?" Mom raised her eyebrows. "What's so different about him?"

"Well, for one thing, he dresses funny." Tom laughed as he remembered. "He had on these clothes that look twenty years old!"

"Maybe his family is short on money," suggested Mom.

Tom shrugged. "His clothes aren't all that's weird about him," he said. "He has a goofy-looking nose that—" He stopped short as he watched his mother sort through the cookies she had just baked. She inspected each one closely and then separated them onto different plates. "What are you doing?" he asked.

Mom picked up the fullest plate and walked toward the trash can. "Some of these didn't turn out quite right," she said. "I'll just dump them."

ACCEPT EVERYONE.

"Don't throw them away!" exclaimed Tom in disbelief.

"But they're not perfect, Tom," explained Mom. "I examined each one, and only a few have the right color and the exact number of chips I like in a cookie."

"They're still good, though," protested Tom. "You have to expect them to be different. . . ." He hesitated and then added quietly, "Just like the new kid, huh?"

Mom nodded. "Just like the new kid," she agreed. "Just like all kids—and all men and women. God made them all different—He made them all special. He loves them all, and we should too."

HOW ABOUT YOU?

Do you have trouble liking people who dress or talk differently from you and your friends? Remember that God created them and loves them. Don't reject them.

TO MEMORIZE:

Thank you for making me so wonderfully complex! Your workmanship is marvelous—how well I know it.

PSALM 139:14

BY DANIEL A. BURNS

March 22

THE LITTLE TOE

Read 1 Corinthians 12:20-27.

Jana sighed as she sat down at the table one morning. "I wish I could do something important for the special services at church," she said. "Carlos and Jack are going to play a trumpet duet; and Melanie, Sherri, and Tara are singing a trio. Holly's playing the piano one evening, and Bonnie was asked to read her poem. Everybody's doing something but me."

"I thought you were helping in the nursery," said Mom.

"I always do that," said Jana, "but I'd like to do something really important."

Jana's older sister, Tracy, limped into the room. "How's the toe you hurt yesterday?" asked Mom.

"Much better," reported Tracy. "Before long, I'll be able to walk normally. I never realized before how important a little toe is!"

"Did you look at your little toes this morning, Jana?" Mom asked.

"Probably not," laughed Jana.

"Did you comb your hair?" asked Mom. "Did you look at your face?"

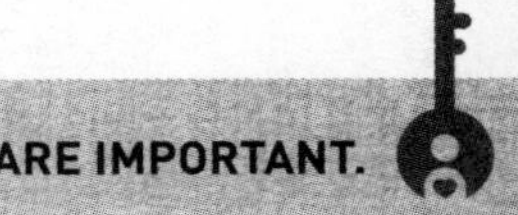

"Sure," said Jana. "What are you getting at, Mom?"

"Well," said Mom, "I'm just trying to point out that although we normally pay more attention to some parts of our body, like our hair and our face, every part is important. Even our little toes. Every member of the body of Christ—that is, every believer—is important too. We tend to pay more attention to those who play instruments or sing or speak. But those who work in the nursery or sweep the church or pray as they sit quietly in their seats are just as important."

HOW ABOUT YOU?

Do you feel unimportant? Some jobs seem more glamorous to us than others, but God won't reward you according to how glamorous your task is. He'll reward you according to how faithfully you perform the task He has given you to do.

TO MEMORIZE:

Some parts of the body that seem weakest and least important are actually the most necessary.
1 CORINTHIANS 12:22

BY HAZEL W. MARETT

March 23

NO SNEAKING IN

Read John 10:1-10.

"Yes, I am the gate. Those who come in through me will be saved." As Mr. Batos, Jonny's Sunday school teacher, read the words of Jesus, Jonny was puzzled. He wondered how Jesus could be a gate.

That night Jonny stayed at Tony's house so he'd be ready to leave on a camping trip early the next morning. After they had gone to bed, Jonny realized that he had forgotten his fishing gear. "Let's run to my house and get it," he said.

"Everybody will be sleeping," said Tony.

"We'll sneak in," said Jonny. "Come on."

Jonny tried the doors at his house, but they were all locked. He decided to pry the screen off his bedroom window and enter that way. The noise woke his parents, so his dad grabbed a bat and went to investigate. Jonny had one foot in the window when his dad yelled, "Stop, or I'll let you have it!"

Jonny froze. "Don't! It's me, Dad!" he said.

ENTER HEAVEN BY THE GATE.

His father flicked on a light. "Jonny? Why are you sneaking in the window? Why didn't you come to the door?" he asked. "I would have let you in."

Jonny gulped.

The next morning the boys told Mr. Batos about their adventure. "I didn't think it mattered how I got in," Jonny said, "but it did."

"That's a good example of why Jesus is called 'the gate.' It's only through Him that we enter heaven. Some people think they can sneak into heaven by doing good works, attending church, or being baptized. But the only way to enter heaven is by the gate—by accepting Jesus as your Savior."

HOW ABOUT YOU?

Are you trying to sneak into heaven? You can't do it. The only way to get into heaven is through Jesus Christ.

TO MEMORIZE:

Yes, I am the gate. Those who come in through me will be saved.
They will come and go freely and will find good pastures.
JOHN 10:9

BY JAN L. HANSEN

March 24

THE FALSE HOOD

Read Matthew 6:1-6.

"Dad, what's a falsehood?" asked Katie as she plunked herself in a chair.

"A falsehood?" Dad asked in surprise. "Well, a falsehood is a lie."

"That's what I thought," said Katie. "But why is it called a falsehood?"

"Hmmm," pondered Dad. "Well, one explanation I've heard is that it comes from something done hundreds of years ago. It was during a time when people wore hoods instead of hats, and they wore cloaks instead of coats."

"Like Little Red Riding Hood?" asked Katie.

"Sort of," answered Dad. "A person like a doctor or lawyer—or whatever profession—wore a certain type and color of hood."

"Then if you saw someone with a certain kind of hood, you would know what he was?" asked Katie.

"Yes, and that's where the falsehood comes in," Dad answered. "Some dishonest people would go to a town where they weren't known, wear a hood they hadn't earned, and set up a practice. They were living a lie. They were wearing a false hood."

BE HONEST AND OBEDIENT.

Katie nodded. "I can see how the word came to mean a lie," she said. "I think it's a good word to use to describe people who pretend to be something they're not. Some kids are unkind at school but pretend to be Christians on Sunday. It's like they're hiding under a false hood."

"That's right!" answered Dad. "Be careful always to be honest before God and others."

"I will," Katie promised.

HOW ABOUT YOU?

Are you pretending to be something you aren't? If you feel the need to pretend, ask yourself why. If you're honest and obedient as God wants you to be, you will not feel the need to hide under a false hood.

TO MEMORIZE:

You have rejected all who stray from your decrees.
They are only fooling themselves.
PSALM 119:118

BY AGNES LIVEZEY

March 25

A DARK PLACE

Read John 12:34-36, 46.

As Cammie listened to the cheerful voices singing choruses at Bible club, she wished she could stay at Mrs. Steiner's house forever. She was glad she had come and heard about Jesus and that she had trusted him as her Savior.

Cammie lingered to help Mrs. Steiner straighten the family room. "Thank you, Cammie," said Mrs. Steiner. "Now, how about a dish of peaches before you go? Would you like to call your parents and make sure it's all right?"

"It'll be okay," Cammie answered. "Mom works late, and Dad will be passed out—I mean, sleeping on the couch."

"Well then, please get a jar of my home-canned peaches from the fruit cellar," Mrs. Steiner said. "I'll get out the dishes and milk." Cammie was limping when she returned from the basement.

"The light didn't go on," Cammie explained, "so I couldn't see very well. I ran into a ladder, but I'm fine."

BE GOD'S LIGHT.

"Oh dear, the bulb must have burned out," Mrs. Steiner said. "I'm sorry. A light is needed in a dark place like the fruit cellar." She opened the jar and dished up the golden fruit. "How are things going at home?"

Cammie sighed and told how her mom worked late hours and her dad was an alcoholic.

"It must be hard for you, Cammie," sympathized Mrs. Steiner, "but Jesus needs you there in your home. Just like the fruit cellar really needed a light, you can be a light in your home to help your parents see the love of Christ."

HOW ABOUT YOU?

Are you the only Christian in your home or in your classroom? It's difficult to stand alone. But it's in the dark that a light is needed the most.

TO MEMORIZE:

Live clean, innocent lives as children of God, shining like bright lights in a world full of crooked and perverse people.

PHILIPPIANS 2:15

BY JAN L. HANSEN

Stand Your Ground

Be on guard. Stand firm in the faith. Be courageous. Be strong.
1 CORINTHIANS 16:13

Having courage can be about standing firm in your faith and trusting God. It can also be about having to *take* a stand. When bullies bully and haters hate, it's time to pray about how best to obey the Bible. Believers have to do more than talk the talk of faith. We have to walk the talk, which clearly says to be brave and strong.

Circle the kinds of actions against which you might take a stand.

```
C R H F K F E O R D M L C M E
D H V R Y F N L A X L I D M R
I H E A Q V M K M L Z T P B S
I E Q A D H M T G B Q T O R G
R I W O T D G H L U Z E L D R
V H A H J I I F C L S R L M A
R A T B H V N C N L U I U P F
E O N Y U K Z G T Y P N T G F
J G X D D S T Y Y I F G I V I
N F D Q A X E X E N O X O J T
R P J P H L B T O G G N N A I
I A G Y D S I P Q V L Y I N G
Y Z H J T M N S T E A L I N G
A A X K S C G Q M B B X Z X R
X Y Q R T Z J G K C M Y E Y D
```

abuse	littering
addiction	lying
bullying	pollution
cheating	stealing
graffiti	vandalism

SEE ANSWER IN BACK

March 26

IN NEED OF A FRIEND

Read John 15:12-17.

Stacie came home in tears. "This is my third week at school, and I still don't have a friend," she wailed. "I wish we had never moved here!"

Mom frowned. "I know you miss your old friends, honey," she said. "I've been praying about this."

"Everyone seems to stare at me," Stacie sobbed. "I'm so lonely."

The door flew open, and Tim blew in like a whirlwind. "Hey, Mom, is it all right if I go over to Paul's for a couple of hours? He needs help with his science project."

Mom nodded. "Just be home by five thirty." The door slammed shut behind Tim. "Now, Stacie, dry your tears and take this casserole to Mrs. Carson next door. She just came home from the hospital today."

Stacie blew her nose loudly. "How do you know that?" she asked. "You seem to know everyone in this apartment building already. Why can't I make friends like you and Tim do?"

TO HAVE A FRIEND, BE ONE.

Mom took a deep breath. "Stacie, you've been looking for someone to be a friend to you, and you haven't found anyone. But Tim and I have found people everywhere who need a friend. Stop looking for a friend, and start trying to be one instead." Mom hugged Stacie gently.

An hour later, Stacie skipped into the apartment. "Guess what, Mom?" She was beaming. "I found someone who needs a friend. Her name is Sara, and she's Mrs. Carson's granddaughter. Can I go over there after dinner?"

HOW ABOUT YOU?

Are you lonely? Look around you. There are lonely people everywhere. The way to make friends is to be one. Try it.

TO MEMORIZE:

This is my command: Love each other.

JOHN 15:17

BY BARBARA J. WESTBERG

March 27

THE OVERDUE BOOK

Read 1 Peter 1:17-21.

As Christie cleaned out her closet, she found a library book in the corner. "Oh no!" she groaned. "I'll never be able to pay the fine on this book. Mom and Dad will be mad, too."

Christie hid the book under the pillow, but she kept worrying about it. Finally she told her parents about the problem. "I'm sorry I forgot to take it back," she said. "Now I don't want to go to the library until I've saved enough to pay the fine. But every day I wait, the fine gets bigger. What can I do?"

"Oh!" exclaimed her mother. "I forgot to tell you. When I was at the library last month, the librarian asked me about that book. It was already so long overdue that it was cheaper to buy it than to pay the fine, so that's what I did."

Christie breathed a sigh of relief. "Thanks, Mom. Here I've been feeling guilty and worried, and all the time the book was paid for!"

"What happened to you is similar to what happens to many people," said Dad. "People often feel guilty for years about things they've done wrong. Just as you were afraid to go back to the library, people avoid talking to God, thinking they must first 'clean up' their lives. But they can't do it. They just keep on sinning more. They don't realize that Jesus paid the price on the cross for all their sins, and all they have to do for it to take effect is accept His gift."

JESUS PAID YOUR DEBT.

HOW ABOUT YOU?

Do you feel guilty about things you have done? Jesus already paid the price for all your sins. Confess them to Him and accept Him as your Savior. Then thank Him for purchasing your forgiveness. Don't feel guilty anymore—feel glad for what God did for you.

TO MEMORIZE:

God bought you with a high price. So you must honor God with your body.

1 CORINTHIANS 6:20

BY SHERRY L. KUYT

March 28

A FAIR CHANCE

Read Matthew 7:1-5.

"There was a new girl in our class today," Maria announced at dinner. "I don't like her, though. She's a snob. She sits just like this." Maria turned her nose up, pushed her shoulders back, and sat very straight. "When Debi asked her if she wanted to jump rope with us, she said, 'No, thank you,' so prissy."

"Hmmm," murmured Mom as she passed the chicken. "Aren't you judging a little prematurely?"

Dad peered at the breaded chicken. "What is this?"

"A new recipe," said Mom.

"I don't want any," stated five-year-old Matteo. "I don't like it."

Maria laughed. "You've never tasted it," she said.

"I want you to try it," said Dad. "Take two bites, Matteo."

Matteo looked at his mom. "You heard your dad," she said. "Two bites." Matteo put a tiny bit on his spoon.

GIVE PEOPLE A FAIR CHANCE.

Matteo grimaced as he put the spoon to his mouth. He chewed and swallowed. "It *is* good!" he exclaimed.

Mom looked at Maria. "You are acting about the new girl just like Matteo did about the chicken. You need to give her a fair chance."

The next day Maria came in from school. "Guess what, Mom? I do like Latrice," she said. "She sits like she does because she wears a back brace. That's why she couldn't jump rope. She just didn't want to tell anybody."

Mom smiled. "I'm glad you gave her a fair chance," she said.

HOW ABOUT YOU?

Are you afraid to try new things or meet new people? If you judge them on the basis of first impressions, you may miss some wonderful experiences. Determine now to give everyone you meet a fair chance to be your friend.

TO MEMORIZE:

Do not judge others, and you will not be judged. Do not condemn others, or it will all come back against you. Forgive others, and you will be forgiven.

LUKE 6:37

BY BARBARA J. WESTBERG

March 29

FOLLOWERS

Read 2 Thessalonians 3:6-13.

"Look at all the people!" exclaimed Andy.

"Yes," replied Dad. "This parade had better be good, or I'll wish I'd stayed home." He inched forward with the traffic. "A lot of cars are turning here," he added. "Maybe they know of a place to park." He made a right turn, following the car in front of him. But instead of finding a place to park, they found themselves on a ramp leading to a freeway. "Oh no," groaned Dad. "I never saw the sign for the interstate!" He scowled at the car ahead of him. "Thanks a lot, mister," he growled.

Mom laughed. "Oh, so it's his fault?"

"What about the car behind us?" asked Andy. "It followed too. Is that your fault?"

"No," Dad said. "They should have watched where they were going."

"Sounds like someone else I know," Mom observed, looking at Andy.

Andy blushed. Just the night before he had excused his rowdy behavior at a family gathering by saying that everybody else was doing the same thing. He was only following the example of some older cousins. At the same time he had insisted that he wasn't responsible for the way his little sister had copied his actions.

FOLLOW JESUS, NOT THE CROWD.

"At times we all tend to forget that God has given each of us a brain. He intends for us to use it instead of blindly following the crowd," said Dad. "On the other hand, He expects us to live in such a way that others may follow us."

HOW ABOUT YOU?

God gave you a brain. Are you using it to think for yourself? Are you being a good example to others? Others are watching you. Lead them in the right way.

TO MEMORIZE:

Don't let anyone think less of you because you are young.
Be an example to all believers in what you say, in the way
you live, in your love, your faith, and your purity.

1 TIMOTHY 4:12

BY HAZEL W. MARETT

March 30

ABOVE THE CLOUDS

Read Psalm 46:1-5, 7-10.

Jeremy was going on his first airplane ride, but he felt as dark and gloomy as the sky above him. His parents were getting a divorce, and he was going to live with his grandparents for a while.

As they boarded the plane, Grandma asked, "Are you scared?"

Inside, he said, *Yes, I'm scared! I'm scared of everything.* But he didn't say anything. As the plane sped down the runway, huge drops of rain splattered the windows. *Just like tears,* Jeremy thought. When the plane lifted from the earth, Jeremy felt his heart fly up into his throat.

Grandma reached for his hand. "Don't be afraid, Jeremy. God will take care of us." Jeremy knew Grandma was talking about more than the plane ride. He wanted to believe her, but he couldn't. "We'll go right through these dark clouds, Jeremy," she explained. "For a few minutes, we'll be in a thick fog. But just wait until we get above the clouds."

DON'T FEAR—TRUST GOD.

Suddenly they were in the clouds. The interior of the plane dimmed. Then, just as suddenly, a brilliant light came streaming through the windows. Jeremy squinted as he pressed his nose to the pane. "It's beautiful," he gasped.

Grandma nodded. "Yes. Above the clouds, the sun is shining." Jeremy turned and looked at his grandmother, who smiled gently. "Our family is going through a storm, Jeremy. Things look pretty dark. But God is in control. One day soon we'll break through the clouds, and life will be filled with beauty and happiness again."

HOW ABOUT YOU?

Are you going through a storm in your life? Are you afraid of the future? Remember, even when you can't see the sun, it is shining. Even when you can't feel God, He is near.

TO MEMORIZE:

See, God has come to save me. I will trust in him and not be afraid.
The LORD GOD *is my strength and my song; he has given me victory.*

ISAIAH 12:2

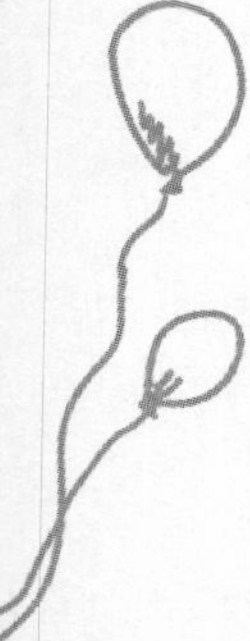

BY BARBARA J. WESTBERG

March 31

WHO'S RIGHT?

Read John 17:20-23.

"Dad, we do things differently at our church than they do at Clint's church," Kenny said one day. "We had an argument about it. He said his church is right, and I said my church is right. Whose way is really right?"

Before Dad could attempt an answer, Kenny's little sister and brother came into the kitchen, carrying a keyboard. They set it on the table. "We want to play a song Daddy taught us," announced Cathy, and they proceeded to do so. At first, they carefully pressed the keys, and Kenny thought he recognized "Twinkle, Twinkle, Little Star." But then it became obvious that they were playing two different songs.

"That sounds awful," declared Kenny. "I think you need a new teacher."

"Wait a minute!" protested Dad. "The teacher's not the problem. They're not following my instructions."

When the children were gone, Dad grinned at Kenny. "That sure wasn't the way I intended their music to turn out," he said. "But what just happened reminds me of what happens to Christians. Can't you almost hear God saying, 'That wasn't what I intended,' as He watches us? Jesus intended for His followers to all play the same song. He wants all Christians to work together."

CHRISTIANS ARE ONE IN CHRIST.

"But which song should we be playing? Whose way is right—Clint's church or our church?" Kenny asked again.

"God's way is right," Dad answered. "And any church that believes and teaches the Bible as the true Word of God is a good one."

HOW ABOUT YOU?

Do you ever argue with people from other churches? If you attend churches that agree with the Bible, then quit arguing. Jesus wants us to work together.

TO MEMORIZE:

There is one body and one Spirit, just as you have been called to one glorious hope for the future. There is one Lord, one faith, one baptism, one God and Father of all.

EPHESIANS 4:4-6

BY KATHERINE R. ADAMS

Let It Go

You need not be afraid of sudden disaster or the destruction
that comes upon the wicked, for the LORD is your security.
He will keep your foot from being caught in a trap.
PROVERBS 3:25-26

What if you never worried about bad things that might happen? God tells us not to fear these things. He even promises that He will keep us from being trapped by danger.

Write down a scary event that you heard about in the news.

____

____

____

____

Now write about something bad that was caused by wicked people.

____

____

____

____

List three worries you have about things that might happen.

____

____

____

Now cross out everything you wrote above. Let it all go. God says not to fear any of them—He is with you. What if you did this in your mind every time you started to worry?

April 1

BROKEN EGGS

Read Romans 5:6-11.

"Let's color some Easter eggs, Grandma," suggested Beth.

Grandma laughed. "Colored eggs don't have a thing to do with Easter," she said. "But if you want to color some for fun, we can do that."

Grandma helped boil the eggs, and Beth dyed them a rainbow of colors.

Then Beth found a book to read. Smokey, Grandma's cat, snuggled down into her lap. He purred as Beth stroked his soft fur. Suddenly a dog began barking outside the window. Smokey leaped out of Beth's lap, ran to the kitchen, and jumped on the counter. Crash! Beth's eggs rolled one by one off the counter and onto the floor. Cracks zigzagged across the colored shells.

"Smokey!" Beth cried. "You've ruined the eggs! You bad, bad cat!"

Grandma picked up the cracked eggs and asked for Beth's colored markers. When Beth brought them, Grandma reached for a pink one. She drew some pink flowers, using the large cracks for some of the lines. Then she drew leaves with a light shade of green. She used a bright purple to make violets on another egg. On some she used the crack lines to make pretty designs. Soon Beth was doing the same thing.

CHRIST MAKES YOU NEW.

"Grandma, they're more beautiful than before," Beth whispered.

"Beth," Grandma said with a happy smile, "we just rescued some cracked eggs, but God rescues broken people—people ruined by sin. God sent His Son, Jesus, to die for them. Broken people need Jesus, and once they accept Him as Savior, they're more beautiful than before."

HOW ABOUT YOU?

Did you know you are a broken person—broken by sin? You don't need to stay that way. Jesus died for you. Ask Him to be your Savior. He'll make you a new person.

TO MEMORIZE:

This means that anyone who belongs to Christ has become a new person. The old life is gone; a new life has begun!

2 CORINTHIANS 5:17

BY JAN L. HANSEN

April 2

GIFT TO SHARE

Read Titus 2:11-15.

"Hi, Jamal." Ken nervously greeted his friend. He felt guilty whenever he saw Jamal. That's because Ken had accepted Jesus as Savior, but he'd never told Jamal. He wanted to—it was just that he was afraid Jamal would laugh.

"What did you get for your birthday yesterday?" Jamal asked.

Ken lifted his left hand and displayed a new baseball mitt. "How about this?"

Jamal smiled. "I could use one like that too."

"My grandparents gave it to me," said Ken, "and this shirt is from my brother. My parents gave me a skateboard."

"Wow!" Jamal let out a long whistle. "I could use all those things."

"Well, you can't have 'em," laughed Ken. Suddenly he thought about the gift of eternal life he had received a month ago. That was a gift Jamal could have. He took a deep breath. "A month ago I got . . ." He stopped, afraid to finish. "I got a gift from God. I got my sins forgiven."

WITNESS FOR JESUS.

"Huh?" Jamal asked. "What on earth are you talking about?"

"I got the gift of eternal life, and if you want to, you can have that gift too," Ken finished in a hurry. "I gotta go. Bye." He hurried down the street as Jamal stared after him. Ken was sure he hadn't done that very well. At the same time, he knew that at least it was a start. *I'm going to invite Jamal to church this week,* he decided. *I'll ask him tomorrow.*

HOW ABOUT YOU?

Do you talk with your friends about anything and everything except the Lord? Are you afraid to witness to them? If you're a Christian, God has given you a wonderful gift, and they can have it too. Tell them about it.

TO MEMORIZE:

The Lord stood with me and gave me strength so that I might preach the Good News in its entirety for all the Gentiles to hear.

2 TIMOTHY 4:17

BY HAZEL W. MARETT

April 3

CARELESS WORDS

Read Romans 15:1-7.

The students at Lakeview Christian Academy looked at each other in disbelief. They had just learned that one of the students had attempted to commit suicide the night before!

"I didn't think that Christian kids ever got that depressed," was Susan's reaction. "Eric knows God loves him. What made him do a thing like that?"

"It's not that simple," responded Kevin. "You have lots of friends." Kevin looked down at his desk as he continued. "I remember when we'd make fun of Eric in gym class. I never thought he took it seriously."

"But he's so smart," emphasized Brad. "Didn't he know that we all wish we could be as smart as he is?"

"We don't always seem to recognize our good qualities," pointed out Mrs. Kelley. "Sometimes our weaknesses seem to get all of the attention." She picked up her Bible. "As Christians, we have the assurance of knowing that God loves us and accepts us just the way we are," she continued. "We also have the responsibility to love others the way God loves us. Listen to Ephesians 4:29: 'Don't use foul or abusive language. Let everything you say be good and helpful, so that your words will be an encouragement to those who hear them.'"

BUILD OTHERS UP.

Kevin looked up soberly. "I sure can't say that all of the things I said to Eric were encouraging. I'd like another chance to really be his friend."

Mrs. Kelley smiled understandingly. "Let's pray you'll get that chance."

HOW ABOUT YOU?

Are you careful about the things you say to others? Sometimes careless words may seem harmless or funny, yet they may hurt others. God wants your life to reflect His love to others. Show God's love through your kind words.

TO MEMORIZE:

Don't use foul or abusive language. Let everything you say be good and helpful, so that your words will be an encouragement to those who hear them.

EPHESIANS 4:29

BY DEANA ROGERS

April 4

HEART, NOT HAIR

Read 1 Samuel 16:1, 3-7.

Christy was excited about the birthday present Aunt Peggy had sent. It was a salon gift certificate so Christy could have her hair cut and colored. It sounded like fun. But that was before Christy knew what the outcome would be!

"Mom, I can't go to school like this!" she wailed after getting her hair dyed. "All the kids will laugh at me!"

"Why should they laugh at you?" teased Christy's brother Joe. "You do look a little funny with black hair, but other than that, you look okay."

"Mom," Christy wailed again.

"That's enough, Joe," said Mom. "Christy feels bad enough without you kidding her. Actually, Christy, your hair looks nice. You just aren't used to the color yet."

Christy looked in the mirror and scowled. She knew her mother would make her go to school tomorrow, and it was just too horrible to think about.

INSIDE BEAUTY COUNTS.

Mom looked at the grouchy expression on Christy's face. "Honey, remember that the Lord said it's not the outward appearance that counts, but what is on the inside. The fanciest hairstyle in the world isn't going to make up for a bad attitude and a grumpy look. On the other hand, if you'll be as kind and cheerful as you usually are, your hair will not be important."

Christy knew it was true. Her heart, not her hair, was what mattered. She would ask the Lord to help her give more attention to her inside appearance than to her outside appearance!

HOW ABOUT YOU?

Do you care more about the latest hairstyles and fashions than you do about your inner beauty? Yes, it is important to be neat and clean and attractive, but God is more concerned about your heart than He is about your curly hair or new shirt!

TO MEMORIZE:

People judge by outward appearance, but the LORD looks at the heart.

1 SAMUEL 16:7

BY LENORA MCWHORTEN

April 5
WHAT A MESS

Read Psalm 25:4-10.

"I don't know how I'm going to get everything done today," Mom said at the breakfast table. "I have several errands to run this morning, and somehow I'll have to find time to bake a birthday cake for Thomas."

"I can make Thomas's cake!" said Julie. "You've told me before that it's easy. Besides, Thomas is only two, and he'll eat anything!"

"Well, okay," agreed Mom hesitantly. "The mix and the frosting are in the cupboard. Be sure to read the directions." Julie started the cake soon after Mom left. She read the directions and was about to pour the mix into the bowl when the phone rang. It was her friend Stephanie.

After Julie hung up the phone, she went about making her cake, remembering what she had read earlier. At least, she thought she remembered. But when the cake was done, it didn't look quite right. When it cooled, she frosted it carefully, but it was no use. The cake was dry, and Thomas, who was known to eat many strange things, wouldn't touch it.

FOLLOW GOD'S DIRECTION.

"What a mess!" Mom exclaimed. "Didn't you follow the directions?"

"I read them, but then Stephanie called, and I didn't look at them again," explained Julie. "I thought I was doing it the right way."

"That's the way many people live their lives," observed Dad. "They hear a sermon or read the Bible occasionally, and then they think they know all they need to know. But they forget what they heard. God gives directions, but some people ignore them, and their lives turn into big messes—just like that cake! Paying attention to directions is an important principle to learn."

HOW ABOUT YOU?

Do you follow the directions the Lord gives in His Word? It's important to spend time each day in God's Word so you will know what those directions are.

TO MEMORIZE:

Seek his will in all you do, and he will show you which path to take.

PROVERBS 3:6

BY LENORA MCWHORTEN

April 6

IN THE DITCH

Read Psalm 26:3-12.

When Ryan's mother picked him up at school, he would not look at her. She had come for him because he and some other boys had been caught smoking, and he was too ashamed to say anything.

Rain pelted the windshield as they rode in silence. When they started up the hill toward their house, the car slipped and skidded. The street was being repaired, and it was a mess! "Be careful, Mom," Ryan exclaimed, "or we'll wind up in the di—"

At that exact moment the car skidded again and slid into a ditch. Mom shifted gears and rocked the car, but it was hopeless. She rifled through her purse to call for roadside assistance. "Bad news," she said with a sigh. "With all the excitement this afternoon, I forgot my cell phone. Nothing to do but walk home and call a tow truck." So they trudged up the muddy hill.

When Dad got home that evening, Ryan did his best to keep Dad's attention on the car. But the dreaded moment arrived when Dad asked what had happened at school. "I didn't want to smoke," Ryan said. "It's just that I couldn't let the other guys think I was a baby."

CHOOSE THE RIGHT FRIENDS.

Dad frowned. "I thought you just told me you didn't like being on a slippery road," he said.

Ryan looked at him, puzzled. "What's that got to do with it?"

"Well," said Dad, "when you spend a lot of time with the wrong crowd, it's like being on a slippery road. And today you slid quite badly at school. You're a Christian, yet you've chosen friends who pressure you into doing things that you know are wrong. With the right kind of friends, life would be a lot smoother."

HOW ABOUT YOU?

Are you hanging out with the wrong crowd? If so, you could be headed for a lot of trouble. Choose close friends who will be a help, not a hindrance, in living for Christ.

TO MEMORIZE:

I hate the gatherings of those who do evil, and
I refuse to join in with the wicked.
PSALM 26:5

BY BARBARA J. WESTBERG

April 7

MACK THE MONKEY

Read Romans 3:10-12, 20-22.

Patti listened eagerly as Mr. Dan began to talk. "I'm glad to be here," said Mr. Dan, "and now I'd like to ask my friend Mack to join me on the platform." For the first time, Patti noticed a brown hairy puppet hanging by its arms from the piano. "Come here, Mack," called Mr. Dan, but Mack didn't move. "Well, I guess Mack is going to be uncooperative," said Mr. Dan. "I think I know what I need to do. I need to snap my fingers, let go, and Mack will spring to life." When Mr. Dan did this, Mack just ended up in a pile on the floor. The children laughed.

Finally Mr. Dan looked at the boys and girls in the front row, where Patti was sitting. "What does Mack need?" he asked them.

Patti's hand shot into the air. "You have to put your hand inside and make him move," she said when Mr. Dan pointed to her.

"You are absolutely right," agreed Mr. Dan. "I could talk to Mack from now until it's time to go home, and he still wouldn't move. Without me, Mack can do nothing." He paused for a moment. "Did you know that the same is true of people? Jesus said to His disciples, 'Apart from me you can do nothing.' We can't get to heaven by ourselves. And we can't live the Christian life by ourselves."

YOU NEED JESUS.

Patti listened carefully to the rest of Mr. Dan's presentation. *I need to find out more about becoming a Christian,* she thought.

HOW ABOUT YOU?

Do you know Jesus as your Savior? If not, talk to a trusted Christian friend or adult to find out more.

TO MEMORIZE:

Yes, I am the vine; you are the branches. Those who remain in me, and I in them, will produce much fruit. For apart from me you can do nothing.

JOHN 15:5

BY CHARLES VANDERMEER

Like a River

Blessed are those who trust in the LORD and have made the LORD their hope and confidence. They are like trees planted along a riverbank, with roots that reach deep into the water. Such trees are not bothered by the heat or worried by long months of drought. Their leaves stay green, and they never stop producing fruit.

JEREMIAH 17:7-8

We trust God and keep our hope in Him. God promises His presence and blessing in return. Use this code to decipher the missing words below.

▼	●	★	♠	♦	✚	✣	♥	✦	♣	✪	✖	■
a	b	c	d	e	f	g	h	i	j	k	l	m

☆	✿	❑	◗	✔	➾	☎	✐	▲	➔	❖	☞	◒
n	o	p	q	r	s	t	u	v	w	x	y	z

■ ▼ ✪ ♦ ➾

He _ _ _ _ _ me to lie down

✣ ✔ ♦ ♦ ☆ ❑ ▼ ➾ ☎ ✐ ✔ ♦ ➾

in _ _ _ _ _ _ _ _ _ _ _ _ _ ;

✖ ♦ ▼ ♠ ➾

He _ _ _ _ _ me beside

➾ ☎ ✦ ✖ ✖ ➔ ▼ ☎ ♦ ✔ ➾

the _ _ _ _ _ _ _ _ _ _ _ .

✔ ♦ ➾ ☎ ✿ ✔ ♦ ➾

He _ _ _ _ _ _ _ _ my soul.

PSALM 23:2-3, NKJV

ANSWER KEY

makes; green pastures; leads; still waters; restores

April 8

GOD'S STRENGTH

Read Mark 4:36-41.

Jared glanced nervously out the school window. All day it had looked stormy. He hoped there wasn't going to be another tornado alert today.

As Jared began the first math problem, a bell rang. "Tornado drill," said Miss Schultz. "Take a large book and file quietly into the hall." Quickly the students obeyed, taking their places in the school's inner hall. Then they put the books over their heads. But there was something different today. Jared could hear a siren signaling that a tornado funnel had been seen nearby.

Jared had never been so scared! But as he sat trembling, he remembered something Dad had said just the weekend before. They had gone swimming, and as Dad walked out into the deep water, Jared's little brother, Brian, hung on to Dad's shoulders. "Are you scared in the deep water, Brian?" Jared had asked.

Brian had said, "Nope, Dad's got me."

Dad had replied, "I'm glad you trust your father." Then he had added, "And remember that you can always trust your Father in heaven, too."

GOD CONTROLS NATURE.

A few minutes later, Jared heard a roaring sound. It got louder and louder. It almost sounded like a train rushing by. He had heard that a tornado sounded that way. *I'm still scared,* Jared thought, *but not so scared. God's my heavenly Father, and He's in control.*

After the all-clear whistle sounded, the children returned to their classrooms and were soon dismissed to go home. They learned that a tornado had indeed passed by, but no one had been hurt.

HOW ABOUT YOU?

Storms can be frightening, can't they? They are powerful and can cause a lot of damage. But God is even more powerful. Remember that God is in control.

TO MEMORIZE:

The disciples were absolutely terrified. "Who is this man?" they asked each other. "Even the wind and waves obey him!"

MARK 4:41

BY HAZEL W. MARETT

April 9

PSALM READER

Read Matthew 6:26-34.

"Where are we going, Dad?" asked Kevin.

"Wait and see," Dad said with a wink.

"Madame Margarite, Spiritualist, Palm Reader," Sarah read as they drove past a sign on Main Street. "Have Your Fortune Told Here."

"I'd like to know the future," Laura said. "Will Brad ask me to the party?"

"How much does it cost to have your fortune told, Dad?" Kevin asked.

"I don't know," Dad answered, "and I will never find out. God's Word warns against going to fortune-tellers."

"Why?" Sarah, Laura, and Kevin spoke in unison.

"It would be fun to know the future," Kevin argued.

"Suppose we had known last Christmas that Grandma Snider was going to have a stroke the next week. Would we have enjoyed Christmas?" Dad asked.

"No, I guess not," answered Laura.

TRUST GOD FOR THE FUTURE.

"And fortune-tellers aren't always right. One young man was told that he would inherit a lot of money," Dad said. "He began buying expensive things on his credit cards. At the end of the year, instead of inheriting a lot of money, he was deeply in debt! People who base their lives on false predictions are living dangerously," Dad warned.

Laura said, "I learned a psalm that said going to a fortune-teller is 'following the advice of the wicked.'"

The kids cheered as Dad drove into the parking lot of a new ice cream shop. "The future is God's secret. He wants us to trust Him, just as you trusted me today. God wisely hides sorrows from us, and He provides many surprises."

HOW ABOUT YOU?

Do you worry about the future? Worry is a sin because it means you are not trusting God. When you are tempted to worry, remember that God loves you and He has everything under control.

TO MEMORIZE:

Oh, the joys of those who do not follow the advice of the wicked,
or stand around with sinners, or join in with mockers.

PSALM 1:1

BY BARBARA J. WESTBERG

April 10

GOOD FOR EVIL

Read Matthew 5:43-48.

"I can't stand Manuel!" exploded Brandon. "He's thinks he's so cool, saying he met the mayor, they got a new car, they're going to Bermuda, his dad's on the city council. Blah-blah-blah!"

"Not jealous, are you?" asked Mom.

"No!" snorted Brandon. "Just sick of his bragging. If he's not doing that, he's swearing. Mom, why does God let him have so many good things when he laughs at Christians and swears?"

"That's a good question," said Mom. "It used to bother me, too." She was interrupted as Misty stomped into the room.

"Mr. Matlock is so mean!" complained Misty. "He put barricades on the sidewalk in front of his house so Denise and I can't ride our bikes there. Denise said we ought to do something to get even with him."

"Oh no!" Mom shook her head. "Remember what we read from the Bible this morning? What did those verses tell you to do to Mr. Matlock?"

LOVE YOUR ENEMIES.

"Love him," mumbled Misty.

"That's not all," Mom reminded her. "What else?"

Brandon answered for Misty. "Pray for him and do good to him."

"Would you like to make some cookies, Misty?" asked Mom. "You could take a few to Mr. Matlock."

"You've got to be kidding!" Misty said, shocked.

Mom shook her head. "No, I'm not. The best way to deal with enemies is to make them your friends." As she got out the cookbook, she turned to Brandon.

"God tells us to pray for our enemies and return good for evil," said Mom. "He's giving them an opportunity to change from enemies to friends."

HOW ABOUT YOU?

Is there someone who is giving you a hard time? Try the formula Jesus used. Love your enemies and pray for those who persecute you.

TO MEMORIZE:

Bless those who persecute you. Don't curse them;
pray that God will bless them.
ROMANS 12:14

BY BARBARA J. WESTBERG

April 11

THE WRONG WAY

Read Haggai 1:5-7.

"You should have seen Brianne today!" laughed Jim as the family began their dinner. His sister sent him a nasty look. "The girls wanted to play touch football with us guys, so we let them play with us today. Know what Brianne did? When she got the ball, she ran toward the wrong goal line! Almost made a touchdown, too—for the wrong team. What a riot!"

Brianne reluctantly joined in the laughter at her expense. "You're in good company," Dad consoled her. "It's happened before! Way back in 1929, a fellow named Roy Riegels played for the California Golden Bears. One time when he got the ball, he headed for the wrong goal with do-or-die determination. One of his teammates finally managed to bring him down just a yard from the goal line. But his team still lost the game."

"Good thing it was only a game," observed Mom. "There's an important lesson for us, though. Some people are running long and hard in the game of life, and they don't realize they're running in the wrong direction."

JESUS IS THE RIGHT WAY.

"That's true," said Dad. "Many people are trying hard to live a good life. In fact, their 'good deeds' sometimes put Christians to shame. But in spite of those 'good deeds,' they're still sinners because they refuse to acknowledge Jesus as the only way to heaven. When all is said and done, they'll find that they went the wrong way. What a tragedy!"

"That's sad," declared Brianne. "Maybe I didn't know which way to run in the football game, but I'm sure glad I know the way to heaven."

HOW ABOUT YOU?

Are you running the wrong way in life? You are if you're trying to get to heaven by any other way than through Jesus Christ.

TO MEMORIZE:

There is a path before each person that seems right, but it ends in death.

PROVERBS 14:12

BY HAZEL W. MARETT

April 12

ANIMAL CHARADES

Read John 3:1-7, 16.

"Okay, kids. We'll end with a short game of animal charades." Miss Ellen looked around at her Bible class. "Tom, can you start? Pretend to be an animal, and the first person to guess the animal will go next."

Tom nodded and dropped to his hands and knees. He crawled a few steps, then panted. "You're a dog!" Parker shouted quickly. Tom laughed and got to his feet.

Parker thought for a minute. Then he got down on his stomach and wriggled his way across the room. "Are you a worm?" someone asked. Parker shook his head. Then he stuck out his tongue several times. "A snake," squealed one of the girls. After several of the kids had a turn, Miss Ellen announced that she would do the final charade.

The children watched as Miss Ellen folded her hands and bowed her head. "You're a praying mantis," suggested Tom.

Miss Ellen shook her head. "Good guess, but I'm a human." She picked up her Bible and pretended to read. Next she solemnly walked to a chair, sat down, and appeared to be listening to someone. She made motions as though she were opening a book. She also opened and closed her mouth several times. "She's in church," whispered someone. Miss Ellen nodded.

Then Leah jumped up. "You're pretending to be a Christian!" she exclaimed.

"That's it," agreed Miss Ellen. "Think about this: pretending to be something doesn't make it so. You're not a dog unless you are born into the canine family, and you're not a Christian unless you are born into God's family." She opened her Bible and read Jesus' words from the third chapter of John.

"It doesn't matter if your parents are Christians or if you go to church every week. The only way to be born into God's family is by trusting in Jesus as your Savior. Then you will be born again—as a child of God!"

HOW ABOUT YOU?

Have you been born again? You may act like a Christian, but you're not one unless you've trusted Jesus and have been "born" into His family. Talk to a trusted Christian friend or adult to find out more.

TO MEMORIZE:

Jesus replied, "I assure you, no one can enter the Kingdom of God without being born of water and the Spirit."

JOHN 3:5

BY HAZEL W. MARETT

April 13

SISTER TROUBLE

Read Psalm 133:1-3.

"This is ridiculous!" exclaimed André. He tapped his pencil impatiently on the paper in front of him. "Whoever thought up this assignment for Sunday school certainly doesn't know Christa! I have to write down ten reasons why I like my sister, and I can't even think of one!"

"Thanks a lot!" Christa called from the living room. "See if I ever help you do the dishes again!"

"Oops! I forgot about that." André wrote it down.

"How about the time last year when you were sick, and Christa helped you with your homework?" suggested Mom.

"And how about the times I've played catch with you before a game?" Christa asked. "Or last week when I let you ride my bike because yours had a flat tire?"

André had forgotten all those things too. He could see that Christa really was a nice sister. He felt guilty for all the times he had called her names or had been a nuisance to her. It was hard to admit, but André said, "I'm really kind of glad we had this assignment. It's made me appreciate you, Christa!"

APPRECIATE BROTHERS AND SISTERS.

"I can't believe I heard you say that," Christa laughed. "I think this calls for a celebration. How about if I, being the wonderful sister that I am, make some popcorn?"

"Sounds great to me!" André said. He wrote one more thing on his paper. "She makes delicious popcorn!"

HOW ABOUT YOU?

Do you appreciate the brothers or sisters the Lord has given you? Do you get along with them, or do you often argue? Brother and sister conflicts are not new. They've been around since Cain and Abel! Brothers and sisters often overlook the good qualities in each other because they're so busy fighting. The Bible says that they should help each other in times of trouble.

TO MEMORIZE:

A friend is always loyal, and a brother is born to help in time of need.

PROVERBS 17:17

BY LENORA MCWHORTEN

April 14

NOT HUNGRY

Read Job 23:10-12.

When Brian came home from school, Mom was gone, so he raided the refrigerator and cupboards. When she returned, he was just finishing an after-school snack of potato chips, chocolate milk, ice cream, and cookies.

Mom frowned. "Next time, don't eat junk food before supper," she said. As she started dinner, she added, "Mrs. Smith's grandson, Nicholas, will be going to Sunday school with us this week."

"I'm tired of Sunday school," said Brian as he took a comic book and settled down in front of the TV. The next thing he knew, Mom was calling him for dinner. At the table he wrinkled his nose. "I don't want any."

"Mrs. Smith sent some cake for dessert," said Mom.

Brian grinned. "I might eat a little of that."

"Not until you eat some meat and vegetables," Dad said.

"But I'm not hungry," protested Brian.

"Because you filled up on junk food," Mom reminded him. As she passed the casserole to him, she added, "And that's exactly why you're not enjoying Sunday school."

WATCH YOUR MENTAL DIET.

Brian snorted. "I don't enjoy church because I eat potato chips? Aw, Mom!"

"You know what your mother means," said Dad. "Unless we keep after you, you feed your mind junk food—TV shows, comic books, and video games."

Mom passed Brian the vegetables. "If you aren't careful, you're going to be sick—spiritually and physically," she added.

HOW ABOUT YOU?

Are you filling your mind with junk food rather than wholesome spiritual food? Make up your mind to change your mental eating habits before you become spiritually sick. Read God's Word. Listen carefully to your Sunday school teacher and your pastor. Spend time with other Christians.

TO MEMORIZE:

I have not departed from his commands, but have treasured his words more than daily food.

JOB 23:12

BY BARBARA J. WESTBERG

You Are Shielded

I love you, LORD; you are my strength. The LORD is my rock, my fortress, and my savior; my God is my rock, in whom I find protection. He is my shield, the power that saves me, and my place of safety. . . . He is a shield for all who look to him for protection.

PSALM 18:1-2, 30

Putting your trust in God provides protection. It's as though a mighty fortress surrounds you, or as if a high tower holds you above danger. God shields those who trust Him. Thank Him for this protection. And remember it's always there.

Draw lines to match the person or object to what it protects.

shepherd	property
wall	biker
safety belt	boater
life jacket	citizens
shield	passenger
parachute	skydiver
police officer	flock
helmet	soldier

ANSWER KEY

shepherd/flock; wall/property; safety belt/passenger; life jacket/boater; shield/soldier; parachute/skydiver; police officer/citizens; helmet/biker

April 15
WAR!

Read Luke 21:9-19.

As soon as Matt walked in the door, his mother knew something was wrong. He was quiet and thoughtful, not his usual happy self.

"How was school today, Matt?" Mom asked.

Matt shrugged. "It was okay."

"You don't seem very happy," observed Mom.

Matt hesitated. "We had a discussion in social studies class. One of the kids started talking about nuclear war and how the whole world was going to end. Mr. Morgan, our teacher, agreed with him."

"What do you think, Matt?" asked Mom.

Matt gave his mother a little smile. "I think it's sort of scary. We talk about war at school. There are shows about it on TV." Matt paused. "Are you afraid?"

"Matt, this world is a messed-up place," answered Mom, "but when people tell frightening stories about war, I take time to thank the Lord that my future is in *His* hands. As Christians, we know that the Lord loves and cares for us. He is still in control. Only what He allows will happen."

TRUST GOD.

"But our teacher says that if everyone would stop making nuclear weapons, the world would be peaceful and no one would fight," offered Matt.

"That sounds good, Matt," answered his mother, "but it's not what the Bible says. Nations want to be powerful and will do anything to gain that power. It's unrealistic to think that all nations will suddenly decide to stop fighting. There will always be war. Again, we must remember to put our trust in the Lord."

HOW ABOUT YOU?

Are you frightened when you hear stories about war? As a Christian, you don't have to be afraid. Jesus says that your future is in His hands. Whatever that future holds, He will be with you and help you through it.

TO MEMORIZE:

Don't let your hearts be troubled. Trust in God, and trust also in me.

JOHN 14:1

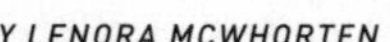

BY LENORA MCWHORTEN

April 16

THE BEST TEAM

Read Romans 5:17-21.

"Our team won!" shouted Erica as she dashed into the house. "Look what I got!" She held out a first-prize ribbon. "We had an archery competition at school today, and my team won!"

"And you always say you're no good in archery," said Mom. "How many points did you make?"

"None, but it didn't matter, because Cheryl was on our team," replied Erica. "She's the best archer in school, and she made enough points for all of us."

"So she really did the winning, but the whole team shared the victory, right?" asked Mom. "Well, I'm glad you had a good time today."

That evening Erica and her parents attended a special service at church. "I know just what the pastor meant tonight when he talked about Christians being righteous in God's sight," remarked Erica on the way home. "When we truly believe in Jesus as our Savior, His blood washes away all our sin. Then God sees His righteousness instead of our sin."

BE ON JESUS' TEAM.

"That reminds me of your archery victory today," said Mom. "Just as you were on the winning team, we could say we're on Jesus' team."

"That's right," agreed Dad, "and just as Cheryl's points counted for all those on the team, the holiness of Jesus counts for everybody on His team. All Christians share in Jesus' victory over sin."

"And the prize we get is wonderful," Mom added. "Eternal life with Jesus!"

HOW ABOUT YOU?

Are you on Jesus' team? There's no way you can win points on your own. Jesus has already won the victory, and He invites you to share in it. Will you accept Him today? Then you'll be on the very best team!

TO MEMORIZE:

But thank God! He gives us victory over sin and death through our Lord Jesus Christ.

1 CORINTHIANS 15:57

BY HAZEL W. MARETT

April 17

BAD EGGS

Read Philippians 4:4-9.

Michael was quiet as he and his father worked on the garden one Saturday. "Dad," he said finally as he leaned on his shovel, "I sometimes wonder if I'm really a Christian. Lately I . . . well, sometimes I have bad thoughts that I know a Christian shouldn't have."

Dad was quiet for a moment. Then he led Michael to a cluster of small trees and moved back a branch to reveal a bird's nest. "I found this when I was pruning some branches," said Dad. "Do you notice anything strange about those eggs?"

"One is bigger than the others."

"That's because it wasn't laid by the bird that built this nest," explained Dad. "It was laid by a cowbird."

"A cowbird?" asked Michael. "Why would she do that?"

"So the other bird would think it was her own and care for the chick when it hatches," Dad replied. "The trouble is, the cowbird baby is usually bigger and stronger than the other baby birds and often takes their food or even pushes them out of the nest."

REJECT BAD THOUGHTS.

"What a mean trick!" exclaimed Michael. "Too bad the other bird can't tell that the big egg isn't her own. Then she could push it out before it hatches."

"That's right," Dad agreed. Then he added, "Satan is like that cowbird. He likes to put things into our minds that don't belong there. We need God's help to think and do the right things. We need to reject Satan's thoughts and push them out."

HOW ABOUT YOU?

Do your thoughts sometimes make you feel like doing something you shouldn't? Don't dwell on these thoughts. Reject them. This is easier to do when you read the Bible regularly. Replace bad thoughts with good ones!

TO MEMORIZE:

And "don't sin by letting anger control you." Don't let the sun go down while you are still angry, for anger gives a foothold to the devil.

EPHESIANS 4:26-27

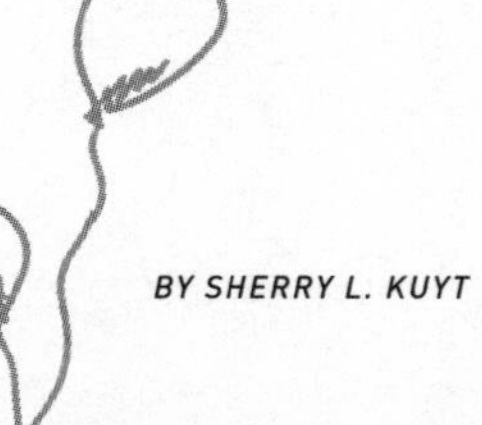

BY SHERRY L. KUYT

April 18

SINGING IN THE RAIN

Read Psalm 78:17-22.

"Oh no! It looks like rain," Ben exclaimed, looking anxiously up at the sky one Saturday morning.

"It sure does," Dad agreed. "I think we'd better postpone our picnic."

Ben was very unhappy about the delay. As the raindrops began to fall, his eyebrows drew together in a frown. And when the rain poured down, he grew downright grumpy. "My whole day is spoiled," he complained.

"Shhhh. Listen." His sister Becky held up her finger. A clear, pure song came from a treetop outside. A robin was singing in the rain.

"Well, let the dumb bird sing. My day is ruined," Ben grumped.

"Why don't you get out one of your games, Ben? We may as well have some fun in spite of the rain," suggested Dad.

Ben grudgingly went to get a game. Soon he and Becky and Dad and Mom were all busy playing and laughing. The time flew by, and Ben forgot all about the rain spoiling his fun. Suddenly Dad looked up at the clock. "Can you believe it's nearly lunchtime?" he asked.

SING TO THE LORD ALWAYS.

"We'll have a picnic right here on the floor," Mom decided. "Becky and I will get things ready, and you guys can clean up."

When the picnic food was brought in, they all sat on a blanket on the floor while they ate. "This is fun!" said Ben. "I even forgot about the rain. That robin had the right idea about singin' in the rain. I had as much fun as if I'd gone on a picnic—well, almost, anyway. I'm sorry I grumbled."

HOW ABOUT YOU?

Do you grumble when it rains in your life—when things don't go your way? There are plenty of reasons to be happy and sing in spite of rain or other disappointments. And best of all, you please God by being cheerful even when you're disappointed.

TO MEMORIZE:

Don't grumble.

1 CORINTHIANS 10:10

BY CAROLYN E. YOST

April 19

JUST ONE STEP

Read Ecclesiastes 3:1-8, 11.

Meg watched her big sister leave the house. "Why can't I go to the library with Tamara?" she asked. "I'll look at books while she studies."

"Meg," Mom said patiently, "it's almost your bedtime. You're eight years old. Tamara's in high school. When you're her age, you'll have a chance to go to the library at night too."

"Tamara has her own phone, and she goes to the mall, and . . ." Meg's words tumbled over each other.

Mom got up from the couch. "Bedtime," she said. "I'll go up with you."

At the stairway, Mom stopped. "Meg," she said, "when you were a baby, you went up these stairs on your hands and knees. Later, you held on to my hand so I could help you. Do you remember that?"

Meg laughed and shook her head. "No, but the little kids at church do that."

"Now you're much bigger," Mom continued, "and you walk up the stairs. Gradually you'll be able to do more and more things. Why, look at all you do now! You stayed overnight with your friend Lisa last week. You ride your bicycle to the street now. You couldn't do those things when you were two or even four, could you?"

BE CONTENT TO BE A KID.

Slowly Meg shook her head.

"God made us so we don't have to learn everything at once," Mom added. "We just have to take one step at a time."

HOW ABOUT YOU?

Do you want to be grown up right now? Do you think you should be allowed to do everything a big brother or sister is allowed to do? God has a time for everything. Take just one step at a time.

TO MEMORIZE:

God has made everything beautiful for its own time. He has planted eternity in the human heart, but even so, people cannot see the whole scope of God's work from beginning to end.

ECCLESIASTES 3:11

BY DEAN KELLEY

April 20

OUT OF TUNE

Read Psalm 51:7-13.

"Are you coming to the Christmas concert at school this afternoon?" asked Katie as she finished her breakfast. "Melanie and I are playing a flute duet."

"I wouldn't miss it," Mom replied. As Katie stood up from the table, Mom gasped. "Where did you get that skirt?"

Katie shrugged. "Candy gave it to me. It was too small for her."

"Well, it's also too small for you!" declared Mom. "Please go up and change into something decent."

"Oh, Mom! You're so old-fashioned!" whined Katie. "All the girls wear skirts like this."

When Katie and Melanie began to play at the concert that afternoon, they realized at once that something was wrong. The notes they played just didn't sound right with the piano. Embarrassed, the girls began to make mistakes. They were glad when the song was over and they could sit down.

FOLLOW GOD'S STANDARDS.

"It was so humiliating," groaned Katie that evening. "Melanie and I made sure our instruments were in tune with each other, but we didn't tune them with the piano."

"Katie, remember what we were talking about this morning?" asked her mother. "You seemed to feel that going along with fads is okay because 'everyone is doing it.' But you might be 'in tune' with the standards of the world and be 'out of tune' with God's standards."

HOW ABOUT YOU?

Are your clothes in style? Do you listen to the same music and watch the same TV programs as everybody else? That's okay as long as you're meeting God's standards too. Make sure you're "in tune" with Him!

TO MEMORIZE:

Don't copy the behavior and customs of this world, but let God transform you into a new person by changing the way you think. Then you will learn to know God's will for you, which is good and pleasing and perfect.

ROMANS 12:2

BY SHERRY L. KUYT

ASK WHAT YOU CAN DO

Read 1 Chronicles 16:23-29.

Carla was tired of her church. She told her mother, "I don't get anything out of the worship services. The music seems so dull, and I can't follow Pastor Reese's sermons. I wish I didn't always have to go!" Mom told Carla she would pray with her about it.

At school that week Carla was assigned to prepare an oral report on John F. Kennedy. She found some interesting facts about him. He was the youngest man ever elected president, and he was shot and killed while still in office.

When Carla finished her report, she asked her mom to listen as she practiced it. She ended with a quote from President Kennedy's inaugural address. "He is very famous for this line: 'Ask not what your country can do for you. Ask what you can do for your country.'"

Mom remained silent.

"Well, what do you think?" Carla asked.

"Oh, I'm sorry," said Mom. "It's good, dear, but that last line started me thinking. Remember what you told me about not being able to get anything out of the church services? Maybe we could apply President Kennedy's quote here. Ask not what your church can do for you; ask what you can do for your church."

BE INVOLVED AT CHURCH.

"Hmmm, maybe so!" Carla responded. She thought a lot about it that week, and she decided to try it.

HOW ABOUT YOU?

Do you just sit around expecting to receive blessings at church, or do you try to be a blessing to others? In church, as in other areas, you generally get out of it as much as you put into it. True worship involves giving glory to God, giving offerings to God, and giving ourselves to God.

TO MEMORIZE:

Give to the LORD the glory he deserves! Bring your offering and come into his presence. Worship the LORD in all his holy splendor.

1 CHRONICLES 16:29

BY RAELENE E. PHILLIPS

Just Be Stubborn

You will keep in perfect peace those whose minds are steadfast, because they trust in You. Trust in the LORD forever, for the LORD, the LORD himself, is the rock eternal.

ISAIAH 26:3-4, NIV

We want the perfect peace promised by God. This peace only comes through putting *all trust* in Him. The word *steadfast* means "immovable or firmly fixed in place." Think of it as a *stubborn* trust. Put your trust in God and dig in your heels. He doesn't want every-now-and-then trust. He wants your trust all the time. When you pray for His help in becoming more steadfast, He will give you peace.

Unscramble the words that mean "steadfast or immovable."

mirf ____

fexid ____

drah ____

bommeili ____

motlesions____

noratsitay ____

botsnurb____

yinludgien ____

ANSWER KEY

firm; fixed; hard; immobile; motionless; stationary; stubborn; unyielding

April 22

A FRIEND OF SINNERS

Read Matthew 9:10-13.

"You didn't invite Joy Blackburn to go to Sunday school with us, did you?" Tiffany already knew the answer before Mom nodded. "Ooohhhh, Mom!" she wailed. "Joy talks loud and is so crude. She's everything you tell me not to be. I'm surprised you would want me to be friends with her." Tiffany picked up a knife and began to peel potatoes for dinner.

"I don't want you to be friends with her in the sense that you do what she does," said Mom, "but I want you to be kind to her."

"Ooohhhh!" Tiffany gasped. "I cut my hand!"

Mom grabbed a clean cloth and pressed it tightly against the cut. After examining it, she decided she had better take Tiffany to the emergency room. There a doctor stitched and bandaged Tiffany's hand. Soon they were ready to go home. "Oh dear, we've made quite a mess," Mom exclaimed as she looked around the room.

"Don't worry about that," the nurse said kindly. "We just want your daughter's hand to heal."

THE CHURCH IS FOR SINNERS.

That evening Tiffany showed her father the bandaged hand. "We got blood all over the emergency room, but they didn't even care," she told him. "They were just concerned about me."

Dad smiled. "That's what hospitals are for—to take care of the sick and hurting."

"Something like church," mused Mom. "The church is a good place for hurting people who need Jesus. What if hospitals only allowed well people in?"

Tiffany sighed. "You're talking about Joy, I know. And you're right, Mom. I'm glad she's going to church with us."

HOW ABOUT YOU?

Do you invite only nice or cool kids to go to church with you? This week look for kids who might feel left out, and invite them to church with you.

TO MEMORIZE:

I have come to call not those who think they are righteous,
but those who know they are sinners and need to repent.
LUKE 5:32

BY BARBARA J. WESTBERG

April 23

A CITIZEN NOW

Read Hebrews 11:13-16.

Todd looked over at his mother as she hung up the telephone. "I heard you tell Mrs. Lewis you'd be a witness. Did she have an accident?" he asked.

Mom smiled. "No, Mrs. Lewis wants to become an American citizen. I'm going to be a *character* witness for her."

"But she lives here," Todd said. "Isn't she an American citizen?"

"No," Mom replied. "Living in America doesn't automatically make her an American. She was born in another country and came here when she got married. Now she has applied for citizenship."

When Mrs. Lewis was sworn in as a United States citizen a few months later, they all went out for ice cream to celebrate. "Why did you decide to become an American citizen?" Todd asked her.

"There was a lot I couldn't do before," Mrs. Lewis explained. "I couldn't vote, hold a public office, or do certain jobs. I'm glad to give up my citizenship in my former country and become a citizen here."

SALVATION ISN'T AUTOMATIC.

"That's what happens when we become Christians," Dad said. "We pledge our loyalty to Christ."

"That's right," Mom said. "No one is automatically a Christian, because in a sense, we're all born in a 'foreign country'—this world. To become a citizen of heaven, we must accept Jesus as Savior."

"And being a Christian gives us privileges," added Dad. "We receive forgiveness from sin and a home in heaven. God cares for our needs. Jesus prays for us, and the Holy Spirit guides us."

"I'm a citizen of the United States now," Mrs. Lewis said proudly. "But I'm a citizen of heaven, too. That's even better."

HOW ABOUT YOU?

Where is your citizenship? Have you personally asked Jesus to forgive your sins and be your Savior? You must make that decision to become a citizen of heaven.

TO MEMORIZE:

We are citizens of heaven, where the Lord Jesus Christ lives. And we are eagerly waiting for him to return as our Savior.

PHILIPPIANS 3:20

BY JAN L. HANSEN

April 24

THE BROKEN WATCHES

Read Isaiah 46:3-4, 8-10.

Justin ran into the house and slammed the front door. "Mom!" he called. "Dad said Grandpa is coming to visit again."

"Yes," replied Mom. "Dad is going to get Grandpa on Saturday morning." She sighed as she poked around in her jewelry box. "My watch is broken, and I was hoping one of my old ones would still work. Look, Justin." She held up a small, gold wristwatch. "This is my high school graduation present from Grandpa and Grandma. This one with the leather strap was my official nurse's watch. And the one I wear now—Dad bought this for me before we were married, but now it won't run either."

Justin nodded, then asked, "Why does Grandpa have to come? He spills things and talks funny."

"I thought you loved Grandpa," Mom said quietly.

"I do," Justin said, "or I did before he had that stroke. He used to do stuff with me. Now he just sits around and . . . gets in the way."

RESPECT OLDER PEOPLE.

Mom pointed to the watches. "These watches won't run, but they bring back memories of happy times," she said. "I don't want to throw them out even though they don't have feelings the way people do." Justin looked at the floor. He knew she meant Grandpa. "I have many happy memories of growing up with Grandpa and Grandma," added Justin's mother. "Grandma is in heaven now, and Grandpa is old. But I don't want to throw him out. I love him too much."

Justin hugged his mother. "I'm sorry, Mom. I don't want to throw him out either."

HOW ABOUT YOU?

Do you value old people? Never "throw them away" just because they can't do all the things they once could. Use every opportunity to show them that you do love and appreciate them.

TO MEMORIZE:

Gray hair is a crown of glory; it is gained by living a godly life.

PROVERBS 16:31

BY BEVERLY KENNISTON

April 25

A NEW FRIEND

Read Daniel 6:3-10.

Chris was frightened. It was his very first day at Jefferson School, and he didn't know anyone! As he walked down the unfamiliar hallway to his class, he prayed, "Lord, help me make a friend!"

Some of the boys and girls in Chris's class smiled at him, but hardly anyone said anything. By lunchtime, he was very discouraged. The teacher showed him where to pay for his lunch and pointed out the section of tables reserved for the fifth graders. Chris sat down and looked around at the other boys and girls. They all seemed to be laughing and talking together.

Then Chris noticed something. One boy was praying! Right there in the cafeteria, he had bowed his head and closed his eyes and was praying. *He must be a Christian,* thought Chris. Getting up, he took his tray and went to sit next to the other boy. "Hi, I'm Chris," he said. "I saw you praying just now. You must be a Christian."

"Yes, I am," the boy answered.

PRAYING IS A PRIVILEGE.

"So am I!" exclaimed Chris. "We just moved to town, and I've been praying that the Lord would help me meet a new friend."

"Wow! That's great!" The boy grinned at Chris. "My name is Jason, and there are some other Christian kids around too. You'll like it here."

Silently, Chris prayed, *Thank you, Lord—thank you for helping me meet Jason.*

HOW ABOUT YOU?

Are you sometimes ashamed to talk to the Lord in front of your friends? You don't need to feel that way. Talking to God is a very special privilege that a Christian has. Dare to pray in public, as Daniel did. It will be a testimony to those who are unsaved. It's also an encouragement to other Christians.

TO MEMORIZE:

Be patient in trouble, and keep on praying.

ROMANS 12:12

BY LENORA MCWHORTEN

April 26

THE INVITATION

Read John 14:1-6.

When Sara returned to school after spring break, she and her friends chatted happily together. Then she noticed that several of them referred to Madelyn's party.

Madelyn's party? thought Sara. She vaguely remembered being handed an invitation, but since it wasn't happening right away and she was very busy, she hadn't paid much attention just then. What had she done with the invitation? She hurried to look in her desk. There it was, sticking out of her math book. She quickly pulled it out and read, "Please come to a party. . . . We'll look for you on April 7." Oh no! The party was last week! Just then Kayla came over to her desk. "You missed a great party!" she exclaimed. "Madelyn's dad took us to her grandparents' place in the country, and we had a tractor ride."

Sara bit her lip to keep from crying. But that evening she did shed a few tears. "I could have gone," she told her parents. "I was invited, but I didn't read the invitation carefully. Now it's too late. I missed it."

"I'm sorry," sympathized Mom.

DON'T IGNORE GOD'S INVITATION.

Dad was sorry too. Then he said, "There is another invitation that many people ignore. God invites us all to spend eternity in heaven with Him, but the day will come when it will be too late to accept that invitation too."

Sara nodded. "I'm glad I won't miss that," she said. "It would be lots worse than missing Madelyn's party."

HOW ABOUT YOU?

Have you been careless with God's invitation to heaven? Have you been too busy to think about it? Do you intend to have a look at it later? Accept the invitation that God is patiently offering now.

TO MEMORIZE:

If you openly declare that Jesus is Lord and believe in your heart that God raised him from the dead, you will be saved.

ROMANS 10:9

BY HAZEL W. MARETT

April 27

GOOD NEWS!

Read Matthew 28:18-20.

"If I watched anything as violent as that, you'd make me turn the TV off," observed Jessica as her father watched the evening news.

"You're right," he agreed, turning it off. "I like to keep up on what's happening in the world, but I think it would be better if they didn't show some of those pictures. Maybe I should rely more heavily on my newspaper."

"Did I hear someone say they want a newspaper?" asked Andrew as he came in the back door. He handed his dad a paper and said, "I just finished my paper route. Seems like everybody I saw talked about all the articles on crime and war. I felt like the bearer of bad news!"

"Well, *I'm* the bearer of *good* news—dinner's ready!" announced Mom. Everyone trooped to the table and together thanked God for the food.

"Mmmmm, this lasagna sure is good news," commented Andrew.

Dad said, "There is some other good news that all of us should be sharing."

SHARE THE GOSPEL.

Andrew and Jessica looked puzzled. "I'll give you a clue," said Dad. "It's found in the Bible."

"Oh, I know—it's the Good News of Jesus!" exclaimed Jessica.

"Right," agreed Dad. "We are to tell others the gospel message. *Gospel* means 'good news.' Perhaps there's so much bad news in the world today because not enough people know the Good News of the gospel. Do you think we can each tell it to at least one person tomorrow?"

HOW ABOUT YOU?

When was the last time you shared the Good News of Jesus with someone? If you are a Christian, it's your responsibility to tell others that Jesus died on the cross for our sins, that He was buried, and that He rose again.

TO MEMORIZE:

He told them, "Go into all the world and preach the Good News to everyone."

MARK 16:15

BY HAZEL W. MARETT

April 28

DAD'S JOB

Read Numbers 21:4-6.

"I sure wish Dad could come to my basketball game tonight," complained Brock to his older brother, Tyler. "He works every Friday night!"

Tyler tried to cheer him up. "Mom and I have been there, Brock."

"But it's not the same," Brock replied. Just then Mom called them to supper.

"Mmmmm, this steak is tasty!" exclaimed Tyler. "Remember how often we wished for a steak when Dad was out of work?"

"I sure do," replied Mom, "and now I need to remember that no work means no gravy." She glanced at Brock, but he refused to smile.

The next evening the family enjoyed having Dad at home. "Tyler, did you choose something for family devotions tonight?" he asked.

Tyler replied, "I've got it all planned, Dad." Tyler took the Bible and read from Exodus and Numbers. Then he said, "Today is an anniversary. Anybody know what for?"

"I do," responded Dad. "It's three months since I got called back to work."

APPRECIATE GOD'S BLESSINGS.

"That's right!" said Mom. "I remember how thrilled we were." She paused, then exclaimed, "Oh, I see your point, Tyler! We've been like the Israelites. At first they were thrilled to have manna, but then they began to complain about it. I confess that I was the first to complain about your dad's job. I hope you'll all forgive me. May God forgive us too! Thank you for teaching us a lesson, Tyler."

HOW ABOUT YOU?

Is there some blessing in your life that you've begun to dislike? Perhaps you prayed for a brother or sister, but now that you have one you sometimes wish you didn't. Or maybe you prayed that your Sunday school class would grow, and now that it has, you don't like it, because there are too many new kids. Be careful. Never criticize God's blessings.

TO MEMORIZE:

We have sinned by speaking against the LORD and against you.

NUMBERS 21:7

BY RAELENE E. PHILLIPS

Let all who take refuge in you rejoice; let them sing joyful praises forever. Spread your protection over them, that all who love your name may be filled with joy.

PSALM 5:11

What if you discovered that trusting God gives you joy? Worrying is not trusting God. Being anxious is not trusting God. Fully trusting Him can make you shout for joy.

Write about something that is troubling you in your life, especially if it's something you continue to worry about.

____

____

____

____

____

Now write directly to God and tell Him you trust Him completely. Tell Him what worries you. He will defend you, like the Bible promises. Be sure to thank Him for His promise of joy.

Dear Heavenly Father,

____

____

____

____

Amen.

What if you practiced trusting Him with everything in your life?

April 29

FRACTURED FRIENDSHIP

Read Proverbs 27:6-10.

"Mom," called Caitlin as she returned from school one day, "can we go get my birthday party invitations?"

Mom shook her head. "I'm sorry, honey, but I promised Mrs. Kettering I'd drive her to the doctor's office this afternoon. Ever since she broke her leg last year, she's had a hard time getting around."

"Well," said Caitlin, "we'd better get the invitations soon. It's only two weeks till my birthday."

Mother smiled. "Have you decided who you'll invite?" she asked. "Remember, five guests is the limit."

Caitlin nodded. "I want to invite Amanda, Brianna, Ashley, Emily, and Marisol."

Mother looked surprised. "What about Brooke from next door?" she asked. "I thought you two were best friends!"

"Oh, we are," Caitlin said, "but I can see her anytime."

TREAT FRIENDS WITH CARE.

Mother was quiet for a minute. "I'm thinking of Mrs. Kettering's broken leg," she said. "Even though the fracture did heal, her leg will never be quite the same. Sometimes it hurts, and she has to be careful not to put too much stress on it. She can't trust it. It's the same way with friendship."

"Friendship?" asked Caitlin.

"If you hurt a friend, she may forgive you. But she may never be able to trust you again." Mom sighed. "I learned that lesson the hard way—I once lost a good friend because of a cruel, thoughtless remark I made. Friends are a precious gift from God, Caitlin."

Caitlin looked thoughtful. "I think I'd better go over my guest list again," she said.

HOW ABOUT YOU?

Do you take your friends for granted? Do you assume that they'll always be willing to forgive you? Even a strong friendship can be broken, and healing can be difficult. Treat your friends as you want them to treat you—with kindness and respect.

TO MEMORIZE:

Never abandon a friend—either yours or your father's.

PROVERBS 27:10

BY SHERRY L. KUYT

April 30

GOD AND ME

Read Isaiah 42:5, 8-12.

"We'll all be late for church if Carmen doesn't hurry up," complained Pablo. "She takes forever to fix her hair!"

Finally they were on their way. When they got to church, Carmen went to comb her hair again. Mom and Dad frowned as she tiptoed into the pew during the first hymn.

That evening Pablo got out a magnifying glass. "It's fun to look at stuff under this," he said.

"Let me see," said Carmen.

Dad wrote something on two small pieces of paper, which he placed on the table with some other things Pablo had lined up to look at. He watched as Pablo put the first paper under the magnifying glass. Pablo looked at it and shrugged. Then Carmen looked. "Why did you write *God* on this?" she asked.

"Because God should be magnified," explained Dad. "Whoa, there," he added as Pablo picked up the second piece of paper. "Don't put that one under your glass, Son. It's not supposed to be magnified."

GLORIFY GOD, NOT SELF.

Pablo read it and handed it to his sister. Written in small letters was the word *me*.

"You see," continued Dad, "sometimes you and I tend to magnify *me* instead of *God*. If we do that, we might spend too much time on appearance."

"Yeah," broke in Pablo, looking at Carmen. "We comb our hair all the time and make everybody late for church."

"On the other hand," said Dad, "when we magnify *God* instead of *me*, we try to please Him in our behavior instead of pointing the finger at someone else."

HOW ABOUT YOU?

Do you spend too much time in front of your mirror? God wants you to look neat, clean, and attractive, but remember that real beauty is seen in actions more than in appearance.

TO MEMORIZE:

Oh, magnify the LORD with me, and let us exalt His name together.

PSALM 34:3, NKJV

BY HARRIETT A. DURRELL

May 1

NO LEMON JUICE

Read Exodus 16:6-12.

Julie felt grouchy as she sat on the couch at the home of her Sunday school teacher, Mrs. Watson. She didn't really want to be on what she called "this stupid old Parents' Night planning committee." She had to miss her favorite TV program to attend this meeting. Maria and Daniel, the other committee members, seemed to be enjoying it, however—or at least they *had* been. They had made several suggestions, but Julie had just scowled at them. Now the others also seemed to be losing a lot of their enthusiasm.

"Julie," said Mrs. Watson finally, "why don't you help me prepare the snacks? Maria and Daniel, I like your ideas. Keep thinking."

Glumly, Julie followed Mrs. Watson into the kitchen and arranged cookies on a plate while her teacher prepared hot chocolate. "Maybe I'll add just a little lemon juice to this chocolate," Mrs. Watson said.

"Lemon juice?" Julie was surprised. "That'll make it sour!"

DON'T BE A COMPLAINER.

"You're right, of course," Mrs. Watson agreed. "And you know, Julie, just like a little lemon juice can ruin this hot chocolate, a bad attitude from one person can ruin the special night we're planning. We want this to be a good Parents' Night, especially since we know there will be unsaved dads and moms attending. Maria and Daniel have come up with some good ideas, and you've 'soured' them all."

Julie stared at the floor. "I'm sorry," she said at last. "I'll apologize to Maria and Daniel. Oh, and Mrs. Watson?" she added.

"Yes, Julie?"

Julie grinned. "Please put the lemon juice away."

HOW ABOUT YOU?

Are you a complainer? Do you often "get into moods" if things don't go the way you want? You might be surprised how quickly your moods can spread. The Lord wants you to be joyful and get along with others.

TO MEMORIZE:

Do everything without complaining and arguing.

PHILIPPIANS 2:14

BY LENORA MCWHORTEN

May 2

A WITNESS (PART 1)

Read Luke 24:46-48.

Krystal was walking home from Bible club and thinking about her good friend Maribeth. Krystal knew she should tell Maribeth about Jesus, but Maribeth might laugh at her!

As Krystal waited at an intersection for the light to change, she saw an old man start across the street against the light. Suddenly a truck came through the intersection and hit him. Soon paramedics arrived, and the injured man was on his way to the hospital.

A few nights later Krystal's dad read in the newspaper, "The police are looking for the red-haired girl who witnessed an accident on the corner of Clay and Main at 2:50 p.m. on Tuesday." Dad looked at Krystal. "It seems that they need you as a witness."

"But I didn't do anything wrong," said Krystal.

"Of course not," Dad assured her. "They're just looking for someone to tell them exactly what happened. Someone must have seen you there. I'll go with you to the police station so you won't be alone. You don't need to be afraid to tell them what happened."

GOD HELPS YOU WITNESS.

When Krystal went to bed that night, the scene of the accident went through her mind. She remembered that she had been thinking about witnessing to Maribeth but she had been scared. Now it seemed she was going to have to be a different kind of witness. She was scared about that, too, but Dad would be with her. Suddenly she realized that her heavenly Father would be with her when she witnessed to Maribeth. If she could trust her earthly father, how much more should she trust her heavenly Father!

HOW ABOUT YOU?

Are you afraid to witness to others—to tell them about Jesus? Remember, you're not alone. Jesus has told you to go and be His witness, and He will go with you. Trust Him.

TO MEMORIZE:

I am with you always, even to the end of the age.

MATTHEW 28:20

BY JAN L. HANSEN

May 3

A WITNESS (PART 2)

Read 1 John 1:1-5.

Some time after Krystal went to the police station with her father, she had to appear in court. "The truck driver could be convicted—and sued—for hitting the man unless he has a witness to testify that he was driving in a proper manner," the police chief had explained. "Your job, Krystal, is just to tell what happened."

Krystal was nervous. She had never been inside a courtroom. But the words came easily once she started giving her testimony. After the case was presented, the truck driver was cleared of any wrongdoing. He came over to shake hands with Krystal. "I'm really sorry that man got hurt," the driver said, "but I'm thankful that you told the truth, Krystal. It takes away the guilt—and the punishment. I could have been sent to jail if I had been convicted."

On the way home Krystal and her dad stopped for hot fudge sundaes. "You're quiet, Krystal. What are you thinking about?"

"I was thinking about my friend Maribeth," Krystal explained. "I've wanted to talk to her about Jesus, but I didn't know what to say. Now I do. When I gave my testimony about the accident, I just told what happened. I'll just tell Maribeth what happened too. I'll tell her what Jesus has done for me."

GIVE YOUR TESTIMONY.

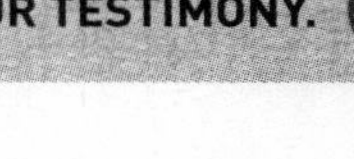

Dad gave her a hug. "Remember how grateful the truck driver was for your testimony because it helped save him from punishment? Perhaps someday Maribeth will be grateful for your testimony too."

HOW ABOUT YOU?

Do you want to witness but you just don't know what to say? A witness simply gives his or her testimony and tells the truth about what happened. You can do that. Remember, Jesus has saved you! Tell somebody.

TO MEMORIZE:

You are to be his witness, telling everyone what you have seen and heard.

ACTS 22:15

BY JAN L. HANSEN

May 4

JUST LIKE US

Read Ephesians 2:19-22.

Amanda and Joelle were on their way to their new home. There were different things to see every day. "What will we see tomorrow?" asked Amanda when they stopped at a motel on Saturday night.

"Tomorrow we're going to church," said Mom, "just like we do when we're home."

"Oh, Mom, do we have to? I'll feel so out of place in a strange church," said Amanda.

Dad smiled. "I think we can find one where we'll feel at home," he assured her.

Early Sunday morning Mom woke Amanda and Joelle and told them to get ready for church. After breakfast they headed for the church they had chosen. When they arrived, a friendly couple met them at the door and took them to their Sunday school class. The pianist was playing a song that Amanda and Joelle knew.

As the morning passed, the girls were surprised to find many things similar to their own church. The kids were friendly, and the teacher told a familiar Bible story.

CHRISTIANS HAVE MUCH IN COMMON.

"Sometimes," said Dad as they got back into their car, "we think we're the only Christians in the world—but that's not true. There are people everywhere who love the Lord."

"And it's fun to meet other Christians," Joelle decided.

"I think so too," agreed Amanda. "After all, we all belong to God's family!"

HOW ABOUT YOU?

Have you ever visited a church in another town? Was it a lot like the one you regularly attend? Christians have much in common—especially their love for the Lord. When you're on vacation or on your way to a new home, you'll find that it's a good time to meet other Christians and fellowship with them.

TO MEMORIZE:

I am a friend to anyone who fears you—anyone who obeys your commandments.

PSALM 119:63

BY LENORA MCWHORTEN

May 5

MAKE UP YOUR MIND

Read Acts 24:24-27; 26:1, 27-29.

On the way to church, Alyssa hummed along as the voices of a choir came over the car radio: "I have decided to follow Jesus. . . ." *I guess I don't really follow Jesus,* she thought. *Actually, I'm not sure I'm saved.*

Her thoughts were interrupted by her sister, Joni. "Look at the big sale sign in the store window!" All Alyssa could think about then was shopping.

In Sunday school class that morning Mrs. Tomkins spoke about Felix and King Agrippa. "Both men heard the gospel from Paul," she said, "but neither made up his mind to accept Christ. I hope none of you put off making such an important decision." Alyssa squirmed. She decided to talk to Mrs. Tomkins after class about being saved. But when class was dismissed, she hurried over to talk to Becky.

After dinner Alyssa put a few leftovers in her dog's dish. She opened the back door and called, "Come, Spunky." He romped toward the door. Then a bird caught his attention. Spunky was off running around the yard. "Spunky, aren't you hungry?" Alyssa asked. Spunky sniffed the grass.

ACCEPT JESUS TODAY.

Suddenly it dawned on Alyssa that she had been acting just like Spunky. She allowed all sorts of things to take her attention away from the most important decision she had to make. Spunky could take his time, but she couldn't linger any longer. It was time for her to trust Christ and to commit herself to Him.

HOW ABOUT YOU?

Have you made up your mind to accept Jesus as your Savior? If not, don't delay. Confess your sin and ask Jesus to come into your life today!

TO MEMORIZE:

Look! I stand at the door and knock. If you hear my voice and open the door, I will come in, and we will share a meal together as friends.

REVELATION 3:20

BY JAN L. HANSEN

Let It Shine

You are the light of the world. . . . Let your good deeds shine out for all to see, so that everyone will praise your heavenly Father.
MATTHEW 5:14, 16

When others see how Christ works through you, it makes it easier for them to see God's light in this world. Think of all you do each day and how you are a light for Him. Let it shine!

Use the clues below to solve the crossword puzzle.

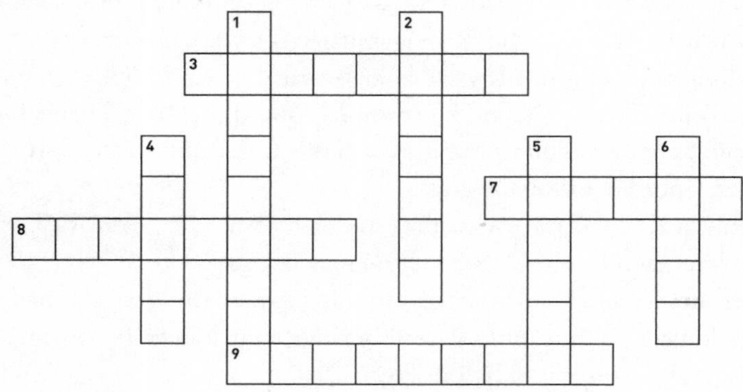

ACROSS

3. God said, "Let there be light in the ______________" (2 Corinthians 4:6).
7. an opening in a wall or door that lets in light
8. to add more light to something or make something more cheerful
9. the group to whom Jesus spoke in Matthew 5:14-16

DOWN

1. a table for a lamp
2. the book of the Bible in which God first said, "Let there be light."
4. "Your word is a lamp to guide my feet and a ________ for my path" (Psalm 119:105).
5. Song title: "This ________ Light of Mine"
6. Jesus' followers are the light of the __________.

ANSWER KEY
ACROSS: 3. darkness; 7. window; 8. brighten; 9. disciples
DOWN: 1. lampstand; 2. Genesis; 4. light; 5. little; 6. world

May 6
LAVA LIPS

Read James 3:3-10.

"Hi, Mom," called Tracie as she opened the front door. "We had the best class today! We learned about volcanoes."

"That sounds interesting," replied Mom. "Volcanoes are a fascinating part of nature."

Tracie nodded. "My teacher, Mr. Hoover, has a small model of a volcano. He could even make it erupt. Do you know what erupts from a real volcano?"

"Lava, hot gases, and rock fragments," answered Tracie's brother Jason, who had also come in from school.

Tracie frowned. "I asked Mom, not you," she growled. Then she went on talking about the volcano. "Pressure builds up and the red hot ash blasts through the surface. Do you know where it erupts from?" she asked, looking at her mother.

Jason answered again. "From the mouth. It's at the top of a cone-shaped mountain," he said.

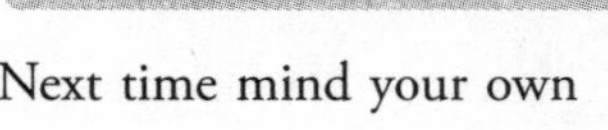

"Wrong!" declared Tracie triumphantly. "That's what it looks like, but the actual opening is lower than the top, or mouth. It's called a vent." She made a face at her brother. "Shows how much you know, dummy. Next time mind your own business and don't answer unless I ask you."

"Tracie," Mom scolded, "a volcano isn't the only thing with a mouth. We have mouths too. Perhaps eruptions don't come from the mouth of the volcano, but our mouths can erupt with hot, vicious words that hurt other people. We can't control volcanic eruptions, but we *can* learn to control our tongues and our mouths."

HOW ABOUT YOU?

Do unkind words sometimes slip out of your mouth? Remember that God made your mouth to praise and glorify Him. Words that hurt others don't please God. Ask Him to help you control your tongue when you feel a hot, vicious eruption building up.

TO MEMORIZE:

Blessing and cursing come pouring out of the same mouth. . . . This is not right!

JAMES 3:10

BY NANCE E. KEYES

May 7

UNUSED GIFTS

Read Romans 12:6-12.

Ryan played the first page of his music. Then he thought about how the guys had snickered when his mother had called him to come inside to practice. He wondered if any kids would make fun of him when he played in church Sunday. He sat at the piano, staring at his music.

"Why did you quit?" Mom called.

"I don't want to play in church," Ryan said. "Piano is for girls."

"That isn't true," protested Mom, placing her hands on Ryan's shoulders. "God gave you an exceptional talent, and He wants you to use it."

"I can't," Ryan answered. Mom didn't insist that Ryan keep on practicing his special number, but she asked him to think and pray about it.

That night Ryan worked on a gift for his sister, Abby. It was a wristband like those many kids at school were wearing.

"Thank you," Abby said when she opened it on her birthday.

USE YOUR GIFTS.

A few days later Ryan complained, "Abby, you never wear the wristband I made for you."

"Well, it's not really like the ones the other girls are wearing," Abby explained.

After Abby left the room, Mom looked at Ryan. "It hurts when you take special care with a gift for someone but that person doesn't use it," she observed. Ryan nodded sadly.

As Ryan considered his mother's words, someone knocked on the door. Ryan answered it. "Want to play ball?" invited Adam, who lived next door.

Ryan hesitated. "I'm going to practice piano first," he said.

HOW ABOUT YOU?

Do you have a gift you aren't using? Maybe you're embarrassed to use it. Maybe you don't want to make the effort to develop it. God gave you gifts. He is pleased when you use them.

TO MEMORIZE:

Once you had no identity as a people; now you are God's people.
Once you received no mercy; now you have received God's mercy.

1 PETER 2:10

BY KATHERINE R. ADAMS

May 8

IN THE BEEHIVE

Read 1 Corinthians 12:18-27.

Neerja slammed the door behind her. "I was looking forward to having the lead part in our spring play, but instead I have to make props," she complained to her father as he put on his beekeeper's outfit. Neerja jumped up. "I want to go with you to the beehives," she said. They exchanged smiles as Neerja, too, slipped into a "bee suit."

At the beehive Neerja watched her father pull out a honeycomb from one of the hives. "Oh! Good!" he said. "I'm glad they're not all queen bees in this hive, aren't you? If they were, there wouldn't be any workers to make the honey, and I like honey!" He checked each of the remaining honeycombs. "The Bible says that every member of the body has a job to do. In the beehive, each one needs to do his own job so the hive works efficiently. The bees can't all be drones. They can't all be worker bees. And they can't all be queens. Each kind of bee is needed. It's that way in life, too."

"Oh, I think I know what you're trying to say, Dad." Neerja's eyes sparkled. "You're trying to tell me that making props is just as important as having the lead part. Without props you can't have a good play."

Dad hugged Neerja. "Exactly."

"Then I'll be a bu-z-z-zy bee making props!" Neerja giggled as she slid her hand into Dad's.

YOU ARE NEEDED.

HOW ABOUT YOU?

Are you content with what God has given you to do? Or do you sometimes wish for more important jobs? God says each one is needed. He doesn't list any job as greater than another. He just asks you to do your best in whatever job you are given. Do whatever you do as if you're doing it for the Lord.

TO MEMORIZE:

Our bodies have many parts, and God has put each part just where he wants it.

1 CORINTHIANS 12:18

BY DOLORES A. LEMIEUX

May 9

WHO MADE WHOM?

Read 1 Chronicles 16:23-31.

When Jeff and his parents moved to Taiwan to help missionaries, Jeff discovered that everything was very strange. He was glad to meet William (his English name), who attended English classes at the mission.

"I show you town," the black-haired boy said one day in his best English. The boys hopped on their bikes. Dodging people, other bikes, and trucks on the narrow streets, they pedaled around the small town. "Come," said William as he parked his bike in front of a large building.

When William pushed open the door, Jeff gasped at what he saw. "God factory," explained William, waving his hand at the rows and rows of half-made idols stacked on the floor of the warehouse. "My father makes. He paint faces. Very nice. Many people buy."

Jeff couldn't believe that people would make their own gods. How could pieces of wood help anybody? "Your father make gods?" asked William.

TELL ABOUT THE LIVING GOD.

Jeff shook his head slowly. Trying to make William understand, he found himself talking just like him. "No, we not make gods. Our God make us!"

Jeff had always known that God had made him, but he had never thought that was anything so special before. Now he realized what a wonderful God he had! He was glad he knew the true God. Silently he prayed, *Thank You, God, for making me. Help me tell William and others about You so they won't have to worship an idol of wood that can't even hear their prayers.*

HOW ABOUT YOU?

Aren't you glad you can know the real living God, who created the whole universe? There are still many people who don't know Him. Begin in your own neighborhood by telling your friends what you know about God. Maybe someday He will allow you to carry His message to other lands.

TO MEMORIZE:

Publish his glorious deeds among the nations.
Tell everyone about the amazing things he does.
1 CHRONICLES 16:24

BY MATILDA H. NORDTVEDT

May 10

TRIPS AND SMALL THINGS

Read Luke 11:9-13.

Megan heaved a big sigh. "I sure wish we could go to Iowa for Grandma and Grandpa's thirty-fifth anniversary party," she said. "All my cousins will be there. Why does your boss have to be so mean and not let you off, Dad?"

"He's not being mean, Megan," replied Dad. "It's just that too many other people requested that week off before I did."

"Why don't we pray about this?" suggested Mom cheerfully.

"Pray about it?" asked Megan. "Do you think we ought to? My friend Jennifer says we shouldn't bother God with unimportant things, because He's busy running a whole universe. Does He want to be bothered with a family trip?"

Dad frowned. "Megan, remember last December when I told you to make a list of what you'd like for Christmas?" he asked. Megan nodded, and Dad continued, "You didn't say, 'Oh, I couldn't do that. You have your job to think about and repairs to make on the house, and so many more important things.'"

"But you're my dad!" interrupted Megan.

BRING REQUESTS TO GOD.

Dad nodded. "That's right," he said, "and I'd feel bad if you weren't comfortable giving me that list." He reached for his Bible and turned to Romans 8:14. "Megan, God calls us His children, and He feels sad when we don't confide in Him. Now, let's pray about that trip."

HOW ABOUT YOU?

Did you know that God is interested in all your requests—even the little ones? Our fathers aren't perfect, but our heavenly Father is. He loves His children even more than an earthly father would. Even though His answer may be "no" or "wait a while," your requests are very important to Him.

TO MEMORIZE:

Don't worry about anything; instead, pray about everything.
Tell God what you need, and thank him for all he has done.
PHILIPPIANS 4:6

BY PHYLLIS M. ROBINSON

May 11

DUMB EXCUSES

Read John 3:16-21.

Danielle stubbornly shook her head. "My dad and mom are going to the college play-offs next weekend," she said. "I want to go with them."

"But everyone else is going on the youth retreat. Why don't you come?"

Danielle shrugged. "I don't have the right clothes for it."

"Oh, honestly!" fumed April. "You make up the dumbest excuses."

Danielle grinned. "Besides, it costs too much."

"Danielle, you know that's not true!" exclaimed April. "Two families have given money to sponsor the group, so it won't cost a thing."

But Danielle refused to go to the retreat.

After Bible club one day, Danielle said to April, "Miss Ellis is always bugging us to 'be saved.' I haven't done anything so bad."

April was thoughtful. "Well," she answered, "no one is good enough for heaven. No sin can enter there, so even the 'little' bad things you've done have to be forgiven."

GO TO GOD FOR HELP.

"Maybe so," said Danielle with a shrug, "but Miss Ellis said that Jesus paid the price for everyone to go to heaven. So the price is paid for my salvation, right? I don't need to worry about it."

April hesitated. "Remember the retreat?" she asked.

"The retreat?" repeated Danielle. "I didn't go."

"No," said April, "but the price was paid for you to go. You just wouldn't accept the offer. It's like that with salvation, too. Jesus paid the price for you to go to heaven, but unless you receive the gift God offers, you won't go there. That makes sense, doesn't it?"

"Yes, I guess it does," Danielle admitted. "I guess I need to accept the offer."

HOW ABOUT YOU?

Have you accepted God's offer of salvation? Or are you saying, "I'll think about it" or "I want to do some fun things first"? Stop making "dumb excuses."

TO MEMORIZE:

To all who believed him and accepted him, he gave the right to become children of God.

JOHN 1:12

BY HAZEL W. MARETT

May 12

DEADLY FLEA BITE

Read 2 Corinthians 6:14-18.

A blast of music hit Mom's ears as she entered the house. "Chan, turn that off!" she called. Click.

Chan's lip curled. "Can't Christians enjoy life?"

"You know they can," Mom replied, "but you enjoy the wrong things."

Chan shook his head. "You'll never understand. You belong to a different generation."

The telephone interrupted him, and Mom went to answer it. "Hello. How are you, Lei? Jian is in the hospital?" Chan listened. "Bubonic plague? Are they sure? I thought bubonic plague was wiped out years ago. Certainly we'll pray for him. As soon as Tom gets home, we'll meet you at the hospital. Tell Jian we're praying for him, okay? Good-bye."

"What's bubonic plague?" Chan asked.

Mom collapsed into a chair. "It's a terrible disease. In the Middle Ages it was called the Black Death, and it killed thousands. The doctor told Aunt Lei there have been a few cases in the States the last few years."

WATCH THE LITTLE THINGS.

"What causes it?" Chan asked.

"Fleas from infected rats are the carriers," Mom answered grimly.

"Fleas?" Chan was astounded. "Little bitty fleas?"

"Little things can be deadly," Mom told him. "They can be just as dangerous as big things—sometimes more so because we tend to overlook them." She paused and looked directly at him. "And little sins can cause spiritual epidemics."

Chan took a deep breath. "Little things like music with hateful words?" Mom nodded. "You might be right," Chan admitted.

HOW ABOUT YOU?

Are little things creeping into your life that will weaken you spiritually? What about the music you listen to, the books you read, the words you say? Check your life now for little sins that you need to destroy.

TO MEMORIZE:

Because we have these promises, dear friends, let us cleanse ourselves from everything that can defile our body or spirit. And let us work toward complete holiness because we fear God.

2 CORINTHIANS 7:1

BY BARBARA J. WESTBERG

You Are Called

Fight the good fight for the true faith. Hold tightly to the eternal life to which God has called you, which you have declared so well before many witnesses.

1 TIMOTHY 6:12

One way we spread the light of Christ is through witnessing. This means sharing our testimony with others. You can witness by explaining the difference faith makes in your life. Or you can tell others how you found Jesus. Our testimony helps others learn how God can work in their lives. The most important thing we can share is how Christ offers salvation to everyone.

Help the child find his way to Jesus.

SEE ANSWER IN BACK

May 13

SEARCH AND DESTROY

Read Romans 8:31-39.

Michael hardly raised his eyes when Dad called. "Come on, Son. We have to clean the basement now." A moment later Michael slowly put down the book he was reading and went to the basement. Dad handed him a broom, and Michael began dusting cobwebs out of corners while Dad cleaned a shelf. "That must be a good book," Dad said.

"It sure is, Dad," confirmed Michael. "It's about some enemy spies on a search and destroy mission. They want to blow up a bridge, cutting the good guys off from escape."

"Well, you'd better get on with your own search and destroy mission," laughed Dad.

Michael waved the broom. "Watch out, spiders! I'm coming after you!"

Dad dumped some trash in a container. "Did you know every Christian has an enemy on a search and destroy mission against him or her?" he asked. "Satan's goal is to steal your love for God, kill your desire to serve Him, and destroy your witness for Him. But if you stay close to Jesus, Satan can't harm you."

FIGHT SATAN.

Dad gave the basement an approving glance. "Thanks for helping. Now you can go back to your book," he added with a smile.

Michael grinned. "Okay. But I'm going to do my Sunday school lesson first. I don't want to let Satan use that book to keep me from staying close to God!"

HOW ABOUT YOU?

Are you aware of Satan's secret mission against you? He knows just how to turn you away from loving God fully. But you can fight him. When you want to disobey your parents, skip church, tell a lie, or do any wrong thing, it's Satan attacking you. Realize that, and ask Jesus to help you follow Him.

TO MEMORIZE:

But you belong to God, my dear children. You have already won a victory over those people, because the Spirit who lives in you is greater than the spirit who lives in the world.

1 JOHN 4:4

BY CAROLYN E. YOST

May 14

EXPERIENCED COMFORTER

Read 2 Corinthians 1:3-7.

"Mom!" called Jaimee loudly. "Mason isn't helping me. Why should I have to pick up all the toys by myself?"

Mom found Mason sitting on the floor, breathing hard. "Jaimee, look at your brother! The dust must have triggered his asthma," Mom said with concern. "Go lie down, Mason, and I'll give you your medicine."

"Oh, Mom," complained Jaimee. "Mason gets out of everything just because he has asthma. It's not fair!"

"I know it seems that way at times," Mom said, "but it isn't his fault."

A few days later Jaimee developed a bad cough and a high fever. "It's bronchitis," the doctor said. "I'll prescribe some medicine, and you'll need lots of rest."

Jaimee stayed inside for several days. She didn't like the medicine, and she missed her friends. Worst of all, it was hard to breathe. She had to sleep propped up on pillows the way Mason often slept. *Imagine feeling like this as often as he does,* Jaimee thought. She closed her eyes and prayed—for herself and for Mason.

BE A COMFORTER.

Finally Jaimee went back to school. At the end of the first day she told her mother, "It sure is great to be feeling good again."

"I imagine you're eager to go out and play with your friends," said Mom with a smile.

But Jaimee hung up her coat instead. "I think I'll play a game with Mason," she said. "He acts tired lately, so I thought I'd try to cheer him up. Now I know how he feels."

HOW ABOUT YOU?

Are you as sympathetic with others as you should be? Do you pray for them? Think of times you've been sick or have had other problems. Try to remember little things people did for you. Give others the same kind of help.

TO MEMORIZE:

He comforts us in all our troubles so that we can comfort others. When they are troubled, we will be able to give them the same comfort God has given us.

2 CORINTHIANS 1:4

BY SHERRY L. KUYT

May 15

GO AND TEACH THEM

Read Mark 1:15.

After traveling all day, Coretta and her parents stopped at a motel. "Dear God," Coretta prayed at bedtime, "please help my friends Joy, Jasmine, and Cesar to accept You as their Savior."

"Have you ever told your friends about Jesus?" Dad asked as he tucked Coretta in bed.

"Well, no," Coretta replied.

"Prayer is important," Mom said, "but we also need to talk to our friends about Jesus."

After everyone had gone to sleep, a loud, blaring noise burst into the night. Coretta, Dad, and Mom jolted straight up in their beds.

"The car horn must be stuck," Dad grumbled, half-asleep. He found the car keys, grabbed his bathrobe, and ran outside. He fumbled in the dark to get the key in the car door. He needed to get into the car to unlock the hood.

TELL OTHERS ABOUT JESUS.

By then people in neighboring rooms were stirring. "You're trying to open my car," a man said. Dad was embarrassed to discover that his car was parked in the next space.

The next night Coretta again prayed, "Please help my friends accept Jesus as Savior."

When Coretta was done, Mom asked, "Remember how Dad's frantic efforts to turn off the horn last night were of no use? Just as Dad needed someone to point out his problem, your friends need you to explain their need for Jesus. Pray for them, and then witness to them."

HOW ABOUT YOU?

Do you sit quietly while your friends run around seeking happiness in things that will not last? You need to pray and then tell others about Jesus.

TO MEMORIZE:

Therefore, go and make disciples of all the nations, baptizing them in the name of the Father and the Son and the Holy Spirit.

MATTHEW 28:19

BY NANCE E. KEYES

May 16

A LOOK AT THE HEART

Read Jeremiah 17:5-10.

"Wow, Mom! I never knew all this stuff before." Blake was doing a report on the heart for school. As he read the encyclopedia entry about the heart, he said, "It's amazing how God has made us!"

"What did you learn?" asked Mom.

"Well, it says here that the heart circulates our blood over 1,000 times in 24 hours. During that time it pumps over 5,000 quarts of blood. And listen to this! If all our blood vessels were laid end to end, they would stretch almost 100,000 miles! The heart is only as big as a fist, yet it can do all that stuff."

Mom said, "In the Bible the word *heart* represents our thoughts, attitudes, values, and emotions. In Jeremiah we read that the heart is deceitful and wicked."

"That bad?" Blake asked.

"Right. We're all born with a sinful nature," replied Mom. "God loves us so much, however, that He gave His Son to take the punishment for our sins. When we believe in Christ as Savior, God gives us a new, clean heart—new thoughts, attitudes, and values."

ASK CHRIST INTO YOUR HEART.

Blake had accepted Jesus as his Savior a few years ago. "Mom," he said, "I'm going to write about the Bible in my report. Our teacher says we're supposed to put down everything we can find about our subject. What a great chance to share about the Lord!"

HOW ABOUT YOU?

Do you have a new heart? In Jeremiah we read about the sinfulness of the heart. That sinfulness can only be taken care of by believing in Christ as our Savior. If you have never taken care of your sinful heart, why not do so today?

TO MEMORIZE:

Create in me a clean heart, O God. Renew a loyal spirit within me.

PSALM 51:10

BY LENORA MCWHORTEN

May 17

A MEMORIAL ROCK

Read 1 Samuel 7:7-12.

The Johnson family stood looking at the big oak tree lying across their yard. During the night a fierce storm had blown the tree down. Mark was the first to speak. "God sure did take good care of us, didn't He, Dad?"

Dad replied, "Yes, He did. And that makes me stop and praise Him."

Mark looked at their house standing just a short distance from the fallen tree, yet not harmed at all. "Yeah," he said in awe, "I hope I never forget all the things God has done for us."

"We had a story in Bible club about Samuel setting up a stone. It was a reminder of how God had won a battle for Israel," Samantha said. "Its name meant 'God has helped us.'"

"You're thinking of the name *Ebenezer*," said Mom. "Do you want to set up a memorial rock of your own?"

Samantha laughed. "No, but I thought we could make a notebook of all the times God helps us. We could keep adding to it."

REMEMBER GOD'S GOODNESS.

"Hey, that's a good idea," exclaimed Mark. "We could put in a picture of all of us standing in front of this big tree. Whenever we see the picture, we'll be reminded of God's help."

Mom and Dad both smiled. "We can call it our 'Ebenezer Book,'" said Dad. "What a good way to remember all that God has done for us."

HOW ABOUT YOU?

Have you received some special answers to prayer? Has God protected you in a dangerous situation? Maybe He's helped you get through a hard class at school. Why don't you try to keep a record of what God has done for you? Do it to be reminded of God's great help when you're faced with a difficult situation.

TO MEMORIZE:

But as for me, I will sing about your power. Each morning I will sing with joy about your unfailing love. For you have been my refuge, a place of safety when I am in distress.

PSALM 59:16

BY DEANA ROGERS

May 18

GUIDING STARS

Read Proverbs 4:14-19.

Zachary looked around at the dark shadows. He was on a campout with some boys from church and their leader, Mr. Jordan. They had gone for a walk, and it had turned quite dark. Zachary shivered and asked, "How are we going to find our camp, Mr. Jordan?"

An eerie sound made shivers run up and down the boys' spines. They stepped closer to their leader. "Now, boys, that was just an owl," said Mr. Jordan. "We'll be at camp in no time." He looked up and pointed. "Just what we need to guide us—the North Star!" He showed the boys how to find it and explained how it could help them find their way. Then they started off across a deserted field, keeping an eye on the bright star.

Soon they were back at camp, sitting around a cozy campfire. "Good thing we had that star to lead us," said Zachary.

"That's right," agreed Mr. Jordan. "Years ago travelers and sailors used the stars to guide them." Then he added, "I hope you boys will shine for God like guiding stars and lead others to Him. How do you think you might do that?"

SHINE FOR GOD.

"Ah-h," began Zachary, thinking hard, "obeying our parents?"

"Being nice to our brothers and sisters," one boy added.

"Playing fair," said another boy.

"And obeying the rules at school," offered still another.

"Those are great suggestions," Mr. Jordan agreed. "As you live in a way that pleases God, you have a good start in guiding others to Him."

HOW ABOUT YOU?

Are you willing to be a guiding light for God? When you do what God wants you to do, those who are watching will be pointed in the right direction. God will bless you for shining for Him.

TO MEMORIZE:

The way of the righteous is like the first gleam of dawn, which shines ever brighter until the full light of day.

PROVERBS 4:18

BY CAROLYN E. YOST

May 19
HEART BLINDNESS

Read Ephesians 4:17-24.

"Mommy!" sobbed Cassie as she struggled through the doorway with her backpack and lunch box.

"What's wrong, honey?" asked Mom as she unzipped her daughter's coat.

"The big kids on the bus called me Four-Eyes." Cassie sniffled as she took off her glasses to wipe away her tears. "I-I don't want to wear my glasses anymore." Mom sighed.

"They said I'm blind, too!" Cassie exclaimed. "I'm not blind, am I?"

"No, honey," answered Mom. "You just need a little help to see clearly. Isn't it wonderful to be able to see better? And you look very nice in your new glasses. The kids just like to tease. Ignore them, and they'll soon get tired of it."

Cassie slipped her glasses back on. "Being teased isn't as bad as not seeing," she said.

Mom got up to answer the phone. When she returned, she sat down with a sigh. "My friend Deborah reminds me of you," she said.

DON'T BE BLIND TO GOD'S WAYS.

"Does she get teased about wearing glasses?" asked Cassie.

"No," Mom shook her head, "she doesn't wear glasses. But she worries that she'll get teased about being a Christian. I'm so glad she has come to know the Lord. But when she's with her old friends, she often acts and talks just the way they do. She's afraid they'll laugh at her if she obeys the Lord. She's not very brave."

Cassie smiled. "I'll be brave tomorrow even if I get teased!" she declared.

HOW ABOUT YOU?

Are you afraid of being teased and laughed at because you're a Christian? Don't be blind to what God wants you to do. The blessings He'll give as you live for Him are worth any teasing you may be asked to endure.

TO MEMORIZE:

Live no longer as the Gentiles do, for they are hopelessly confused.
EPHESIANS 4:17

BY VICKI L. REINHARDT

Spread the Light

Then [Jesus] told them, "Go into all the world and preach the Good News to everyone. Anyone who believes and is baptized will be saved."

MARK 16:15-16

Missionaries travel the world. In some places, they make Bibles available. In other parts of the world, they help build homes and wells. They share their faith wherever they go. Thank God for the brave people who spread the Good News around the world.

Find the names of some countries where missionaries live and work.

```
Y K B A G K J V H D F M G L T
E Y V B B X C O N G O I S Q R
E Y D N X T Y X Z R E C X C G
V P C J U S K Y C K I R T O K
D Y H Q Q X G H A V V O I R S
C K I W A R G E N T I N A T G
Y P L N I Q K E O M A E K D R
O X E A B S W D S F N S S L U
W E X S O U T H A F R I C A S
E J R R D U E C M Q P A B A S
I H I E P Z X I O I R W R Q I
P W P C I T B U A W N I A Z A
G T Y L S X C H O T S D Z K C
C I E G L P Z T D Y N N I E M
J B S J E A Z B Q K C Z L A T
```

Argentina	India
Belize	Micronesia
Brazil	Russia
Chile	Samoa
Congo	South Africa

SEE ANSWER IN BACK

May 20
HIDDEN TREASURE

Read Proverbs 8:5-14.

Raul laid his report card on the table and grabbed the newspaper, looking for Part 3 of "Hidden Treasures," a five-part article about deep-sea treasures. Raul eagerly read and then cut out the article. He often daydreamed about what it would be like to find a hidden treasure and get rich!

After dinner Raul's parents were reading the paper. "What's going on?" Dad asked. "I see that another article has been cut out."

Raul's eyes got big and dreamy as he told his dad all about the treasure articles and how he hoped to become a treasure hunter someday.

Then Dad brought out Raul's report card. "It looks to me as if you've been concerned with the wrong kind of treasure lately," he observed. "Your school grades have gone down."

Raul sighed. "Oh, well, treasure hunters don't have to be so smart—just lucky!"

"The report card isn't all," said Mom. "Your Sunday school teacher says you haven't been paying attention. You know, Proverbs says we must look for wisdom with the same persistence that a treasure hunter searches for silver. The Bible describes wisdom as being 'more valuable than rubies.'"

WISDOM IS A TREASURE.

"Your mom's right," agreed Dad. "You need to get your treasure-hunting priorities in order, Son. It's time to put a little more effort into your work—at school and Sunday school."

"It's okay to dream of being a treasure hunter," added Dad, "as long as you find the treasure of wisdom first."

HOW ABOUT YOU?

Do you search for wisdom? Are you growing in Bible knowledge and learning to live as a Christian? Nothing can be compared to the treasure of wisdom that God wants to teach you from His Word.

TO MEMORIZE:

For wisdom is far more valuable than rubies.
Nothing you desire can compare with it.
PROVERBS 8:11

BY VICKI L. REINHARDT

HOLY HOLLY

Read Colossians 4:2-6.

"I know I should keep inviting McKenzie to Sunday school," Holly told her mother as they walked across the parking lot. "But I don't want to anymore. Sometimes she swears at me or hits me. But the worst thing is that she always says, 'Holy Holly. Ho! Ho! Ho!' when she sees me. I hate that!"

When they were almost to the grocery store, Holly asked if she could run ahead. "I'll wait for you just inside the door," she promised.

"Oh," said Mom. "I'm surprised you want to go into the store."

"Why?" asked Holly in surprise.

"The door is in the way," Mom pointed out.

Holly eyed her mother suspiciously. "The door swings open by itself—almost like magic!"

"But how do you know it's going to open? Electric doors can fail," persisted Mom.

TRUST GOD TO OPEN DOORS.

"They never have before," replied Holly.

"Aha!" Mom chuckled. "It sounds to me like someone has more faith in that store to keep its door in working order than in an all-powerful God to open doors He tells her to go through."

"What do you mean by that?" asked Holly.

"Just that if God wants you to do something, He'll make a way!" replied Mom. "He'll 'open the door' to make it possible. Holly, we both know God wants you to keep reaching out to McKenzie, don't we?"

"You're right, Mom," admitted Holly. "I know I should keep trying and that God will help me if I do. And I guess 'Holy Holly' isn't such a bad name after all!"

HOW ABOUT YOU?

Are you discouraged and ready to give up doing something God wants you to do? Don't quit. Pray about it and trust God to open doors at just the right time.

TO MEMORIZE:

Pray for us, too, that God will give us many opportunities to speak about his mysterious plan concerning Christ. That is why I am here in chains.
COLOSSIANS 4:3

BY SARA L. NELSON

May 22

DO ROOSTERS LAY EGGS?

Read 2 Timothy 3:13-17.

"Why don't roosters lay eggs?" asked Martin as he watched his aunt and his cousin, Lynne, stuff a Rhode Island Red rooster.

"Oh, but they do," Lynne said. "Martin, please get the meat thermometer from the cupboard." When Martin came back, Lynne pulled an egg from inside the bird. Martin was very surprised.

Aunt Marcia hid a smile. "Martin," she said, "Lynne is playing a joke on you. Go take a look at the book about birds on the coffee table."

As he paged through the book, Martin read, "The male fowl does not lay eggs."

He went back to the kitchen. Lynne said with a chuckle, "When you got the thermometer, I put an egg in the rooster to fool you."

"Lynne was just teasing," said Aunt Marcia. "But it's much more serious when Satan tries to deceive us. He's not doing it just for fun. Do you know ways he tries to fool us?"

"He wants us to think that we're good kids who have no need of a Savior," suggested Lynne.

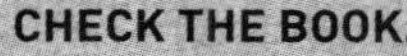

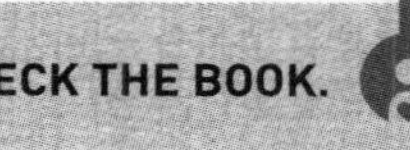

CHECK THE BOOK.

"Yeah," agreed Martin, "and he wants us to think we don't need to go to Sunday school."

Aunt Marcia nodded. "And just like Martin checked a book to learn the truth about roosters, we all must keep checking God's Book, the Bible, so we will not be fooled."

HOW ABOUT YOU?

Have you ever felt foolish over being deceived? It's not so serious when someone just teases you, but don't let Satan deceive you. He may try to convince you that it's okay to tell a "little" lie. He may say it's all right to cheat. He may encourage you to disobey your parents. He'll keep trying to deceive you, so keep checking the Book!

TO MEMORIZE:

He must have a strong belief in the trustworthy message he was taught; then he will be able to encourage others with wholesome teaching and show those who oppose it where they are wrong.

TITUS 1:9

BY PHYLLIS M. ROBINSON

May 23

THE UMBRELLA

Read Psalm 19:7-11.

"Mommy, I want that 'brella," pleaded little Ashley, pointing to a brightly colored umbrella on display in the children's department.

Mom said, "I was just thinking it would be a good idea for you to have your own umbrella." So Mom bought it and showed Ashley how to carry it over her wrist when it wasn't raining.

The next day, to Ashley's delight, it rained. "Can I go outdoors with my 'brella?" she asked.

"All right," Mom agreed. "Just for a while."

A minute later Ashley hurried up the front walk, her new umbrella swinging on her arm while the rain pelted down on her head. Mom hurried to the door. "My 'brella doesn't work," complained Ashley. "I'm all wet!"

"The umbrella works all right," Mom replied. "But you have to open it and hold it over your head." She helped Ashley change into dry clothes and then let her go out once more, this time with the umbrella opened and held high. That evening the rest of the family laughed when they heard the story, but Ashley pouted.

OPEN YOUR BIBLE AND READ.

"It's okay, sweetheart," Dad told her, reaching for the Bible he used in family devotions. "Sometimes we all act like you did."

Ashley's face brightened. "You do?"

"Yep," said Dad. "You left your umbrella closed, and sometimes we leave the Bible closed. God's Word teaches us about Him and keeps us from sin. Just as you needed to open your umbrella to get any use from it, we need to open our Bibles. Let's do that right now."

HOW ABOUT YOU?

Do you open your Bible and read something from God's Word every day? You should. It can't help you if you leave it closed.

TO MEMORIZE:

The instructions of the LORD are perfect, reviving the soul. The decrees of the LORD are trustworthy, making wise the simple.

PSALM 19:7

BY HAZEL W. MARETT

May 24

STAGE FRIGHT

Read Exodus 4:10-15.

Kira could hardly believe the assignment. "We're going to give speeches next week," said Ms. Davis. "Pick a topic and be ready to talk about it for three minutes."

After class Kira approached Ms. Davis. "Please don't make me give a speech," she pleaded. "I just can't talk in front of people!"

Her teacher smiled. "Part of being a good speaker is learning to forget about yourself and to concentrate on your topic. Don't worry about what others will think. You'll do fine."

During the next few days Kira often thought and prayed about her speech. When her turn finally came, she swallowed hard and walked to the front of the room. "My topic," she said in a squeaky voice, "is stage fright. It's something I really feel like an expert on." The kids smiled, and Kira began to feel better. She talked about the causes of stage fright and about some famous people who had problems with it. Then she said, "A verse in the Bible that has helped me this week is Philippians 4:13: 'I can do everything through Christ, who gives me strength.'"

As Kira went back to her seat, she thought, *That wasn't so bad after all. I know God helped me!*

GOD HELPS HIS CHILDREN.

HOW ABOUT YOU?

Does talking in front of people make you nervous? Some people are more shy than others. But it will help if you are honest about your nervousness and if you stop worrying about what others will think of you. Pick a subject that's important to you, and use the opportunity as a witness to God's help and power. If He wants you to speak, He will help you find the words to say.

TO MEMORIZE:

Now go! I will be with you as you speak, and
I will instruct you in what to say.
EXODUS 4:12

BY SHERRY L. KUYT

May 25

BAD BANANAS?

Read Psalm 18:30-32.

"Ah-choo!" Peter sneezed as he wandered into the family room. "Mom, why do I have to have a cold? It's Saturday, and Dad promised to take me fishing with him!"

"Your dad would have enjoyed taking you," said his mom, "but it's a little too chilly to go out with that cold."

"I even prayed about it," Peter moaned, "but it didn't help. Now I'm stuck at home with nothing to do." He opened the cupboard and peered inside. "Hey, Mom!" he exclaimed. "Did you notice these rotten bananas?" He pulled out some shriveled, brownish-black pieces of fruit.

"Don't throw those away!" said Mom. "I'm saving them for banana bread."

Peter made a face. "You mean you wanted these bananas to turn rotten?"

Mom smiled. "Maybe ripe would be a better word," she said. "Dark, mushy bananas make the best banana bread."

"That sounds crazy," said Peter.

TRUST GOD IN ALL THINGS.

"You know," said his mom, "your cold is like these bananas. You can't see anything good about it, but God can still use it for His purposes."

Peter sniffed and thought about what his mom had said. "I did get some extra homework done this morning," he told her. "And since I had some free time, I talked to Kevin on the phone and invited him to go to church with us tomorrow!"

"I hope you'll feel better by then," said Mom. "But we'll have to wait until God thinks the time is 'ripe.' You can trust the Lord to turn bad situations into good!"

HOW ABOUT YOU?

Have you ever been in a situation that seemed to keep getting worse and worse? Perhaps you've even prayed about it but haven't heard an answer. Maybe God was using that situation in a way you never realized. Keep trusting Him. Thank Him for bad bananas!

TO MEMORIZE:

God arms me with strength, and he makes my way perfect.

PSALM 18:32

BY SHERRY L. KUYT

May 26
BE READY

Read Luke 12:37-43.

Kelly and Shawn were excited. Dad had promised that if they had their rooms cleaned by the time he got home, he would take them to the carnival for the rest of the day.

"We can watch cartoons before we clean our rooms," Shawn said after Dad left. "We have plenty of time."

After the program, Shawn's friend Neil came over to play, and Kelly got a phone call. Before they knew it, it was lunchtime. "Let's go to the Ice Cream Shoppe after lunch," suggested Kelly, and Shawn quickly agreed. By the time they got home, it was almost three o'clock. "I guess we'd better get started on our rooms," sighed Shawn.

"Yeah. Mine is really a mess," said Kelly.

They were just about to go to their rooms when their father came home.

"Dad!" Shawn exclaimed. "You're back early! We were just going to clean our rooms."

"You mean you two haven't even started on your rooms yet?" asked Dad. "I'm sorry, kids, but we'll have to forget our trip to the carnival."

BE READY FOR JESUS.

"But, Dad," said Kelly, "if we'd known when you were coming, we'd have been ready."

Dad smiled but looked sad. "Jesus warned us to be ready for His return too, because we don't know just when that will be."

"I sure don't want to miss Jesus' return too," Shawn said. "There's a lot to do for Him first."

Kelly agreed. "We'd better get busy."

HOW ABOUT YOU?

Would you be ready if Jesus came back today? Do you know Him as your Savior? If so, are you busy serving Him and obeying Him? Don't be taken by surprise. Be ready!

TO MEMORIZE:

You also must be ready all the time, for the Son of Man will come when least expected.

LUKE 12:40

BY SHERRY L. KUYT

I Am a Child

"O Sovereign Lord," I said, "I can't speak for you! I'm too young!" The Lord replied, "Don't say, 'I'm too young,' for you must go wherever I send you and say whatever I tell you. And don't be afraid of the people. . . . I have put my words in your mouth!"

JEREMIAH 1:6-9

What if we were always ready to witness to others? Write about a time when you felt too young or afraid to share the Good News.

What did you do?

What could you have done differently?

What if we prayed to speak only God's words when we share our faith?

May 27

BUNDLES OF BOOKS

Read John 6:5-13.

"Wow, Ethan, I can't believe all the books you borrowed from the library!" exclaimed Lucas as his brother came into the house and put a stack of reading material on the table.

Mom came into the family room. "Reading is a good way to learn about animals, other countries, sports from around the world, or any number of things."

"Right," Ethan agreed. "You can learn how to do things too. Last year Dad built Romeo's doghouse from plans he found in a book at the library."

"Well, I like reading adventure stories," Lucas said. "And I like those books we have about science experiments."

"How about the Bible? Do you enjoy reading God's Word?" Mom asked.

Ethan nodded. "I like reading about the miracles Jesus did—like the one where He used a little boy's lunch to feed five thousand people."

"I like the story about Jesus calming the storm when His disciples were afraid. Just think—without the Bible, we wouldn't know about those miracles," Lucas added.

READ THE BIBLE.

Mom said, "The Bible says that the world couldn't even contain all the books that would have to be written if everything that Jesus did was recorded!"

"What a fantastic library we would have then!" Ethan exclaimed.

HOW ABOUT YOU?

Reading can be fun. Reading the Bible is most important because that is how you learn about God the Father, Jesus, His Son, and the plan of salvation. There's so much to know that even the oldest Christians will tell you they're still learning as they keep reading the Bible.

TO MEMORIZE:

Jesus also did many other things. If they were all written down, I suppose the whole world could not contain the books that would be written.

JOHN 21:25

BY LENORA MCWHORTEN

May 28

GOODY-GOODY

Read 1 Peter 3:12-17.

Jon went to get a glass of milk from the refrigerator. "Wow, what a day!" he said.

"What happened?" asked Mom.

"During recess a bunch of boys were running around the gym, and Nate King asked if he could run with them. Well, Nate tripped and fell flat on his face the way he does a lot. You should've heard the boys tease him! I saw he was hurt. So I went over, helped him to his feet, and went to the nurse's office with him. When I came out again, the kids started calling me a goody-goody."

"Then what?" Mom asked.

"After school two boys followed me, calling me Mr. Goody-Goody all the way home."

"It's hard to be called names for being good, isn't it?" asked Mom.

Jon nodded. "Yeah. It sure is."

"You have to remember, Jon," Mom told him, "as a Christian it's your responsibility to be kind to others. But you can't expect everyone to understand. The apostle Paul wrote that the gospel seems foolish to those who don't believe in Christ. Because unbelievers choose to think the Bible is foolish, they may think you are foolish for following God's guidelines."

GOD'S WAY IS BEST.

Jon nodded. "Those kids didn't understand why I should be friendly to Nate. But I'm glad I was. Nate needs friends!"

HOW ABOUT YOU?

Is it hard for your non-Christian friends to understand why you won't join them in cheating, swearing, or treating someone unkindly? Do you get teased for doing what is right? God says it's better to suffer for well-doing than for evil-doing. Continue to follow His way, even when your friends don't understand.

TO MEMORIZE:

The message of the cross is foolish to those who are headed for destruction! But we who are being saved know it is the very power of God.

1 CORINTHIANS 1:18

BY LENORA MCWHORTEN

May 29

I BLEW IT ALREADY

Read Romans 7:15-25.

Emma took her pen and wrote carefully on a piece of paper, "I resolve never to fight with my brother, David, again." Then she taped the paper on her bedroom door so she wouldn't forget what she had written. All went well for two hours—until David came home! "You dummy," he yelled at Emma. "You were riding my bike, weren't you?"

"I was not!" Emma yelled back at him.

"You were too!" screamed David.

Emma screamed even louder. "Oh, yeah? Just try proving it!"

Later, Emma was discouraged. "I promised myself never to fight with David again, and already I broke my promise," she told Mom. "It'll never work, so why bother trying?"

"You sound like the apostle Paul," said Mother. "In Romans 7 he wrote that he often did things he knew were wrong and didn't do things he knew were right. He knew it was because his old sin nature was still active within him."

CHANGE COMES THROUGH THE LORD.

"What did Paul do about it?" Emma asked.

"He understood that we can't do what's right without Jesus' help," Mom replied. "You see, honey, saying that you will never fight with David again doesn't work if you try to do it in your own strength. You and David are both human. Instead of saying, 'I will never fight with my brother,' why not try doing something nice for him each day? I think the end result will be less fighting as well."

HOW ABOUT YOU?

Do you set impossible goals for yourself, such as "I'll never be bad again"? We all have a sin nature within us. Even Christians don't do what is right all the time. Recognize that you cannot make a change in your life without the Lord's help. Be positive in your goals, make sure they are reasonable, and rely on Jesus to help you achieve them.

TO MEMORIZE:

So now there is no condemnation for those who belong to Christ Jesus.

ROMANS 8:1

BY LENORA MCWHORTEN

May 30

THE FORGOTTEN SMUDGE

Read James 1:22-27.

Madison was ready for Sunday school—at least she thought she was. "Oh no," she said with a sigh. "How did I get that?" She had seen herself in the hallway mirror. There was a dark smudge across her forehead.

As Madison went to wash off the smudge, three-year-old Kara stopped her. "Madison, help me put on my shoes, please." So Madison helped her sister and forgot the smudge.

On the way to church they passed the home of Gabrielle, a new girl on their street. Madison knew she should have told Gabrielle about Sunday school, but she had not done so. Madison thought, *She probably wouldn't come anyway.*

When Madison walked into her classroom, her friend Jennifer laughed. "You didn't wash your face!" Madison remembered the smudge on her forehead and hurried to wash it off.

DO WHAT GOD SAYS.

When Madison returned, the teacher was reading from Scripture about a man who looked in a mirror. But when he left the mirror he forgot what he'd seen. *That's like me this morning,* Madison thought, holding back a giggle.

"When you learn what God wants you to do but you don't obey it," the teacher said, "you're like that man. You see what God's Word says, but you don't do anything about it."

Madison thought about a smudge in her life—something she knew God wanted her to do but she hadn't done. She would go see Gabrielle after church.

HOW ABOUT YOU?

Do you have any forgotten "smudges" in your life? Has God shown you from His Word that you should not lie? Cheat? Lose your temper? Has He shown you that you should be friendly? Helpful? Obedient? It's wonderful that you are learning how God wants you to live. But when you look in the mirror of God's Word, don't forget what you see there.

TO MEMORIZE:

Don't just listen to God's word. You must do what it says. Otherwise, you are only fooling yourselves.

JAMES 1:22

BY KATHERINE R. ADAMS

May 31 FIRE!

Read James 3:5-10.

Alexis and her mother watched in horror as fire swept through the wheat field. "How did it start, Mom?" Alexis sobbed.

"We can't be certain, Alexis," answered Mom. "Someone driving by could have thrown out a cigarette. Or there may have been a spark from the tractor. A little spark is all it takes to start a fire."

The wheat crop would be lost. "But I'm thankful we were able to keep the fire from spreading to buildings or other fields," said Dad that evening.

Just then the phone rang, and Alexis answered it. It was her friend Rachel.

After Alexis hung up, Mom said, "The fire this afternoon was not nearly as harmful as the fires you just started," she said.

"What?" Alexis was shocked. "I've never started a fire. What are you talking about?"

"I'm talking about the rumors I heard you tell Rachel," Mom replied.

"About Erika? Well, if she didn't cheat, how could she get such a good grade without studying?" Alexis asked.

DON'T SPREAD RUMORS.

"Alexis, you said some very unkind things about a girl you don't even know," scolded Mother. "You can't be certain that any of those rumors are true, but they'll all spread like a fire. I think you ought to have the courage to stop the fire instead of spreading it."

"But, Mom," Alexis protested. "I was just—"

"You were just starting a fire," Mom finished. "I hope you'll call Rachel and make an effort to put out the fire you helped start."

HOW ABOUT YOU?

Do you ever say unkind words? Do you help spread gossip and rumors that will hurt other people? God says that a mouth that is used to bless and praise Him should not be used to hurt others. How will you use your tongue?

TO MEMORIZE:

The tongue is a flame of fire. It is a whole world of wickedness. . . . It can set your whole life on fire.

JAMES 3:6

BY BRENDA DECKER

June 1

FOOLISH PIGS AND PEOPLE

Read Matthew 7:24-27.

Stacy climbed into the car after Sunday school, eager to share her lesson with her family. "My teacher talked about the three little pigs today," she said.

Matt scowled. "Yeah, right."

"She did," insisted Stacy. "She said the Bible tells us about a builder who was even more foolish than the first two little pigs. Bet you don't know who it was." Matt thought for a few minutes before giving up. "It was the person who built a house on the sand," Stacy said. "When the storms came, the house fell down."

"Well, I don't see how that builder was more foolish than the little pigs. Their houses fell too," argued Matt.

Stacy couldn't think of an answer for a moment. "Well, the builder was more foolish because that person was a human being, not just a pig," she decided. "The wolf ate the pigs and that was the end of them. But the person who built on the sand is like all people who don't obey Jesus and don't accept Him as Savior. They don't go to heaven—so they're lost forever."

"BUILD" ON JESUS.

Matt had to admit that this was worse than what happened to the pigs.

"Now tell us the good part of the story," suggested Dad.

"Another person—a wise person—built a house on the rock," said Stacy. "It stood through even the worst storms. That builder is like people who hear and believe what Jesus says. They accept Him as Savior, so they live forever in heaven."

HOW ABOUT YOU?

Where are you building—on the sand or on the Rock, Jesus Christ? All the good things you do won't last unless you are building your life on the right foundation—unless you've accepted Jesus as your Savior.

TO MEMORIZE:

For no one can lay any foundation other than
the one we already have—Jesus Christ.
1 CORINTHIANS 3:11

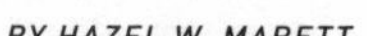
BY HAZEL W. MARETT

June 2

THE GUARDRAIL

Read Proverbs 4:1-10.

As the Tylers' car edged up the mountain road, Jeffrey pouted. "Picnics are boring," he grumbled. "Why couldn't I stay with Connor?"

Mom sighed. "We already told you—Uncle Lee and Aunt Sue aren't home. We don't think you should be there while they're gone."

Jeffrey frowned. "You treat me like a kid."

Suddenly, five-year-old Jessica squealed as she looked at the valley below. "Be careful, Daddy!" Her nose was pressed hard against the car window. "It's a long way to the bottom."

Dad said, "I'll be careful. But if I should slip off the road, the guardrail will keep us from going over the edge."

When they reached the picnic area, Jeffrey's spirits lifted. He couldn't stay mad.

The trip home was quiet. Jessica went to sleep. Even Jeffrey and Dad dozed.

"Wake up, everyone!" called Mom as she drove into the garage. "Oh, I hear the telephone."

OBEY YOUR PARENTS.

Jeffrey and Dad were unloading the picnic supplies when Mom came back out. "I have bad news. Your cousin Connor had an accident this afternoon on his dirt bike."

Later, as they returned from visiting Connor at the hospital, Jeffrey said, "If I had stayed with Connor, it could have been me."

Dad nodded. "Uncle Lee told Connor not to ride that bike while he and Aunt Sue were gone, but Connor didn't listen."

"Parents are like guardrails," Jeffrey said. "They keep us from danger . . . if we obey them."

HOW ABOUT YOU?

Do you obey your parents? You need their guidance, and God commands you to obey them. Next time you're tempted to disobey, remember that He often uses parents to guard you from danger—just like a guardrail.

TO MEMORIZE:

"Honor your father and mother." This is the first commandment with a promise: If you honor your father and mother, "things will go well for you, and you will have a long life on the earth."

EPHESIANS 6:2-3

BY BARBARA J. WESTBERG

Plan to Prosper

"For I know the plans I have for you," says the LORD. *"They are plans for good and not for disaster, to give you a future and a hope."*
JEREMIAH 29:11

God already knows His plans to bless your life. Sometimes you don't feel very hopeful. But always remember His plan is to bless you. Jesus talked about His blessings in Matthew 5. Use this code to decipher the missing words below.

▼	●	★	♠	♦	✚	✣	♥	✦	♣	✪	✖	■
a	b	c	d	e	f	g	h	i	j	k	l	m

☆	✿	❑	◗	✔	⊸	☎	✐	▲	➔	❖	☞	◒
n	o	p	q	r	s	t	u	v	w	x	y	z

Blessed are the poor in spirit, for theirs is the

✪ ✦ ☆ ✣ ♠ ✿ ■   ✿ ✚   ♥ ♦ ▼ ▲ ♦ ☆

_ _ _ _ _ _ _   _ _   _ _ _ _ _ _ .

Blessed are those who mourn, for they

⊸ ♥ ▼ ✖ ✖   ● ♦   ★ ✿ ■ ✚ ✿ ✔ ☎ ♦ ♠

_ _ _ _ _   _ _   _ _ _ _ _ _ _ _ _ .

Blessed are the meek, for they shall

✦ ☆ ♥ ♦ ✔ ✦ ☎   ☎ ♥ ♦   ♦ ▼ ✔ ☎ ♥

_ _ _ _ _ _ _   _ _ _   _ _ _ _ _ .

MATTHEW 5:3-5, NKJV

ANSWER KEY
kingdom of heaven; shall be comforted; inherit the earth

June 3

THE BAND-AID KID

Read Psalm 32:1-5.

Dad sighed as he arrived home and saw Noel sweeping the garage. When Noel did work without being asked, it usually meant he'd done something wrong.

"Travis has chicken pox," said Mom when Dad came inside. "And Noel shot Mr. White's dog with Kyle Roe's BB gun."

Dad frowned. "I've told him never to play with Kyle's gun! Did he hurt the dog?"

"No—just scared him and made Mr. White angry," replied Mom.

"Look, Daddy!" said three-year-old Travis. Dad laughed when he saw Travis. "I got the chicken poxes. I put Band-Aids on them."

"How dumb can you get?" grumbled Noel as he entered the room and saw his brother. "You can't cure chicken pox by covering up the spots!"

"That's true," agreed Dad. "But I've noticed that whenever you do something wrong, you try to cover it up by doing something good. When you disobeyed your mother, you washed dishes. Now you've disobeyed me, and you've been sweeping the garage as if that would make up for what you did this afternoon."

CONFESS AND FORSAKE SIN.

"Kyle dared me—" Noel stopped.

"When you do something wrong, Noel, don't blame it on anyone else. The only cure for sin is to be sorry and ask God to forgive you."

Noel looked sad. "I'm sorry, Dad. Will Mr. White forgive me? Will God forgive me too?"

Dad sighed. "I surely hope Mr. White will forgive you. And as for God, well, you should read what Psalm 32 says."

Noel went to his room. He knew he had some reading and praying to do.

HOW ABOUT YOU?

Are you a "Band-Aid" kid? Don't try to cover your sins with good deeds or excuses. You need to repent, and you need to do it now.

TO MEMORIZE:

People who conceal their sins will not prosper, but if they confess and turn from them, they will receive mercy.
PROVERBS 28:13

BY BARBARA J. WESTBERG

June 4

THE LONG WAY HOME

Read Ezekiel 18:30-32.

"Thanks for inviting me to go to church with you next Sunday, Uncle Al." Hector and his uncle were on their way to Bonny Lake to fish. "But I'm not sure I want to go."

Uncle Al looked surprised. "You sounded interested last week," he said.

"Yeah," Hector said. "But the kids at school might not understand, and I like being with them. Someday I'll start going to church, but I think I'll just go on the way I am for a while."

Hector's uncle drove on silently for a few minutes. "Oh no!" he exclaimed as they passed a road sign. "I missed the turnoff. We should have gotten off this road five miles back."

"Guess we'll have to turn around and go back now, huh?" asked Hector.

Uncle Al shook his head. "I don't feel like turning around right now," he said. "I guess we'll just keep going this way. I kinda like this road."

"But we have to turn around to get to Bonny Lake," Hector said. "If we wait too long to turn around, we might not get there in time to fish."

TURN TO JESUS.

Uncle Al smiled at Hector as he slowed down for the next turn. "You're right," he said. "And what you told me just now is what I've been trying to say about your spiritual life. When you're traveling down the wrong road, the sooner you turn around, the better. If you wait too long, you might never get to your goal—heaven."

HOW ABOUT YOU?

Do you need to turn around and go in a different direction to get to heaven? You do if you've never accepted Jesus as Savior. Don't let habits, the opinions of others, or even your own feelings of laziness keep you from taking the right road. Don't wait until it's too late to turn to Jesus.

TO MEMORIZE:

Turn from your sins. Don't let them destroy you!

EZEKIEL 18:30

BY SHERRY L. KUYT

June 5

THE HOME RUN THAT WASN'T

Read Romans 8:26-30.

David sat on the bench and waited for his turn at bat. His team was losing by a couple of runs, and it was the last inning. *I know,* David thought. *I'll pray that I get a home run.* So he whispered a prayer.

Finally it was David's turn. Confidently, he picked up his bat and walked to home plate. The pitcher threw the ball twice, and David missed—twice. Again, the pitcher threw the ball. This time David hit it, and it slowly rolled toward the third baseman. An easy out to end the game!

David walked over to meet his parents. How could he have missed? "I don't understand it," David said as they drove home. "I prayed that the Lord would give me a home run, but He didn't."

"Hmmm," Dad said. "The Gray boys were on the other team, and they're Christians too. I wonder what they were praying!" David smiled. That was true. "Seriously, David," his father went on, "when we pray we need to be willing to accept the answer that God gives."

PRAY FOR GOD'S WILL.

"But doesn't God care about the ball game?" David asked.

"Yes, God does care. He cares that you have a good attitude and that you do your best."

Next game, David decided he would ask the Lord to help him be a good sport whether he hit a home run or not.

HOW ABOUT YOU?

Do you pray that you will hit a home run or that you will receive an A on a test (when you haven't even studied), or that you will get a new bike? You can ask God for anything, but you need to accept His answer. The Lord knows what is best for you.

TO MEMORIZE:

We are confident that he hears us whenever we ask for anything that pleases him.

1 JOHN 5:14

BY LENORA MCWHORTEN

June 6

JANA'S PASSPORT

Read Philippians 3:4-9.

Ted and Jana were going to spend the summer in England with their older sister. "Did you forget anything?" Dad asked when they were on their way to the airport. "If so, now is the time to remember before we get too far from home."

"Do you have the tickets and passports?" Mom asked.

"Right here." Jana patted her purse. "But I hate my passport picture."

"Let me see it again." Ted held out his hand.

"No way!" Jana held her purse tightly.

"Well, give me my ticket and passport," Ted insisted.

Jana opened her purse and took them out. "Oh no!"

Dad took his foot off the accelerator. "What's wrong?"

"I have Mom's passport instead of mine," wailed Jana.

"It's a good thing you discovered it!" Dad looked for a place to turn around.

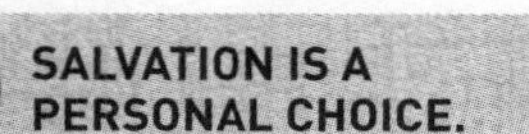

Mom looked thoughtful. "Hmmmm," she mused. "I'm going to have to tell Mrs. Lewis about this experience. I've had a couple of opportunities to witness to her, and whenever I ask if she has accepted Christ, she tells me about the wonderful Christian parents she had. She seems to think that makes her a Christian too."

"I see what your mom is getting at," said Dad as he headed back home. "Maybe when Mrs. Lewis hears about this, she'll see that just as your mother's passport won't get Jana into England, the salvation of her parents won't get her into heaven."

HOW ABOUT YOU?

Do you have your "passport" to heaven? Your own righteousness—your fine family, your Christian parents, your own good works—will not get you to heaven. You must receive God's righteousness by accepting Jesus as your Savior. It's a decision you must make for yourself.

TO MEMORIZE:

I no longer count on my own righteousness through obeying the law; rather, I become righteous through faith in Christ.

PHILIPPIANS 3:9

BY BARBARA J. WESTBERG

June 7

THE HURT THAT HELPS

Read Romans 8:18-23, 28.

Benjamin cried loudly as his mother led him into the doctor's examining room. Benjamin's sister Lisa said, "Don't cry. You haven't even gotten your shot yet!"

"I don't wanna get shot!" cried the little boy.

When the nurse came, Benjamin screamed. "You'll feel a little prick," the nurse said, "but it will be over soon." Before Benjamin could give another yell, the nurse had finished.

Benjamin walked out to the car with a big smile. "That wasn't so bad, was it?" asked Lisa.

Benjamin shook his head. "Not so bad," he said. "But I still don't like shots. They hurt!"

"We know, honey," said Mom. "But the hurt doesn't last long, and the medicine in the shot keeps you healthy. If you didn't get shots, you might get sick and hurt for a long time."

Lisa watched her brother play with a toy car. "Someday he'll be glad he got the 'hurt,' won't he, Mom?"

TRUST GOD IN ALL SITUATIONS.

"I'm sure he will," Mom said. "And that's a good lesson for you and me. If we go through hard times, we may wonder if God really cares about us. But all of our experiences—even pain and sadness—are for our good and God's glory. If we look at things from His point of view, we'll think about our troubles in a different way."

HOW ABOUT YOU?

Is it hard to be patient when you're not feeling well? Or when things just aren't going well? Perhaps God has something to teach you, or He may want you to be an example of His love. Maybe He wants to clean some sin from your life or to protect you from an even greater danger in the future. Whatever His purposes are, you will find peace and joy when you fully submit to Him. He knows best!

TO MEMORIZE:

We know that God causes everything to work together for the good of those who love God and are called according to his purpose for them.

ROMANS 8:28

BY SHERRY L. KUYT

June 8

THE MONKEY TRAP

Read Luke 12:16-21.

Jordan's parents were missionaries in central Africa. One day Jordan's friend Joseph helped him make a monkey trap. Joseph said, "Make a hole in this gourd, just big enough for a monkey to put his hand through." He watched Jordan work. "That's big enough. We'll put some nuts and fruit in the gourd. Then we'll fasten it to a tree branch at the edge of the village."

"I don't get it," said Jordan as the boys walked toward a tree. "I can see that a monkey might reach into the gourd to get the food, but what will keep him from getting away?"

"When he has nuts in his fist, his hand won't go through the hole," explained Joseph. "If he'd just let them go, he could get away. But he won't. He'll hang on even though he's caught." Joseph helped Jordan attach the gourd to a tree. "There. By tomorrow morning, you'll have a monkey."

That night Jordan told his mother about the monkeys. Mom nodded. "I was just as foolish myself at one time. I didn't want to give up my things and come to the mission field. But God showed me that when I obeyed Him, I wasn't giving up anything important. I was just letting some things go for better things. I've never been as happy as I've been here in Africa, bringing the message of salvation to the people here."

LOVE GOD, NOT POSSESSIONS.

HOW ABOUT YOU?

What things do you want to keep? What things do you want to have when you grow up? Don't let your things trap you into missing what God wants for you. It may be that the things you want will be in His plan for you, but you need to be willing to let them go. If they are not in His plan, you can be sure He has something even better.

TO MEMORIZE:

Think about the things of heaven, not the things of earth.

COLOSSIANS 3:2

BY HAZEL W. MARETT

June 9

WHY GO TO CHURCH?

Read Psalm 66:4-13.

Antonio gazed at his friend Adam, not sure what to say. Adam had asked a simple question, but Antonio was stumped for an answer. "Why do I go to church?" he repeated.

"Yeah," nodded Adam, sounding as though he really wanted to know.

"Because it's Sunday," Antonio said finally.

Adam looked at him. "That's a stupid answer," he said. "That's like saying, 'I go to school because it's Monday or Friday.'"

Antonio thought about the question as he headed for home. Did he go to church just because his parents took him there? Was it because it was part of their family life? He talked with his father about it that evening.

"That's a question you need to answer for yourself," his father said. "I go to worship the Lord."

"Can't you worship Him someplace other than church?" Antonio asked.

Dad nodded. "Yes, you can worship the Lord anytime and anyplace. But if you don't go to church, you'll miss the fellowship you need to have with other Christians. The Bible tells us that we should gather together with others who believe like we do."

WORSHIP GOD IN CHURCH.

Antonio thought about that. When the people of his church got together, it was a time to praise the Lord through singing and preaching. When the pastor preached from the Bible, Antonio always got something special from it—something he wouldn't learn from the Bible by himself. "I'm going to talk with Adam again," he called to his parents. "I think I can give him a better answer now."

HOW ABOUT YOU?

Do you attend church just out of habit? It's a good habit to have, but you should also go to worship the Lord, to sing praises to Him, to hear His Word, and to fellowship with other Christians.

TO MEMORIZE:

I was glad when they said to me, "Let us go to the house of the LORD."

PSALM 122:1

BY RUTH I. JAY

Faith in Action: My Devotional Journey

The Lord stood with me and gave me strength.
2 TIMOTHY 4:17

This summer, keep a record when you witness your faith in action. Specifically focus on God's strength as it relates to the themes for this season (blessings, friendship, and obedience). Or make a note when you apply your devotional studies in everyday life. This way, you can see your faith in action!

God's strength was revealed to me . . .

JUNE: BLESSINGS

WHEN ____

____

WHERE ____

____

HOW ____

____

MORE ____

____

____

JULY: FRIENDSHIP

WHEN ____

____

WHERE _______________________________________

____

HOW ____

____

MORE ____

____

____

AUGUST: OBEDIENCE

WHEN ____

____

WHERE _______________________________________

____

HOW ____

____

MORE ____

____

____

June 10

SPICE IN YOUR LIFE

Read Ephesians 5:18-20.

Jenna piled her taco shell with the things her father had prepared—meat, cheese, lettuce, tomatoes, and his own special taco sauce. Between bites Jenna said, "This sauce is different from what you get in a restaurant. What makes it different?"

"Well, Jenna, I double the amount of ground cumin in my sauce," said Dad with a smile. "The cumin gives Mexican foods their special flavor."

The memory of that supper stayed with Jenna. One day she saw the bottle of ground cumin in the spice drawer. She opened the bottle, shook a little of the powder into her hand, and licked it. "Oh, yuck!" she gasped, nearly choking. She ran to the sink and rinsed her mouth with water three times.

When Jenna told her father what had happened, she asked, "Why doesn't that spice taste good? It sure makes the tacos good."

"I think this is an example of having too much of a good thing," said Dad, laughing. "Have you ever heard people refer to something as the 'spice of life,' Jenna? They're usually talking about one of the fun things they enjoy—vacations, holidays, and so on. Sometimes we think we'd like those things all the time. But if we did, soon they would mean nothing. It would be like having too much of a good spice. The hard times God allows to come our way are needed too. They help us enjoy the good times."

ALL GOD SENDS IS GOOD.

"Hmmmm," said Jenna with a smile. "Whoever thought life as a Christian would be like eating tacos?"

HOW ABOUT YOU?

Do you think it would be nice to play all the time and never work? Just as there are many kinds of spices that lend their special touch to foods, God sends you many kinds of experiences to make your life special. He knows just what you need to help you live life at its best.

TO MEMORIZE:

Give thanks for everything to God the Father
in the name of our Lord Jesus Christ.
EPHESIANS 5:20

BY CATHERINE RUNYON

Read James 1:13-15.

"Hey, Taylor," whispered Kirk. "Look over there by the bushes."

"Wow!" Taylor whispered back. "Mr. Jones has a new dog. He's big, but he looks harmless."

"We'll still take our regular shortcut through his backyard," said Kirk.

"But look, Kirk." Taylor pointed to a sign on a tree. "It says, 'Beware of the Dog.'"

"Sure! Just look at that baby face!" exclaimed Kirk as he slowly walked toward the dog. The dog began to growl. "Nice doggy," said Kirk.

"Hey, Kirk," warned Taylor, "maybe we'd better not go any closer. That's a long chain!"

"He's as gentle as a lamb," Kirk said.

Suddenly, the dog made a dash for Kirk. "Help!" yelled Kirk as he tried to free his pant leg from the dog's teeth.

The boys heard a shout. "What are you doing in my backyard?" Mr. Jones asked angrily as he walked toward his dog. "Come here, Max!" Max wagged his tail and trotted to his master. "You boys should read signs more carefully," Mr. Jones spoke firmly. "Max may look gentle, and most of the time he is, but he's been known to scare a few people. Warnings are given for a reason. Obey them."

BEWARE OF SIN.

Kirk and Taylor were quiet as they walked home. "Kirk," Taylor broke the silence, "Mr. Jones sounded a lot like Pastor Parker."

Kirk nodded. They were remembering last Sunday's message. "Sin may look harmless," Pastor Parker had said. "But God warns against all sin. Say no when Satan tempts you."

HOW ABOUT YOU?

Would you like to be like "everybody else" once in a while? Do you think it wouldn't hurt you to go where they go and do what they do, even though you know it wouldn't please the Lord? You're wrong. God warns that sin has dreadful consequences. Heed His warning and live for Him.

TO MEMORIZE:

These desires give birth to sinful actions. And when sin is allowed to grow, it gives birth to death.

JAMES 1:15

BY VICKI L. REINHARDT

June 12
A NEW HEART

Read Psalm 51:1-4, 7-10.

"Wow!" Brent's eyes were wide. His parents had just been explaining that Grandpa was going to have a heart transplant as soon as a donor could be found. "That's neat!" said Brent.

"It's amazing," agreed Dad. "We must remember, though, that the operation is not always successful. Let's trust the Lord to bring Grandpa through it."

"What if he has the heart transplant and then dies?" asked Brent's little brother, Samuel. "He wouldn't go to heaven."

"Of course Grandpa would go to heaven," said Mom. "He's a Christian."

"But my Sunday school teacher said we won't go to heaven unless we've asked Jesus to come into our hearts," replied Samuel. "So if Grandpa has a new heart, he won't be a Christian anymore."

"Oh, I see the problem," said Dad. "Think about this: If I say you have a big place in my heart, do I mean you are really inside my heart?"

LET JESUS LIVE IN YOU.

Samuel thought for a moment. "No. I guess you mean that you love me a whole lot."

Dad nodded. "Right! And when we say we ask Jesus to come into our hearts, we don't mean He is really in our hearts. What we mean is that we love Jesus very much. No matter what heart is inside Grandpa's body, he loves Jesus."

Samuel smiled. He was happy again.

HOW ABOUT YOU?

Have you wondered what it means to ask Jesus to come into your heart? The word *heart* often does not refer to the physical heart in your body. Instead, it refers to your real "self"—the real you. It's the part of you that goes on living after the body dies. It's the part that sins and needs to be saved. Have you asked Jesus to take those sins away?

TO MEMORIZE:

Christ will make his home in your hearts as you trust in him. Your roots will grow down into God's love and keep you strong.

EPHESIANS 3:17

BY HAZEL W. MARETT

June 13

A HARD JOB FOR MICHAEL

Read John 7:1-5.

After Sunday school Michael waited until the others had left so that he could talk to Mrs. Winfield alone. "What is it, Michael?" she asked gently. "You were very quiet today."

"It's my family," Michael told her. "I'm the only one who believes in Jesus. I come to church with my neighbors. I'd like to witness to my parents, but my dad always tells me that church is crazy, and my mother laughs when I try to tell her about the Bible."

"It is hard to be the only Christian in the family," said Mrs. Winfield. "I know, because I started going to church with a friend too, and it was at church I accepted the Lord. I prayed for my parents daily, but they seemed to grow angry about what I was learning."

"What did you do?" Michael asked.

"I talked to my Sunday school teacher, and she reminded me that the Lord understood the problems I was having at home. Then she showed me a verse I hadn't seen before." Mrs. Winfield opened her Bible. "Did you know, Michael, that the Lord's own brothers didn't believe in Him? Look at John 7:1-5."

PRAY FOR UNSAVED RELATIVES.

"I never knew that before," Michael said. "Jesus does understand my problem, doesn't He?"

"He sure does, Michael," agreed the teacher. "Remember that truth as you pray for your parents, and live each day so that they can see Christ in you."

HOW ABOUT YOU?

If you or any of your friends are the only Christian in your families, remember that Jesus does understand. There was a time when His own brothers did not believe in Him. Talk to the Lord about your feelings. Pray for your family. Pray for your friends and their families. Jesus will help.

TO MEMORIZE:

He came to his own people, and even they rejected him. But to all who believed him and accepted him, he gave the right to become children of God.

JOHN 1:11-12

BY LENORA MCWHORTEN

June 14

LIKE A DONKEY

Read Luke 19:29-35.

"What can you do to serve Jesus, boys and girls?" asked Mr. Jim.

Good question, thought Mikayla. She didn't see how the Lord could use her. Some kids gave money to help people, but she didn't have any money of her own. Some kids sang in the children's choir, but Mikayla didn't have a good voice. Some kids talked easily about Jesus, but she knew she'd stutter if she tried to do that.

Just then Mr. Jim asked, "Are you smarter than a donkey?" The kids laughed. "Then," said Mr. Jim, "you can serve Jesus." He read Luke 19:29-35, explaining how a donkey was a perfect picture of a servant. "First of all," said Mr. Jim, "the donkey was where God wanted him to be. He was available."

Hmmm, thought Mikayla. *I qualify there, because I want God to be able to use me.*

"Second," added Mr. Jim, "the disciples untied the donkey, as Jesus said they should. Maybe you need to let Jesus untie your fears." Mikayla had to admit that she was afraid to try to sing or talk about Jesus.

BE A SERVANT.

"Also, the donkey didn't buck in fright when Jesus sat on him. He let Jesus control him. Do you let Jesus control you?" asked Mr. Jim. Mikayla had never asked Jesus to control her life.

When Mr. Jim asked the children to pray quietly, Mikayla asked Jesus to untie all her fears and take control of her life. "Let me be a servant like the donkey," she prayed.

HOW ABOUT YOU?

Are you afraid to try to speak out for Jesus? Are you afraid that if you try to sing a song or play an instrument to serve Him, you will make a mistake? Take a lesson from the donkey. Be available. Be loosed. And be controlled. The Lord needs you!

TO MEMORIZE:

The disciples simply replied, "The Lord needs it."

LUKE 19:34

BY RAELENE E. PHILLIPS

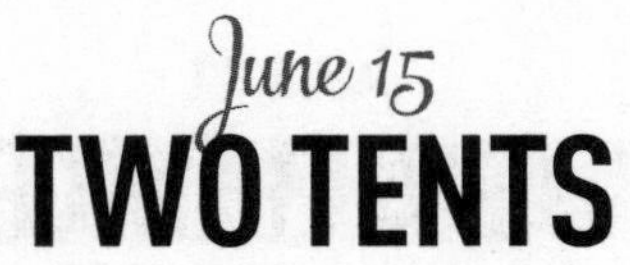

June 15 TWO TENTS

Read Philippians 4:6-11.

"I wish my dad had time to spend with us like yours does," Sonya said. "He's always so busy!"

Bethany looked at Sonya's beautiful home. "Well, your dad must make lots of money. At least you have nice things," she said with a sigh.

Then Sonya's mother asked the girls to go visiting with her for the church welcoming team.

At the first stop a young mother invited them in. "You'll have to excuse this mess," she sighed. "I have so much to do. And I don't like this town. No one is friendly here." For thirty minutes Mrs. Marshall kept talking about how terrible her life was.

When they left, Bethany whistled. "Wow! I wonder if she's happy about anything."

Then the girls followed Sonya's mother up the steps of another house. A smiling lady answered the door. "We're so happy here," Mrs. Perry said with a smile. "We're thankful we found a loving church family so quickly."

BE CONTENT.

On the way home Sonya's mother said, "There are two tents in which we can live. One is contentment, and the other is discontentment. Mrs. Marshall and Mrs. Perry live on the same street and attend the same church. Mrs. Marshall has chosen to live in discontentment, but Mrs. Perry lives in contentment." Then Sonya's mother said, "It's not how much time or money you have that makes you happy. It's which of those two tents you choose to live in."

Sonya and Bethany grinned at each other. Sonya said, "It looks like we need to move. We've been camping in the wrong tent!"

HOW ABOUT YOU?

Do you live in the tent of discontentment? Do you find yourself complaining about what you don't have instead of counting your blessings? If so, now is the time to move into contentment, no matter what your situation is.

TO MEMORIZE:

Not that I was ever in need, for I have learned
how to be content with whatever I have.
PHILIPPIANS 4:11

AUTHOR UNKNOWN

June 16

THE SODIUM CHLORIDE OF THE EARTH

Read Matthew 5:13-16.

Steven waited patiently as his father offered a prayer of thanks for the food. Then he spoke up. "Please pass the sodium chloride."

Dad laughed. "I know what you're talking about, but where did you hear that?"

"In school today," Steven said. "We had a lesson on salt."

"Well, if you were trying to impress us," Mom said, "you did."

"Salt's important," Steven informed his family. "Our teacher said that it's used in science and medicine."

Dad agreed. "She's right. Chemical compounds of sodium are used in photography and industry, too."

"Not to mention the way we use salt right here in our home," Mom added. "Salt is used to flavor food and also to keep it from spoiling."

BE A USEFUL CHRISTIAN.

"Did you know that sodium chloride is mentioned in the Bible?" asked Dad.

"In the Bible?" repeated Steven.

"Well, not by that name," said Dad with a smile. "But it does tell us that Christians are the salt of the earth. We can help preserve and flavor the earth. Unless—"

"Unless what?" Steven asked.

"Unless the salt has lost its flavor. The Bible says that if the salt doesn't have the power to flavor anything, then it's actually good for nothing except to step on."

"So Christians have to be careful to live in such a way that they have the power of Christ in their lives," Mom added. "Christians are to be like salt—helping, preserving, and being useful."

Steven said, "Well, I hope people can tell I'm part of the sodium chloride of the earth."

HOW ABOUT YOU?

Are you being "salty" to your schoolmates? To your family? Jesus didn't say you could be like salt if you wanted to be. No, He said you are the salt of the earth. It's your job to help, preserve, and be useful. Live that way!

TO MEMORIZE:

You are the salt of the earth.

MATTHEW 5:13

BY RUTH I. JAY

A Blessed Home

How abundant are the good things that you have stored up
for those who fear you, that you bestow in the sight of all,
on those who take refuge in you.
PSALM 31:19, NIV

To "fear" God means to respect and obey Him. It means honoring and worshiping Him. When we take "refuge" in God, He becomes our shelter, our protection against the world. When we find safety in Him, God blesses us with an abundance of good things.

Draw lines to match each creature to its place of refuge.

beaver	den
bee	hill
bird	hive
horse	lair
rabbit	lodge
spider	nest
ant	stable
lion	warren
tiger	web

ANSWER KEY
beaver/lodge; bee/hive; bird/nest; horse/stable;
rabbit/warren; spider/web; ant/hill; lion/den; tiger/lair

June 17

A DISAPPOINTING BIRTHDAY

Read Luke 17:11-19.

When Lauren's birthday arrived, she found an envelope for her in the mailbox. She clapped her hands. She had known it would be there. Every year Aunt Joy sent twenty dollars. Quickly, she tore the envelope open and found a beautiful card. Lauren opened the card, expecting twenty dollars, but there was no money. The card was signed, "All my love, Aunt Joy."

"I can't believe this!" Lauren exclaimed. "Mom, I got a birthday card from Aunt Joy, but there's no money in it!"

Mom said gently, "Aunt Joy told me she was going to leave it out this year."

"But why?" asked Lauren.

"Last year you never wrote to thank her for it," answered Mom. Lauren remembered the many times Mom had reminded her, but she had never gotten around to writing. Mom went on, "Aunt Joy loves you very much, and she wants to help you learn to be a thankful person.

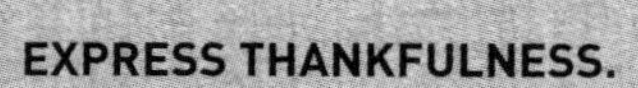

"Do you remember the story of ten lepers? They must all have been happy to be healed, but only one came back to tell Jesus how he felt. Jesus was pleased with that one. The others may have been thankful, but they didn't show it."

Lauren said, "I was wrong not to write Aunt Joy. From now on, I'm going to thank people for things they do for me."

HOW ABOUT YOU?

Do you remember to thank others when they do something for you? How about thanking your parents for all the washing, cooking, shopping, and errands they do? How about thanking them for providing a home for you? Think of other people who do things for you and thank them. It takes practice to show thankfulness, but that's what God wants you to do.

TO MEMORIZE:

Jesus asked, "Didn't I heal ten men? Where are the other nine?"

LUKE 17:17

BY CAROLYN E. YOST

June 18

COSTLY BUT FREE

Read Romans 6:20-23.

Gabriella went with her mother to the drugstore and then to Mrs. Navarro's house. Mom often visited the older woman, bringing cookies or cake. Today she brought medicine.

"I don't have money to pay for that right now," Mrs. Navarro said.

Mom smiled. "I know. That's why Gabriella and I got it today—so we could bring it to you as a small gift."

Mrs. Navarro shook her head. "Oh, no," she argued. "I won't take it unless I can pay for it."

Mom spoke softly and kindly. "There are two reasons why we want to give this to you. The first reason is that we love you and want to see you get well again."

The elderly woman looked up. "And what's the second reason?" she asked.

"To use it as an illustration," answered Mom. "We've talked with you about receiving Christ as your Savior, but we don't know if you've ever done it."

JESUS PAID FOR SIN. 

The sick woman said, "No, I haven't. I never felt like I had anything to offer God."

"All we need to do is offer ourselves," Mom answered. "Salvation is free."

"Free?" Mrs. Navarro repeated. "But I think it should cost something."

"It did! It cost Jesus His life," said Mom. "He was willing to die because He loves us, but He also came back to life. Now He's offering free salvation to all who will accept it."

Gabriella said, "It's just like the medicine. If you accept the gift, the medicine is free to you."

"Gabriella's right," Mom continued. "Will you accept both our gift—and God's?"

HOW ABOUT YOU?

Salvation was provided by Jesus Christ. It cost Him His life. But He offers it to anyone who will accept it, and there is no charge. It's free!

TO MEMORIZE:

People are counted as righteous, not because of their work,
but because of their faith in God who forgives sinners.
ROMANS 4:5

BY RUTH I. JAY

June 19

THE WRONG BULBS

Read Ephesians 2:1-10.

Six-year-old Nadine pointed to a picture of some tulips. "Can we get seeds and grow some of these?" she asked.

Her mother looked at the picture. "Those are tulips, and they grow from bulbs," she said.

The next day Nadine planted some bulbs by the fence. She had seen a neighbor, Mr. Jenks, throw them away. Every day Nadine checked to see if the flowers were coming up. When the dirt became dry, she watered it. Several weeks later she dug in the dirt and brought the bulbs to her mother. "They aren't growing," said Nadine.

"Oh, honey!" Mom gave her a hug. "These are light bulbs, not flower bulbs. There's no life in these. Even flower bulbs seem to have no life in them for a long time.

"I'll tell you what—we'll go buy some flower seeds and plant those now. Then we'll get some tulip bulbs in the fall. They will need to be in the ground all winter, and next spring you will see them come to life as the tulips come up."

JESUS GIVES LIFE.

That evening Nadine told her dad about the bulbs that wouldn't grow. He smiled. "Yes, there has to be life for there to be growth," said Dad.

Nadine answered, "My Sunday school teacher said Jesus gives us life, and we're to grow to be like Him."

"She's right," agreed Dad. "Sometimes we expect people to grow when there's no life—when they've never accepted Jesus as Savior. They try to do good, but they're dead in sin—as dead as those light bulbs you planted. They need the life only Jesus can give."

HOW ABOUT YOU?

Are you growing in the Lord—developing the characteristics He wants to see in you, such as love, kindness, helpfulness, and honesty? If not, search your heart—you can't "grow in Jesus" unless you have His life planted there.

TO MEMORIZE:

Once you were dead because of your disobedience and your many sins.

EPHESIANS 2:1

BY HAZEL W. MARETT

June 20

POISONED ARROWS

Read James 3:8-13.

"I don't know why Dan had to invite Avi to our Bible club. He's crazy like his mom," Alan said. "She's in a mental institution, y'know."

"Shame on you, Alan," said Mrs. Parker. "I'm glad Dan invited Avi. As club sponsor, your father's goal is to reach unsaved boys."

The next afternoon after Mr. Parker finished the Bible lesson, the boys went out to play with Alan's archery set.

The boys had a great time shooting at the target—and missing. "Your turn now, Avi." Dan handed the bow to him.

When Avi missed, Alan mumbled, "I knew he'd miss. What a dumb shot!"

As Avi walked away, Mr. Parker followed him. "I'm glad you came today, Avi."

Avi shook his head. "I'm not. These guys don't want me here."

Just then four-year-old Kiley ran across the lawn toward her dad. "Mom said the food is—"

"Kiley! Get out of the way!" screamed Alan. But it was too late! An arrow struck Kiley's forehead!

WORDS CAN WOUND.

Later Mr. and Mrs. Parker brought Kiley home from the hospital. "The doctor put six stitches in her forehead," Mr. Parker told Alan. Then he added, "I only wish Avi's wounds would heal as easily as Kiley's."

"Was Avi hurt?" asked Alan in surprise.

"Yes," replied Dad. "He was hurt. The Bible says that words can be like poisoned arrows shot out by the tongue, which wound and even kill."

Alan hung his head. "I'm sorry, Dad. I didn't realize we were shooting him with words. I'd better call him and apologize."

HOW ABOUT YOU?

Have you been shooting poisoned arrows? Do you need to apologize to someone? Do it today. And if you know families that are having problems, be especially kind.

TO MEMORIZE:

Telling lies about others is as harmful as hitting them with an ax, wounding them with a sword, or shooting them with a sharp arrow.

PROVERBS 25:18

BY BARBARA J. WESTBERG

June 21

BUILDING BLOCKS

Read 1 Thessalonians 5:11-15.

Lisa and her friend Shawna sat at the table talking. Little Tucker sat on the floor nearby, playing with his new building blocks. "Did you see Rachel today?" asked Shawna. "She got her hair all chopped off, and it looks just awful!"

"Did you know that Mona dyes her hair?" asked Lisa.

"No!" Shawna gasped. "Well, she's so fat, she may as well do something to try to improve herself."

Mom began to speak, but just then a horn sounded outside. "There's my mom," said Shawna. "Bye, everybody." As she headed for the door, her long coat brushed against the tall block building Tucker had just finished, knocking it over. Tucker began to cry.

Mom put her arm around Tucker. "It was an accident. Why don't you build it back up again? It will make you feel better." As Tucker got busy, Mom looked at Lisa and added, "Shawna's not the only one who knocked down in a moment what it took a long time to build."

DON'T CRITICIZE.

"I didn't touch Tucker's blocks," said Lisa.

"No," said Mom, "but you helped Shawna tear apart your friends. Isn't that more serious than knocking down a few blocks?"

Lisa stared down at the table. "I guess so."

"People are like Tucker's building," said Mom. "They need to be built up with kind words, not torn down by criticism. And you'll feel a lot better about yourself when you build people up."

"But how do I do that?" Lisa asked.

"Whenever you hear a criticism of another person, try to replace it with a compliment," suggested Mom. "Why not begin by calling Shawna and telling her something nice about each person you knocked down?"

HOW ABOUT YOU?

Do you compliment or criticize? The Bible says to speak evil of no one. Don't tear down—build up instead!

TO MEMORIZE:

Get rid of all bitterness, rage, anger, harsh words, and slander, as well as all types of evil behavior.
EPHESIANS 4:31

BY VICKI L. REINHARDT

June 22

A WELCOME MESSAGE

Read 2 Timothy 3:14-17.

"Grandma, I'm glad Mom and Dad went to that conference and let me stay with you. It will be a vacation for me," Megan said with a smile.

That morning Grandma and Megan played board games. For lunch they had ham sandwiches and chips. Then Grandma took out her Bible.

"This is when I usually have my daily Bible reading," she said. "I thought we could take turns reading to each other."

"Oh, Grandma, I'm on vacation," said Megan. "I just want to have fun." Grandma looked sad, but she let Megan run outside and climb the apple tree.

As Megan got ready for bed that night, she began thinking of her parents and feeling a little lonely. "I wish Mom and Dad were here to tuck me in," she told Grandma.

Grandma smiled and said, "Your parents knew you'd be lonesome. They asked me to give you this." She pulled a note from her pocket. Megan read the note her parents had left her. Then she felt much better.

DON'T VACATION FROM GOD.

"Some people are so important to us that we never want to take a vacation from them. Aren't you glad your parents left that message for you?" Grandma asked. Megan nodded. "Someone else had a message for you today, but you wanted to take a vacation from Him," added Grandma.

Megan knew Grandma was talking about God. As she thought about it, she knew she had missed reading about His love today. "Grandma, can we read your Bible together before I go to sleep?" she asked.

HOW ABOUT YOU?

When you're on vacation, do you also take a vacation from God's Word? You sometimes need a rest from your normal routine, but you need to hear from God every day no matter where you are. Be sure to give Him an opportunity to speak to you through His Word—with no vacations.

TO MEMORIZE:

I will pursue your commands, for you expand my undestanding.

PSALM 119:32

BY KATHERINE R. ADAMS

June 23
THE GOOD DEAL

Read Colossians 1:11-14.

"I wish I had enough money to buy that new game I've been wanting," said Alex to his friend Finn. Then Alex said, "Didn't you want to buy the tires from my old bike, Finn? I'll sell them for twenty dollars."

"Okay," Finn said. So Alex took part of the money and bought the game. The boys enjoyed it nearly every day.

As the days grew warmer, Alex and Finn began taking long bike rides. One day Alex ran over a bottle and slashed a tire. "I should have kept my old bike tires," he groaned.

"I only used one, so I'll sell the other back to you," offered Finn.

"All right!" agreed Alex. The boys got the tire and went to Alex's house to fix his bike.

"I thought you sold those tires to Finn," said Alex's dad.

"I bought this one back," Alex explained.

BE REDEEMED BY JESUS' BLOOD.

Dad smiled. "You redeemed it."

"Redeemed it?" asked Alex. "Isn't that a Bible word?"

Dad nodded. "The word *redeemed* just means 'bought back.' God wanted to buy us back from being slaves of sin. He knew that the only way we could be redeemed from sin was for His Son to die. We were redeemed by Jesus' death."

"Wow!" said Alex. "That's awesome!"

HOW ABOUT YOU?

Have you been redeemed? If you are not a Christian, you are a slave to sin. You can't stop doing things that are wrong. This sin separates you from God. He had to pay the price to redeem you—to buy you out of sin and back to Himself. No amount of money can do that. It's only through Jesus' death on the cross that you can be redeemed from sin. Accept what Jesus has done for you.

TO MEMORIZE:

God paid a ransom to save you from the empty life you inherited from your ancestors. And it was not paid with mere gold or silver, which lose their value. It was the precious blood of Christ, the sinless, spotless Lamb of God.

1 PETER 1:18-19

BY LENORA MCWHORTEN

Generous Father

Study this Book of Instruction continually. Meditate on it day and night so you will be sure to obey everything written in it. Only then will you prosper and succeed in all you do.

JOSHUA 1:8

Sometimes it's not easy to obey God. But He is a generous Father. He provides everything we need to know. It's all in one book, His Word. And He promises to bless His children who live out His Word.

Unscramble the words that mean "prosperous and successful."

gnombio ______________________________

shilifungor ______________________________

neldog ______________________________

thelayh ______________________________

shul ______________________________

garroin ______________________________

virntigh ______________________________

antupimhrt ______________________________

ANSWER KEY

booming; flourishing; golden; healthy; lush; roaring; thriving; triumphant

June 24

SPRING CLEANUP

Read Colossians 3:8-16.

"Mom, what are you doing?" asked Tiffany. Piles of old clothes, jewelry, and broken furniture were scattered around the living room.

"I decided to do a big cleanup," Mom replied. "Why keep clothes or jewelry I never wear or furniture that I'll never get around to fixing?"

"Good point, Mom," said Tiffany.

"Honey," Mom called, "why don't you go through some of your things too?"

"But I use everything I have," Tiffany said. A short time later, however, she brought a big box downstairs. She pulled out an old stuffed animal. "Look at this, Mom—hardly any stuffing left. And this sweatshirt is three sizes too small."

Mom nodded. "You know," she began, "this reminds me of when I was saved."

"How's that, Mom?" asked Tiffany.

"Well, after I was saved I had to get rid of a lot of old, bad habits and replace them with new, good ones like church attendance and prayer."

THROW OUT BAD HABITS.

"I was saved when I was just a little girl," replied Tiffany. "I didn't have any bad habits."

"No?" Mom's brows went up. "I seem to remember that you used to tell a lot of lies."

"Oh yeah," Tiffany said, blushing. "I forgot about that. I used to get mad a lot too, didn't I? I still have some garbage to get rid of sometimes."

"Each of us needs to check our life every day to see if it pleases the Lord," said Mom. "When we belong to Him, we want our lives to show that."

HOW ABOUT YOU?

Are there bad habits you should throw away? Cheating? Selfishness? Yelling? Get rid of bad habits and make room for new, good ones. Live as a "new creature" in Christ.

TO MEMORIZE:

Since God chose you to be the holy people he loves,
you must clothe yourselves with tenderhearted mercy,
kindness, humility, gentleness, and patience.
COLOSSIANS 3:12

BY VICKI L. REINHARDT

June 25

LEADER NEEDED

Read Matthew 16:24-28.

Daniel and Thomas went camping with their Sunday school class. The first thing the class did was hike through the woods. Mr. Ward, their teacher, led the way. After a while, Daniel saw another path. "Come on, Thomas!" he said.

"But we'll lose the group," said Thomas.

"So what?" Daniel said. "We can make it on our own. We'll just come back to this main path and follow it to the camp when we're ready. We'll tell all about our adventure tonight."

So Thomas went with Daniel down the side path. Quite a while later Thomas looked at his watch. "Daniel, look what time it is!" he said. "We'd better get back to camp before dark."

The boys hurried back the way they had come. Then they reached a fork in the path. "Now where do we go?" puffed Thomas.

"I don't know," Daniel admitted.

Just then, they heard a shout. "Thomas! Daniel!" It was Mr. Ward. The two boys were very happy to follow their teacher once again.

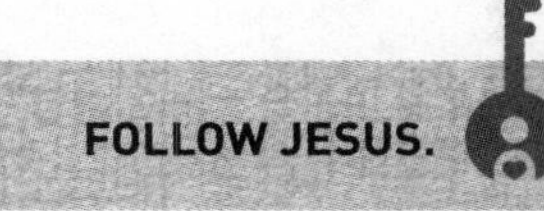

Around the campfire that night Mr. Ward spoke to the group. "When Thomas and Daniel got lost today," he said, "it reminded me of people who think they can find their own way through life. Even Christians sometimes go their own way rather than depending on God to show them how to live. Boys, it's important for you to follow Jesus. He's the only true leader for you."

HOW ABOUT YOU?

Do you want to do something your own way instead of doing what you know is right? Jesus wants to help you and lead you. But you have to be willing to follow where He takes you. He knows the way you should go.

TO MEMORIZE:

Anyone who wants to serve me must follow me, because my servants must be where I am. And the Father will honor anyone who serves me.

JOHN 12:26

BY DEBORAH S. MARETT

June 26

JUST A LAMB'S KEEPER?

Read Luke 22:25-32.

"Good morning, Hendrick," William greeted his lamb as he entered the fenced enclosure. He groomed Hendrick until it was time for lunch.

"Hendrick is going to win that blue ribbon at the fair this summer, Mom," William said.

His mother smiled. "He just might," she agreed. "By the way, have you called Kevin to see if he'll be going to church with us tomorrow?"

"No." William shook his head. "But it doesn't matter, because he became a Christian last week."

William went back to see his lamb, only to discover that he had left the gate open and the lamb was gone. Quickly he ran to the house, calling for his mother. Before long they found him in a field—right in the middle of some weeds that stuck in his coat.

"Oh, Hendrick," William moaned. "I had you all cleaned and brushed. Now look at you!"

STRENGTHEN NEW CHRISTIANS.

Mother said, "We wouldn't want this to happen to Kevin, would we?"

William was puzzled. "What do you mean?"

"Hendrick needs help and direction even after he has been brushed and fed. By himself, he gets all messed up again," explained Mom. "Kevin needs help too. He needs to be around people who can show him how to live as a Christian."

"I get it," William said. "I'll ride over to Kevin's and ask him to go to church with us—as soon as I get this naughty lamb locked up."

HOW ABOUT YOU?

Do you think new Christians should take care of themselves? All Christians need help and direction, especially those who have just received Jesus. You can help them.

TO MEMORIZE:

I have pleaded in prayer for you, Simon, that your faith should not fail. So when you have repented and turned to me again, strengthen your brothers.

LUKE 22:32

BY DOLORES A. LEMIEUX

June 27

SPOILED APPETITE

Read 1 John 2:15-17.

"Sarah! Brian!" called Mrs. Swanson. "Time to get ready for church!"

"Oh, Mom!" grumbled Brian from the family room. "Do we have to? We just started playing our new video game."

"Yeah!" agreed Sarah. "It's neat, Mom! Can't we stay home from church just once?"

"I'm surprised at you children," said Mom. "You both know that studying God's Word is more important than playing a game. Now go and get dressed!"

After church the Swansons came home to a delicious dinner of roast turkey with dressing, mashed potatoes, corn, and apple pie. But Sarah just picked at her food. When her parents asked her why, she looked embarrassed.

"Well," she admitted, "my Sunday school teacher brought cupcakes today. She had three left, and she said I could bring them home. But I ate them instead."

"So that's what spoiled your appetite!" said her mother. Then Mom asked, "Do you remember the video game that you wanted to play instead of going to Sunday school?"

GIVE JESUS FIRST PLACE.

"Yeah, we remember," Brian said.

"I think the excitement of that game made you 'lose your appetite' for spiritual things," said Mom. "Video games can't give our souls the spiritual food they need any more than cupcakes can give our bodies the vitamins we need. True happiness can only come as we serve the Lord and 'feed' on the Word of God!"

HOW ABOUT YOU?

Is there something you'd rather be doing than going to church or reading the Bible? That activity may not be bad in itself, but it is bad if it takes you away from what you should be doing for the Lord. If you want to be a healthy, growing Christian, don't spoil your appetite!

TO MEMORIZE:

Do not love this world nor the things it offers you, for when you love the world, you do not have the love of the Father in you.

1 JOHN 2:15

BY SHERRY L. KUYT

June 28

GONE FISHIN' (PART 1)

Read Matthew 4:17-22.

Todd quickly scribbled a note for his mother—"Gone fishin'. Todd." Then he grabbed his pole and bait and hurried out the door. As Todd reached the river, he saw a boy sitting in his favorite fishing spot. "Catchin' anything?" he asked.

The boy looked up and mumbled, "Naw, this isn't a very good spot."

Todd couldn't believe his ears. This was the best spot on the whole river! "Well, you gotta be patient when you're fishin'," he reminded the boy.

"I've been sitting here all morning without any bites," the boy complained, giving his pole such a jerk that his line popped out of the water.

"How much do you pop your line out of the water like that?" Todd asked.

"Oh, every few minutes—just to see if a fish has eaten the worm yet," the boy replied.

"You fish much?" asked Todd.

"My first time," the boy answered.

BE A FISHER OF MEN.

"What's your name?" Todd asked.

"Pete Fisher," the boy said.

Todd sat down. "Pete," he said, "we've gotta talk."

At dinner that night, Todd told his family about Pete. "We sure had fun! He's learnin' to fish so he can live up to his name."

"That's funny," Dad said, smiling. "It reminds me of the Peter in the Bible. He was a fisherman too. And one day Jesus said to Peter, 'Come, follow me, and I will show you how to fish for people!' Todd, you have a perfect opportunity to 'fish' for Pete. Your friendship could help lead Pete to Christ."

HOW ABOUT YOU?

Do you go fishing? You should if you're following Jesus. This kind of fishing doesn't even require handling wiggly worms! It requires a smile or maybe an invitation to go to church with you. Ask God to show you how you can become a fisher of people.

TO MEMORIZE:

Jesus called out to them, "Come, follow me, and
I will show you how to fish for people!"
MATTHEW 4:19

BY LENORA MCWHORTEN

June 29

GONE FISHIN' (PART 2)

Read James 5:7-8.

Todd lay in bed, thinking of what his dad had said about being a fisher of people. He knew that if he was going to use God's Word he would need to have it in his heart and mind. He worked hard at learning Bible verses so he could share them with his new friend, Pete.

Many times he asked Pete to go to church, but Pete always refused. And Pete didn't seemed interested when Todd tried to talk about God, either. Todd was frustrated. "I give up, Dad," he said. "Pete never wants to come to church."

"Todd," Dad reminded him, "you have to be patient when you're fishing, remember? You can't keep popping your line out of the water."

"Huh?" grunted Todd.

"You don't have to ask Pete to go to church with you so often," said Dad. "I suggest that you first strengthen your friendship with Pete. Tell him what you enjoy at church and the fun you have with the other kids. Then maybe Pete will become interested enough to come sometime. Remember, though, don't lie to make it sound like it's just all fun. You must be honest."

WITNESS WITH PATIENCE.

For the next three weeks, Todd practiced what his dad had suggested. Finally, he felt the nibble he'd been waiting for. "Dad!" he shouted as he burst into the house. "Guess what happened today?"

"I found your note about going fishing, so I'd say you caught a fish." Dad smiled.

"Did I ever!" Todd beamed. "And his name is Pete! You were right, Dad. A good fisherman must be patient if he really wants to catch a fish."

HOW ABOUT YOU?

Are you an impatient fisher of people? Does it seem as though you're never going to get a bite? Don't give up. The salvation of a friend is worth waiting for.

TO MEMORIZE:

You, too, must be patient.

JAMES 5:8

BY LENORA MCWHORTEN

June 30

GUESS WHO'S COMING?

Read 2 Peter 1:16-21.

"Guess who's coming to our house!" Cathy said as she skipped down the street with her friend Brittany. Her eyes were bright with excitement.

"I don't know. Who?" Brittany asked. "It must be someone important! You're so excited!"

"Oh, Brittany," squealed Cathy. "Remember when we read that book at school about the orange elephant?"

Brittany nodded. "Sure, I remember. That was a good book! Now tell me who's coming to your house—the orange elephant?"

"Almost!" laughed Cathy. "No, it's Martha Briggs—the woman who wrote the book! See, my mom knew Mrs. Briggs in college, except her name was Martha Alberg then, since she wasn't married yet. My mom didn't realize it was the same Martha! But now she . . ."

"Wait a minute," Brittany interrupted. "Slow down, Cathy. You mean the author of *The Orange Elephant* is coming to your house?"

GOD WROTE THE BIBLE.

"That's right," bubbled Cathy, "and you could come over and meet her while she's here!"

Brittany had to admit that Cathy had reason to be excited. "I wish I knew an author personally," she said to her mother later.

Mom smiled. "You do, Brittany—an author who is even more important than Mrs. Briggs."

"I do?" Brittany couldn't believe it! "Who?"

"You're a Christian, a child of God," Mom told her, "and God is the author of the Bible."

"That's right, Mom!" agreed Brittany. She giggled. "I can tell Cathy that I know the most famous author of all!"

HOW ABOUT YOU?

Do you know any authors? You do if Jesus is your Savior! Through the Holy Spirit, God told writers (such as John, Paul, and Moses) what to write in the Bible. So it is God who is the author of the Bible, not people. And He wrote it especially for you!

TO MEMORIZE:

Those prophets were move by the Holy Spirit, and they spoke from God.

2 PETER 1:21

BY LENORA MCWHORTEN

Your Inheritance

Don't repay evil for evil. Don't retaliate with insults when people insult you. Instead, pay them back with a blessing. That is what God has called you to do, and he will grant you his blessing.

1 PETER 3:9

What if God blessed you every time you blessed others? What if you were blessed for blessing those who are mean to you? That's God's promise when you refuse to repay one wrong with another.

Describe a time when someone said something mean to you.

Write about what you said in response.

Now write about what would have happened if you had blessed that person instead.

What do you think might happen if you remember God's blessing promised to you the next time someone is mean?

July 1
RUMOR SEEDS

Read Psalm 19:12-14.

"There goes Melinda, the new girl on my block," said Dee to her softball teammates. "She wears funny clothes. And her father has a big scar on his face—he looks like a criminal."

"Do you think he's really a criminal?" asked Natalie. "What do you suppose he did?"

Dee shrugged. "Robbed a bank maybe."

As Dee began her warm-up run about the bases, she heard Natalie tell Pam, "Melinda's dad is a bank robber."

The rumor flew and grew until everyone on the team was whispering about Melinda and promising to avoid her. A little voice in Dee's heart said, *Dee, what have you done?* But she tried not to listen.

After softball practice, Dee picked a dandelion that had gone to seed. She blew on it, and the seeds floated off like dozens of tiny parachutes.

SPEAK KIND WORDS.

"Oh dear!" said Mom, who came out to wash windows. "Those seeds are going to take root and become more pesky dandelions!"

"Sorry, Mom," said Dee.

"Well, if you hadn't blown them, the wind would have," Mom said. Then she added, "Those seeds are gone forever. Words are like that. Once we've said them, they're gone. The good ones bring happiness, and the unkind ones bring sorrow." Dee squirmed as she remembered her words about Melinda and her father. "Before we speak about anyone," continued Mom, "we should ask ourselves, 'Is what I'm about to say true? Is it kind? Would God be pleased to hear me say it?' "

Dee's words about Melinda's father had certainly not been kind or pleasing to God. They probably weren't even true! "Mom," she said as she started for the house, "I've got some phone calls to make. I'll tell you about it later."

HOW ABOUT YOU?

What kind of words do you speak? Are they true? Kind? Pleasing to God? Do they build, or do they destroy? Ask God to help you watch your words.

TO MEMORIZE:

Take control of what I say, O LORD, and guard my lips.

PSALM 141:3

BY MATILDA H. NORDTVEDT

TOO FAR

Read Hebrews 10:22-25.

Rob's radio-controlled car zipped down the driveway. "Ready, Dad?" he asked as his father stepped out the front door with another car in his hand. "Let's hit the parking lot!"

When they reached the nearby parking lot, Rob and his father found a couple of boys already there. "There's room for all of us," said Dad.

They had a good time. Dad made his Chevy model jump off the curb, flipping it back onto its tires. Rob skidded his Turbo through some sand, turning it sharply to catch up with Dad's car.

"Look! My car is going crazy!" Rob exclaimed. "It won't follow my directions!"

"I think it's too far away to receive your signals," Dad observed. "Look—it's too close to those other boys. I think it's following the directions one of them is giving."

One of the boys looked up. He laughed and waved. "I'll send it back to you," he called. Soon Rob's car was again under his control.

STAY CLOSE TO SPIRITUAL HELP.

On the way home Dad said, "You know, just like your car, it's important for us as Christians to stay close to the right source to guide us. If we get too far away—for example, if we skip Bible reading and prayer or stop spending time with Christians at church—we may not get the spiritual guidance we need. And it's easy to be influenced in the wrong direction by people who don't follow Jesus."

Rob nodded. "My car will help me remember that," he said.

HOW ABOUT YOU?

Do you find yourself going along with the crowd? Are you easily influenced to join in when friends are trying to get you to do something that isn't right? Perhaps it's because you've gotten too far from the Lord. Remember that steady Christian fellowship, Bible reading, and prayer will help you live as a Christian should.

TO MEMORIZE:

Let us hold tightly without wavering to the hope we affirm, for God can be trusted to keep his promise.

HEBREWS 10:23

BY NANCE E. KEYES

NOT A TAURUS

Read Isaiah 47:12-14.

"Mom, Linnea told me I'm a Taurus!" exclaimed Kelly as she burst through the front door. "Her mom says the stars can show us what we should do according to what day we were born. She says we can read the paper every day to find out what the stars say."

Kelly's mother asked, "Does it make sense to you to believe that the stars have power over a person's life? Does it make sense for people to have to wait until the newspaper arrives to find out what to do that day?"

Kelly thought about that. She remembered a girl from summer camp last year who'd always worn a rabbit's foot on her belt, even to go swimming. She had believed it would bring her luck, until another little girl had asked, "How much luck can a foot bring? Look what happened to the rabbit, and he had four of them!" Kelly decided that believing in the power of the stars to direct her life made about as much sense as believing in a rabbit's foot.

DON'T TRUST SUPERSTITIONS.

Kelly glanced at the family Bible lying on a nearby shelf. "Linnea may say I was born under the sign of Taurus," she said, "but I've been born again." She smiled at her mother. "I'm a Christian, not a Taurus. Jesus is more powerful than any star—He made all of them! And I don't have to wait for the newspaper. I have God's Word to tell me how to live!"

HOW ABOUT YOU?

Do you ever find yourself avoiding the cracks in the sidewalk? Crossing the street to dodge a black cat? Reading the horoscope section of the paper? Astrology and superstition have no place in a Christian's life. Get rid of these things. God hates them!

TO MEMORIZE:

Let all the world look to me for salvation! For I am God; there is no other.

ISAIAH 45:22

BY LORNA B. MARLOWE

July 4
MORE THAN SAND

Read Psalm 40:5; 139:14-18.

"Nine, ten, eleven," Julie painstakingly separated tiny pieces of sand from the pile she held in her hand and dropped them, grain by grain, into her pail.

"Are you just going to sit on this beach blanket, trying to count sand?" asked her brother, Rick.

"There must be more sand than anything else in the whole world," Julie exclaimed, ignoring her brother. Rick rolled his eyes and headed toward the water.

Julie stayed on the blanket, counting sand. After a little while her father looked up from the book he was reading. "How's the counting? Do you think you'll be able to finish the whole beach this afternoon?" he teased.

Julie sprinkled the remaining sand she held over her feet. "I give up," she said. "I can't even count one handful. How much sand is there, Dad?"

Dad laughed. "There is no way we could begin to count all the sand in the world," he said. "Isn't that wonderful?"

Julie was puzzled. "Wonderful?" she asked. "Why is that wonderful?"

YOU ARE SPECIAL.

Dad reached into the tote bag packed with books, towels, and lotion. He took out a small Bible and turned to Psalm 139. "It says here that God's thoughts concerning us outnumber the grains of sand," he said. "Just think of that!"

Julie filled her bucket to the top with sand. Then she tipped it over and watched the millions of grains pour out. "Yes," she agreed. "It is wonderful."

HOW ABOUT YOU?

Do other kids sometimes say things that leave you feeling worthless? God made each person special. The next time you feel less than special, think about all the sand there is. Then thank God that you are so special to Him that His thoughts about you are far more than all the grains of sand in the world.

TO MEMORIZE:

How precious are your thoughts about me, O God.

PSALM 139:17

BY NANCE E. KEYES

WHY BOAST?

Read James 4:13-17.

Dad shook Owen's shoulder gently. "Time to go," he whispered. "Fishing is best early in the morning, you know."

Owen rolled out of bed. Soon he and Dad pushed offshore in a rowboat. Owen yawned as he pulled at the oars. "Better wake up," said Dad. "I heard you tell your friends yesterday you were going to catch the most fish."

"I will, too," Owen boasted.

Dad was the first to reel in a big bass, and then he caught several others. Owen snagged a small sunfish, which he threw back into the water. After a few hours Owen was ready to quit.

"I've gotta get back for our ball game today," said Owen. He looked at his father. "Are you coming to the game? I'm gonna knock a ball right out of the ballpark!"

Dad laughed. "I want to be there to see that," he said. "But you'd better be careful about what you say. Not long ago you were going to catch the most fish. Now you're going to be the best ballplayer. It's not good to boast like that and then come up empty handed."

PLAN—SEEKING GOD'S WILL.

"That's for sure," Owen admitted, glancing at the few small fish he had caught.

"The Bible warns against boasting about plans without thinking about God's will," said Dad. "We can't be sure what will happen today or tomorrow, you know. We need to live each day with a desire to do God's will instead of bragging about our own plans."

HOW ABOUT YOU?

Do you have plans for today, tomorrow, or next week? Do you make plans without thinking about God's will for you? He is in control of all that happens, and your plans will come to pass only as He allows them to. Make all your plans with that knowledge in mind.

TO MEMORIZE:

How do you know what your life will be like tomorrow? Your life is like the morning fog—it's here a little while, then it's gone.

JAMES 4:14

BY BRENDA DECKER

July 6

DELAYED ACTION

Read Ecclesiastes 8:11-13.

Mark's uncle Jeff was scheduled to have back surgery. "The doctor says an old injury is causing the trouble," said Dad. "Jeff was butted by a goat years ago."

"How'd that happen?" asked Mark.

"Our grandpa had a mean old billy goat," said Dad. "Grandpa warned Jeff and me not to go into the stall where the goat was, but Jeff did anyway. When he tried to get out, the goat got him."

"Was he hurt bad?" Mark asked.

"Pretty bad, but he never told anyone because he was afraid he'd be punished," answered Dad. "He said he fell. He was stiff for a long time and had a big bruise. Now that spot is giving him a lot of trouble. After all these years he's paying for his disobedience. If he had admitted what happened right away, he could have gotten help and wouldn't need an operation now."

The next week Dad and Mark came home with a bush Mom wanted. She came out to watch Dad dig a hole. Then Mark suddenly remembered that a few months ago he had tossed a ball in the house and had broken a vase. He had buried the pieces in this very spot. In a few minutes Dad turned up some of the pieces.

CONFESS RIGHT AWAY.

Mark said, "I guess I'm just like Uncle Jeff." Then Mark told his story and apologized.

"Mark, I would have forgiven you the day it happened if you had told me," Mom answered. "It's not pleasant, but it's always best to confess what you did wrong at the time you did it."

HOW ABOUT YOU?

Are you hiding some sins, thinking they will never be found out? Do you think you are getting away with something? God knows all about it. Confess your sins, take the consequences, and receive forgiveness.

TO MEMORIZE:

I, the LORD, search all hearts and examine secret motives. I give all people their due rewards, according to what their actions deserve.

JEREMIAH 17:10

BY AGNES LIVEZEY

July 7

THE GUIDING HAND

Read Psalm 31:1-5.

Nine-year-old Marco watched as his father guided the aluminum fishing boat across the lake. The wind was strong, and the waves were high! Dad had to fight to keep the small boat on course.

Marco asked, "Can I steer for a while?"

"I'm afraid you can't handle it alone," Dad said, raising his voice above the motor sound.

Marco still wanted to guide the boat across the lake to the spot where he and his father were to spend the day fishing. "When you see I'm not doing it right, you can help me."

Carefully Marco and his dad changed places in the boat, and Marco began to guide it across the rough waters. Suddenly a big wave stood before them, and Marco turned the boat with a jerk. The boat began to zigzag back and forth until Dad came to the rescue. Placing his hand over Marco's, he guided the boat until things were once again under control.

LET GOD GUIDE YOU.

"Boy," Marco said with relief in his voice. "It's a good thing you were there to take over."

His father smiled. "This is a good example of our Christian life. We sometimes think we can handle our problems by ourselves, and God lets us try. Then just about the time when things seem to be completely out of hand, God puts His hand over ours and guides us through the situation."

HOW ABOUT YOU?

When things seem to be going well, do you forget that you need God? Do you think you can handle that math test alone? That you don't need help with your paper route? When you try to get along without God's help, sooner or later you'll run into trouble. God wants to help. Let Him!

TO MEMORIZE:

You are my rock and my fortress. For the honor of your name, lead me out of this danger.
PSALM 31:3

BY RUTH I. JAY

My Friends

You are my friends if you do what I command. I no longer call you slaves, because a master doesn't confide in his slaves. Now you are my friends.

JOHN 15:14-15

In the verse above, Jesus is speaking to His closest friends, the disciples. Finish the crossword below to see how well you know some of His friends' names.

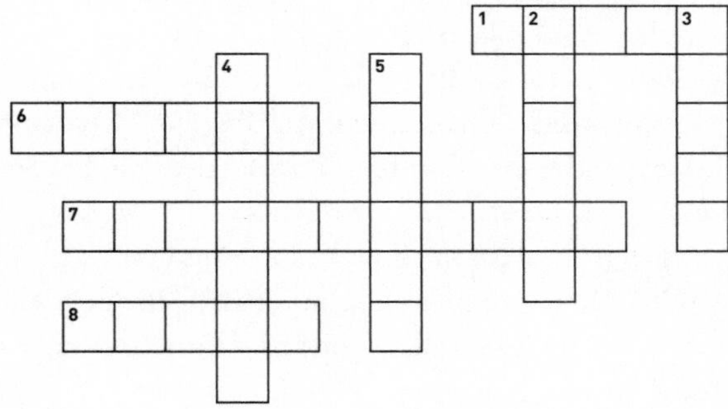

ACROSS

1. This friend was John's brother and the son of Zebedee.
6. Called a "doubter" by some, he was also named Didymus.
7. Also known as Nathanael, he was Philip's friend.
8. This son of Alphaeus was either younger or smaller than the disciple in clue no. 1 Across, who had the same name.

DOWN

2. This fisherman friend told Jesus about the little boy with loaves and fishes.
3. There were two disciples by this name; one was also called Peter.
4. This disciple was a tax collector from Capernaum.
5. This disciple was from Bethsaida and a friend to Bartholomew.

ANSWER KEY

ACROSS: 1. James; 6. Thomas; 7. Bartholomew; 8. James

DOWN: 2. Andrew; 3. Simon; 4. Matthew; 5. Philip

July 8
TAKING ROOT

Read Romans 6:1-2, 11-14.

Isaiah stopped to wipe the sweat from his face. "Let's take a break."

Grandpa dropped his hoe. "Sounds good!"

They walked around the garden. A row of peas was sprouting where Grandpa had planted them a few weeks earlier. Otherwise the garden was still full of weeds.

"Weeds grow in a hurry," Grandpa said.

"Why did God make weeds?" asked Isaiah.

"They're the result of sin," said Grandpa. "Farmers need to destroy weeds to keep them from spoiling their crops. In the same way, we have to get rid of the sinful things in our lives so they don't take over!"

"What do you mean?" asked Isaiah.

Grandpa pulled a tall weed. "I have a temper," he said. "My temper is like this weed. It has tough roots and grows fast. It could take over my life and cause me to be angry all the time."

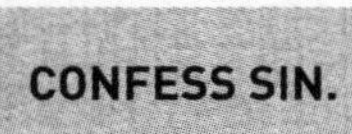

CONFESS SIN.

Isaiah thought for a minute. "I'm not always nice to Jennifer," he confessed. "That's like a weed, too, isn't it?" Grandpa nodded. "So what can I do about it?" asked Isaiah.

"First tell God," advised Grandpa. "Ask Him to forgive you and help you to be the kind of brother He wants you to be." Grandpa sat down on a bench near the garden. "Then you need to ask Jennifer to forgive you."

Isaiah sat down next to him. "That's almost harder than asking God to forgive me. But I know you're right. If I really mean it when I tell God I'm sorry, He'll help me apologize to Jennifer, too."

HOW ABOUT YOU?

Is there a weed that you need to remove from your life? Do you have a bad temper? A habit of disobeying? Whatever it is, seek God's forgiveness first. Then ask for forgiveness from anyone you've hurt.

TO MEMORIZE:

Do not let sin control the way you live; do not give in to sinful desires.

ROMANS 6:12

BY GAIL L. JENNER

July 9

JUST ONE STING

Read 1 Corinthians 15:54-57.

"Get away! Get away!" Jessica swung her arms wildly as a bee buzzed around her head. "Mom!" she screamed. "He's going to get me!" She dashed toward her mom, who was putting the lawn mower away. Mom held out her arms, and Jessica rushed into them, wrapping her arms around her mother's waist. The angry bee followed.

Mom stood still, waiting for the bee to leave, but it kept looking for a victim. As Mom brushed the bee away from Jessica, it landed on her own arm. "Ow!" Mom yelled. Then she said, "Honey, the bee stung me, so you don't need to be afraid of it anymore." Jessica looked at her mother's arm. She drew back as she saw the bee still crawling there. "It can't hurt you now," Mom said. "It can only sting once."

"Oh, Mom! Does it hurt a lot?" Jessica asked as the bee tumbled to the ground. "You took the sting for me!"

"I'm glad I was there to do it," said her mother.

As Mom treated the sting, Jessica said, "Last Sunday my teacher told us that Jesus took the punishment for our sins. I didn't understand it then, but now I do. Just like you're suffering for me, He did too—only more. I'd like to ask Him to save me now."

JESUS TOOK YOUR PUNISHMENT.

Jessica and Mom prayed together and forgot all about the bee sting!

HOW ABOUT YOU?

Do you understand that Jesus was punished for your sins? Because He died for you, you no longer need to fear death. When you accept Him as your Savior, He removes the "sting." If you've never asked Jesus to save you, won't you do that right now?

TO MEMORIZE:

Thank God! He gives us victory over sin and death through our Lord Jesus Christ.

1 CORINTHIANS 15:57

BY HAZEL W. MARETT

July 10 THE HIKE

Read Psalm 119:33-40.

"Let's go for a hike," Mandy said after the big meal at the family reunion. "Let's take one of the nature trails." Several children headed toward the beginning of the trails, where a large map was posted. No one stopped to study it, though.

After walking awhile, they came to a place where the trail went two ways. "Let's take the path to the left," said Mandy.

"I want to take the trail that goes up the mountain and around the lake," said Grant.

"How long is it?" asked Cassie.

"And where does it end?" asked Mandy.

Grant shrugged. "I guess it circles back to the road. C'mon—let's go!" He led the way.

It was fun at first, but after an hour everyone was tired. "How much farther?" asked Mandy.

READ YOUR BIBLE.

"How should I know?" Grant snapped.

"Didn't you read the map?" asked Cassie.

"No," said Grant. "But this trail should lead back to the road—sooner or later."

Mandy stood still. "Well, I'm going back the way we came." Cassie agreed.

When they came to the map, they stopped to look at it. Mandy said, "I can just hear Granny Williams saying, 'You're like all those people who try to get through life without reading the Bible,'" she said in her best Granny voice.

"And don't depend on someone else to lead you," Cassie added in shaky tones. "Read the map for yourself."

HOW ABOUT YOU?

Are you studying God's "map"—the Bible—or are you depending on someone else to tell you what God says? Good teachers who love the Lord can be a great help, but you need to read the Bible for yourself, too.

TO MEMORIZE:

Show me the right path, O LORD; point out the road for me to follow.

PSALM 25:4

BY BARBARA J. WESTBERG

July 11 SURPRISE PARTY

Read 1 John 4:7-12.

"What's Beth's problem?" asked Matt as his sister left. "She was acting awful gloomy."

"This is the day her friends leave for camp," sighed Mom. "Beth can't afford to quit her job—but she loves camp so much!"

"We should do something special for her so she won't be so mopey. I know. Let's have a surprise family party."

"All right," said Mom. "I'll fix her favorite dinner, and you can decorate the dining room."

"What about presents?" asked Matt.

Mom thought for a minute. "Why don't we make 'love coupons'? I'll make one with a promise to make her bed and clean up her room every day this week. Then she can sleep later. You could wash the dishes when it's her turn," suggested Mother.

Matt groaned. "We want her to feel better, but there's a limit!"

His mother laughed and gave him a quick hug. "This is a great idea, Son. God says we should show love to one another, and you're doing that."

SHOW LOVE WITH ACTIONS.

When Beth came in from work, she saw a big banner on the dining room wall—"We love you, Beth." The table was set with the best china, and there were streamers and balloons everywhere.

After dinner Beth looked at her family. "I love all of you," she said. Looking at the dishes, she winked at Matt. "Especially you, little brother. I hope you don't get dishpan hands!"

HOW ABOUT YOU?

Does someone in your family need a pick-me-up? As you remember all that God did to show His great love for you, will you, in turn, go out of your way to show love to that person? Maybe you can plan a party, do more than your share of the chores, or help in some special way. You'll be surprised to find how much it will lift everyone's spirits.

TO MEMORIZE:

Dear friends, since God loved us that much,
we surely ought to love each other.

1 JOHN 4:11

BY BARBARA J. WESTBERG

July 12

FRUITFUL BRANCHES

Read John 15:1-8.

Randy bounced beside Grandpa in the pickup truck. They stopped at the vineyard, and Grandpa got out the long-handled clippers. "I'm going to do some pruning," he said.

"What's pruning?" asked Randy.

"When I prune a grapevine, I take out some of the vines or branches."

"How do you know which branches to cut off?" Randy asked.

"The ones that are attached to the main vine are the branches that I leave," answered Grandpa. "They're the strongest and will grow nice, fat grapes. The branches that grow from other branches won't grow good grapes, so I cut those off." Grandpa showed Randy how he followed a branch to its beginning to see whether or not it was attached to the main vine.

"Whenever I prune grapevines, I remember what Jesus said about them," said Grandpa. "Jesus compared Himself to the main vine, and He said people are like the branches. Some are the true branches attached to the vine and will be fruitful. Others are just branches to be cut off."

BE ATTACHED TO JESUS.

"Which people are the true branches?" asked Randy.

"Those who trust in Jesus as the way to heaven," answered Grandpa. "The other branches are those who try to get there on their own."

"I've asked Jesus to forgive my sins, and I love Him. So I'm a true branch, right?" Randy asked.

"Right you are," said Grandpa.

HOW ABOUT YOU?

Are you attached to Jesus, the Vine? Or are you attached to your church, your baptism, or your good works? There is only one way to get to heaven, and that is to trust Jesus to forgive your sins. If you do that, you'll be like a fruitful branch attached to the vine. If you've never asked Jesus to be your Savior, you can do it right now!

TO MEMORIZE:

I am the vine; you are the branches. Those who remain in me, and I in them, will produce much fruit. For apart from me you can do nothing.

JOHN 15:5

BY CAROLYN E. YOST

July 13

A NEW BEGINNING

Read Lamentations 3:18-26.

Nathan hadn't been very happy lately. His father's company had moved the family from the Midwest to the South, and Nathan missed his friends. He felt it was no use to even try to be happy here.

One day the family took a trip to the beach. They all went swimming, but Nathan wouldn't admit it was fun. Later the family hunted for shells. Nathan found a starfish, but two of its arms were broken off. He was about to throw it away when Dad said, "Let me see it." Nathan handed the starfish to him, and Dad turned it over. "See the little moving feet?"

"You mean it's alive?" Nathan asked. Dad nodded. "But it's gonna die," continued Nathan. "It has only three arms instead of five."

Dad said, "Starfish can regenerate."

"What does that mean?"

"In time the starfish will grow new arms to replace the old ones," Dad explained.

"And I thought it was useless," Nathan said.

ACCEPT NEW SITUATIONS.

"Nathan, right now you're something like that starfish. You've been cut off from your old friends and you're hurting. It's scary to begin again, but with God's help you can make new friends," said Dad.

Nathan looked at the starfish and smiled. "If he can begin again, I guess I can too."

HOW ABOUT YOU?

Do you accept new situations as a challenge to learn and grow? Or do you just feel sad and refuse to try again? Perhaps someone special to you has died, a friend has moved away, or you have a new mom or dad, and things seem so uncertain for you. Ask God for strength to accept your new situation. Then look for ways you can reach out and be friendly to those around you.

TO MEMORIZE:

The faithful love of the LORD never ends! His mercies never cease.
Great is his faithfulness; his mercies begin afresh each morning.
LAMENTATIONS 3:22-23

BY JAN L. HANSEN

July 14

FOR HIS GLORY (PART 1)

Read Psalm 8:3-9.

Crickets chirped, and June bugs buzzed. Mike and his friend Steve lay in their sleeping bags, looking up at the sky. They were camping out in Mike's backyard. "I'll bet we could count a thousand stars up there if we tried," said Mike.

"Yeah, and that's just the ones that are close enough for us to see without a telescope," Steve replied. "My science teacher said there are hundreds of millions of galaxies, and each galaxy has about ten billion stars."

Mike said, "I can see why God created the earth and sun and moon—maybe even the other planets in our solar system. But why did He make the rest of the universe? I mean, what's the use of making something so great and wonderful if no one's ever going to see it?"

"Well," said Steve, "I guess it's like what Mom told me when I was cleaning my room yesterday. I said I didn't see why I had to clean under my bed since nobody would see it."

GOD IS GREAT.

"What did your mom say?" asked Mike.

"She said that having it clean was important to her. She says she likes order and beauty, and God does too."

"I guess all mothers are like that," said Mike. "Maybe God didn't make the universe just for us," he added, "but for Himself. I guess it's silly for us to think that the universe is wasted just because we can't see all of it."

"Besides, all those stars help us realize how great God really is," added Steve.

HOW ABOUT YOU?

When you think about the greatness of the universe, does it make you feel small and unimportant? Does it make you realize the huge difference between God and human beings? You can never fully understand His greatness or all the things He has done. All you can do is worship Him with praise and thanksgiving.

TO MEMORIZE:

The heavens proclaim the glory of God.
The skies display his craftsmanship.
PSALM 19:1

BY SHERRY L. KUYT

Stick Close

There are "friends" who destroy each other, but a real friend sticks closer than a brother.
PROVERBS 18:24

We know our true friends. They are the ones we can always trust, the ones who never give up on us. Being friendly is how we make friends, but staying close is how we keep them.

Help the child find her friend at the park.

SEE ANSWER IN BACK

July 15

FOR HIS GLORY (PART 2)

Read Psalm 148:1-13.

As Mike and Steve ate breakfast the morning after their campout, they told Mike's mother that they had talked about the huge universe. "It made me feel small," said Mike.

Mom said, "God is interested in small things too. Mike, have you shown Steve the microscope you got for your birthday?"

"Yeah, he did. It's neat!" exclaimed Steve.

"I've got something on a slide you haven't seen," said Mike. The boys hurried off.

As Steve looked through the lens, he saw what appeared to be a giant, horned monster. "Yuck!" he exclaimed. "What's that thing?"

"It's just a flea from my dog!" Mike said, laughing.

Steve took another look. Then he said, "Let's find some other things to look at." Soon the boys had examined an ant, a leaf, a worm, and part of a flower.

Then the boys looked at a drop of water from a puddle. They were amazed at all the tiny things swimming in it. "I can't believe it," said Steve. "There must be billions of these things all over the world, and we never even see them."

GOD CARES ABOUT SMALL THINGS.

"Even though no one sees these little creatures, each one of them was created by God." Mom's voice came from the doorway.

"I'm glad He's interested in little things as well as in big things," said Mike. "That means He's interested in us, too."

HOW ABOUT YOU?

Do you realize that God cares about you—that you are important to Him? He created you and has a purpose for your life. You could not even live if it were not for His loving care every day. Don't you think you can trust Him for everything?

TO MEMORIZE:

When you open your hand, you satisfy the hunger
and thirst of every living thing.
PSALM 145:16

BY SHERRY L. KUYT

July 16

A HIGHER VIEW

Read Romans 8:28-32.

Kayla and Derrick grinned at each other as they rode the elevator with their family to the observation deck of the skyscraper in Chicago. Their ears popped as they whizzed by floor after floor, going higher and higher. Getting off the elevator, the children ran to a window to look out at the view below.

"Everything looks so tiny!" Kayla exclaimed. "The cars look like toys."

Mom nodded. "You can see a long way from here. See the boats on the lake?"

"Look way ahead, over to your right," Dad instructed. "Traffic's stopped there."

"Yes, but look right below us," Derrick said. "See that red car? It keeps changing lanes, trying to get ahead of everyone else."

"Probably in a hurry," Kayla suggested.

"Probably," agreed Dad. "That guy is in such a hurry he's foolishly and dangerously passing everyone. But he's going to be slowed down because it looks like there's a roadblock up ahead. That will stop him."

"Too bad he can't see the roadblock like we can," Kayla said. "Then he'd know there's no point to be in such a hurry."

GOD'S WAYS ARE GOOD.

"You know," said Dad, "as Christians, we sometimes act a lot like that fellow. God has a plan mapped out for each of us, but we often try to hurry ahead of His ways. We complain when we have to wait, but we don't stop to think that there is a purpose for the delay."

Mom nodded. "The higher view—God's view—is better, isn't it?"

HOW ABOUT YOU?

Do you fret when your plans are changed? Do you grumble when someone gets sick or hurt, making it necessary to cancel an activity? Changes aren't always pleasant, but they can be good for you. Trust God to work through your interrupted plans.

TO MEMORIZE:

What shall we say about such wonderful things as these?
If God is for us, who can ever be against us?
ROMANS 8:31

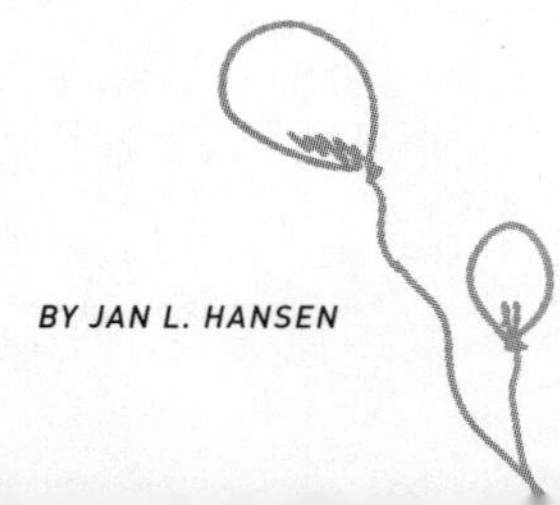

BY JAN L. HANSEN

CLOSER TO THE LIGHT

Read Psalm 119:129-135.

Brian and his family went to visit his aunt and uncle on the farm. Brian loved seeing the animals, climbing on haystacks, swinging on the rope in the barn, and wading in the creek. "This is a neat place!" he said at supper one evening.

Mom smiled. "I'm glad you can enjoy yourself without ballparks or ice cream stores!"

After supper, Dad looked over at Brian. "Your uncle Mark and I have a surprise for you, Son. We thought you might enjoy camping out in the woods with us tonight."

Three hours later, they sat by the campfire. "Time for devotions," Uncle Mark announced, pulling out his Bible.

As Brian reached in his duffel bag for his own Bible, he looked at all the stars. "Wow," he cried. "We can't see this many stars at home. They must be a lot closer here."

SPEND TIME ALONE WITH GOD.

Dad and Uncle Mark laughed. "No, the stars aren't closer," Dad replied. "But we're out in the country, away from city lights, which tend to blot out the smaller lights of the stars."

Uncle Mark leafed through his Bible. "Just as the lights of the city blot out the stars, so the busyness of everyday activities can make it hard to see how God is working in our lives. That's why it's good to go to a quiet place—a place where you can be alone and think about God's Word and His love."

Brian listened very carefully as Uncle Mark read from the Bible.

HOW ABOUT YOU?

Is your time so filled with activities that you hardly ever think about God or the Bible? Be careful! If you don't set aside "quiet times" to be alone with God, you'll miss many of the wonderful blessings the Lord has planned for you.

TO MEMORIZE:

After sending them home, he went up into the hills by himself to pray. Night fell while he was there alone.
MATTHEW 14:23

BY SHERRY L. KUYT

July 18

ROSES AND ROOTS

Read Colossians 2:1-7.

"Can I go play at Cesar's house?" asked Julio.

Mom looked up from the book she was reading. "Is your Sunday school lesson done?" she asked. Julio nodded. "Say your verse then."

"Aw, Mom," protested Julio, but he went to his room to learn the verse. After a while he came back. "I know the verse now, but I don't understand it." Julio recited Colossians 2:7.

Just then Julio's little sister, Carmen, came in. "My rose died!" she cried. She led her mother out to the flower bed. Julio followed. Carmen pointed to a wilted rose sticking out of the ground. "I picked that rose and planted it."

"Oh, honey," replied Mom, "when you pick roses, they don't have roots and can't grow."

Mom looked at Julio. "Plants need to be rooted in the soil so they can take in food and water. And we, as Christians, need to be rooted in the Lord. As we study His Word and pray and learn more about Him, we're taking in spiritual food. And we're developing strong roots so that when troubles come we can stand and grow."

BE ROOTED IN CHRIST.

"That's what my verse means, huh?" Julio said. "And the last part of it means I should be thankful for everything God does—like giving me a mother who makes me study my lesson before I play!"

HOW ABOUT YOU?

Do you take advantage of opportunities to be rooted in the Lord? Do you study your Bible? Listen in church? Take time to pray? You need to do those things. You need to be firmly rooted and established in your faith in Christ.

TO MEMORIZE:

Let your roots grow down into him, and let your lives be built on him. Then your faith will grow strong in the truth you were taught, and you will overflow with thankfulness.

COLOSSIANS 2:7

BY HAZEL W. MARETT

July 19
THE HERO

Read John 13:13-17.

"Did you see Galdino hit that last ball?" asked Chan as his father started the car. "It went so far I bet the other team hasn't found it yet! I want to be just like him when I get to high school."

"Me, too! Galdino's the best player we have," Chan's friend Travis continued the hero worship.

"Can we stop at this next restaurant, Dad?" asked Chan. "The team's going to eat here."

The three of them were just starting to enjoy their food when the team came into the restaurant. Chan and Travis were delighted when Galdino and three other players took a table near their booth. But as the boys watched, they saw the team members—led by Galdino—blow the paper from their straws onto the floor, throw food at the busboy, and shout rudely until the coach threatened to send them out to the bus. They heard Galdino swear and saw him laugh at the waitress. Chan and Travis felt sad that their hero's behavior was not something to admire.

LET JESUS BE YOUR HERO.

As the boys returned to the car Chan said, "I don't like Galdino anymore. How can such a neat ballplayer be such a rotten person?"

"You can admire Galdino's athletic ability," Dad said. "But it's not a good idea to make people into idols. Sooner or later they let you down. Jesus is the one you should choose for your role model. He'll never let you down."

HOW ABOUT YOU?

Has a sports figure you admire been found guilty of taking drugs? Does a television personality you like use bad language and brag about an immoral lifestyle? Beware of making people into idols. Only Jesus is perfect. Choose Him for your hero.

TO MEMORIZE:

Dear children, keep away from anything that might take God's place in your hearts.
1 JOHN 5:21

BY RUTH MCQUILKIN

July 20

PART OF THE FAMILY

Read Romans 5:15-19.

Joshua's uncle Dan and aunt Judy, missionaries in Africa, were returning home on furlough. Everyone was eager to see them and their two-year-old boy, who had been born in Africa. At the airport Joshua watched while the grown-ups hugged and kissed one another. Then Uncle Dan turned toward him and said, "This must be Joshua. You have your dad's eyes."

"I'm eight years old now," said Joshua. "Is that your baby?"

"Yes, that's our Benjamin."

"He looks just like you, Dan," Mom said.

Uncle Dan laughed. "Yes, he's my boy!"

On the way home that night Joshua was full of questions. "How did I get Dad's eyes, and why does Benjamin look like Uncle Dan?" he asked.

"Children inherit certain characteristics—size or shape or color of hair and eyes—from their parents," replied Mom. "Benjamin inherited his father's looks, and you inherited your father's eye color."

SALVATION IS A CHOICE.

"That's right," nodded Dad. "But we inherit more than just physical traits."

"What do you mean?" Joshua asked.

"The Bible tells us we are all descendants of Adam, the first man God created. Adam sinned against God, so everyone inherits his sinful nature," explained Dad. "But we don't have to remain in our sin. If we accept Jesus as Savior, we become children of God. And God's family is the best family to be a part of!"

HOW ABOUT YOU?

Even though God created you, that doesn't automatically make you His child. Your sinful nature is inherited, but salvation is a definite choice. Have you chosen Christ as your Savior? If not, do so today, and you'll be part of God's family forever!

TO MEMORIZE:

Because one person disobeyed God, many became sinners. But because one other person obeyed God, many people will be made righteous.
ROMANS 5:19

BY JAN L. HANSEN

July 21

LESSON IN A FISHBOWL

Read Matthew 5:38-47.

"It's too hot to mow the lawn," groaned Joey.

"Well, it's not going to get cooler. You'd better start now," advised Mother.

"The Bible says, 'Don't make your children angry by the way you treat them.' And I feel angry right now," grumbled Joey.

"You're taking that verse out of context, Son," said Mom firmly. "The same chapter says, 'Children, obey your parents.'"

Later that day Joey played with his little brother, Nick. Soon Mom heard Nick crying, so she went outside. "Joey pushed me down," sobbed the little boy.

"Well, he ran into me," Joey defended himself. "The Bible says, 'If an eye is injured, injure the eye of the person who did it.'"

"There you go again, taking a verse out of context. The Bible also says, 'Be kind to one another,'" Mom replied sternly.

"What does context mean?" Joey asked. "You said that earlier today."

USE GOD'S WORD CAREFULLY.

"Taking something out of its context means to take it out of its proper surroundings," Mom explained. "If you do that to Goldy, your goldfish—you take it out of water—it will soon die. If you take a Bible verse out of its proper surroundings—that is, if you use it any way you want, without considering other Bible verses—you can make it seem like the verse is saying something different from what it really means."

HOW ABOUT YOU?

Do you use Bible verses to try and get your own way? God's Word is sacred, and you should never use it in a wrong way. Don't use it in a way that doesn't agree with the principles taught in the Bible.

TO MEMORIZE:

When the Spirit of truth comes, he will guide you into all truth.

JOHN 16:13

BY SARA L. NELSON

Better Than One

Two people are better off than one, for they can help each other succeed. If one person falls, the other can reach out and help.
ECCLESIASTES 4:9-10

These verses from Ecclesiastes help remind us that people aren't meant to be alone. True friends lift us up. We do the same for them. And together, two friends can accomplish so much more than a single person can do on his or her own.

Circle the words that mean "friend" in this puzzle.

```
F C O M R A D E X S A H R C K
L H S G S C O M P A D R E C N
P U K O X L H H D I H R U K V
C M F I V N U N T V D R K F A
H W M G H R E X H Y J T J C W
R F K T Y I Z D S P X N M B J
X F P J R G G M Y A A C U A J
T R F F A R A M I G O L S B Q
S B U D D Y U R L I N S K N R
M D M M G K J P V E X L E F F
C E T U C O N F I D A N T Z H
L E G V T M Y D W R R P E E Z
K P G C A J E J X S Z C E W G
B S B T C M Z D H T K X R Z P
E P O C C R O N Y O B Q K C R
```

amigo	confidant
buddy	crony
chum	friend
compadre	musketeer
comrade	pal

SEE ANSWER IN BACK

July 22

THE SOONER THE BETTER

Read Psalm 107:1-8.

"Becky, would you share your testimony next week?" Mr. Helton asked after Bible club.

Becky said, "I don't have anything to share."

"I thought you asked Jesus to save you at one of our meetings last year," answered the teacher.

"Yes, but people who give testimonies always tell about all the bad things they did before Jesus came into their heart," Becky said. "I didn't do a lot of bad things."

Mr. Helton smiled. He knew Becky was remembering the rally to which he had taken his Bible club. First a pro football player had talked about his life on drugs. Then a woman had talked about how she had wanted to take her life until a friend stepped in and told her about Jesus' love. "Becky, since you accepted Jesus into your heart at a young age, the Lord has kept you away from some of the horrible sin that might have entered your life as you grew older. You can express thanks to God for this."

ALL CHRISTIANS HAVE A TESTIMONY.

"But do you think anyone is interested in hearing what I have to say?" Becky wondered.

"Oh yes," Mr. Helton assured her. "Many others in our Bible club may feel just as you do—that they have little to testify about. Hearing what you have to say may help them realize how blessed they are too. And some who are not saved may see the value of accepting Jesus now, while they are young."

Becky smiled and nodded. "Plan on my testimony next week," she said.

HOW ABOUT YOU?

Are you one of those who accepted Jesus as Savior before you ever got deeply involved in a life of sin? If so, never be sorry that you have not experienced some of the evil in the world. Instead, thank the Lord for protecting you.

TO MEMORIZE:

Has the LORD redeemed you? Then speak out! Tell others he has redeemed you from your enemies.

PSALM 107:2

BY RAELENE E. PHILLIPS

July 23

THE UNCRUSHABLE CAN

Read 1 Peter 4:16-17.

Alex ran to the car as Dad drove up in front of the building where he took a summer class. "Have a good afternoon?" Dad asked. Alex shrugged. "Are you unhappy with me for not letting you go to that movie?" Dad asked softly.

Alex shook his head. "No. I'm glad you said no."

"Did your friends give you a hard time?" asked Dad.

"Yeah. Even Ben thought I should tell you I was going somewhere else and then go to the movie." Ben was his friend from church.

When they got home, Dad found an empty soda can and handed it to Alex. "Crush this can," Dad said. Alex started to ask a question, but then set the can on the floor and smashed it.

"Now crush this can," Dad said, handing Alex a full can of pop.

Alex replied, "I can't. It's full."

"Think about which can you are like," said Dad. "I bet you felt empty when your friends made fun of you. But you're not actually empty. God's Holy Spirit came into your life when you became a Christian. He fills you with His strength so that no one can 'crush' you or defeat you."

DON'T BE DISCOURAGED.

Alex gave Dad a little smile. It wasn't easy having others against him, but God would help him do the right thing.

HOW ABOUT YOU?

Does it bother you when others—especially other Christians—try to get you to do things you know are wrong? Do you feel "down" when someone makes fun of you for doing right? Remember, if you're a Christian, God is living in you. You are "uncrushable."

TO MEMORIZE:

We are pressed on every side by troubles, but we are not crushed. We are perplexed, but not driven to despair. We are hunted down, but never abandoned by God. We get knocked down, but we are not destroyed.

2 CORINTHIANS 4:8-9

BY KATHERINE R. ADAMS

July 24

WHATEVER THE WEATHER

Read 1 Timothy 6:6-8; Psalm 103:1-5.

"Whew!" Dad said as he picked up the newspaper. "This hot weather is unbearable! After this summer, I'll never complain about being too cold again."

With a twinkle in his eye, Brad ran from the room. He returned quicly with his mom's smartphone. Sneaking up behind Dad, Brad hit a button on the phone.

"Whew!" Dad's voice boomed from the speaker. "This cold is unbearable! I'll never complain about being too warm again. I wish we had a hot sun right now."

"What!" Startled, Dad dropped the newspaper and twisted around in his chair to look at Brad. "When did you record that?" demanded Dad.

Brad laughed. "Last winter," he replied. "We hear the same thing every summer and every winter. We just wanted you to hear it yourself."

Dad laughed too. "Caught by my own words. I guess we're hard to please, aren't we?"

Mom said, "We often complain about what we don't like instead of giving thanks for what we have."

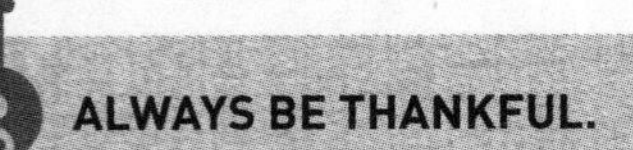

"I don't complain about the weather," said Brad. "I like summer, and I like winter." He grinned at his parents.

"I wasn't talking only about weather complaints," said Mom.

"I know," Brad admitted.

"Good!" said Mom. "Then I assume you'll do the lunch dishes without complaining. You'll be remembering with gratitude the good meal you just ate."

"Oh, Mom," protested Brad, but he began to clear the table.

"I'd better go pull weeds in the garden and give thanks that I don't have to shovel the driveway today," said Dad. He put his arm around Brad's shoulder and gave it a squeeze. "I appreciate the good lesson!" added Dad. "Did you record this conversation too? I might need to be reminded of it again when the snow starts to pile up."

HOW ABOUT YOU?

Are you content with what you have? Are you unhappy because you can't get a new shirt, or do you give thanks for your new shoes? Be content with what you have, and thank God for the gifts He's given you today.

TO MEMORIZE:

True godliness with contentment is itself great wealth.

1 TIMOTHY 6:6

BY HAZEL W. MARETT

July 25

BRAND NAMES

Read Ephesians 4:24-32.

Stacy and her friend Valerie ran to the window of a store in the mall. "Mom, hurry!" Stacy pleaded. "Look at this outfit! Could I have that for my birthday?"

"I don't know," Mom answered. "It's a bit expensive. And really, I think it looks a little too grown up for you."

"I love it!" Stacy exclaimed. "Everyone's wearing shirts like that."

"The jeans are great too," Valerie added.

"Yeah," agreed Stacy. "Everyone at school wears that brand. Oh, please, Mom!"

Mom frowned. "I've seen jeans at the discount store that look just as nice."

Stacy wailed, "I don't want those. Everyone would know they were the cheap kind."

"Well," said Mom, "the stores are closing, so we won't get any jeans today." As they drove home, Mom said, "Girls, the names on clothing labels seem so important to you. Yet you wear a name much more important than the one on any pair of jeans."

CHRISTIAN IS YOUR LABEL.

"What do you mean, Mom?" asked Stacy.

"Since you have trusted in Christ to save you," Mom explained, "you wear Christ's name—the name *Christian*. Brand names are really advertisements, and our lives should advertise for Jesus. I wonder, girls, can your friends tell that you wear Christ's name?"

"Wow!" Stacy exclaimed. "I don't know. I've never thought about it that way."

"Me either," Valerie agreed. "That's awesome—we wear the most important name of all!"

HOW ABOUT YOU?

Have you trusted Jesus Christ as your Lord and Savior? If so, you belong to Him. As Christ's follower, you are known by His name—you are called a Christian. Let others see by your words and actions that you belong to God. Let your life be a pleasing advertisement for Christ.

TO MEMORIZE:

Do not bring sorrow to God's Holy Spirit by the way you live. Remember, he has identified you as his own, guaranteeing that you will be saved on the day of redemption.

EPHESIANS 4:30

BY BRENDA DECKER

July 26

THE ANTIQUE MIRROR

Read 1 Peter 2:21-24.

"Mom, look at this old mirror!" Carrie exclaimed. She giggled at her short, squat reflection. "It makes me look so funny."

Mom came up to the attic behind her and looked. "That's very old," she said with a laugh. "It was your great-grandmother's."

"Can we take it downstairs?" asked Carrie.

"Sure," agreed Mom, "everyone would like to see it. But first let's take down the things for the garage sale."

That evening the Stevens family laughed together over their reflections in the antique mirror. "It's fun to look in that old mirror, but I sure am glad we have better ones to use now," said Carrie as they ate their supper.

"Oh?" asked Dad. "Why is that?"

Carrie giggled. "Because the old one doesn't reflect me the way I really am," she said. "It makes me look all squashed."

REFLECT CHRIST'S LOVE.

"Yeah," agreed her brother, Gary. "A good mirror shows you just as you are."

"I wonder how well all our mirrors are working," said Mom as she cut a melon.

"What do you mean?" asked Carrie.

Mom smiled. "I mean us."

"Us! We're people, not mirrors," said Gary.

"We are also mirrors," said Mom. "As Christians we should reflect Christ in everything we say and do."

"And when we do, we should reflect a true image," added Dad. "People should see Christ living in us, the way He really is—not a squashed reflection."

HOW ABOUT YOU?

Do you reflect Christ's love in your life when you talk with your friends and when you play? Or is your reflection of Jesus squashed by unkind actions? Each moment of the day let your life be a true reflection of Jesus' love.

TO MEMORIZE:

Now you must be holy in everything you do,
just as God who chose you is holy.
1 PETER 1:15

BY JEAN A. BURNS

July 27

GOD'S HANDIWORK

Read Genesis 1:26-27.

"Just look at Kellie's hair," Emily whispered to Amy. "It must have been made with straw from Mr. Brown's barn." The girls quieted down as their Sunday school teacher entered the room.

"I'm happy to see each of you today," said Ms. Ruth. "I'm especially glad you're back, Kellie." Then Ms. Ruth told the class, "We're going to draw numbers and divide into teams to make a mural of the story of the Prodigal Son."

Each girl chose a slip of paper. Emily drew a six, and so did Kellie. "Anyone want to trade?" asked Emily. When Ms. Ruth looked shocked, Emily mumbled, "Never mind." She told Kellie, "You draw the pigpen. I'll draw the Prodigal Son." Emily soon saw that Kellie was a very good artist, but she didn't tell her so.

"Boy, that's a good drawing," said Stacy, pointing to the pigpen. Then she giggled. "Is that a two-legged pig or a four-legged man in the middle?" Everyone laughed. Emily felt like she'd been hit in the stomach.

DON'T MAKE FUN OF OTHERS.

When the dismissal bell rang, Emily ran to the door, but Ms. Ruth called her back and put her arm around the girl's shoulders. "It hurt you when the girls laughed at your picture, didn't it?"

Emily sniffed. "That was mean," she said.

"Yes," Ms. Ruth agreed. "Now think about how God must feel when we make fun of Him. You created the picture, so it hurt you when the girls laughed at it. God created Kellie, so it hurts Him when you laugh at her. He knows it hurts her, too."

HOW ABOUT YOU?

Are you guilty of making fun of God's creation? Not only do you hurt others when you laugh at them, but you laugh at their Creator. God made people in His image. You wouldn't laugh at God, would you?

TO MEMORIZE:

Those who mock the poor insult their Maker; those who rejoice at the misfortune of others will be punished.

PROVERBS 17:5

BY BARBARA J. WESTBERG

July 28

JOEL'S MACHINE

Read 1 Corinthians 6:19-20.

"It's a great car, huh, Dad?" Joel watched as his father polished the hood. The car shone in the sunshine, the dark red interior contrasting sharply with the gleaming white paint.

"It sure is," agreed Dad, putting the cleaning rags away. He found a hammer and held it out to his son. "Here. Slam this into the windshield for the fun of it."

"Dad! You've gotta be kidding! What would I do that for?" asked Joel.

"I'm glad you have better sense than to do that," said Dad with a smile. "Let's talk for a minute. When you were born, God gave you a beautiful, precision-built 'machine,' your body. He asks that you treat it well. That's not expecting too much, is it?" Joel shook his head, smiling at the comparison, and Dad continued. "You've seen the TV ads showing young men and women who have drug problems, haven't you?"

Joel nodded. "Yes, Dad, I've seen them."

KEEP YOUR BODY PURE.

"Well, Son," continued Dad, "there may come a time when people you know will suggest that you try drugs just once. 'Just for kicks,' they may say, or maybe to prove you're not 'chicken.' But just as it would be crazy for you to slam that hammer into our new car," Dad nodded toward the driveway, "it would be even crazier to do something to destroy your wonderful body."

Joel nodded. "You can trust me to keep my 'machine' in good shape." Then he added, "Thanks for talking about this. I'll remember!"

HOW ABOUT YOU?

Has anyone asked you to do something you know is wrong? It may happen, and if it does, just say no. If you're a Christian, your body is the temple of the Holy Spirit. Use it to glorify God.

TO MEMORIZE:

My child, if sinners entice you, turn your back on them!

PROVERBS 1:10

BY PHYLLIS I. KLOMPARENS

At All Times

A friend loves at all times.
PROVERBS 17:17, NKJV

What if you focused on your love for a friend every time the two of you disagreed? Think about what it means to focus on love. It means choosing loving words. It also means using a loving *tone* of voice. All the time.

Write about a time you and a friend had a conflict that wasn't settled lovingly.

____

____

____

Describe how you and your friend felt and acted after the disagreement.

____

____

____

Now write three things you could do in a conflict that would show your love.

____

____

____

The Bible says that a friend loves at all times. This means in both good times and bad times. What if using the love in our hearts is the secret to lasting friendship?

July 29

SOME BRIGHT MORNING

Read 2 Corinthians 5:6-9.

The long row of cars moved slowly from the church to the cemetery. There, standing between her parents, Laura struggled to keep her tears from overflowing again.

"Kim is now in the presence of Jesus," said Pastor Drew. "She sees His kind face and hears His gentle voice. Kim is able to run and laugh now. And God's Word says that those who belong to Jesus will see her again some bright morning in heaven." The minister's thoughtful words gave assurance to the family and friends who had assembled after Kim's funeral service.

For as long as Laura could remember, she and Kim had gone to school and Sunday school together. Both had accepted Jesus as Savior when they were little. Now Kim was gone, and Laura's heart was sad. She looked around at Kim's other classmates. Each carried a balloon.

The minister's quiet words broke into Laura's thoughts. "These balloons will picture the freedom of Kim's spirit. The Bible tells us that the spirit of the one who believes in Jesus goes to be with Him. Kim's spirit is home now."

CHRISTIANS LIVE FOREVER IN HEAVEN.

The pastor held up a pink balloon. "Let's release our balloons together in celebration of Kim's new home," he said. In an instant, as all eyes were raised skyward, a cloud of balloons danced in the summer breeze.

"Good-bye, Kim," Laura whispered. "I'll be seeing you."

HOW ABOUT YOU?

Have you known someone who has died? Perhaps you wonder what it would be like to die. Jesus has promised to take Christians to heaven when they die. They live forever with Him there. The Bible says that for a Christian, to "be away from these earthly bodies" is to "be at home with the Lord."

TO MEMORIZE:

Then, together with them, we who are still alive and remain on the earth will be caught up in the clouds to meet the Lord in the air. Then we will be with the Lord forever.

1 THESSALONIANS 4:17

BY PHYLLIS I. KLOMPARENS

July 30

THE THIRTY

Read Matthew 20:25-28.

Jason pointed a stick at a bush. An imaginary enemy was behind it!

"Winning the war again?" asked Dad, who had been in a real war. "You know I don't like you to even pretend to shoot anyone, Son."

"I'm going to be a real hero someday," said Jason.

"I hope you get to be a hero some other way than by being in a war. What do you want to be?"

Jason said, "I want to be important, like David in the Bible. He killed Goliath and was a king."

"How about being as important as the Three or the Thirty?" asked Dad. Jason looked puzzled. "We'll talk about them later," Dad promised. "Right now I hear your mother calling."

Soon the whole family was helping Mom take some groceries to the basement, some to the pantry, some to the kitchen. "She's like a general in the army," Jason muttered.

BE A SERVANT.

During family devotions Dad said, "We're going to read about the Three and the Thirty." He read 2 Samuel 23:18-23 to introduce his family to some of David's mighty men.

"They were famous only because they served with King David," observed Jason.

"Think so?" asked Dad. "Or was King David famous because he had those mighty men?" Dad looked at his family. "For every general there are thousands of soldiers. They carry out his plans, and he becomes famous. We have one Lord—Jesus Christ—and it's our responsibility to glorify Him, not to make a name for ourselves. I'd love to be like one of the Thirty in God's army."

HOW ABOUT YOU?

Does serving Jesus and others seem dull? Do you wait for the time when you can be independent and not have to take orders anymore? Jesus instructed His people to serve. That's the way to true greatness.

TO MEMORIZE:

Among you it will be different. Whoever wants to be a leader among you must be your servant.

MATTHEW 20:26

BY CATHERINE RUNYON

July 31
ALWAYS TUNED IN

Read Psalm 86:1-7.

David looked at all the people lying on the beach and swimming in the ocean. He squinted in the sunlight to see people bobbing up and down in the water. Everyone was making noise—laughing, talking, shouting, or singing.

Suddenly a lifeguard jumped into the water. With quick strokes, he swam out into the deep water. In a few minutes a crowd gathered and watched as he rescued a drowning girl.

David asked later, "Dad, how did the lifeguard know that girl was drowning? I was standing right here. But there was so much noise all around me, I didn't hear her call for help."

"That's because your ears and eyes weren't tuned to hear or see that she was drowning," David's father replied. "Lifeguards have to take a lifesaving course," he explained. "They learn that when they are on duty, they must keep very alert. They must be able to see right away if someone is in trouble. And they must listen carefully so they hear a person's call for help."

GOD IS TUNED IN TO YOU.

David asked, "Isn't there a Bible verse that says God always hears us when we call?"

"Yes," replied Dad. "Throughout the psalms we learn that God hears and answers when we call to Him in prayer."

David looked up some of those verses. He was glad that God is always tuned in and ready to hear him.

HOW ABOUT YOU?

Can you think of some verses that assure you that God's eyes and ears are tuned in your direction? Learn the one below and see how many more you can find in your Bible. Then don't forget to thank God for His love and care.

TO MEMORIZE:

Call to me and I will answer you.

JEREMIAH 33:3, NIV

BY RUTH I. JAY

August 1

UNUSED LIGHT

Read Psalm 119:97-105.

It had been a busy day for Daniel, who was on a camping trip with his uncle Bob and cousin Eric. As the sun went down, two tired boys stretched out beside the campfire. "That was the best fish I ever ate," declared Daniel.

Uncle Bob nodded. "Now let's have some spiritual food before we turn in for the night," he said. "I hope you boys remembered your Bibles."

Eric nodded, but Daniel shook his head. "I don't need it," he said.

Uncle Bob raised his eyebrows. "The Word of God is a very important part of my life," he told Daniel. "Listen to what God says about it—He calls it a light." Uncle Bob turned to Psalm 119. The boys listened quietly as he read several verses and then prayed.

As the boys were unrolling their sleeping bags later, Daniel groaned. "The mosquitoes are terrible! Where's the bug spray?"

"It's in the car," said Uncle Bob. He picked up the flashlight. "I'll get it."

"Let's go with him, Daniel," suggested Eric. "Maybe we'll see a bear!"

READ YOUR BIBLE.

As they headed into the darkness, Daniel stumbled over a log. Then he saw Uncle Bob bump into a branch. "Why don't you turn on the flashlight, Uncle Bob?" he asked. "I can't see where I'm going."

"Flashlights are okay," Uncle Bob replied, "but I don't think I need one."

Daniel chuckled. "Okay, Uncle Bob, I get the point—we need light in the dark, and we need the Bible to give us light in our lives. Now, would you please turn on that flashlight?"

HOW ABOUT YOU?

It's foolish to stumble along and not use the light that's available, isn't it? Only the light of God's Word will keep you from stumbling into sin. Are you using it?

TO MEMORIZE:

[Your parents'] command is a lamp and their instruction a light.

PROVERBS 6:23

BY BARBARA J. WESTBERG

August 2

DON'T TELL

Read Proverbs 15:1-9.

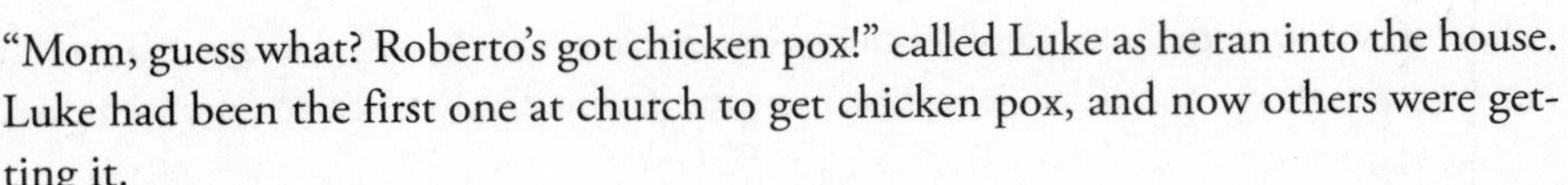

"Mom, guess what? Roberto's got chicken pox!" called Luke as he ran into the house. Luke had been the first one at church to get chicken pox, and now others were getting it.

Mom held up her hand and continued her phone conversation. As Luke listened, he figured out that his Sunday school teacher, Mr. Taylor, was moving to Texas.

"Don't tell anyone," Mom said when she hung up. "Mr. Taylor's boss is on vacation, so Mr. Taylor hasn't told him yet."

Luke didn't tell anyone about the Taylors—until Sunday. Then he told Eric that their teacher was moving. "But don't tell anyone," he added. And Eric didn't—until he told his sister, who told her friend Karen.

By the end of that week several more children had chicken pox—and several more people knew about the Taylors' move. Karen told her parents. They didn't know it was a secret, so they told another family. After a woman told the Taylors she would miss them when they moved, Mrs. Taylor told Luke's mother, "The news is out."

CONTROL YOUR TONGUE.

"Luke," said Mom, "did you tell anyone about the Taylors?"

"Well, just Eric. But I told him not to tell."

"Mr. Taylor wanted to tell his boss before someone else does, but now the news is all over town," said Mom. "News spreads fast."

"Like the chicken pox?" asked Luke.

"Yes," agreed Mother. "Once you exposed your friends to the chicken pox, there was nothing you could do to stop it. And when you tell a 'secret,' the story is sure to spread."

Luke went to the Taylors to apologize. He told the Lord he was sorry too.

HOW ABOUT YOU?

Are you a good friend? A good friend knows how to keep a secret. That means not telling even one person. When you're taken into someone's confidence, talk about it only to the Lord.

TO MEMORIZE:

The tongue of the wise makes knowledge appealing,
but the mouth of a fool belches out foolishness.
PROVERBS 15:2

BY LENORA MCWHORTEN

August 3

KEEP THE LIGHT ON

Read Psalm 119:97-105.

"Son, come here, please," Mom called from Patrick's room.

"What is it, Mom?" Patrick asked.

"This." Mom was holding up Patrick's Bible. "It's all covered with dust."

"Sorry, Mom," said Patrick. "I keep forgetting to dust that shelf by the bed."

"That's not what I meant," explained Mom. "When was the last time you read your Bible?"

Patrick shrugged. "Since we go to church on Sundays—twice—I figure I hear enough from the Bible there to last me through the week."

At bedtime Mom followed Patrick to his room, switched on the light, and then turned it off again. "Mom!" exclaimed Patrick. "I can't see!"

"But the light was on for a minute," said Mom. "Can't you remember where things are? Can't you make do with the light you got then?"

"Don't be silly," grumbled Patrick as he turned the light back on. "Once it's off, it doesn't do anything for me. So don't turn it off, okay?"

READ GOD'S WORD DAILY.

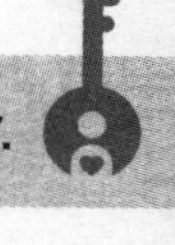

"But Patrick," said Mom, "isn't that what you've been trying to do with God? You told me that by going to church twice on Sundays, you learn enough about God to be able to skip reading your Bible during the week. But it doesn't work that way. You need to read God's Word every day in order to grow as a Christian."

"By not reading my Bible, I turn off the light on myself, huh?" asked Patrick. "Well, can I leave my light on awhile longer tonight? I want to read my Bible and 'turn on' my other 'light.'"

HOW ABOUT YOU?

Do you think that by going to church you can get through the rest of the week without bothering with daily devotions? That isn't true. Every day you need to turn on the light of God's Word for spiritual direction.

TO MEMORIZE:

The teaching of your word gives light, so even the simple can understand.

PSALM 119:130

BY DEBORAH S. MARETT

August 4

TREES NEED LEAVES

Read John 15:1-7.

Once a year Tyler visited his uncle and aunt. There he had a great time playing with his cousins and helping in his uncle's apple orchard. One day after Tyler had helped pick apples for a of couple hours, he was resting beneath one of the trees. Uncle Mike came and sat next to him. "Here, how about having an apple?"

"No thanks, Uncle Mike," Tyler replied. "I've had several already. I've just been sitting here wondering why apple trees grow so many leaves. Without leaves there'd be more room for apples."

"Oh, but Tyler, without the leaves there would be no apples," Uncle Mike stated.

"Are you sure?" Tyler wanted to know.

"Very sure," came his uncle's reply. "The leaves absorb sunshine, which gives the tree the strength to make fruit."

"How about that!" Tyler exclaimed.

"Here's something else that's important," Tyler's uncle continued. "Just as leaves soak up the sun, spelled s-u-n, in order to bear fruit, we need the Son, s-o-n, if we are to produce fruit."

LIVE IN THE SON-SHINE.

"What do you mean, Uncle Mike?"

"Many people try to live good lives and do good things," said Uncle Mike. "But without Jesus, the Son of God, their fruit—or good living—is worthless. We need Jesus living in our hearts and lives. That's why it's important to accept Him as Savior while we're young and learn all we can about Him as we grow up. He can help us live the way we ought to."

HOW ABOUT YOU?

Do you think you can get along without the Son of God? Do you try to produce fruit, or good deeds, in your own strength? You can do nothing good by yourself. You need God's Son, Jesus.

TO MEMORIZE:

I am the vine; you are the branches. Those who remain in me, and I in them, will produce much fruit. For apart from me you can do nothing.

JOHN 15:5

BY CHARLES VANDER MEER

Who Loves Me

Those who accept my commandments and obey them are the ones who love me. And because they love me, my Father will love them. And I will love them and reveal myself to each of them.

JOHN 14:21

We show Christ our love when we obey Him. He asks us to go through this process. And He promises His Father's love in return. When obedience is difficult, pray for strength. Jesus is always there for you. He promises to show Himself to those who know His commands and obey them.

Use this code to decipher the missing words below.

▼	●	★	♠	♦	✚	✣	♥	✦	♣	✪	✖	■
a	b	c	d	e	f	g	h	i	j	k	l	m

☆	✿	❑	◗	✔	➾	☎	✐	▲	➔	❖	☞	◒
n	o	p	q	r	s	t	u	v	w	x	y	z

I can do ▼ ✖ ✖ ☎ ♥ ✦ ☆ ✣ ➾
_ _ _   _ _ _ _ _ _

through ★ ♥ ✔ ✦ ➾ ☎
_ _ _ _ _ _

who ➾ ☎ ✔ ♦ ☆ ✣ ☎ ♥ ♦ ☆ ➾
_ _ _ _ _ _ _ _ _ _ _ me.

PHILIPPIANS 4:13, NKJV

ANSWER KEY
all things; Christ; strengthens

August 5

THE FLOATING KNIFE

Read Hebrews 4:12-16.

Malcolm and his father were enjoying one last fishing trip before the new school year began. "I know we're supposed to love everyone," said Malcolm as he stared at the river, "but I don't think I'll ever love Byron. He's a bully, and he makes me mad. How can I love him?"

Dad reeled in his line. "Malcolm," he said, taking out his pocketknife, "what do you think will happen if I toss this knife in the water?"

Malcolm looked at the knife. "It will sink like a rock, of course."

Dad said, "I think it will stay at the top."

"Don't throw it in the water," protested Malcolm. "Give it to me if you don't want it."

But Dad was taking out the biggest cork bobber he could find. He tied it to his fishing line. Just above it, he attached the knife. Malcolm watched Dad throw it all into the river. First it sank, but then it began to float.

GOD CAN DO THE IMPOSSIBLE.

"No fair," said Malcolm. "The cork is floating and the knife is just riding along."

"I didn't say it would float by itself," replied Dad. "That would be impossible. But with the help of the cork, it's carried along at the top of the water. It reminds me that God gives many commands that would be impossible for me to carry out by myself. But when I trust Him to help me, He holds me up and carries me along."

"I get the point, Dad." Malcolm grinned. "I'll ask God to help me love Byron. I really will."

HOW ABOUT YOU?

Is it hard for you to witness for Jesus? To quit complaining? To be cheerful? To be unselfish? God gives many commands that you can't obey by yourself—but with His help, you can.

TO MEMORIZE:

I can do everything through Christ, who gives me strength.

PHILIPPIANS 4:13

BY HAZEL W. MARETT

August 6

DEBBY'S DIARY

Read 2 Peter 3:13-15, 18.

Debby and her mother were cleaning the attic when Debby found a small book with a key. "Look! My old diary!" she exclaimed. "I started writing in this when I was five." She pointed to the large, crooked letters on one page. "I can hardly read it," she said with a laugh.

Her mother smiled. "Your writing improved through the years, though."

"Yeah, it keeps getting better," agreed Debby. "Look at this page. I wrote this two years ago, when I was nine. This writing looks almost like the way I write now."

"Yes, it does," said Mother, and your spelling hasn't changed much either. You still spell *friend* 'f-r-e-i-n-d,' the way it is here."

Debby blushed. "I always did have trouble with that word."

Mom grew thoughtful. "Sometimes our learning seems to stop—even our learning about how to live as Christians," she said. "When I first asked Jesus to be my Savior, I was always learning new things from God's Word. But the changes and improvements started coming more slowly after a while. I wonder if I'm any more like Jesus now than I was five years ago."

KEEP GROWING IN CHRIST.

"I asked Jesus to be my Savior just three years ago," Debby said, "but I know what you mean, Mom. What do you think happens?"

"It's easy to get lazy," said Mom. "I'm going to confess that to the Lord and ask Him to help me start learning to be more like Him."

"Me, too!" Debby agreed. "Let's start today."

HOW ABOUT YOU?

Have you accepted Jesus as your Savior? If so, think back to that time. Were you more enthusiastic and committed to Him then than you are now? Ask Him to renew your devotion to Him. Until you reach heaven, there will always be room for improvement.

TO MEMORIZE:

Look how far you have fallen! Turn back to me and do the works you did at first.

REVELATION 2:5

BY SHERRY L. KUYT

August 7

ICE, WATER, AND STEAM

Read 1 John 5:5-8.

"This is the life," said Samuel as he sat with his back propped against an old log. He and his cousin, Shawn, were spending the day in a state park with their grandfather.

"I feel close to God out here," said Grandpa.

Shawn nodded. He said, "Our youth leader told us God is one God but three persons. There is God the Father, God the Son, and God the Holy Spirit. That's hard to understand."

"I don't understand it either," said Samuel. "But I'm hungry—let's start lunch, Grandpa. Should we get water from the spring?"

Grandpa walked over to the ice chest. "Let's use some ice for cooking water," he said, dropping several ice cubes into a pan that he set on a rack over the campfire. "I think it might help us understand something." The boys watched as the ice began melting into water. Soon the water was steaming.

GOD IS THREE IN ONE.

"Did you notice that first there was ice, then it melted into water, and then some of that water turned into steam?" asked Grandpa. "It's the same substance, but in three different forms."

Shawn looked at Grandpa. "That's a little like God, right? He's one God, but he has three different forms."

Grandpa nodded. "Of course, God is much greater than water. After all, He made water! But seeing water in these three forms can help us understand God in three persons."

The boys agreed. "It's good to think about God and His greatness," added Samuel. He grinned. "And now I'd like to change some food to a different form. I'm still hungry!"

HOW ABOUT YOU?

Do you find the Trinity hard to understand? God does not ask you to understand it perfectly. Just remember that we serve one God, not three—but He does have three forms. Give thanks for our great Creator God.

TO MEMORIZE:

So we have these three witnesses—the Spirit, the water, and the blood—and all three agree.

1 JOHN 5:7-8

BY CAROLYN E. YOST

August 8

THE BEAR FACTS

Read Ephesians 5:14-20.

Tamara was excited. It was the first time Dad had taken her bow hunting. As Tamara squinted into the low sun, she noticed rows of corn in the field nearby. Glancing around, her gaze froze on something large and black. Black? Deer are tan! Tamara shivered. Then she whispered, "Dad, something is out there!"

Just then the animal stood on its hind legs, revealing that it was a large black bear. It raised its head and sniffed the air. Tamara and Dad stood still in amazement at this rare sight. Still sniffing, the bear slowly moved to the edge of the woods. It gazed longingly at the corn. After several minutes the bear lumbered toward the field. Soon, however, it returned to the woods.

Driving home later, Tamara asked, "Did you see how much the bear wanted that corn?"

"Yes, but it sensed danger, so it wouldn't stay out in the open," replied Dad. "The Bible tells us that, just like that bear, we should be careful how we live."

"What does that mean, Dad?" asked Tamara.

WALK CAREFULLY.

"Well, it means that Christians are to be careful about what we do and where we go—looking around to spot temptations. Then we won't get trapped by sin or a trick of the devil."

When they got home, Mom asked about their hunting trip. "Don't make up a story about hundreds of deer," she joked. "Just tell me the bare facts."

Dad grinned and winked at Tamara. "All right. We'll just tell you the 'bear' facts!"

HOW ABOUT YOU?

Are you foolish about the way you live, or are you careful in all that you do? Do you stay away from places where you might be tempted to do wrong? Do you avoid people who encourage you to sin? Be careful to live as God wants you to live. Be wise.

TO MEMORIZE:

Be careful how you live. Don't live like fools, but like those who are wise.

EPHESIANS 5:15

BY LOIS A. TEUFEL

August 9

THE TRANSLATORS

Read Isaiah 43:10-12.

Rodney rolled a piece of paper into a ball and flicked it toward Joshua. Eric snickered.

Rodney turned toward Eric. He was glad Eric had come along to Sunday school today to hear the missionary speaker from Africa.

Mr. Telsen, the missionary, was saying something, but Rodney didn't understand a word of it. Mr. Telsen was speaking in a tribal language. "How many of you understood what I said?" he asked. When no one raised a hand, Mr. Telsen again spoke in the foreign tongue. This time Mrs. Telsen repeated his words in English.

"We translate the Bible into languages that people can read," said Mr. Telsen. "But many of our people cannot read. So we translate God's message to them by our lives. Besides telling them what it means to be a Christian, we show them by helping them, sharing with them, and being kind to them."

Mr. Telsen looked around the group. "Maybe you have friends who don't understand the Bible. Maybe you need to translate what it means to be a Christian," continued Mr. Telsen. "How can you do that?"

WITNESS WITH YOUR LIFE.

Joshua raised his hand. "By sharing our toys and stuff," he said.

"By bringing them to Sunday school," added Rodney.

But he gulped when he heard the next suggestion: "By sitting quietly in church so they won't be disturbed and can hear the message."

"Good!" said Mr. Telsen. "Ask God to make all of us good translators of His Word."

HOW ABOUT YOU?

What kind of translator are you? Are you kind? Forgiving? Willing to share? Obedient? Friendly? Do those around you get a correct idea of what it means to be a Christian? Think about it.

TO MEMORIZE:

You will receive power when the Holy Spirit comes upon you. And you will be my witnesses, telling people about me everywhere—in Jerusalem, throughout Judea, in Samaria, and to the ends of the earth.

ACTS 1:8

BY HAZEL W. MARETT

August 10
CUT OFF

Read 1 Corinthians 12:20-27.

"I just think it's silly. I don't want to go!"

As Tammy slammed down the phone, her mother asked, "Where don't you want to go?"

"Oh, some kids in my Sunday school class are going to take cookies to the retirement home. I wanted to take them to the day care center—but we have to do what Becky wants."

"Didn't your class just have a party?" Mom wanted to know.

Tammy responded, "I didn't go. They play stupid games! Becky's always got to be the leader, and Regina thinks she's so cool."

Mom watched as Tammy went out to get the newspaper. When Tammy came inside, she pointed to an article and picture in the paper. "Listen! 'Local Boy's Hand Restored.' That's Eddie!" she said excitedly.

Together they read about the accident in which the young boy's hand had been severed from his arm. The doctors were able to sew his hand back on, and there was a good chance he'd be able to use it again.

WE NEED ONE ANOTHER.

After a restless evening, Tammy went to bed. Later Mom stopped at the door of her room. "What's the matter, honey?" she asked gently.

"I'm so lonely," Tammy sobbed. "Why can't I get along with my friends?"

Mom said, "You've cut yourself off from them, Tammy. If they don't do things your way, you refuse to have anything to do with them. Without Christian friends, you're like a hand that's no longer connected to the body."

"I guess I have cut myself off from the group," Tammy said slowly. Then she brightened. "But now I know what's wrong, and I know what to do about it. Good night, Mom. And thanks."

HOW ABOUT YOU?

If things don't go your way, do you refuse to cooperate? Are your actions cutting you off from your friends? Christian friends are important, so ask God to forgive your selfishness. Be willing to sometimes do things someone else's way.

TO MEMORIZE:

Yes, the body has many different parts, not just one part.

1 CORINTHIANS 12:14

BY BARBARA J. WESTBERG

August 11

A HOUSE DIVIDED

Read Luke 11:14-20.

"Look at the way Kim is wearing her hair," snickered Beth to her friend Cayla.

Just then Kim turned and looked at the girls. She seemed to know they were talking about her, but she just said hello quietly and sat down.

This is how Mrs. Newton began the Sunday school class. "Someone said, 'A house divided against itself cannot stand.' Who was it?"

Beth's hand shot up. "Abraham Lincoln. We just studied the Civil War in school."

"Right," said Mrs. Newton. "Our country's people were fighting each other, and Abraham Lincoln wanted to teach Americans that they needed to be united if they wanted to be a strong country. But did you know that Jesus first spoke almost those exact words?"

There were many looks of surprise as Mrs. Newton continued, "Unity among Christians is even more important." For the rest of the class time Mrs. Newton read many Scripture verses to teach the class how to show Christian unity. "When we talk about others in an unfriendly way or do things that hurt other Christians rather than help them, we're dividing our own house," concluded Mrs. Newton.

CHRISTIANS SHOULD BE UNITED.

Beth thought of her unkind words about Kim's hair. She knew she had divided God's family instead of helping it grow strong. Silently she asked God to forgive her, and after class she went up to Kim. She asked, "Would you like to come over to my house this afternoon?"

Kim smiled. "I'd like that," she said.

HOW ABOUT YOU?

Do you sometimes say unkind things about other Christians? Do you think it will make you look better? Not so. You not only hurt that person, but you also hurt yourself and other Christians. When Christians are divided against each other, the whole church suffers. Work together, not against one another.

TO MEMORIZE:

Any kingdom divided by civil war is doomed. A family splintered by feuding will fall apart.

LUKE 11:17

BY CAROLYN E. YOST

All Your Heart

Joyful are those who obey his laws and search for him with all their hearts.
PSALM 119:2

As we search for God, we show our desire to learn more about Him. We gain knowledge of what He wants. And when we desire obedience, obeying His laws is easier. God promises joy and blessings in return.

Draw lines to match each of the Ten Commandments in numeric order. (*Hint: Look up Exodus 20 if you need help.*)

1.	a. Use God's name with respect.
2.	b. Don't wish for others' things.
3.	c. Tell the truth.
4.	d. Don't kill.
5.	e. Rest on the seventh day to honor God.
6.	f. Don't make anything more important than God.
7.	g. Respect your parents.
8.	h. Don't steal.
9.	i. Love God more than anything.
10.	j. Be faithful in your marriage.

ANSWER KEY
1./f.; 2./i.; 3./a.; 4./e.; 5./g.; 6./d.; 7./j.; 8./h.; 9./c.; 10./b.

August 12

NEVER TOO BUSY

Read Psalm 17:5-8.

"Dad," said Craig, "can I talk to you?"

"I'm sorry, Son," Dad replied, "but I need to get an oil filter before the auto store closes."

Craig wandered out to the yard where his mother was raking leaves. "Mom, today in math class Taylor Matthews said—"

"Can't it wait, Craig?" asked Mom. "I'm going inside to make a few phone calls right now. We can talk while we're eating supper."

But during supper Dad and Mom kept talking about Dad's job and family finances. That evening Craig called his friend Bob. "Wait till you hear what Taylor said today," Craig began. But Bob cut him short.

"Sorry, Craig. I gotta go. My favorite TV show's on."

Later, as Craig was climbing into bed, his parents came in to say good night. "Did you want to talk about something?" asked Dad.

GOD ALWAYS LISTENS.

Craig smiled. "Well, I did—but I don't anymore." Then he explained. "I wanted to tell you about Taylor Matthews, who's in my math class and always makes fun of me. But you and Mom were both busy, and Bob was too. So I talked to God about it! After that I began thinking that Taylor might be jealous because I get better grades than he does. I think I'll offer to help him."

Both Dad and Mom looked surprised and pleased. "I'm sorry we didn't listen, Son," said Dad, "but it sounds like you learned that God is never too busy to listen to His children!"

HOW ABOUT YOU?

Are your parents sometimes too busy to talk? Do you wish you had a friend who would always listen to what you have to say? Let Jesus be that friend. Talk to Him whenever you have a problem, or if you just feel lonely. He's never too busy!

TO MEMORIZE:

I look to the LORD *for help. I wait confidently for God to save me, and my God will certainly hear me.*

MICAH 7:7

BY SHERRY L. KUYT

August 13

NO TIME TO EAT

Read 1 Peter 2:1-5.

Fernando grabbed his schoolbooks and ran out the door. If he didn't hurry, he'd be late for class! It was that way every day—he'd sleep too long and then have to hurry to get ready. But no matter how late he was, he'd always take time for a big breakfast.

One day a nutritionist, Mr. Pierson, came to speak to the youth group at church. He spoke about Fernando's favorite subject—eating! "How many hours are there between breakfast and lunch?" Mr. Pierson asked one of the girls.

"About four or five," she replied.

"How many hours between lunch and supper?" he continued.

"About the same," was the answer.

He pointed to Fernando. "And how many hours from supper time until you eat again?"

"Too many," moaned Fernando.

"Now let's ask those same questions about our spiritual food," Mr. Pierson said. "How long does your spiritual body have to wait for food from the Word of God?"

EAT SPIRITUAL FOOD.

Fernando was glad he did not have to answer that question out loud. He hadn't been very faithful about having his spiritual food lately. Sometimes he'd go from one Sunday to the next without even opening his Bible.

"If you skip meals," the nutritionist was saying, "your physical body suffers. And if you do not regularly read the Word of God, your spiritual body will suffer. Don't forget Peter's reminder to cry out for spiritual food just as a baby cries for milk. We grow only when we eat."

As the youth meeting ended, Fernando decided he'd get up early from now on. He would read the Bible and pray before breakfast.

HOW ABOUT YOU?

Did you eat your meals today? Did you also read God's Word? It's important to take care of both your physical and spiritual needs on a daily basis.

TO MEMORIZE:

God blesses those who hunger and thirst for justice, for they will be satisfied.

MATTHEW 5:6

BY RUTH I. JAY

August 14

KEEP ON SWINGING

Read Proverbs 14:23-27.

As soon as he got home from school, Kevin went to his room and got out pencils, paints, and poster paper. Kevin wanted to win the library's art contest. So every afternoon that week he hurried home to work on his poster.

By Friday the poster was finished, and Dad drove him to the library. Kevin's heart beat heavily as he waited for the judges' decision. He watched while one of them put a third-prize ribbon on one of the posters. It wasn't Kevin's. The second-prize ribbon went on another poster, but it wasn't his either. Finally one of the judges picked up the first-prize ribbon, walked over to a poster, and attached it. Tears boiled up in Kevin's eyes. He had not won a prize.

When Mom came home later she asked, "How did the poster contest go, Kevin?"

"Terrible! I'm never going to enter a contest again," Kevin said.

Mom said, "Did you know that Babe Ruth, the famous ballplayer, struck out many times?"

KEEP TRYING.

"But I thought he was so good," said Kevin.

"He was," Mom replied. "He was the first player to hit sixty home runs in a season. But he was a good player because he kept swinging that bat when others would have given up."

"I guess you're telling me I shouldn't give up in art," sighed Kevin.

Mom smiled. "You enjoy art and you do have talent. Besides, God blesses hard work. Even if you never win a prize, you'll become a better artist if you keep practicing."

Kevin hesitated. "The missions committee at church is having an art contest. I think I'll take a 'swing' at that."

HOW ABOUT YOU?

Do you keep trying even though you're discouraged? If God has given you an interest in something, and a talent for it, keep on trying even if you're not the best in it yet. Ask God to bless your efforts.

TO MEMORIZE:

Work brings profit, but mere talk leads to poverty!

PROVERBS 14:23

BY CAROLYN E. YOST

August 15

PART-TIME FRIEND

Read John 15:8-14.

As Lynn got on the school bus, she looked for Stacy, her best friend from church. Stacy was transferring to her school. Of course, Stacy was a grade ahead of her, but they would see each other at lunch and ride the same bus. *Now that I have a Christian friend at school, I'll witness like I should,* Lynn said to herself.

Stacy hadn't been on the bus that morning, because her mother had taken her to school to enroll. Lynn had missed her at lunch, too, so now she was eager to see Stacy.

Soon Stacy and two other girls boarded the bus. They were giggling and having a great time. "Stacy, I've saved you a seat," said Lynn.

"Oh, that's okay. I'm with Beth and Amy."

All the way home Lynn heard the happy chatter of the three girls. Sobs stuck in her throat. At her stop she jumped off the bus. Once inside the house, she couldn't hold back the sobs.

"What's wrong?" her older sister asked.

Lynn hid her face on her big sister's shoulder. "S-S-Stacy already has fr-friends at s-s-school. She's just my friend at ch-church."

BE A TRUE FRIEND OF JESUS.

"That's too bad," said Lynn's sister after she had heard all about it. "But isn't that the way you've been treating your best Friend?"

Lynn shook her head. "I'd never ignore her."

"Not her, Lynn, Him—Jesus. You always say you don't want to talk to anyone about Him."

"Oh!" Lynn gasped. "You're right—I have hurt my best Friend. I've been ignoring Him when I'm with kids who don't know Him. I've got some apologizing to do to Jesus."

HOW ABOUT YOU?

Are you a friend Jesus can depend on, or do you act as if you don't know Him when you're with people who aren't Christians? Be a true friend to Jesus—show that you love Him at all times. Talk to Him and talk about Him.

TO MEMORIZE:

A friend is always loyal.

PROVERBS 17:17

BY BARBARA J. WESTBERG

August 16

A GOOD FUSE

Read 1 Corinthians 10:12-14.

Nikolai thought, *Mrs. Gray's rule is stupid. What if I cheat just once?* The rule was that those who spelled all the words right on a trial test in the middle of the week could go out early for recess on Friday while the rest of the class repeated the test. Nikolai and his friends planned a way to peek at the answers so they'd be sure to get extra recess time.

As a Christian Nikolai knew it was wrong to cheat, but the others were counting on him. He didn't know what to do.

Dad was cleaning up after dinner that evening when the lights went out. "Oh no! I blew a fuse by using too many appliances at once."

Nikolai watched his father replace the burned-out fuse. "How do those things work?" Nikolai asked.

"Well," said Dad, "wires run through the walls to switches and electrical outlets. If too many things are turned on at once, it requires so much electricity that the wires could get hot and cause a fire. But the fuse burns out and stops the flow of electricity when it's not safe."

YOU DON'T HAVE TO SIN.

Nikolai and Dad started back up the stairs. "The fuse reminds me of what God does for us," Dad added. "He'll never let such a great temptation come our way that we can't handle it. He stops it before it can get that bad."

As Nikolai went to his room, he knew he didn't have to cheat. God would help him be honest. He took out his list of words and began to study.

HOW ABOUT YOU?

Do you sometimes feel that you can't help doing something wrong—that the temptation is just too great? You're wrong. No matter what the temptation, you can be sure that God will help you overcome it if you'll let Him.

TO MEMORIZE:

The temptations in your life are no different from what others experience. And God is faithful. He will not allow the temptation to be more than you can stand. When you are tempted, he will show you a way out so that you can endure.

1 CORINTHIANS 10:13

BY HAZEL W. MARETT

August 17

NOBODY'S PERFECT

Read Luke 18:10-14.

"Oh well! Nobody's perfect!" laughed Jody as she missed the basket. The other girls laughed with her. They always knew when they would hear Jody say, "Nobody's perfect."

Later Jody went with her friend Robin to an after-school Bible class. She did not agree with the Bible teacher. "No matter how good you are," said Mrs. Gates, "you're not good enough for heaven. You're a sinner. The only way you can get into heaven is to believe that and accept Jesus as your Savior."

As the girls walked home Jody said, "Mrs. Gates makes it sound like everybody's a terrible sinner. I'm not that bad!"

"You may be a decent kid," replied Robin, "but you know you've done things that are wrong. I remember when you and I sneaked—"

Jody laughed. "But even that wasn't so bad. And there are good people like Uncle Joe, who gives lots of money to church."

Suddenly she stopped. "We passed my street, and I forgot to turn. Oh well! Nobody's perfect!"

SIN CANNOT ENTER HEAVEN.

"You said it," said Robin, laughing. "I didn't. But God said it too. He said we've all sinned, and no sin can enter heaven. No matter how much good you or your uncle do, you still have to get rid of your sin. Only Jesus can take it away."

Jody thought about that as she turned and headed back toward her own street.

HOW ABOUT YOU?

Are you fit for heaven? No lying, disobedience, cheating, gossip—nor any other sin—is allowed to enter heaven. In today's Scripture one man had done good things. The other admitted he had done bad things. Jesus says the one who asked for God's mercy is the one who was saved. You can confess your sin too, and ask Jesus to forgive and save you.

TO MEMORIZE:

Nothing evil will be allowed to enter, nor anyone who practices shameful idolatry and dishonesty—but only those whose names are written in the Lamb's Book of Life.

REVELATION 21:27

BY HAZEL W. MARETT

August 18

READ AND OBEY

Read 2 Timothy 3:14-17.

Kelsey slipped quietly through the kitchen, hoping to avoid her mom. She hung her jacket in the closet and tried to sneak to her bedroom, but Mom appeared in the doorway. "Hi, honey," Mom greeted cheerfully. "How did you do on that math test?"

"Not so hot," Kelsey answered. "And I studied hard." She handed the test to her mother.

"You didn't follow directions," Mom said. "When will you learn to read directions first?"

"I don't know," Kelsey mumbled.

"Yesterday you tried to make cupcakes without following the recipe. What happened?"

"I blew it," admitted Kelsey, head down.

"And what about the time I told you how to do the laundry, but you didn't follow directions?"

FOLLOW GOD'S DIRECTIONS.

Kelsey giggled this time. "Dad ended up with pink underwear."

Mom smiled too, but only briefly. "Kelsey, failure to follow directions could harm you—both physically and spiritually."

"What do you mean?" Kelsey asked.

"God's Word is full of instructions for us. When we neglect to follow those instructions, we cause ourselves a lot of grief," Mom explained.

"Or sometimes we don't even bother to read the instructions at all," Kelsey added.

"Right," Mom agreed, "and unless we read them—on math tests or in the Bible—we can't possibly obey them."

"Mom, I'm going to make a real effort to do better from now on. I don't want to fail any more tests!" Kelsey said with determination.

HOW ABOUT YOU?

When was the last time you read God's Word? The Bible contains many specific directions and many principles to follow. Read it and follow the instructions God gives.

TO MEMORIZE:

All Scripture is inspired by God and is useful to teach us what is true and to make us realize what is wrong in our lives. It corrects us when we are wrong and teaches us to do what is right.

2 TIMOTHY 3:16

BY BRENDA DECKER

A Way Out

God is faithful. He will not allow the temptation to be more than you can stand. When you are tempted, he will show you a way out so that you can endure.

1 CORINTHIANS 10:13

Temptation to do the wrong thing happens. We know what's wrong (for example, bullying, gossiping, or saying mean things). When you are tempted, remember God's promise. There is a way out. You can walk away. And He promises to help you handle it.

Unscramble the words that are related to the term *obey*.

debai ______________________________

eareg ______________________________

plomyc ______________________________

cornmof ______________________________

feedr ______________________________

veers ______________________________

mistub ______________________________

dererruns ______________________________

diely ______________________________

ANSWER KEY

abide; agree; comply; conform; defer; serve; submit; surrender; yield

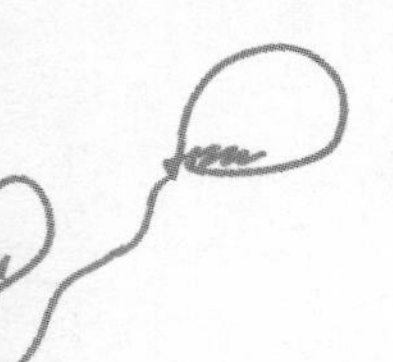

August 19

BIG LITTLE THINGS

Read Ephesians 4:24-32.

It had been a terrible day for Lanita! In the first place, Mom had said they were out of bread and Lanita would have to buy her lunch at school. Then Dad had said he couldn't take her to school, so she had to ride the bus.

Lanita was mad when she went to school, she was madder when she came home, and she was maddest now! She was old enough to know when to go to bed without being sent there like a baby!

Lanita didn't even feel like praying. She had just pulled the sheet over her head when there was a gentle knock on the door.

Mom came in and handed Lanita her robe. She said, "Put this on, honey. There's something outside Dad wants you to see."

Outside, Dad pointed to the moon. "It looks so big and close," murmured Lanita.

Dad reached into his pocket. "Now hold this dime in front of you like this." He held it out from his face an arm's length. Then he handed it to Lanita. "What do you see?" he asked.

DON'T FUSS ABOUT LITTLE THINGS.

"Just a dime," Lanita replied.

Dad nodded. "You can block out a big, beautiful moon with one little dime," he said. "And you can shut yourself off from beautiful things like love, happiness, and even God when you make a big fuss about little things."

Lanita gave her father his dime. Then she gave him a hug. "Thanks, Dad. I needed that!"

HOW ABOUT YOU?

Do you make a big fuss about little things? Anger can ruin your day, your week—even your life. Make up your mind now not to let little things get between you and happiness—or between you and God.

TO MEMORIZE:

This false teaching is like a little yeast spreads quickly through the whole batch of dough!
GALATIANS 5:9

BY BARBARA J. WESTBERG

August 20

THE PROBLEM

Read Psalm 119:18.

Ric was upset. No matter how hard he tried, he just couldn't solve his math problem. "This book has to be wrong," he said.

His father looked up from the stove. "What's your problem, Ric?"

"This math book is the problem," said Ric.

Dad turned off the burner. "Let me see it, Son. Maybe we can solve the problem together."

Rick's father compared his son's work with the book's instructions. Then he studied the examples in the text. "I see what went wrong, Ric. You divided when you should have multiplied," he said.

"I guess you're right, Dad," Ric admitted. "Why didn't I notice that?"

"You were so sure the book was wrong that you gave up trying to understand," Dad replied. "The problem wasn't the book. It was your lack of understanding."

"I heard that," said Mom, coming into the room. "It sounds like the way some people treat the Bible. Just because they don't understand all of God's Word, they think the Bible is wrong."

GOD'S WORD IS WITHOUT ERROR.

Dad nodded and said, "God's Word is true, but sometimes our understanding of it is faulty. Some things in the Bible might remain a mystery to us until we get to heaven, but that's okay. We don't need to understand all of it now."

"I'm glad," Ric said with a grin. "I have a big enough problem understanding math!"

HOW ABOUT YOU?

Do you excuse yourself from reading God's Word because you don't understand all of it? You don't need to understand everything to believe it's all true. Ask God to give you wisdom as you read it. Look up unfamiliar words in a dictionary. The more you read God's Word, the more you will understand it.

TO MEMORIZE:

Every word of God proves true. He is a shield to all who come to him for protection.

PROVERBS 30:5

BY JAN L. HANSEN

August 21

ANYONE FOR GARBAGE?

Read Philippians 4:4-9.

When Harrison came home from school, he was very hungry. He hadn't had an after-school snack because he had stayed for soccer practice. He peered into the pot of spaghetti sauce simmering on the stove. "My favorite!" He smacked his lips. "When do we eat?"

"In fifteen minutes," answered Grandma. "I have some chores for you to do first."

By the time Harrison finished his chores, he was starved. Grandma had one more chore for him—taking out the garbage. Before handing it to him she said, "Wait a minute." Then, taking a plate off the table, she carefully scooped some of the garbage from the bag onto the plate.

Harrison stared in disbelief at the peelings, coffee grounds, and leftovers heaped together in one soggy mess. "What in the world is that for?" he asked in surprise.

"This is your dinner," said Grandma.

"My dinner!" He stared at his grandmother. "I can't eat smelly garbage!"

Grandma said, "Garbage is what you're feeding your mind, so I figured we could feed garbage to your body, too." She took some magazines from the top of the refrigerator. "I found these under your blankets when I changed the sheets today. It upset me—so think how the Lord must feel about your reading these."

Harrison knew his grandma was right. Those magazines and the pictures in them were garbage. His mind shouldn't feed on them. Ever since he'd bought them, he'd felt guilty and unhappy. "I'll throw them out right now, Grandma," he said. "And I won't buy any more. Honest."

HOW ABOUT YOU?

Do you refuse to look at pictures in magazines, on TV, or on the Internet that make your mind and heart dirty? If not, ask God to forgive you for feeding your mind on the world's garbage. Ask Him to help you think about pure, good things instead.

TO MEMORIZE:

I will refuse to look at anything vile and vulgar.

PSALM 101:3

BY MATILDA H. NORDTVEDT

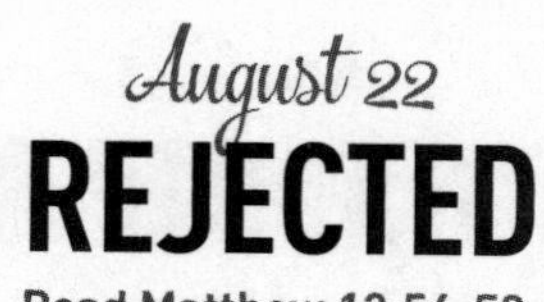

REJECTED

Read Matthew 13:54-58.

Tears streamed down Melanie's face as she came in the back door. "Nancy is having a birthday party on Saturday," she cried. "She invited all the girls in our class except me. Mom, why didn't she invite me? It's not fair."

Mom put her arms around Melanie and hugged her. "I'm sorry, honey," she said. "I know it hurts to feel rejected. We want our friends and family to accept us. When they don't, our hearts ache."

Melanie wiped her eyes and looked at her mother in surprise. "Have you ever felt rejected?"

"Do you remember when I wanted to work part-time at the school?" asked Mom. "They hired someone else, so I didn't get the job. That was rejection, and it hurt." She smiled. "I got over it, though, and you will too. Maybe it will help to remember that no one felt unloved more than Jesus did."

"Yeah, but Jesus' friends didn't reject Him. It was His enemies who crucified Him," Melanie pointed out.

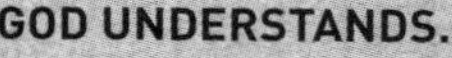

"Let's read something," said Mom, getting a Bible. Together they read about one day when Jesus taught in the synagogue at Nazareth.

"Does this mean Jesus' friends didn't believe Him?" Melanie asked.

Mom nodded. "They rejected Him," she said. "One of His own disciples betrayed Him. And the others left Him when He was arrested."

"I guess He does know how I feel right now," Melanie said, surprised.

"Yes," Mom assured her. "He understands and cares."

HOW ABOUT YOU?

Do you feel rejected when someone says no to you or forgets you? Remember that Jesus knows how rejection feels. He knows and cares how you feel. Let that comfort you, and then think about those who have hurt you and treat them the way you think Jesus would treat them.

TO MEMORIZE:

Give all your worries and cares to God, for he cares about you.

1 PETER 5:7

BY MARILYN J. SENTERFITT

THE DYNAMITE BLAST

Read Psalm 34:17-19.

Bethanne didn't feel like going on the class field trip to the rock quarry. She just wanted her lost kitten to come home. And she wanted her daddy to get his job back.

The quarry superintendent met their bus and handed out hard hats. "We're going to have a dynamite blast today to break up the stone in the quarry," he said.

A loud horn sounded a warning. A moment later it sounded again. "The horn goes off three times before the blast," the superintendent explained. "We blow it one time after the blast to let everyone know it's safe again." The third horn blared. Then, *boom*! A loud explosion sounded while the children watched the side of the pit break up and rise into the air. When the "all-clear" horn sounded, the superintendent allowed the children to take a closer look. They also saw the men who had controlled the operation.

As Bethanne told her family about the trip that evening, she picked up a picture of her cat. "It seems like we've had a dynamite blast in our house," she said. "Everything's fallen apart."

GOD IS IN CONTROL.

"Sometimes our world does seem to be blowing to pieces," Mom agreed. "But those men at the quarry who control the blasts remind me that God is in control of our lives. And just as the stone company profits from their explosions, we can profit from troubles by learning to trust God through tough times." She smiled. "Bethanne, the quarry's horn sounds to make sure everyone gets to a safe place. In our case, God is with us throughout every experience we face, so we are always safe."

HOW ABOUT YOU?

Are you having a rough day? When difficult things happen, remember that God is in control and will work through the hard situations to strengthen your life for Him.

TO MEMORIZE:

The righteous person faces many troubles, but the
LORD comes to the rescue each time.
PSALM 34:19

BY NANCE E. KEYES

August 24

THROW IT OUT

Read Leviticus 19:16-18.

"Let's go to the sidewalk sale," said Paige.

Mom sighed. "I'd love to, but we'll have to clean up the kitchen first."

"Okay," agreed Paige. "I'll clean the fridge."

After working silently for several minutes, Mom asked, "Would you like to invite Melissa to go with us?"

"No," Paige answered sharply as she unloaded the refrigerator shelves. "Melissa is Amy's friend now."

"You could invite Amy, too," Mom suggested.

"No," snapped Paige. Then she added, "Melissa knows I can't stand Amy. Last year Amy said some mean things about me, and she—phew! What do I smell?"

Mom grimaced. "You must have uncovered something spoiled," she said.

Paige gingerly picked up a bowl. "It's this old tuna casserole. Phewweee!"

Mom reached for it. "Let's get rid of this."

A few minutes later Mom said, "Paige, sometimes we keep old things inside of us until they spoil and cause our attitude to stink. The grudge you've been carrying against Amy is beginning to stink."

DON'T HOLD GRUDGES.

"But, Mom," began Paige, "she said . . ."

"I know. You've told me at least twenty times," Mom reminded her. "And you have said some pretty nasty things about her, too." Paige hadn't thought of that. "Maybe it's time to throw that stinking grudge out," Mom said gently.

A few minutes later Paige called Amy. "Would you and Melissa like to go shopping with my mom and me today?"

HOW ABOUT YOU?

Are you carrying a nasty, stinking grudge? Ask God to help you get rid of it today. Ask Him to give you a sweet and forgiving spirit.

TO MEMORIZE:

Don't grumble about each other, brothers and sisters, or you will be judged. For look—the Judge is standing at the door!

JAMES 5:9

BY BARBARA J. WESTBERG

August 25
OVERLOAD

Read Luke 12:15-21.

"There's a For Sale sign at the house on the corner," said Mikayla one morning. "Can we look at it, Dad? It's so neat!"

"It's too expensive," said Dad.

Mom added, "I think the only way we could pay for that house would be to live on canned spaghetti and powdered milk for thirty years."

Mikayla sighed. "I wish we were richer. Couldn't you and Dad get second jobs?"

"Mikayla," said her mother, "do you remember what happened when we tried to make a super-duper buffet lunch last week?"

"Yeah." Mikayla laughed. "We had the oven going, and every appliance we own was plugged in. And we blew one fuse after another!"

"Yes," said Mom. "We ended up with a lot of half-cooked food because we tried to do too much. Can you see how we might learn something from that experience?"

"Well," said Mikayla thoughtfully, "do you mean that we could overload ourselves, like we overloaded the wiring?"

THINGS DON'T SATISFY.

Mom nodded. "More possessions, along with more debt, might make us lose track of what really matters," she said. "Let's just thank the Lord for leading us to a safe and comfortable home we can afford."

HOW ABOUT YOU?

Do you sometimes wish your parents were richer? Surprisingly, many rich people worry so much about their possessions that they can't enjoy them. Money provides physical comforts, but it cannot satisfy the hunger and thirst of the spirit. It's much better to have a rich relationship with God than to be rich in the things of this world. Don't overburden yourself seeking riches that don't satisfy.

TO MEMORIZE:

Seek the Kingdom of God above all else, and he will give you everything you need.

LUKE 12:31

BY LORNA B. MARLOWE

Pass the Test

God blesses those who patiently endure testing and temptation. Afterward they will receive the crown of life that God has promised to those who love him.

JAMES 1:12

What if obedience were simply a test to take every day? It seems that practice would make perfect. And God promises us so much more than good grades in return.

Describe what you did during a time when you felt led into temptation by others.

____

____

____

What would you do now?

____

____

Describe another time when you faced temptation on your own, without other people tempting you. What did you do then?

____

____

____

What would you do now?

____

____

What if we practiced resisting temptation as hard as we practice for the subject we love best?

August 26

STANDING THE TEST

Read 1 Corinthians 3:10-15.

Kaleen looked at the pictures in her Bible storybook. "Isn't this one pretty, Dad?"

Her father smiled. "Yes," he said. "That's a copy of *The Last Supper* painted by Leonardo da Vinci more than five hundred years ago. The original painting was badly damaged and has had to be restored multiple times."

"What happened to it?" asked Kaleen.

"The artist used an experimental painting technique because he thought it would work better than the usual one. Unfortunately, the new method couldn't stand the test of time. The paint peeled and flaked when it was exposed to sunlight, moisture, and dust. The end result is a dim shadow of what the artist intended."

"I'll bet if he could, he'd do it all over again the right way," Kaleen said.

Dad agreed. "You know, honey, it would be good for us to remember that everything we do will have to stand a test by the Lord. All the things we have done out of love for Christ will stand the test and be rewarded. But other things we have done will be worthless, because we did them out of pride or a desire to impress others."

SERVE CHRIST WITH YOUR LIFE.

Kaleen nodded. "I'm going to try to do all I can for the Lord—and to do it in the right way so I won't be wishing I could do it over again."

HOW ABOUT YOU?

Do you want to be a success? No matter how hard you work or how many good things you do, it will all come to nothing if it's not done for the Lord. Ask the Lord to guide you in all that you do. Only what's done for Christ will last!

TO MEMORIZE:

Because of God's grace to me, I have laid the foundation like an expert builder. Now others are building on it. But whoever is building on this foundation must be very careful.

1 CORINTHIANS 3:10

BY SHERRY L. KUYT

August 27

SEEDS FIRST

Read Mark 4:26-29.

"It looks like these tomatoes will be perfect for the fair next week," noted Mom as she examined Kara's vegetable garden. "You certainly have worked hard, honey."

"It was fun most of the time," said Kara. She moved the hose over to the carrots as she continued to think about the fair. "I wonder how Consuela is doing on the quilt she's making for the sewing exhibit."

"I'd like to see it sometime," said Mom, picking up the weeds she had pulled from the garden. "She's such a sweet girl. Has she enjoyed coming to church with us?"

"I think so," replied Kara, turning to her mom with a look of concern. "I wish she'd become a Christian, though! I thought as soon as she heard about Jesus, she'd trust Him as her Savior."

"The Bible says that when we tell someone about Jesus, it's like planting a seed," answered Mom. "Remember waiting for these vegetable seeds to grow?"

Kara nodded. "Some of them sprouted almost right away. Others didn't come up for several days."

KEEP WITNESSING.

"You didn't stop taking care of the seeds that didn't come up right away, did you?" asked Mom.

"No," answered Kara. "I don't think I'll ever understand exactly what goes on inside the ground to change small, dry seeds into radishes or cucumbers! But I knew that if I kept on watering the ground where we planted the seeds, eventually they would grow. Some just took longer than others."

"As we keep watering the gospel seeds by continuing to witness to our friends, God will make these seeds grow too," said Mom.

HOW ABOUT YOU?

Have you been discouraged because someone you've been witnessing to hasn't trusted in Jesus as Savior and Lord yet? Don't give up!

TO MEMORIZE:

I planted the seed in your hearts, and Apollos watered it, but it was God who made it grow.

1 CORINTHIANS 3:6

BY DEANA ROGERS

August 28
THE TRAIL

Read Psalm 31:19-24.

"Mom, can we hike that trail?" asked Kim, pointing to a path a few feet from their campsite. "The sign says it's only a thirty-minute walk."

"It's okay with me if your dad doesn't mind waiting with little Timothy for half an hour," said Mom.

Dad laughed. "Go!" he ordered. "Timothy is sound asleep, and I have a good book to read."

Kim and her mother began their hike, walking at a fast pace. Kim talked about school. "Sometimes Jane is friendly and even seems interested in coming to Sunday school," she said. "But yesterday she and some other kids laughed at me when I prayed before I ate my lunch. It doesn't seem to do any good to try to witness."

Soon the trail became more difficult. They climbed hills, pushed away branches, and stumbled over rocks. Kim stopped to rest. "Tired?" asked Mom as she sank down onto a fallen log beside her daughter.

Kim nodded. "This trail seemed easy at first, but now it's tough! I didn't realize there were so many hills and valleys. I feel like giving up!"

"You know, Kim, the Christian walk is a little like this," observed Mom. "There are some rough trails to follow, and we get tired. It's very tempting at times to stop and give up. Life has a lot of ups and downs—hills and valleys, you might say. But the Bible says we must run with patience."

"I know you're right," said Kim as she got up. "I'm not going to give up in my Christian witness or on this hike. Let's go!"

HOW ABOUT YOU?

Are you weary in your Christian walk? Do kids at school laugh at you because you live for the Lord? Are you tempted to stop and give up? Remember that your Christian walk will have both lows and highs. Don't give up now!

TO MEMORIZE:

Be strong and courageous, all you who put your hope in the LORD!

PSALM 31:24

BY VICKI L. REINHARDT

August 29

NEW FATHER, NEW RULES

Read John 15:9-14.

Mr. Arends held the adoption papers as he hugged Alex. "Now you're really mine!" he said.

Alex hugged him back. "I'm glad you wanted me . . . Dad. I'm going to be the best kid in the whole world for you."

Alex meant what he said. He had already learned that he had to obey the rules in his new home. At first Alex didn't like having to come straight home from school, hang up his clothes, and do his homework. But as he learned to love his new parents, he found that he wanted to please them. And it wasn't long after his adoption was final that he accepted Jesus as his Savior.

One day Alex was writing with a new pen. "Where did you get that pen?" asked his father.

"It's Jerry Stern's," Alex answered. "He broke mine on purpose, so I took his."

"Son," said Dad, "when you came into my family, I had some rules for you to obey. When you asked Jesus to be your Savior, you came into God's family. One of His rules is, 'You shall not steal.' You must return the pen to Jerry."

OBEY YOUR HEAVENLY FATHER.

"But, Dad, he broke mine!" protested Alex.

"You said yourself that the pen is Jerry's," Dad pointed out. Then he asked, "Alex, why have you tried so hard to obey my rules?"

"Because . . . well . . . because I love you, Dad, and you love me." Alex paused as he thought about his words. "I love God, too," he added slowly, "and I should also obey Him. Okay, Dad. I'll give the pen back to Jerry."

HOW ABOUT YOU?

Have you become a child of God by receiving Jesus as your Savior? Do you obey your heavenly Father? His rules are in the Bible. If you love Him, you'll want to obey Him.

TO MEMORIZE:

If you love me, obey my commandments.

JOHN 14:15

BY AGNES LIVEZEY

August 30

FIVE-FINGER DISCOUNT

Read Proverbs 4:20-27.

At the department store, Sherman met his friends Joshua and Henry. "Hi," he said.

"Hi. Want to play five-finger discount with us?" Joshua asked.

"What's that?" asked Sherman.

"You find something that you can pick up with five fingers, and you hide it in your hand," whispered Joshua. "The discount is when you walk out of the store without paying for it."

"That's stealing," gasped Sherman.

"Shhh," Henry whispered. "Sometimes you can't get what you want any other way."

Sherman cupped his hand around a little car. For a long time he had wanted a car like that for his collection.

"Go on," his friends urged him. "It's easy."

Sherman put the car down.

"Think about it," said Joshua. "You can come back for it tomorrow."

PLEASE GOD, NOT YOURSELF.

Dessert that night was chocolate fudge cake. Mom sat down and looked at her piece. Suddenly she got up and put it back on the cake plate. "When I see a dessert, I think it looks good, so I eat it," she said. "Then I get upset when I find out my diet isn't working. Sometimes it's hard to resist something you enjoy doing no matter what it will cost you in the long run."

Sherman knew what she meant. He had been tempted to do something wrong just because he would enjoy having a little car. Even if he hadn't gotten caught, the car would have cost him a guilty conscience and many uncomfortable moments. He was glad he had resisted.

HOW ABOUT YOU?

Are there things you think you need right away just to please yourself? The excitement you'd enjoy at first isn't worth the long-term results. Trust God to meet your needs in His own good time.

TO MEMORIZE:

We reject all shameful deeds and underhanded methods.

2 CORINTHIANS 4:2

BY NANCE E. KEYES

August 31

OUTGROWN

Read Romans 11:33-36.

When Nico's mother reminded him that he still hadn't studied his Sunday school lesson, he looked up from his work on an airplane model. "Aw, Mom, I know all that stuff," he argued. "I go to church and Sunday school and Bible club." But when Mom gave him a stern look, he began working on his lesson.

The following morning Dad told Nico to get ready for church. Unwillingly, he went to his room to change, but in a few minutes was back again. "Look at this shirt!" he exclaimed. "The sleeves are short on me."

Dad agreed. "We'll have to buy you some new shirts this week."

The next day Dad bought two new shirts. Nico tried one of them on that evening. "The sleeves are just the right length," Dad said with a big smile. Then he became serious. "But, Son, you seem to think God is like your old shirt."

"What?" Nico asked.

"Well, you've acted as if you've outgrown God. But it takes a lifetime to learn about God, and then you still know just a little about Him."

YOU CAN'T OUTGROW GOD.

Nico looked down at his new shirts. "I'll try to remember that next Sunday when I'm wearing one of these shirts."

Sure enough, the next week as he thought about the words of the songs and listened to his Sunday school teacher, he heard several things he hadn't known before. *I'm glad I'll never outgrow God like I did my old shirt,* he thought.

HOW ABOUT YOU?

Do you think that you've heard all the Bible stories before? Although it may seem that you know everything, you'll always be able to discover new things about God and His ways. You can never outgrow God.

TO MEMORIZE:

Oh, how great are God's riches and wisdom and knowledge! How impossible it is for us to understand his decisions and his ways!

ROMANS 11:33

BY CAROLYN E. YOST

September 1
THE WORST PAIN OF ALL

Read 1 John 3:21-24.

Eric kicked a stone, sending it flying along the sidewalk. He heard someone coming up behind him and turned. It was Doug, one of the few kids at school who didn't make fun of Eric's bald head. "What's wrong?" Doug asked.

"Oh, not much," mumbled Eric. "It's just that the kids have been making fun of me again."

"Does having leukemia make your hair fall out?" Doug asked.

Eric shook his head. "That's caused by the treatments I have to take," he explained. "Thanks for never teasing me, Doug," he added.

"Oh, that's all right." Doug smiled. "Want to come over and play with my race car set?"

After getting permission from his mother, Eric followed Doug to his basement. The boys had a good time sending their cars around the track. Then Doug asked, "Does it hurt to have leukemia?"

LOVE OTHERS FOR JESUS' SAKE.

"Some of the tests hurt, and the treatments make me feel sick. But what I hate most is that my hair falls out," said Eric, stopping his car. "And the teasing just makes it worse. How come you don't tease like the others?"

"Because Jesus wouldn't want me to," Doug said. "It's that simple."

"I wish more kids knew about Jesus," said Eric. "I don't know much about Him either."

Doug smiled. "Let's go upstairs, and I'll tell you more about Him," he said.

HOW ABOUT YOU?

Do you know someone who is teased because he or she looks or acts different? You can make life easier for that person by refusing to join in the teasing. Others will want to learn about Jesus when they learn He is the reason why you refuse to hurt people's feelings.

TO MEMORIZE:

And this is his commandment: We must believe in the name of his Son, Jesus Christ, and love one another, just as he commanded us.

1 JOHN 3:23

BY CAROLYN E. YOST

Lift Him Up

You are my God, and I will praise you! You are my God,
and I will exalt you!
PSALM 118:28

Praise lets God know that you are aware of His greatness. Praise helps you show God that you love Him. You can praise Him in song or spoken word, including prayer. God hears and receives it all.

The Bible includes many examples of praise. Learn more about them by solving the crossword puzzle.

ACROSS

3. He took the baby Jesus in his arms and praised God for sending salvation.
5. He was a father who ended a long period of silence with praise.
6. "I will praise the name of God with a ______" (Psalm 69:30, NKJV).
7. This harp player thanked and praised God.

DOWN

1. They praised God for all the things they heard and saw in the fields when Christ was born.
2. She played the tambourine and led the children of Israel in a dance and song of praise.
4. He rode a donkey while the disciples praised God loudly.

ANSWER KEY
ACROSS: 3. Simeon; 5. Zechariah; 6. song; 7. David
DOWN: 1. shepherds; 2. Miriam; 4. Jesus

September 2

THE IMPORTANT BOOK

Read Revelation 21:21-27.

As Mike helped clean the garage, he heard snatches of a message his father was listening to on the radio. It was about the "Book of Life." The minister said that only people whose names were written in that book would be allowed in heaven. Mike wanted to be sure his name was there, so he decided he'd be very good.

When Mike started to tease his sister, Jordan, later that day, he thought about that "Book of Life," so he gave Jordan a ride on his bike instead. He also took out the garbage without being asked.

Mike showed his Sunday school teacher a list of the good things he had done. "Will God write my name in His book now?" he asked.

"Let me ask you something," Mrs. Lewis said. "Should I write down your name as a winner in our Bible reading contest because you have done all these good things?"

Mike shook his head. "I didn't read enough chapters yet," he said.

"Right," said Mrs. Lewis. "To be a winner the requirement is reading the assigned chapters, not being good. In the same way, you must meet God's requirement to get your name in His book. He requires that you trust Jesus to be your Savior. God knew that no one could do enough good things to go to heaven," explained Mrs. Lewis.

HAVE YOUR NAME WRITTEN IN HEAVEN.

As they talked about it, Mike realized that he needed Jesus to take his sins away. Mike bowed his head and told God how sorry he was for his sins, and he asked Jesus to come into his life. Then he smiled, for he could almost see Jesus writing his name in a big book in heaven: "Mike Roberts."

HOW ABOUT YOU?

Is your name written in the Book of Life? If not, receive Jesus as your Savior. Then thank Him for writing your name in His book and preparing a place for you in heaven.

TO MEMORIZE:

Rejoice because your names are registered in heaven.

LUKE 10:20

BY MATILDA H. NORDTVEDT

September 3

THE STONE BRACELET

Read Romans 5:1-5.

"Grandpa! Kaitlyn is moving!" Abbie looked very sad. "Why does everything have to go wrong? First my kitten disappeared, then I ruined my favorite shirt, and now this."

"I'm sorry, honey," said Grandpa. "Can you trust God to teach you through these things?"

"I don't want to learn," mumbled Abbie.

Grandpa left the room. Soon he returned, carrying a box. "These are some stones your Grandma and I picked up on a trip to the Black Hills. Want to trade your bracelet for these?"

Abbie looked at her polished-stone bracelet and shook her head. "The stones in this box are rough and dirty. Mine are smooth and shiny."

Grandpa smiled. "Well," he said, "Grandma and I planned to have these stones polished and made into jewelry, but we never did. So they've just been lying around. The stones in your bracelet have been tumbled around with sand and other stones. The rough edges have been ground off, and they've been rubbed until they shine.

LEARN FROM PROBLEMS.

"You know," continued Grandpa, "our lives are like that. When we face difficult times, some of the rough edges get polished off. We learn from our troubles and become more like Christ."

"I don't see how," mumbled Abbie.

"Losing Patches helps you to understand how others feel when they lose someone they love," suggested Grandpa. "Ruining your shirt may have taught you to be more careful. Having your best friend move can help you be friendly to children who don't have a best friend. Those things will make you a better person."

HOW ABOUT YOU?

Do you feel like you're being bumped around by difficult times? Maybe the Lord wants to polish off some rough edges. What can you learn from what is happening in your life right now? Thank God for polishing you and making you more like Him.

TO MEMORIZE:

We can rejoice, too, when we run into problems and trials,
for we know that they help us develop endurance.
ROMANS 5:3

BY HAZEL W. MARETT

September 4
THE X RAY

Read 2 Timothy 3:14-17.

Pablo's mother took him to the dentist for a checkup. Pablo hopped up into the chair, leaned his head back, and opened his mouth wide. "Good," said the dentist. "I see only one cavity. Now I'm going to X-ray your teeth."

"But why?" Pablo asked.

"I want to know if there are any problems that I can't see on the outside," the dentist explained. "Now hold very still for the X ray, Pablo."

The X ray showed that Pablo had one more cavity. So his mother made an appointment to have both cavities filled. "I don't see why the dentist had to take that X ray," grumbled Pablo on the way home. "Now I have to have two cavities filled instead of just one!"

"That's true," agreed Mom, "But it would have shown up later. By then it would have gotten much bigger and you'd have needed a big filling instead of just a little one."

GOD'S WORD SHOWS SIN.

That evening Pablo told his Dad about the X ray. "X rays can be a big help," said Dad. "In a way, they remind me of the Bible."

"How?" asked Pablo, surprised.

"Well," replied Dad, "when we read God's Word, He uses it to examine us deep inside where we can't see. The Bible helps us recognize our sin so we can ask God to forgive us. He will take away our sin and help us stay away from it."

"Yeah," said Pablo. "I'm glad God gave us the Bible—and dentists, too."

HOW ABOUT YOU?

Do you read the Bible to see what it has to say to you? Is there a sin to avoid? Is there a commandment to obey? A lesson to learn? Study the Bible for your profit!

TO MEMORIZE:

The word of God is alive and powerful. It is sharper than the sharpest two-edged sword, cutting between soul and spirit, between joint and marrow. It exposes our innermost thoughts and desires.

HEBREWS 4:12

BY JAN L. HANSEN

September 5

THE POOR RICH MAN

Read 1 Timothy 6:9-11, 17-18.

Jason whistled as he rang the doorbell of the big house on the hill.

Mr. Atkins jerked the door open and stood there, frowning. "What do you want?"

"I'm Jason Parker, your new paperboy. I'd like to collect five dollars for the paper."

"And I suppose you expect a tip. Well, you aren't going to get it!" The old man counted out the exact amount and slammed the door.

Jason's next stop was Ms. Patterson's little house. "Yes? Oh, it's the new paperboy. I'll get your money." Soon she was back with the money and a plastic bag. "I appreciate getting the paper on my porch. I'd like to give you a tip, but I don't have any extra money. So I put some homemade cookies in this bag."

Later Jason told his mother about Mr. Atkins. "Poor old man," was her response.

"Poor?" Jason snorted. "He's rich!"

"He's also poor," replied Mom. "He has made lots of money. But he has turned his back on God and on his friends."

MONEY DOESN'T BRING HAPPINESS.

When Jason told his mother about Ms. Patterson, she smiled. "Everyone loves her. She may not have much money, but she's what the Bible would call 'rich in good works.' She's also rich in friends. She's a good example of the way Christians ought to love and care for others."

"So Mr. Atkins is a poor rich man, and Ms. Patterson is a rich poor lady," Jason decided.

HOW ABOUT YOU?

Do you want to be rich? There's nothing wrong with money, but a strong desire for lots of money is dangerous. Don't make the mistake of thinking money brings happiness. There is a better kind of "riches." Invest your time and efforts in making friends, helping others, and serving the Lord.

TO MEMORIZE:

Tell them to use their money to do good. They should be rich in good works and generous to those in need, always being ready to share with others.

1 TIMOTHY 6:18

BY BARBARA J. WESTBERG

September 6

THE SUN STILL SHINES (PART 1)

Read Colossians 4:2-6.

Vic met his friend Matt before school one day. "Do you know what my aunt gave me for my birthday?" asked Matt. "A Bible! What would I want with a Bible?"

"You could read it," suggested Vic.

"I could never understand it," said Matt. "Give me one good reason why I should read it."

"Well . . . the Bible tells us how to . . . uh . . . how to live," stammered Vic. He knew he should witness to Matt, but he didn't know what to say.

"How to live?" echoed Matt. "Man, I know how to live! An old-fashioned, outdated book couldn't tell me how to live. Why, the Bible must have been written before there were cars or planes or telephones."

"The Bible is more up-to-date than today's newspaper," replied Vic. "My dad said so."

"Yeah? Well, my dad says it's old-fashioned. Hey, there's the bell. Let's run or we'll be late!"

BE READY TO WITNESS.

That evening Vic told his dad what had happened. "I messed up. I couldn't think of any good answers."

"That's too bad," Dad said. "The Bible tells us we should always be ready to give an answer concerning our faith. If you study God's Word, meditate on it, and pray each day, I'll pray with you. I'll ask God to give you another opportunity to witness to Matt. When He does, He will give you the right words to use."

HOW ABOUT YOU?

Are you ever caught off guard, unprepared to witness? Do you sometimes keep quiet because you just can't think of what to say? Read God's Word every day, talk with Him, and as opportunities come, do speak up, trusting God to use the words He gives you for His glory. He will do it.

TO MEMORIZE:

You must worship Christ as Lord of your life. And if someone asks about your hope as a believer, always be ready to explain it.

1 PETER 3:15

BY BARBARA J. WESTBERG

September 7

THE SUN STILL SHINES (PART 2)

Read 1 Peter 1:23-25.

Matt's uncle was building a new home with a solar energy system. With his uncle's permission, Matt invited Vic to go along to look it over. "Whew! Quite a layout," whistled Vic.

"Yeah! Most of the power for heating and cooling will come from the sun. That old sun's been around a long time. I wonder why people are just starting to use it for energy."

Vic recalled their conversation about the Bible and had an idea. "Using the sun for heating and cooling sounds silly!" he declared. "Like you said, the sun has been around a long time. Your uncle should use something more up-to-date."

"Have you gone bananas?" exclaimed Matt. "Solar energy is modern technology."

Vic pointed to a piece of equipment. "What's that thing?"

"Aw, Vic, I don't understand all about it," Matt admitted.

"There you go," Vic told him. "You don't understand solar energy, but you believe it. The sun is as old as creation, but you still believe it's useful." Vic paused a moment, then added, "If the old sun is still useful and powerful, why can't that be true of the Bible, too?"

THE BIBLE IS FOR TODAY.

"Well . . . I . . ." stammered Matt.

Vic continued, "If you ask God to help you understand the Bible, He will. The Bible can affect your life even more than the sun does."

"How do you know?" Matt asked.

"The Bible says so," answered Vic. "If you read it, you'll learn lots of things."

HOW ABOUT YOU?

Have you felt that the Bible is outdated? The things it teaches are just as appropriate today as when they were first written down. Read it daily. It teaches many things (such as love, kindness, honesty, obedience) that you need in your life. Best of all, it teaches you how to get to heaven.

TO MEMORIZE:

Heaven and earth will disappear, but my words will never disappear.

MARK 13:31

BY BARBARA J. WESTBERG

September 8

NO MORE TROUBLES

Read 2 Corinthians 4:7-10.

The man on TV waved his arms. "Do you have health problems? Problems with money? Family problems? To get rid of your troubles, just follow Jesus!" he shouted.

Turning off the TV, Alexis went outside. She looked up when she heard the tap of a cane. It was old Mrs. Koning, who could see only dimly. Alexis skipped up to her and put her small hand in the old lady's wrinkled hand.

"Guess what! I heard a preacher on TV say you'll have no troubles if you follow Jesus."

Mrs. Koning smiled. "I do follow Jesus."

"Then why doesn't God help you see again?" asked Alexis.

"God is powerful enough to make people see. But He never promised that all my troubles would go away because I follow Jesus. Instead, He promised He'd be with me in times of trouble, take care of all my needs, and be my friend."

"But the preacher said you could be well," said Alexis, "and rich, too—if you trust Jesus."

GROW THROUGH TROUBLE.

"In a way, he is right," said Mrs. Koning, squeezing Alexis's hand. "My sins are gone, so my soul is healthy. And I'm rich in love for God and others. Never try to use Christianity as a way to make life easy," she advised. "Christians have troubles too. But they have God to help them get through those troubles."

"I see," said Alexis. "Following Jesus does make you healthy and rich—but not in the way you might think at first."

HOW ABOUT YOU?

Have you gotten the idea that God wants all Christians to have lots of money, beautiful clothes, and perfect health? This may be God's plan for you. Or it may be His plan that, through troubles, you will come to know Him in a special way. God knows what you need to best serve Him.

TO MEMORIZE:

[The Lord] said, "My grace is all you need.
My power works best in weakness."
2 CORINTHIANS 12:9

BY CAROLYN E. YOST

Faith in Action: My Devotional Journey

You crown the year with a bountiful harvest; even the hard pathways overflow with abundance.
PSALM 65:11

This fall, keep a record of when you witness your faith in action. Specifically focus on God's abundance as it relates to the activity themes for this season (praise, serving, and faith). Or make a note when you apply your devotional studies in everyday life. This way, you can see your faith in action!

God's abundance was revealed to me . . .

SEPTEMBER: PRAISE

WHEN ____

____

WHERE ____

____

HOW ____

____

MORE ____

____

____

OCTOBER: SERVING

WHEN ______________________________

____

WHERE ______________________________

____

HOW ______________________________

____

MORE ______________________________

____

____

NOVEMBER: FAITH

WHEN ______________________________

____

WHERE ______________________________

____

HOW ______________________________

____

MORE ______________________________

____

____

September 9

I REMEMBER

Read Malachi 3:14-18.

Tony's grandfather had just died. He felt nervous about attending the service. "Remember the wonderful things Grandpa taught you," his mother said. "And keep in mind that it is only his body in the casket. He is with the Lord in heaven."

Tony nodded. He knew that everyone will die someday until the time when Jesus comes back. And he knew that when Christians die, they go to be with Jesus.

"Death is not to be feared if we are part of God's family," his mother added. "Of course, we'll miss Grandpa, and that makes us feel sad. But we can be happy for him. And until we join him, we can be thankful for the wonderful memories we have."

Tony's father asked, "Tony, what do you remember most about your grandfather?"

Tony thought for a minute. "I remember how kind he was to me, how he helped other people, and how he prayed for me."

"Your grandfather would be pleased to know he was remembered for those things," said Dad with a smile. "We should all live in a way that leaves good memories."

HOW ABOUT YOU?

When God calls you to heaven someday, what memories will you leave behind? More important, what will be written in God's "scroll of remembrance"? Will it be recorded that you were honest, kind, helpful, and loving? That you prayed for others and served the Lord? Live so that you'll be happy to have God and others remember your deeds.

TO MEMORIZE:

Then those who feared the LORD spoke with each other, and the LORD listened to what they said. In his presence, a scroll of remembrance was written to record the names of those who feared him and always thought about the honor of his name.

MALACHI 3:16

BY RUTH I. JAY

September 10

GET OUT OF THE DUMP

Read 2 Peter 3:10-14.

Steve and his family lived in an area where there was no trash pickup, so each week he and his dad put the garbage cans in their truck and took them to the county dump. One afternoon, as he and his dad were unloading the truck, Steve noticed some mice among the trash.

"I can see why a mouse would love to nest in that trash," Dad said. "There's always plenty of food and lots of papers for building materials. But some men are going to burn all this trash. The mice will lose their homes and everything in them."

As Steve and his dad drove away, Steve couldn't resist one last look at the mice, who were scampering about as though they had nothing to worry about.

When they arrived home, Steve went to his bedroom to change his clothes. As he opened the closet door, a bunch of his belongings fell out. "This place is a dump," he muttered. As he glanced around the room, he saw his posters, video games, and comic books. He saw his baseball mitt, soccer ball, and model spaceships. He saw his books and his Boy Scout manual. *Hmmm,* thought Steve. *I'd hate to be like those mice, spending all my life on things that won't last. Maybe it's time to get out of the dump and start spending more time on things that really matter!* Steve took his Bible from the dresser drawer and placed it beside his bed.

LIVE FOR JESUS.

HOW ABOUT YOU?

Are you so wrapped up in your own plans, projects, and activities that you have little time for God? Now is a good time to concentrate on doing things that help you become more like Jesus. Remember, this life is only temporary. Only the things we do for Jesus will last forever.

TO MEMORIZE:

Since everything around us is going to be destroyed like this, what holy and godly lives you should live.

2 PETER 3:11

BY SHERRY L. KUYT

September 11

THE PROWLER

Read Romans 6:11-14.

Doug sat up in bed with a start. The floor was creaking downstairs. Maybe he was just imagining things. Then he heard drawers opening and closing. Doug was scared now. He tiptoed across the hall and knocked on his parents' bedroom door. "Dad!" he whispered.

Dad opened the bedroom door. "Doug! It's the middle of the night," Dad began.

Doug replied, "I heard a prowler." Just then there was the sound of a door opening.

"Stay here," Dad cautioned, "and I'll investigate." Slowly he sneaked down the stairs. The outside door was open, so Dad tiptoed outside. He saw a shadow by the tree. Someone was walking away with a brown bag in his hand. Dad went after him, caught him, and then led him into the house and up the stairs.

"Doug, here's your prowler," Dad said. "Your brother, Randy, has been walking in his sleep. Go to bed now."

"I can't believe I could walk in my sleep last night and not know what I was doing," Randy said the next morning.

WAKE UP AND LIVE.

"You did," laughed Doug. "You looked funny. You were walking barefoot carrying a lunch."

"That's right," Dad said. "I guess you were on your way to school. You know, sinners are like sleepwalkers. They go through the motions of living, but they're dead in their sins, unaware that they face eternal death without Christ. Going through the motions in the dark doesn't give eternal life. Only Christ, the Light, can do that. We must wake everyone up with the truth!"

HOW ABOUT YOU?

Do you go through the motions of being a Christian—being good, attending church, praying, reading your Bible—without trusting Christ as your Savior? Going through the motions won't save you from your sins, but accepting Christ will.

TO MEMORIZE:

At night there is danger of stumbling because they have no light.

JOHN 11:10

BY JAN L. HANSEN

September 12

WORLD OF WARS

Read Matthew 24:4-14.

"Boy, have I got a hard assignment tonight," Stephen announced as he and his brother and sister began to do their homework. "I have to memorize a bunch of dates about the Civil War."

"And *I'm* learning about the battles of the Revolutionary War," said John.

"All I have to do is go through the newspaper and cut out articles for our current events project," Jolene told her brothers. "That doesn't sound too hard compared to what you guys have to do."

"Just make sure you don't cut any of the comics," said Stephen, grinning.

The three children worked quietly for a while, then Jolene sighed. "Almost all the articles in this paper are about troubles and wars in one place or another."

"I wonder why," said Stephen. "I thought people are supposed to be making the world a better place."

"That's true," agreed Mom, who had just walked into the room, "but as Christians, we shouldn't be surprised. The Bible says there will always be wars and rumors of war. Politicians talk about peace, but their desire for power often gets in the way. God is left out of the picture."

GOD GIVES PEACE.

"It's scary," Jolene said. "It makes me glad I'm a Christian."

Mom smiled and said, "As Christians, we can have peace of mind no matter what happens."

HOW ABOUT YOU?

Do you ever wonder why the world is not getting better? Do you wonder why there are so many wars? Because the world's leaders are human, they have difficulty getting along with each other. They often refuse to follow God's way. Isn't it good to know that in spite of the chaos in the world around you, you can put your trust in God and have peace?

TO MEMORIZE:

Don't worry about anything; instead, pray about everything. Tell God what you need, and thank him for all he has done. Then you will experience God's peace.

PHILIPPIANS 4:6-7

BY LENORA MCWHORTEN

September 13

PEAS OR PEELINGS

Read Psalm 23:1-4.

It was lunch time, and Karen watched as her little brother, Isaac, sat stubbornly shaking his head, refusing to eat the strained peas Mom was offering.

"Maybe you should give him applesauce," suggested Karen. "He likes that."

"Yes, he can have some," responded Mom. "But he also has to learn to eat other foods that he needs." Mom took Isaac out of his chair and set him on the floor. "We'll try feeding him again in a few minutes."

A short time later, Karen heard a rustling noise coming from behind the kitchen door. There was Isaac, rummaging in the trash bag. "Oh, Mom!" said Karen.

Their mother rushed to the rescue, but Isaac cried when she took a banana peel out of his mouth.

"Wasn't that silly, Mom?" asked Karen, turning on the TV to see what was on. "Isaac sure doesn't know what's good for him, does he?"

"No," Mom replied, "he doesn't." She paused, then added, "Very often Christians don't either. We pay no attention to the gifts God provides for us to help us be joyful and grow to be like Him. Instead we try to fill our needs with things from this world that aren't important or necessary or even good for us. Those things are 'garbage' compared with the things of the Lord. They are peelings, not peas."

GOD MEETS NEEDS.

Karen agreed with her mother, turning off the TV. "I think I'll go do my Sunday school lesson."

HOW ABOUT YOU?

Do you have a need in your life? A need for fellowship? For spiritual growth? For emotional fulfillment? For a sense of achievement? The things of this world will never satisfy those needs. Let God do it. Whatever your need, give God the chance to satisfy it.

TO MEMORIZE:

And this same God who takes care of me will supply all your needs from his glorious riches, which have been given to us in Christ Jesus.

PHILIPPIANS 4:19

BY SHERRY L. KUYT

September 14

TIME TO LEARN

Read Galatians 5:22–6:1.

As Alexa helped her mother clear the table and put food away after dinner one evening, she said, "There's something I'm confused about. Courtney acts like she's better than some kids at school, and she says mean things to them," replied Alexa. "She told me she accepted Jesus as her Savior recently, but if she really did, she should be nicer."

As Alexa loaded the dishwasher, her gray kitten jumped up on the counter, causing a big mess. "Coco! Get down!" scolded Alexa, and Coco jumped down. "Now I have to clean up this mess!" Alexa sputtered. "Sometimes I wish I didn't even have a cat. He can be such a pain!" grumbled Alexa as she wiped the counter. When she finished, she stomped outside and sat down on the porch.

Mom joined her. "Still mad at your kitten?" asked Mom. "Do you want to give Coco away?"

Alexa shook her head. She picked up Coco and stroked his soft fur. "I can't expect you to know all the rules yet. You're still a baby, so I'm not going to give up on you."

BE PATIENT WITH NEW CHRISTIANS.

Mom slipped an arm around Alexa. "That's right," she said. "You need to teach him the rules. And you have to be patient with him." Mom paused, then added, "I'm sure you don't really want to give Courtney away either."

Alexa looked puzzled. "Give Courtney away? What do you mean?"

"I mean you don't want to give up on her," said Mom. "She's a baby too—a 'babe in Christ.' She needs time to learn from God's Word. Be patient with her and help her learn those things."

"But how can I help her learn?" asked Alexa.

"Be a good friend and teach her by your example," suggested Mom. "Invite her to Bible club for good Bible teaching and to meet other Christian kids."

Alexa grinned. "Sounds like a plan," she said. "I'll talk to her tomorrow."

HOW ABOUT YOU?

Do you expect too much from others? Remember that one of the fruits of the Spirit is patience. As you pray for new Christians, also be patient with them.

TO MEMORIZE:

The Holy Spirit produces this kind of fruit in our lives: love, joy, peace, patience, kindness, goodness, faithfulness, gentleness, and self-control.

GALATIANS 5:22-23

BY VICKI L. REINHARDT

September 15

JUST LIKE JESUS (PART 1)

Read John 13:12-17.

Bethany laughed as she watched her little brother, Nathan, playing in the living room. He had climbed up into Dad's favorite chair and was pretending to read the newspaper. He shouted, "I'm just like Daddy!"

Bethany just couldn't resist giving Nathan a big hug. "Wait right there so we can show Mommy what a big boy you are."

By the time Bethany returned to the living room with her mother, Nathan had put the paper down on his lap and was pretending to fall asleep. He was even leaning back with his hands behind his head, just like Dad did when he was finished reading the paper.

"Isn't that cute, Mom?" whispered Bethany, giggling. "He's trying to be just like Dad."

Mom smiled. "That's how children learn. They imitate people."

"Did I ever do that?" asked Bethany.

IMITATE JESUS.

"Sure you did," replied Mom. "You used to pretend you were making dinner. You would get the pots and pans out of the cupboard and tell me that you were making mashed potatoes." Bethany went over to pick up her brother as Mom continued to speak. "That reminds me of an important lesson in the Bible, Bethany. As Christians, we need to imitate Jesus in order to learn how to live as mature Christians."

"But if we can't see Jesus, how can we imitate Him?" Bethany asked. "Oh, wait—I know. We have the Bible. That tells us how He lived."

HOW ABOUT YOU?

Are you learning to imitate Jesus? Studying God's Word will help you. Then when you are in a situation at school or at home, try to think of what Jesus would do if He were in your place. Imitate Him.

TO MEMORIZE:

Imitate God, therefore, in everything you do,
because you are his dear children.
EPHESIANS 5:1

BY DEANA ROGERS

Praise the Lord

I called on the L*ORD, who is worthy of praise, and he saved me from my enemies.*

2 SAMUEL 22:4

David is known for praising God many times during his life. The book of Psalms is full of songs David wrote for God. David praised God for saving him, protecting him from his enemies, and helping him. David's life reminds us to praise the Lord.

Help David find his way to the battlefield to defeat Goliath.

SEE ANSWER IN BACK

September 16

JUST LIKE JESUS (PART 2)

Read John 4:7-14.

Bethany gave a lot of thought to her mother's words about learning to be like Jesus, and she was eager to be more like Him. She decided to read about Jesus in the Gospel of John. Every time she read about something Jesus did that she could follow, she wrote it down in a little notebook.

Thursday morning Mr. Singleton, the school principal, brought a new girl named Kim into Bethany's class. Some kids snickered because Kim's clothes were out of style and she had straggly hair.

As Kim found a seat, Melissa slipped Bethany a note with a mean remark about Kim. Bethany smiled at her friend, but she wished that she hadn't. She had just read about how Jesus had been friendly to a Samaritan woman. Jesus was Jewish, and in those days Jewish people didn't associate with people from Samaria. But Jesus talked with her anyway. Bethany had written in her notebook, "Be friendly to everyone, even when others are not."

Dear Lord, she prayed silently, *I think You would want me to be Kim's friend. Please give me courage to make her feel welcome.*

BE FRIENDLY.

As soon as the bell rang, Bethany made her way toward Kim. "Hi," she said, introducing herself. "Would you like to go to lunch with me?"

In the following days, Melissa and some of Bethany's other friends acted snobbishly toward Kim. But Bethany continued to treat her as a friend. It wasn't long before all of the girls accepted Kim too.

HOW ABOUT YOU?

Do you find it hard to make friends with someone who might seem different, especially when some of your other friends make fun of that person? Jesus would be friendly, though, and He wants you to be kind to others too. Follow His example. Be friendly even if others are not.

TO MEMORIZE:

Love each other with genuine affection, and
take delight in honoring each other.
ROMANS 12:10

BY DEANA ROGERS

September 17
NO LOOKING BACK

Read Luke 9:57-62.

Scott had been a Christian only a short time. His old friends kept after him to join them in doing things they used to do together.

"Scott, would you help me get my garden ready for spring planting?" asked Mr. Lockwood, Scott's Sunday school teacher.

"Sure," said Scott.

The next day Mr. Lockwood showed Scott how the garden tiller worked. "Start here, and don't take your eyes off that post down there," said Mr. Lockwood. "Make a straight row toward it. When you come back this way, you follow the furrow you've just made."

Scott's confidence began to build as row after row of neatly turned earth appeared. He was almost finished when he saw his teacher.

"Shut it off and take a break," shouted Mr. Lockwood.

LOOK TO JESUS.

Grinning, Scott turned back to shut off the machine. To his dismay, he saw that the tiller had made a big swerve to the right while he had been looking back. Mr. Lockwood saw what had happened too. "Come and have your lemonade," he said, "and then we'll figure out how to straighten this last row."

As they sat under a tree, Scott talked about the problems he was having with his old friends.

Mr. Lockwood gazed over the garden. "Looking back messes up a field, and looking back can mess up a life, too. Sometimes we have to break friendships to follow God. Don't look back on your old life, Scott. Look to Jesus."

HOW ABOUT YOU?

Do you have old friends who want you to join them in doing things that you know are wrong? Do those old ways seem attractive? Ask the Lord to help you not to look back.

TO MEMORIZE:

Jesus told him, "Anyone who puts a hand to the plow and then looks back is not fit for the Kingdom of God."

LUKE 9:62

BY RAELENE E. PHILLIPS

September 18

WHEN THE TREE NEEDS HELP

Read Proverbs 6:20-23.

David watched his father pull out the stake that had been wired to a small tree ever since it had been planted.

"A small tree often doesn't have the strength or ability to stand alone," Dad said. "This stake acted as a support, but now I believe the tree is big enough to take any winds that may come along. And it can teach us a lesson about life," added Dad.

"What do you mean?" David asked.

"When you were small, your mother and I held on to your hand every time you took a step," Dad explained. "We didn't want you to fall and get hurt. As you began to grow, we let you go by yourself, but we still watched you."

David nodded as he thought about it. Even now he often needed his parents' advice and help. He asked his father if he'd always have to depend on them.

"We're committed to helping you grow to be a strong follower of Jesus Christ," Dad replied, smiling. "As you grow up, you'll be ready someday to go on without us. Proverbs 22:6 is a verse that your mother and I try to follow as we raise you: 'Direct your children onto the right path, and when they are older, they will not leave it.'"

WELCOME HELP.

"Sort of like the tree, isn't it?" David asked. "When it was small and frail, you had to keep the stake beside it all the time. But now that it's old enough, it will keep growing straight without the supporting stake."

HOW ABOUT YOU?

How do you feel when you are restricted in some way by your parents' rules and guidance? Don't get angry. Every young tree needs help to grow big and strong and straight.

TO MEMORIZE:

My son, obey your father's commands, and don't neglect your mother's instruction.

PROVERBS 6:20

BY RUTH I. JAY

September 19

THE LIGHTHOUSE

Read Philippians 2:13-16.

Jeff's class was on a field trip to a lighthouse, and the caretaker took them up to the top room to see the powerful light. "This big light runs on electricity," he said, indicating the heavy cables that went into the light. Walking over to a counter, he pointed to an old lamp about one-fourth the size of the modern one. "This kerosene lamp was used before they had electricity," he continued.

"But that light is smaller," one of the kids piped up. "Could it shine very far over the ocean?"

"Actually, the old lamp shone just as far as the modern one does," the caretaker answered. He picked up two odd-shaped pieces of glass from the counter. "These are prisms. They are cut to bend the rays of light that hit them and to reflect that light back—not once, but several times. By using prisms, the beam of the kerosene lamp could be magnified up to a thousand times. A sailor far out at sea could see the beam of reflected light."

BE A PRISM FOR GOD.

That night all Jeff could talk about was his visit to the lighthouse. "They used a small kerosene lamp in the old days," he said. "They used prisms to reflect the beam of light to make it strong."

Mom smiled. "Prisms remind me of how the Bible says Jesus is the Light of the World. And because we are Christians, it's our job to reflect that ight for everyone to see."

HOW ABOUT YOU?

What are you doing to reflect the light of Jesus? Are you using the talents He has given you to glorify Him? Are you telling others about Him? Are you kind and loving?

TO MEMORIZE:

Live clean, innocent lives as children of God, shining like bright lights in a world full of crooked and perverse people.

PHILIPPIANS 2:15

BY DEBORAH S. MARETT

September 20

A COMFORTER

Read 2 Corinthians 1:3-5, 7.

Jenna and Jill. People who didn't know them thought they were twins. The two girls seemed inseparable. But one day that all changed.

"Jill, aren't you going to stay for pep assembly?" Jenna asked.

"No, I don't feel well," Jill said. "I called my mom to come and get me."

"See you tomorrow then," said Jenna.

But Jill didn't come to school the next day. Jenna stopped to see her at home, but she was resting. Jill did come back to school the next week, but she seemed very tired. And before long, she was in the hospital.

Jenna went there and brought their favorite flower, a pink rose. She could tell Jill liked the rose even though she didn't say much. She was hooked to several tubes, and nurses kept checking her.

The longer Jill stayed in the hospital, the less Jenna visited her.

"Jenna, who's your best friend?" asked Mom one day.

Jenna looked puzzled. "Jill, of course!"

COMFORT THE ILL.

"I thought best friends liked to be together," her mother answered. "You haven't seen Jill in days."

Jenna burst into tears. "Mom, I can't go there. Jill can barely talk. And she looks so different. What can I say?"

"You don't need to say anything," answered Mom. "Just be there. Or take your Bible along and read to her. Jill really needs a friend now. Her mom told me that she thinks you no longer care about her."

"But I do, Mom!" exclaimed Jenna. "I care so much it hurts!"

"Then go be with her," encouraged Jenna's mother. "Show her you still care."

HOW ABOUT YOU?

Do you know someone who is ill? Be a comforter. Visit if possible. Read a few comforting Bible verses. Send a card, a note, flowers, or a favorite item.

TO MEMORIZE:

He comforts us in all our troubles so that we can comfort others.

2 CORINTHIANS 1:4

BY JAN L. HANSEN

September 21

THE ALARM

Read Romans 13:8-14.

Greg fumbled for the snooze button on the alarm clock and burrowed deeper into his blanket. When the alarm roused him again, he hit the snooze button once more and nestled back in his bed. Several minutes later Mom called, "Get up, Greg. Hurry or you'll miss your bus."

Greg sat up quickly, then stumbled from his bed. "I'll hurry." He did, and he was ready just in time to catch the bus.

"My alarm didn't go off this morning," Greg complained at the dinner table that evening. "I almost missed my bus."

His mother laughed. "It went off all right," she assured him. "I heard it. But you kept hitting the snooze button. So I finally called you myself."

"You sound like some Christians I know," said Dad. He grinned at Greg's quizzical look and reached for his Bible. "Why don't you read Romans 13 for us, Greg? It tells us that Christians need to 'wake up.'"

WAKE UP AND LIVE FOR GOD.

When Greg finished reading, Dad nodded and said, "God is sounding an 'alarm' here. He says we'd better wake up and live as we should because our time here is getting shorter and shorter. Soon it will be too late to win people to Jesus or to do other things God wants us to do. But so often we hit the snooze button and ignore the warning. We don't even realize what's happening. We need to wake up and live for the Lord."

HOW ABOUT YOU?

Have you hit the snooze button in your Christian life? Time is passing quickly. It's time to wake up and do the things you know God wants you to do.

TO MEMORIZE:

This is all the more urgent, for you know how late it is; time is running out. Wake up, for our salvation is nearer now than when we first believed.

ROMANS 13:11

BY HAZEL W. MARETT

September 22

A DIFFICULT MOVE

Read Joshua 1:1-5.

At the close of the church service, Carrie listened in disbelief as Pastor Allen said, "After much prayer, we feel the Lord is calling our family to serve Him at an Indian reservation. We'll be leaving in a month." Carrie was upset by the news. Her best friend was Becky, the pastor's daughter.

When the service ended, Carrie dashed out to the car. She was too angry to even speak to Becky. "How could Pastor Allen do this?" Carrie sobbed on the way home.

"He must obey the Lord's leading," Dad said gently.

"But I don't want him to leave," Carrie wailed. "Becky's my best friend."

Carrie was upset all day. At bedtime Mom gave her a hug. "Honey," she said, "your old crib is set up in the guest room. How would you feel about sleeping in it tonight?"

Carrie laughed. "I don't want to sleep in a crib. Besides, I wouldn't fit."

Mom smiled. "That's true," she agreed. "Part of growing up means leaving behind old things and adjusting to new ways. You left your crib a long time ago, and that was good. People sometimes leave their homes, and that can be good too. When friends leave, God is still with us, planning things for our good. And keeping the Allens here apparently doesn't fit into God's plan."

ACCEPT GOD'S LEADING.

"Right," said Dad. "Let's thank God for the good years we've had with them and make their last days at our church extra special."

HOW ABOUT YOU?

Are you faced with a move, a new family member, or a new church or school? Are you angry about changes or new circumstances in your life? It isn't easy to let the familiar go, but God will still be with you in your new situation.

TO MEMORIZE:

I will be with you as I was with Moses. I will not fail you or abandon you.

JOSHUA 1:5

BY JAN L. HANSEN

Set a Reminder

Yours, O LORD, is the greatness, the power, the glory, the victory, and the majesty. Everything in the heavens and on earth is yours, O LORD, and this is your kingdom. We adore you as the one who is over all things.

1 CHRONICLES 29:11

We tell God our secrets. We ask for His help. We thank Him for His mercy. But sometimes we have to remind ourselves to praise Him. This can be as simple as writing a reminder on a post-it note or tying a string around your finger. It's wonderful to know God's always there for us. Praising Him is a way to show God we're always there for Him, too. Circle the words that mean a kind of "praise."

T Z U S R E J L F P D G B Z P
T A T P Q O X C K C P H U T Q
S B E S F F T E C P H A H P P
T N F J F H X L A E R I P O D
P F Z J G O Q E S J X L L X S
T L Y E N N O B L E J T D P B
D R Q T E O P R M C X Y O Q E
B I F E D R V A A J G Z H L V
B R G Q L X W T D M Y K M Q Y
X X Y N F E P E Z T K D A M D
Z K M H I K G D Y S Z T G X Z
A R J I D F U P D F D N N I K
G L O R I F Y M J U R Z I U N
Y R J G E L E V A T E O F T H
L P Q E T U Q L G I J I Y T K

celebrate
dignify
elevate
ennoble
extol
glorify
hail
honor
laud
magnify

SEE ANSWER IN BACK

September 23

IN REMEMBRANCE

Read 1 Corinthians 11:23-28.

Caleb and Camille tucked pansies and geraniums into the soil. They were helping Dad decorate their grandparents' graves. "Look at all the flags waving in the breeze," said Caleb as he glanced around the cemetery.

Camille looked up from her work. "Daddy, how come only some graves have flags flying beside them?" she asked.

"Those flags honor the soldiers who gave their lives to protect our country's freedom," Dad explained.

"They paid a big price to keep us free, didn't they?" Caleb asked thoughtfully.

"Yes, they did," agreed Dad. He gathered the tools they had been using. "But someone else paid a greater price for our freedom than the soldiers did," he observed as they started toward the car.

Caleb and Camille looked puzzled. "Who?"

"Jesus. He died on the cross to free us from the penalty of sin," answered Dad. "He arose from the dead and is alive in heaven now, so there's no need to decorate a grave for Him. But there is a way we can remember His sacrifice."

REMEMBER CHRIST'S SACRIFICE.

"How?" Caleb asked.

"By participating in the Communion service at church," Dad explained. "When believers take Communion, they remember Christ's sacrifice on the cross. They are also looking forward to Christ's return. The Communion service and all that it means should fill our hearts with thanksgiving."

HOW ABOUT YOU?

Before you celebrate the Lord's Supper in church, make sure you are a Christian. Then examine your heart by asking yourself these questions: Am I obeying the Lord in my life? Have I confessed all known sin? If you have done anything that would hurt your fellowship with the Lord, confess it to Him before you take Communion. Then participate with a joyful and grateful heart.

TO MEMORIZE:

Every time you eat this bread and drink this cup, you are announcing the Lord's death until he comes again.

1 CORINTHIANS 11:26

BY JAN L. HANSEN

September 24

ORDINARY DAYS

Read Ecclesiastes 3:11-14.

The Murrays were concluding their family devotions by reading from an exciting missionary book. "The jungle closed in around Pedro," read Dad. "He knew his enemies were looking for him. Since Pedro had become a Christian, other members of his tribe were determined to kill him. Pedro prayed as he ran."

"This is so scary," Mary whispered.

Dad continued reading. "Suddenly a dark-skinned man stepped out of the bushes just ahead. He motioned for Pedro to follow him. *Should I follow him?* Pedro thought. *Is this man an enemy too?* Pedro didn't know what to do." Dad looked up, put a bookmark in the book, and closed it. "Bedtime!" he said.

"Oh no!" groaned Kurt.

"Just one more page?" pleaded Mary.

Mom shook her head. "There's school tomorrow."

Kurt stretched. "Boy, some people live such exciting lives, and mine is so ordinary. School, practicing trumpet, studying, eating, sleeping, and school again."

THANK GOD FOR EACH DAY.

"Well, I suspect Pedro was glad when his life became somewhat ordinary after he escaped from his enemies," Dad said.

"Then he does get away!" Kurt laughed heartily at his unexpected discovery. "Well, I still think my days are pretty dull."

"God planned for ordinary days in our lives," said Dad. "He knows we need them. Even men of the Bible had ordinary days. Daniel didn't face lions every day. He also worked in the king's court doing many ordinary jobs. And Paul was a tentmaker. He no doubt spent many days sewing, measuring, and cutting. We need to see all those ordinary days as gifts from God."

HOW ABOUT YOU?

Do you sometimes feel that the exciting things are happening to everyone else? Ordinary days of going to school, eating, and sleeping are a part of God's plan for you. Think of each day as a gift from God.

TO MEMORIZE:

For everything there is a season, a time for every activity under heaven.

ECCLESIASTES 3:1

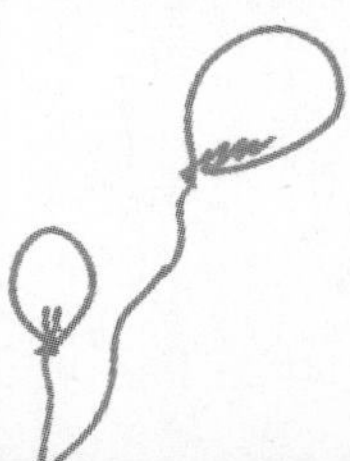

BY JORLYN A. GRASSER

September 25
PUMPED UP

Read Hebrews 10:19-25.

Every Sunday morning Bart grumbled about going to church. He complained about having to get up early, about his clothes, and about anything else he could think of. "Why do we always go to church?" he whined.

Dad rumpled Bart's hair as he walked by. "It's good for you," he said.

That afternoon Bart and his dad decided to take a bike ride. "My tires are a little soft," said Bart as they started out. "I meant to pump them up at the gas station yesterday, but I forgot. I think they'll be fine, though."

"We could pump them up before we go," suggested Dad.

"I don't feel like bothering," replied Bart. "They'll be fine. Let's go."

Before long, Bart began to get tired. "Whew, it's hard to pedal with soft tires," he exclaimed. He was glad when they finally reached home. He ran and got the tire pump. After the tires were filled, Bart tried the bike. "It pedals easy as pie now," he said.

Dad nodded. "Good," he said. "But now it's time to put your bike away and get ready for the evening service."

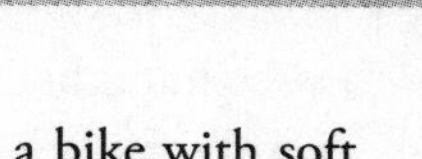

"Aw, Dad," whined Bart. "It seems like we just got back from church. I was thinking of taking another spin on my bike."

"I was thinking too," said Dad. "Just as it's hard work to ride a bike with soft tires, it's hard work to live for God without the things we learn in church and Sunday school. It's hard work to live without the encouragement we get from other Christians. We need to get 'pumped up' regularly with God's Word and with Christian fellowship. It pays to take time to do that."

HOW ABOUT YOU?

Do you sometimes complain about having to go to church? You need constant encouragement to live as God wants you to live.

TO MEMORIZE:

Think of ways to motivate one another to acts of love and good works.

HEBREWS 10:24

BY CAROLYN E. YOST

September 26

TRACE IT

Read 1 Peter 2:21-25.

"I don't see why it's so important to read the Bible every day," said Brianna. She picked up a book with pictures of birds. "If we go to church and Sunday school every week, that should be enough." She studied a picture of a beautiful red cardinal. "I'd sure like this picture for my bird project at school," she said.

"Why don't you trace it?" said Mom.

"Good idea." Brianna went to get paper.

Mom watched as Brianna worked. "Why do you put the paper right on top of the picture?" asked Mom.

"So I can see the picture through the paper," replied Brianna, surprised at her mother's question.

"But you just saw the picture," said Mom. "And you can look at it again now and then."

"When you trace, your paper has to touch the picture," said Brianna. She looked at her mother. "But you know that. Are you asking those questions for a reason?"

LIVE CLOSE TO JESUS.

"I am," admitted Mom. "The Bible says that our lives should be like Christ's. Just as you need to touch the picture with your paper in order for you to trace it, we need to 'touch' Jesus—to live close enough to Him so our lives are copies of His. We do that through daily prayer and Bible reading as well as through church and Sunday school."

Brianna lifted her paper and looked at the picture she had made of the cardinal. "While I color this, I'm going to talk to Jesus," she decided. "It's important."

HOW ABOUT YOU?

Do you realize that you should spend time each day with God? You can't expect to live the way He did if you think about Him only now and then. Constant contact with the Lord is important.

TO MEMORIZE:

God called you to do good, even if it means suffering, just as Christ suffered for you. He is your example, and you must follow in his steps.

1 PETER 2:21

BY HAZEL W. MARETT

September 27

ATTRACTIVE BAIT

Read 1 Peter 5:8-11.

"Dad, my fishing line is pulling!" shouted Ron.

Dad laughed. "That's because there's a fish on the end. Start reeling it in."

Soon the little sunfish was lying on the sand, but it was too small to keep. Reluctantly Ron put it back into the water. It flipped its tail, and in a moment it had disappeared.

"Whoa!" said Dad as Ron tossed his line back into the lake. "Aren't you forgetting something?" Ron looked at him, puzzled. "The bait," Dad explained.

Ron laughed. "Oh yeah," he said, pulling his line back in. "I guess no fish would be dumb enough to bite on the bare hook, would it? I'll disguise it and make it look good with this juicy worm. The fish won't know there's any danger, so it'll open its mouth and swallow the hook. Then I'll have it!"

"That reminds me of the way Satan works," Dad mused.

Ron was curious. "What do you mean, Dad?"

AVOID SATAN'S BAIT.

"Satan tries to make sin look attractive," explained Dad. "Sometimes we're uneasy about something, or maybe we've been warned that it's wrong. Yet it looks good or our friends are doing it, and we're tempted to try it. Satan is a master at disguising sin and making bad things look good. So when you're tempted by a questionable activity, remember the fish. It wouldn't have gotten caught if it had stayed away from the hook."

HOW ABOUT YOU?

Does Satan catch your attention with a good movie so that you become careless about what you watch? Does he make playing video games so much fun that you do it even though you know you're spending too much time and money? What other methods does he use? Be careful.

TO MEMORIZE:

Put on all of God's armor so that you will be able
to stand firm against all strategies of the devil.
EPHESIANS 6:11

BY PHYLLIS M. ROBINSON

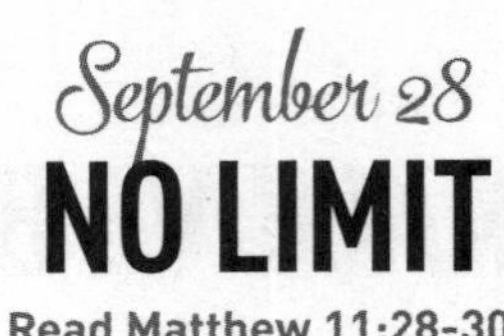

NO LIMIT

Read Matthew 11:28-30.

The wind whipped through Tucker's hair, and salt water washed his face as the boat approached Liberty Island. "Look! There she is," he yelled.

"The Statue of Liberty is beautiful!" exclaimed Mom.

As they docked, Tucker skipped down the gangplank. He couldn't wait to get inside the Statue of Liberty.

After they had enjoyed a guided tour, they headed back to their hotel. "I can remember my grandparents telling what it was like to come to America from Holland," said Dad. "They said the Statue of Liberty was the first sight to welcome them in a strange land."

"I'll bet they were glad to get here," said Tucker.

"Yes, they were," Dad replied. "They were also glad when they became citizens of this country and could finally call America their home."

"Do immigrants still come to America?" Tucker asked.

BECOME A CITIZEN OF HEAVEN.

"Yes," Dad answered, "but not as many as before."

"Why?" asked Tucker.

"Things have changed," said Dad. "The poem on the statue says, 'Give me your tired, your poor, your huddled masses yearning to breathe free,' but the door is no longer open to everyone. Since so many people have wanted to come to America, our government has had to put restrictions on the invitation. Criminals and the insane aren't accepted, and there's a quota now on the number that can come each year from any one region. It seems sad, but I suppose it's necessary."

"That reminds me of another gateway to freedom," said Mom, "and it is still open to everyone. Jesus invites all to come to Him. He offers freedom from sin and grants citizenship in heaven to anybody who will come."

HOW ABOUT YOU?

Have you accepted the invitation of Jesus? Is your citizenship in heaven? His offer is open to everyone.

TO MEMORIZE:

We are citizens of heaven, where the Lord Jesus Christ lives. And we are eagerly waiting for him to return as our Savior.

PHILIPPIANS 3:20

BY JAN L. HANSEN

September 29

PATCH IT UP

Read Proverbs 10:11-21.

Angela looked at her brother. "There's a hole in your pants!" she said.

Mom shook her head and sighed. "His only good pair is in the wash, so he'll have to wear these," she said. "Just make sure you don't pick at the hole and make it bigger, Jason."

Angela pouted. "Why do we have to wear such worn-out clothes?"

Mom sighed again. "You know we can't afford new clothes since the divorce, honey," she said. "I could work more hours, but then I wouldn't have much time left for you kids. I think family life is more important than clothes."

"Maybe if you had been a better wife, Dad wouldn't have left us," grumbled Angela. She tried not to see the tears in her mother's eyes.

On the way home from school, Angela noticed that the hole in Jason's pants was bigger. "You've been picking at that hole," she scolded. "Every time you pick at it, you only make it harder for Mom to patch it up."

DON'T MAKE PROBLEMS WORSE.

Jason looked ashamed. "I don't want to make things harder for Mom." He paused, then added, "You do the same thing, you know."

"I do not!" retorted his sister.

"I'm talking about the way you treat Mom," explained Jason. "You always pick at her about getting divorced and not having much money."

Angela was silent for a few moments. "I guess I do," she admitted.

"Mom will patch my jeans tonight," Jason said, "and I think we should do some patching too. Let's try to 'patch up' our family problems rather than making them worse."

HOW ABOUT YOU?

Do you have a problem at home? Instead of feeling angry or discouraged, do what you can to make the situation better. Pray about it, be as cheerful as possible, and be supportive and loving toward others.

TO MEMORIZE:

Too much talk leads to sin. Be sensible and keep your mouth shut.

PROVERBS 10:19

BY SHERRY L. KUYT

Celebrate God

Are any of you suffering hardships? You should pray.
Are any of you happy? You should sing praises.
JAMES 5:13

What if we praised God every time we felt good? We remember to thank Him. We remember to pray to Him. And we're quick to ask for His help. But how often do we praise Him?

Describe the last time you felt cheerful, content, or happy. Include where you were and the cause of your good feelings.

Now focus on that sense of good cheer, and write a few lines that praise God. Use words that lift Him up. Then take a moment after you write to read those words out loud.

What if we focused on praising God? What if we simply praised Him every time we're happy?

September 30

REFLECTIONS

Read Exodus 34:29-35.

"Well?" Lisa looked at her sister, Beth. "Do I look like Tara?" Lisa held a picture in a magazine under her chin as she gazed into the mirror. She had worked a long time to get her hair arranged like that of the movie star.

Beth shrugged. "A little, maybe. Come on, we've got to go." They were on their way to the lake before Lisa mentioned the movie star again.

"Tara's so beautiful." Lisa sighed.

"Why do you want to be like her?" asked Beth.

"Hasn't she been married several times?" asked Mom.

"But this magazine says she has the most exciting life in the world," Lisa said.

When they reached the lake, everyone piled out of the car. Soon they were enjoying a picnic lunch. "The lake's lovely. Look how blue it is," Mom observed.

"The water isn't really blue, though," said Dad. "It is reflecting the sky."

After the picnic they had fun hiking, fishing, and swimming. "It looks like rain," said Dad when he noticed the gathering clouds. "We'd better go."

REFLECT JESUS. 

"Look at the lake now." Mom pointed toward the water.

"It's gray now. It's reflecting the clouds," said Beth.

"And it isn't beautiful anymore," added Lisa.

"The lake doesn't have a choice about what it reflects," said Mom, "but in our lives, we can choose."

Lisa knew Mom was thinking about Tara Tarton. *Tara's life is gray compared to the beautiful life of Jesus,* Lisa admitted to herself. *I should be reflecting Him.*

HOW ABOUT YOU?

Is your life reflecting the beauty of Jesus? Compared to Him, the life of any singer or ballplayer, or of any friend or relative, is gray. Reflect Jesus and His way of life, not that of someone else.

TO MEMORIZE:

All of us who have had that veil removed can see and reflect the glory of the Lord.
2 CORINTHIANS 3:18

BY KATHERINE R. ADAMS

October 1

ALMOST!

Read Acts 26:1-3, 27-29.

Ever since Sunday David had been thinking off and on about the pastor's sermon. He knew he needed to ask Jesus to be his Savior, and he had almost made that decision last Sunday. But right now he had other things on his mind—soccer, for instance. Becoming a Christian could wait.

David shook the thoughts from his mind as he got out of bed. Today was the big day! His team, the Lions, would be playing the Bears, a team from the south side of town, for the city championship. David was the goalie for his team, and he was eager to play.

The coaches had been saying that the two teams were equal in ability, and it soon became obvious that this was true. First the Lions were ahead, then the Bears, then the Lions evened the score with another goal. Unfortunately for David and his teammates, the Bears made a goal in the shoot-out and won the championship.

"That was a good game!" Dad said later.

ACCEPT CHRIST.

"But, Dad, we lost!" David protested.

"You still can feel good about it," Mom said. "Being the second-place team in the city is an honor too!"

"Yeah, David," his sister agreed. "You almost won!"

"Almost isn't enough!" David complained.

Dad gave him a thoughtful look. "That's true, David. Almost isn't enough—not in winning soccer matches, nor in getting to heaven."

David was startled. He hadn't thought about it that way before! He knew he needed to make the decision to become a Christian, and he was almost ready to do it. Now he realized that almost being a Christian wasn't enough.

HOW ABOUT YOU?

Are you almost a Christian? Perhaps you listen to your parents, your pastor, and your Sunday school teacher talk about Christ. What's holding you back? Why not become a Christian today?

TO MEMORIZE:

Agrippa interrupted him. "Do you think you can persuade me to become a Christian so quickly?"

ACTS 26:28

BY LENORA MCWHORTEN

October 2

THE DONKEY'S TAIL

Read Ephesians 5:1-8.

It was the day of the church party, and Mrs. Gates, the teacher, tied a blindfold over Jeremy's eyes. His class had decided to play an old party game called "Pin the Tail on the Donkey." Against the wall was the picture of a donkey. Each child had a turn to be blindfolded and turned around a few times before attaching the tail.

"There you are," said Mrs. Gates, turning Jeremy around.

Jeremy took an uncertain step. This wasn't as easy as he had expected. He walked forward, wobbling just a little. He reached out with his hand and—there! It was done. The other children laughed as he snatched off his blindfold. There stood the donkey with a tail growing right out of its nose!

When the game was over, Mrs. Gates called the group together before refreshments. "Think about the game we just played," she said. "It would be easy for any one of you to go right now and pin that tail in the right place. What made it hard during the game?"

"We were blindfolded," said one of the children.

GET RID OF SPIRITUAL BLINDNESS.

"And dizzy from being turned around," added Jeremy.

"That's right," agreed Mrs. Gates. "As Christians, we're sometimes like that too. We have spiritual blindfolds—things like laziness, selfishness, hate, or stubbornness. And worldly things such as TV and bad companions turn us the wrong way. Let's ask God to help get rid of our 'blindfolds' and stay facing in the right direction."

HOW ABOUT YOU?

Are you wearing a spiritual blindfold? Are you turning away from pleasing the Lord because of your friends, things you read, or music you choose? Ask God to help you walk straight ahead—to live a life that is pleasing to Him.

TO MEMORIZE:

For once you were full of darkness, but now you have light from the Lord. So live as people of light.
EPHESIANS 5:8

BY HAZEL W. MARETT

October 3

RAGAMUFFIN (PART 1)

Read Romans 5:6-11.

Rick and Yolanda were helping their dad in his meat shop. Part of their job was to take the trash out to the big bin behind the store. Rick lifted the trash bin cover, then he slammed it back down quickly. "Yolanda, there's something in there!"

"You're just trying to scare me," laughed Yolanda.

"I'm telling the truth," Rick persisted, grabbing a stick. Bravely he pulled up the lid and poked at the rubbish with the stick. A high-pitched squeal jarred the air, and Yolanda screamed.

Dad rushed outside. "What's wrong?" he asked in alarm.

"Something's in the trash," Yolanda yelled.

Looking doubtful, Dad approached the trash bin and looked inside. "Why, it's a puppy!" he exclaimed. "Let's see if we can help him."

"Can we take him home, Dad?" Rick begged. "He looks like a stray."

"Ugh!" Yolanda made a face. "He smells! I bet Mom won't want him."

JESUS LOVES SINNERS.

"He's a mess all right," said Dad. "We'll clean him up and see if we can find him a home."

When they arrived home, the children told their mother all about the puppy. At her suggestion they named him Ragamuffin. "You know, children, Ragamuffin would make a good illustration for my Sunday school lesson tomorrow," said Mom as she looked at the pup. "What you did for Ragamuffin, God did for us—and even more! God found us spiritually dirty, lost, and trapped in our sins. Yet He reached down to rescue us. He loved us when there was nothing lovable about us."

Ragamuffin barked and Yolanda laughed. "He agrees with you, Mom. I think Ragamuffin is glad he's been found!"

HOW ABOUT YOU?

Have you been found? God sent Jesus to rescue you from sin. Have you accepted His forgiveness and trusted Him as Savior?

TO MEMORIZE:

When we were utterly helpless, Christ came at just the right time and died for us sinners.

ROMANS 5:6

BY JAN L. HANSEN

October 4
RAGAMUFFIN (PART 2)

Read Psalm 111:1-10.

Rick and Yolanda enjoyed romping with Ragamuffin, the stray puppy they found. They taught him tricks and took him on walks. They were delighted that no one answered the newspaper ad seeking Ragamuffin's owners.

But not everything was pleasant. Ragamuffin got into trouble. Sometimes he tracked mud into the house or knocked things over and broke them. Though Rick and Yolanda were patient, they often had to punish their puppy.

During dinner one day, the children scolded Ragamuffin for snitching food off the table. They worried that their dog might not like them after being punished. But Ragamuffin was as loyal as ever. He ran to meet them, wagging his tail and following them around. "Ragamuffin makes us feel like we're really important to him," observed Rick.

"You are," said Mom. "You rescued him and you take care of him. Ragamuffin knows that, and he loves you in return."

"Reminds me of someone who has rescued us," said Dad. Seeing the children's puzzled looks, he continued, "Our heavenly Father loves us. He saved us, and He provides for us. But I wonder if we remind God how important He is to us?"

BE DEVOTED TO GOD.

"I never thought of it like that," Yolanda said. "I guess I sometimes act mad when God doesn't let things work out the way I want them to."

"And sometimes I get impatient when God doesn't answer my prayers right away," admitted Rick.

Mom nodded. "I'm afraid we're all guilty. We need to learn to give to God the kind of unconditional devotion that Ragamuffin gives to you."

HOW ABOUT YOU?

Is God important to you? Do you give Him your time? Show God that you love Him by being obedient to His Word and serving Him. Tell Him you love Him when you pray and go about your day!

TO MEMORIZE:

We love each other because he loved us first.

1 JOHN 4:19

BY JAN L. HANSEN

October 5

THE ANSWER

Read Nehemiah 4:6-13.

Erin and her brother, Greg, had been praying that some of their friends would become Christians. Greg was overjoyed one Sunday when Chuck joined him at church. On the way home, Greg told his family that Chuck had accepted Jesus during Sunday school.

"That's great," Dad said with a smile.

"Wonderful!" added Mom. "Your prayers have been answered."

Erin spoke up. "I pray for Lynn. But God doesn't answer my prayers."

"Don't be discouraged," advised Dad. "Sometimes it takes a long time before a person is ready to accept Christ."

"Yeah," added Greg, "I invited Chuck to Sunday school a whole year ago."

"That's right," agreed Mom. She turned to Erin. "How often have you invited Lynn to go to church with you?"

"I haven't exactly invited her," stammered Erin. "But I let her know I go."

PRAY AND WORK.

"Have you ever told her about Jesus?" asked Greg.

"Well, not exactly," admitted Erin. "I pray for her, though—a lot!"

"Hmmm," murmured Dad. "Remember the Bible story of Nehemiah and the people of Israel building a wall around Jerusalem? When they heard their enemies were coming, they prayed, and they prepared to fight. It's good that you pray for Lynn, but sometimes the Lord wants to use you to answer your own prayers."

HOW ABOUT YOU?

Are you praying about something special—for someone's salvation, for money you need, or perhaps for help with your lessons? Prayer is very important, but don't just pray if there's something you could also do to help. Maybe the Lord wants you to talk to somebody, to rake leaves, to be a friend, to study hard. Pray, and then with the Lord's help, do all you can to accomplish the task.

TO MEMORIZE:

We prayed to our God and guarded the city day and night to protect ourselves.
NEHEMIAH 4:9

BY HAZEL W. MARETT

October 6

LOOSE LIPS

Read Psalm 119:12-16.

Stephanie and her brother were having fun looking through old trunks in Grandpa and Grandma's attic. "Aren't these clothes funny?"

"Yeah," agreed Caleb as he tried on one of Grandpa's old hats. "Hey, look at this trunk! It's full of army stuff."

Stephanie came over to look. "I wonder what this means?" She held up a poster with the words "Loose Lips Sink Ships." It had a picture of a sinking ship above the words.

"Let's go ask Grandpa," suggested Caleb.

They climbed down the narrow stairs, clutching the old poster. When they asked Grandpa about it, his face grew serious. "These signs were posted in areas where military secrets were discussed. 'Loose lips' are lips that talk a lot, so the signs were a reminder that talking about such things could bring disaster. If someone carelessly gave out our plans to enemy spies, it might mean death to hundreds of our sailors or soldiers."

TALK ABOUT JESUS.

"Wow!" exclaimed Caleb. "Hundreds of lives depended on whether or not you happened to say a few words to the wrong person!"

Grandpa gazed at the old poster. "You know, 'loose lips' aren't always bad," he said. "In fact, sometimes we need to loosen up our lips in order to save lives."

"What do you mean by that?" asked Stephanie in surprise.

"God has given us the gospel, a very special message about His Son," explained Grandpa. "But He doesn't want us to keep it. He expects us to share it so that many lives can be saved."

HOW ABOUT YOU?

Are you tight lipped when it comes to telling others about Jesus? Do you think it's enough that your lifestyle pleases the Lord—that you're honest, kind, helpful, cheerful? That's good, but God also wants to use your lips to spread His message. Don't be afraid to talk about Him.

TO MEMORIZE:

I have recited aloud all the regulations you have given us.

PSALM 119:13

BY SHERRY L. KUYT

My Servants

Anyone who wants to serve me must follow me, because my servants must be where I am. And the Father will honor anyone who serves me.

JOHN 12:26

We honor God when we serve Christ. In return, God honors us. Jesus clearly tells us in His Word to serve and follow Him. And He promises His presence in our lives—and in heaven—for this service.

Use this code to decipher the missing words below.

▼	●	★	♠	♦	✚	✣	♥	✦	♣	✪	✖	■
a	b	c	d	e	f	g	h	i	j	k	l	m

☆	✿	❏	◗	✔	➾	☎	✐	▲	➔	❖	☞	◒
n	o	p	q	r	s	t	u	v	w	x	y	z

▼ ☆ ♠   ■ ☞   ✚ ▼ ■ ✦ ✖ ☞

But as for me _ _ _   _ _   _ _ _ _ _ _ ,

➾ ♦ ✔ ▲ ♦   ☎ ♥ ♦   ✖ ✿ ✔ ♠

we will _ _ _ _ _   _ _ _   _ _ _ _ .

JOSHUA 24:15

ANSWER KEY

and my family; serve the LORD

October 7

NUTCRACKER

Read Isaiah 53:3-8.

"Mom, in Bible club today we learned that some people will miss heaven when they die." Mia was troubled as she reached for a pecan and placed it between the jaws of the nutcracker. "It scared me. What if I miss heaven?" She squeezed the ends of the nutcracker, but the nut slid out.

"You asked Jesus to be your Savior," Mom reminded her.

Mia nodded. "Yes, but I still worry about it sometimes," she confessed. She squeezed the nutcracker again, this time holding the pecan with her fingers. "Ouch!" she wailed as the nut again slipped away and the nutcracker closed on her finger. Tears filled Mia's eyes, and she put her finger to her mouth. "I'm keeping my fingers out of there," she declared.

"I'm not scared to put my finger in the nutcracker," boasted her brother Anthony. "Look!" He put his finger in the nutcracker, but before squeezing down on it, he placed a stick beside his finger. When he squeezed down, the stick held the jaws of the nutcracker open, preventing them from touching his finger. "See," he laughed. "It doesn't even hurt."

JESUS TOOK YOUR PUNISHMENT.

Mia made a face at her brother, but Mom said, "You've given us a good illustration, Anthony." She turned to Mia. "You see, honey, Anthony's finger deserves to be hurt since he's being so cocky, right? But the stick is taking the punishment his finger deserves. Jesus took all our punishment. So you don't need to worry about missing heaven."

HOW ABOUT YOU?

If you have accepted Jesus as your Savior, you don't need to worry about missing heaven. If you haven't trusted in Jesus to forgive your sins and give you eternal life, talk to a trusted Christian friend or adult about how you can do that.

TO MEMORIZE:

He was pierced for our rebellion, crushed for our sins. He was beaten so we could be whole. He was whipped so we could be healed.

ISAIAH 53:5

BY HAZEL W. MARETT

October 8

THE RIGHT SOUNDS

Read Psalm 119:9-16.

As Jeff turned the dial of his new radio, he counted the stations it could pick up. "Dad, how can I pick up so many stations?" Jeff asked. "I counted thirty."

"Sound waves from all those stations are right here in this room. Your radio is a 'receiver,' so it picks out the various sound waves and makes it possible for you to hear them."

"The man who invented the radio must have been pretty smart," Jeff said.

"Yes," agreed Dad, "but you know, the One who made your ear to hear the sounds is even smarter."

"You mean God, don't you, Dad?" Jeff asked.

"That's right," said Dad. "Your ear can pick up the softest voice, but it can handle very loud noises as well. In a noisy room your ear can pick out a certain voice you want to hear while tuning out other noises. And since you have two ears, you can tell what direction a sound is coming from and also about how far away it is!"

LISTEN TO GOD.

"So the ear is like a radio," said Jeff. "They both receive sound waves."

Dad nodded. "And even as your radio can be tuned to receive all kinds of sounds from different stations, so your ears can receive all sorts of different sounds. Do you always treat your ears to the right kind of sounds?"

Jeff looked down, remembering jokes he had listened to with his friends.

"Jeff," continued Dad, "be careful not to drown out God's voice with the sounds of the world."

HOW ABOUT YOU?

Are you using your ears to listen to the right kinds of things? Does the music you choose honor God? Do the jokes, stories, and programs you listen to please Him? Thank God for your hearing, and promise Him you'll use your ears to listen to good things!

TO MEMORIZE:

Ears to hear and eyes to see—both are gifts from the L*ORD.*

PROVERBS 20:12

BY CHARLES VANDERMEER

October 9

SPEND IT WISELY

Read Psalm 92:12-15.

Linda and her mother went to a nursing home one afternoon. First they saw Hattie Smith.

"It's about time someone came to visit!" snapped Mrs. Smith. Then she grumbled about the food, the nurses, and the rainy weather.

Linda felt sad as they walked down the hall, but when they got to Aunt Clara's room, everything changed. The thin old woman in the wheelchair greeted them with a smile on her rosy, wrinkled face. "Praise the Lord! It's nice to see ya!" she said. "I've got so much joy bubblin' up in me today that I've been prayin' for someone to share it with. This here's Leona White. I've been talkin' to her about the Lord, and she asked Him into her heart." Leona smiled.

After they left, Linda asked, "Mom, why are those ladies so different? They're both old, but Aunt Clara is happy and Mrs. Smith is grumpy."

"Let's think about it," Mom suggested. "Do you remember the shirt we bought for your father at the garage sale yesterday? We bought a skirt and shirt for you, too. We got all that for ten dollars."

LIVE WISELY.

"That's a lot for ten dollars!"

"Yes, we spent the money well," said Mom. Then she said, "I think Aunt Clara is happy because she has spent her life well and continues to do that, witnessing and praising the Lord. Perhaps Mrs. Smith looks back on her life with regret. Does that make sense?"

"I think so," Linda said. "I'm going to dedicate my life to God. Then, when I'm old, I'll be happy, too."

HOW ABOUT YOU?

Are you afraid of growing old and dying? Don't be! Invest your life in serving God and others. He'll reward you in heaven. Whether your life on earth is long or short, spend it wisely!

TO MEMORIZE:

Gray hair is a crown of glory; it is gained by living a godly life.

PROVERBS 16:31

BY SHERRY L. KUYT

October 10

IT TAKES TWO

Read 1 Thessalonians 5:9-15.

Mom sighed deeply as she heard raised voices coming from the basement. Soon Brad came bursting into the kitchen. "Mom, Logan's being mean again! I wish he wouldn't come over if he's going to act like that."

"I know you boys haven't gotten along very well lately," said Mom, "but why can't you be the one to stop the arguing that goes on between you?"

"Why me? Logan's the one who always starts it," Brad said.

"It takes two to quarrel," Mom pointed out. "If you refuse to fight, and if you ignore his teasing, there won't be an argument."

"If I don't stand up for my rights, he'll think I'm a sissy," protested Brad.

"Do you know what God thinks about all this?" asked Mom. "He says, 'Avoiding a fight is a mark of honor; only fools insist on quarreling.' Read it in Proverbs chapter 20, verse 3. Anybody can quarrel, you know, but it takes a wise person to stop a quarrel. The same verse says that it's a fool who insists on quarreling."

DON'T QUARREL.

"Tell that to Logan!" demanded Brad.

"I'm not Logan's mother. I'm yours, so I'm telling you," said Mom.

Brad took a deep breath. "All right, I'll try not to quarrel."

Several times in the next few days, Logan tried to pick a quarrel. He rode Brad's bike without permission, he tossed pebbles at him, and he called him a sissy, but Brad just walked away. Finally Logan could stand it no longer. "What's the matter with you?" he asked.

Brad grinned. "Read Proverbs 20, verse 3," he advised.

HOW ABOUT YOU?

Do you often argue with others? Remember what God says about someone who is quick to quarrel. Even if you think it's really the other person's fault, avoid arguing and fighting.

TO MEMORIZE:

Avoiding a fight is a mark of honor; only fools insist on quarreling.

PROVERBS 20:3

BY BARBARA J. WESTBERG

October 11

CHRISTIAN FILTERS

Read Romans 12:1-3.

Leslie clapped a hand over her mouth. As Mom took out the coffeepot, she looked at her daughter. "Don't use that word again," she said.

"I'm sorry, Mom," apologized Leslie. "I didn't mean to say it, but I hear it all the time at school." She watched Mom put a white paper into the coffeepot. "What's that for?"

"This filter," said Mom, "lets the water through but keeps the coffee grounds from going into the coffee. You need to be a filter too, filtering the things you hear and see. Allow only good things to settle down and stay with you. God will help you."

"I'll try, Mom," agreed Leslie. She showed her mother a listing of a TV show on their DVR. "Can I watch this show tonight?"

Mom read the description and shook her head. "This isn't the type of program you should see," she said.

"Oh, it'll be all right," teased Leslie. "I'll filter out all the bad stuff."

Mom shook her head. "Would it be okay to put garbage in the coffeepot and expect the filter to make it fit to drink?"

KEEP THOUGHTS PURE.

"Yuck," exclaimed Leslie. "Deep down I know I shouldn't watch that show, but what you just said makes it more clear. We shouldn't dump garbage into our minds on purpose. But when we can't help what we see and hear, that's when we should use our filters."

HOW ABOUT YOU?

Do you find yourself automatically saying or doing things you know are wrong? The best policy is to avoid being where you will hear or see bad things. If that's impossible, ask the Lord to help you filter out the bad influences and to keep only the thoughts and ideas that are good.

TO MEMORIZE:

Fix your thoughts on what is true, and honorable, and right, and pure, and lovely, and admirable. Think about things that are excellent and worthy of praise.

PHILIPPIANS 4:8

BY HAZEL W. MARETT

October 12

A FEW GRAY HAIRS

Read Titus 2:1-7.

Danny dragged his feet as he approached Mr. Grant, the man in the wheelchair. He was visiting the old man as a "Christian work assignment" for his youth group. "Uh, I'm Danny Harper from church," he managed to say.

Mr. Grant invited the boy to sit beside him. Then the old man began telling how he had helped start the church Danny now attended. "That was in the old days when I was a new Christian," said Mr. Grant. "I went door to door, inviting people to come to our new church. I had so much energy then! Oh, to be young again! That's when a person can really serve the Lord."

Danny laughed. He said, "And I've always thought that a kid like me can't do much for Jesus. I keep thinking that when I'm older, I'll really start working for the Lord."

Mr. Grant shook his finger in Danny's face. "Don't think that way," he said. "Young people can do much for the Lord. They're so fresh and excited about life! Already you've helped me realize that I ought to start serving God again like I used to. But I'll have to work pretty hard to keep up with a young whippersnapper like you!"

USE THE GIFT OF YOUTH.

"Thanks, Mr. Grant!" said Danny. "You've helped me, too. Next time I won't be so afraid to visit someone just because he's got a few gray hairs!"

HOW ABOUT YOU?

When was the last time you made friends with someone much older than yourself? You may feel that older people look down on you because of your youth. But actually you can do much for them by visiting and by helping with shopping or yard work.

TO MEMORIZE:

Don't let anyone look down on you because you are young, but set an example for the believers in speech, in life, in love, in faith and in purity.

1 TIMOTHY 4:12, NIV

BY SHERRY L. KUYT

October 13

THE WRONG FRIENDS

Read 2 Corinthians 6:14-17.

Alan's little sister reached up. "Hold my hand, Alan," she said.

"I don't need to hold your hand," he answered. "You're not a baby, Melinda!"

"But Mama holds my hand when—oh! I almost falled," Melinda exclaimed as she tripped over a crack in the sidewalk.

"If you'd look where you're going, you wouldn't trip!" Alan grabbed her hand. "Now hurry up!" Melinda chattered happily, but her big brother wasn't listening. He was still annoyed because Mom had insisted that he take Melinda to play in the park. He'd much rather play video games. But Mom didn't like him hanging around the arcade. And she didn't like the boys he hung around with either. Steve and Clay weren't so bad.

When Alan and Melinda returned home, they saw Mom in the yard. Melinda dashed ahead, tripped on the hose, and fell. "She never looks where she's going," said Alan in disgust.

Mom helped Melinda stand up. "She's not the only one," she said. "You need to look where you're headed too, Son. I just learned that Steve and Clay were caught shoplifting this afternoon. I'm glad you weren't with them. But if you keep hanging around those two, you are headed for a big fall."

CHOOSE CHRISTIAN FRIENDS.

Melinda reached up to her brother. "I'll hold your hand, Alan, so you won't fall."

Mom smiled at her. "I'm afraid you couldn't keep him from falling, but there's someone who can. Alan had better let God hold his hand."

HOW ABOUT YOU?

Have you looked down the road you're traveling to see what is ahead of you? If you're following the wrong crowd, you're headed for a fall. Choose friends who will help you to do what is right.

TO MEMORIZE:

"Quick!" he told the people. "Get away from the tents of these wicked men, and don't touch anything that belongs to them. If you do, you will be destroyed for their sins."

NUMBERS 16:26

BY BARBARA J. WESTBERG

Those Who Serve

The kingdom of God is . . . righteousness and peace and joy in the Holy Spirit. For those who serve Christ in these things are acceptable to God and approved by people.

ROMANS 14:17-18, NKJV

Righteousness means "free from guilt or sin." We serve Christ when our actions are free from sin. We also serve Him when we're filled with peace and joy. Jesus' first servants were His closest followers.

Draw lines to match the disciples' names to their descriptions.

Andrew	called Nathanael (or Bartholomew) to meet Jesus (John 1:45)
John and James	followed John the Baptist before serving Christ (John 1:40)
Judas	left his wealth behind when Christ said, "Follow me" (Matthew 9:9)
Matthew	brothers together known as the "Sons of Thunder" (Mark 3:17)
Peter	raced to Jesus's empty tomb with John (John 20:2-3)
Philip	said, "My Lord and my God" to the risen Christ (John 20:28)
Thomas	served as the disciples' money keeper (John 12:4-6)

ANSWER KEY

Andrew first followed John the Baptist; John and James were the "Sons of Thunder"; Judas was in charge of the disciples' money; Matthew left his wealth; Peter ran with John; Philip called Nathanael (Bartholomew); Thomas said "My Lord and my God."

October 14

TOOTHPICKS OR TREASURE

Read Psalm 90:10, 12-17.

"Carl!" called Dad as he hung up the phone. Carl knew by the tone of Dad's voice that there was going to be trouble.

"That was your principal," said Dad. "He told me you were sent to his office today for goofing off in class and talking disrespectfully to your teacher."

Carl looked uncomfortable. "It wasn't my fault," he protested. "Jack started it. Besides, that class is boring!"

"Maybe it wouldn't be so boring if you studied your lessons more often," Dad replied sternly.

Carl shrugged. "Aw, Dad, if I studied all the time, I wouldn't have any fun!"

Dad was quiet for a moment. Then he said, "Come down to my workroom. I want to show you something."

After rummaging around in a box, Dad pulled out a small, thick piece of wood. "This belonged to Grandpa Williams," he said.

USE YOUR LIFE CAREFULLY.

Carl looked at it curiously. "That can't be worth much," he said finally.

"Oh, but it is. It's solid cherry," said Dad. "Remember the hand-carved figure Mom has on the coffee table? Grandpa Williams used to carve those and sell them to collectors. They were made from the same kind of wood as this piece."

Carl whistled. "Wow! I guess that is valuable after all."

"On the other hand," said Dad, "if it were cut up into toothpicks, it wouldn't be worth much. The wood must be used properly. And the same thing is true of a life. Life is a gift from God. It's important to use it well. Don't be careless with it and waste it."

HOW ABOUT YOU?

Do you think the most important thing in life is having fun? Are you careless in your schoolwork or lazy about prayer and Bible reading? Life passes quickly. Don't waste it.

TO MEMORIZE:

Whatever your hand finds to do, do it with all your might.

ECCLESIASTES 9:10, NIV

BY SHERRY L. KUYT

October 15

A BETTER OFFER

Read Matthew 19:27-30.

Jana plopped down on the couch. "I don't think Sara will ever become a Christian. I've witnessed to her lots of times, but it doesn't do any good. She just keeps on going to raunchy movies and watching those television shows you won't let me watch. I've told her what I think about all that, but she just laughs."

"She'll do those things until she has the Lord's power to overcome sin," Mom reasoned.

"But she doesn't want to overcome sin," Jana said as she shook her head. "She enjoys it."

Mom nodded. "That's natural. There are temporary pleasures in sin, but living for God is much bett—"

"Big Paw! Come back with that!" Brian's cry rang down the hall. "Mom! Big Paw has my marker!"

The dog ran under the dining room table. "Give it to me, Big Paw," ordered Mother. Big Paw growled softly.

THE CHRISTIAN LIFE IS BEST.

Mom reached for the marker as she spoke. This time Big Paw growled louder.

Jana laughed. "You two are doing it all wrong!" She took a small piece of cold meat from the refrigerator. "Here, Big Paw! Want some meat?" Immediately the dog dropped the marker and gobbled the food.

As Mom picked up the marker, she grinned. "To get the marker, all we had to do was offer him something better."

Then Mom said to Jana, "Have you offered Sara something better than sin, Jana? You've told her all she shouldn't do, but have you told her all the good things she would get as a Christian?"

Jana looked surprised. "No, I guess not."

HOW ABOUT YOU?

Do you witness by telling people all the things they are doing wrong and what they have to give up? Instead, tell them about the advantages of being a Christian.

TO MEMORIZE:

The blessing of the Lord makes a person rich,
and he adds no sorrow with it.
PROVERBS 10:22

BY BARBARA J. WESTBERG

October 16

A WONDERFUL MEAL

Read Psalm 119:9-16.

Abigail picked up her Bible and brushed off the dust that had gathered since she used it last Sunday. This Bible had been a gift from the church for perfect attendance, and Abigail wanted to keep it looking new.

"It won't do you any good if you don't read from it," her mother warned.

One day Abigail picked up her mother's Bible and leafed through it. "How come you let your Bible get so old looking?" she asked.

Mom smiled. "You don't mean old looking do you?" she asked. "You mean used looking, right?"

Abigail shrugged her shoulders. Suddenly, she burst into laughter. "Look what you wrote in it," she said, showing her mother the Bible. "It says, 'Another wonderful meal.'"

"You'll find those words all through the Bible," Mom replied.

"Why would you write that in your Bible?" Abigail asked, flipping through more pages.

READ THE BIBLE.

"God's Word is food for my spiritual life just like the meals I make are food for my physical needs," Mom explained. "The Bible gives strength, life, and maturity. It helps us to grow in love, and it shows us how to stay away from sin."

Abigail thought about her mother's words. Her Sunday school teacher had said almost the same thing last week. Abigail went to her room. She picked up her beautiful Bible and opened it carefully. It was nice to keep it looking new, but it was more important to use it and benefit from God's teaching. She began to read and think about the words she was reading. Maybe someday she, too, would write in her Bible, "Another wonderful meal."

HOW ABOUT YOU?

Does your Bible look nice but unused? Is the Bible a part of your everyday life? Remember, it's your spiritual food. Don't neglect those meals.

TO MEMORIZE:

I will study your commandments and reflect on your ways.

PSALM 119:15

BY RUTH I. JAY

October 17

THE LAST WORDS

Read Psalm 19:12-14.

"I hate you!" Julie screamed as she ran out of the house. She was glad to see the school bus coming around the corner. She climbed on quickly before her mother had a chance to call her back, but she knew she would have to answer for her words when she got home from school.

Later Julie's anger began to go away, but she didn't want to lose it. When she felt it weakening, she would feed it bitter thoughts. *Why does she always say no? Why can't she be like Hannah's mother? Her mom lets her do what she wants to do.*

At lunchtime Julie scowled. Thanking God for her food didn't fit her mood, so she skipped it. Feeling guilty, she pulled her favorite sandwich from her lunch box. Tucked in the sandwich bag was a note. "Julie, I love you. Mom." Julie felt a bit ashamed, but not too much. *She's just feeling guilty for not letting me go to Hannah's party,* she reminded herself.

By the time school was dismissed, Julie had made a long list of complaints to present to her mother. She was thinking about them when she got off the bus. Then she glanced over at the garage and saw that the door was open and the garage was empty. Mom always came home from work before Julie got home. Where was her mother now?

WATCH YOUR WORDS.

Julie began to panic, but then she saw her mother come around the corner and pull into the garage. Julie ran into her mother's arms. "I'm sorry," she whispered. "I love you!"

HOW ABOUT YOU?

Do you ever leave home with sharp words hanging between you and your family? Do you feed those feelings of anger with bitter thoughts? Right now, make up your mind to stop. Determine to say only words you would not regret if you knew they were the last words you would ever say to that person.

TO MEMORIZE:

Too much leads to sin. Be sensible and keep your mouth shut.

PROVERBS 10:19

BY BARBARA J. WESTBERG

October 18

RHIZANTHELLA GARDNERI

Read 1 Corinthians 4:1-5.

"Dad, are you in here?"

"Back here with the orchids, Joel," Dad answered. Joel plodded to the back of the greenhouse where his father was patting down the soil in a flowerpot. "Well, how was your first day at Mr. Callaway's store?" asked Dad.

"Terrible," said Joel. "I worked hard. And all Mr. Callaway said was, 'You can stack those cans better. You missed some dirt. You didn't put enough paint on the brush.' I was mad."

"I know he can be gruff," said Dad. "But I hope you were polite anyway. You can be a witness for the Lord by your attitude, you know."

Joel looked glum. "You can be like the *Rhizanthella gardneri*," added Dad.

"The what?" gasped Joel.

Dad laughed. "That's the scientific name for an all-white orchid from Australia. The orchid spends its whole life underground, except when it pokes its pod above the ground to empty out its seeds." Dad took the flowerpot he had been working with and asked Joel to follow him into a dark room. Digging carefully, Joel's father pointed to a small, white flower under the soil.

WITNESS THROUGH YOUR ATTITUDE.

"Neat!" Joel said. "But what does my working for Mr. Callaway have to do with that?"

"You can be like the white orchid by poking your head above Mr. Callaway's gruffness and spreading Christian seeds of kindness, patience, and love," explained Dad. "You can serve the Lord by serving Mr. Callaway. In time he's almost sure to notice. Even more important, God sees. He's the one who really matters."

HOW ABOUT YOU?

Do you stay kind, loving, and thoughtful even when it seems you're not appreciated? Your actions and attitudes are an important part of your witness for the Lord. Don't look for the praise of people. Instead, look for God's future praise of, "Well done, My good and faithful servant."

TO MEMORIZE:

In the same way, let your good deeds shine out for all to see,
so that everyone will praise your heavenly Father.
MATTHEW 5:16

BY DOLORES A. LEMIEUX

October 19

WRONG WAY

Read Ephesians 6:10-18.

Zachary looked up. "I told you to mow the lawn," said Dad. "Instead, you're playing ball. Last night when we talked about the way a Christian should live, you said obeying your parents was one of the most important things you could do."

Zachary took off his baseball mitt. "Sorry, Dad. I'll get the lawn mower right away."

"It's time to leave now," said Dad. "But when we come home, you need to mow that lawn."

Soon Zachary and his family were on their way to see six-year-old Sammy's first soccer game. "Keep the ball in front of you and run fast!" advised Dad.

At the beginning of the second period the ball came to Sammy. He kept it in front of him and ran as fast as he could. "Oh no!" moaned his family. Sammy had kicked the ball through his own team's goal!

On the way home Sammy's family did their best to comfort him. "It's your first game. You'll learn," said Dad as they drove into their yard. Dad looked at the lawn and then at Zachary. "I hope you learn which side you're on too, Zach."

ALWAYS CHOOSE GOD'S SIDE.

Zachary, who knew what Dad meant, said, "A Christian is on the Lord's side. And when he doesn't obey his parents, he is acting as if he were on the world's side." Zachary jumped out of the car and hurried to get the lawn mower.

HOW ABOUT YOU?

Are you living as if you're on the world's side or on the Lord's side? The world teaches you to do whatever feels good to you. God says, "Be holy as I am holy." The world teaches you to disobey and to be unkind to your parents. God says, "Honor your father and mother." Don't listen to the world's view or be swayed to its side in any area of your life. Be strong in the Lord.

TO MEMORIZE:

A final word: Be strong in the Lord and in his mighty power.

EPHESIANS 6:10

BY LENORA MCWHORTEN

October 20

STRONG IN THE LORD

Read Psalm 29:10-11.

"You missed!" Anson shouted as he dodged a handful of leaves his sister Gwen had thrown. He laughed as he tossed a bunch of leaves back at her.

"No fair—you're stronger than me!" Gwen protested. They were having a great time at their aunt and uncle's home for a weekend visit.

Uncle Tom came outside, and they all decided to go for a walk in the woods.

As they started down the trail, Uncle Tom suddenly stood still. "Don't move," he said softly. "Look over there!" They saw an eagle in a tree.

"Cool!" Gwen grinned. "We've seen eagles in a zoo, but never out in the open."

Then with a powerful flap of its wings, the eagle took off over the treetops.

"Wow!" exclaimed Anson. "That's a strong bird!"

"It certainly is," Uncle Tom agreed. "You kids can be strong like that, too."

Anson looked at his sister. "I don't think Gwen could ever be that strong," he teased.

GOD MAKES US STRONG.

Uncle Tom smiled. "Have you heard this verse?" he asked. "Those who trust in the Lord will find new strength. They will soar high on wings like eagles."

Gwen frowned. "I've heard that verse in church," she said. "I'm not sure what it means, but I know it doesn't mean we can fly."

"That's true," Uncle Tom said, "but the verse gives a picture of the strength God offers us. When we trust the Lord, He supplies the strength we need, especially when we face difficult situations—like when your dad was in the hospital last year."

"And girls can wait on the Lord and be strong just like boys, right?" Gwen asked, looking triumphantly at her brother.

Uncle Tom nodded and smiled. "Absolutely," he agreed.

HOW ABOUT YOU?

Are there hard things you face throughout the day? Jesus will help you. Your problems won't necessarily go away, but He will give you the strength you need to handle them. The next time you see a bird soaring through the sky, think of God's promise.

TO MEMORIZE:

Those who trust in the Lord will find new strength.
They will soar high on wings like eagles.

ISAIAH 40:31

LENORA MCWHORTEN

Do It Heartily

Work willingly at whatever you do, as though you were working for the Lord rather than for people. Remember that the Lord will give you an inheritance as your reward, and that the Master you are serving is Christ.

COLOSSIANS 3:23-24

The Bible tells us to do our work as though we were serving the Lord. Imagine if Christ asked you to finish your chores. What if He told you to make dinner? How about if He asked you to help clean out the garage? You would pitch in heartily, which means happily or cheerfully. And your inheritance from God is an eternal reward for serving this way.

Unscramble the words that mean "inheritance."

stubeeq ______________________________

slabwote ______________________________

ghrithitrb ______________________________

leintmetent ______________________________

moleohir ______________________________

arightee ______________________________

glycea ______________________________

ANSWER KEY

bequest; bestowal; birthright; entitlement; heirloom; heritage; legacy

October 21

STREAKS ON THE WINDOWS

Read John 3:19-21.

Kent worked hard all morning. First he had to climb up a ladder to wash a window. Then he had to rinse it and dry it with a clean, soft rag. Next he had to climb down the ladder and move it to the next window.

When Kent came in to tell his mother he was done, she gave him four oatmeal cookies and a glass of milk. He was feeling good!

In the afternoon the sun came out. Kent was jumping on his bike to go visit a friend when Mom called. "Kent Anthony Simmons, come here!" Kent knew that when Mom used his full name, he was in trouble! "Kent, you have to wash the windows again."

As Kent looked at the windows, he couldn't believe his eyes! With the sun shining on the glass, he could see big streaks all over. "But, Mom, I couldn't see the streaks before!"

"I warned you about that," said Mom. "I said that you wouldn't see streaks until the sun came out."

JESUS IS THE LIGHT.

As Kent got the ladder out of the garage again, he thought about how his heart used to be dirty with sin. Until he learned about Jesus, he had not even known that he was a sinner.

It's just like the windows, Kent thought. *I didn't see the streaks until the sunshine was on them. And I didn't see the dirt of sin in my heart until God's Son shined His light on it.*

As Kent carefully washed the streaks away, he thanked God for His Son, Jesus, who had washed away the sin from his heart.

HOW ABOUT YOU?

Has the light of Christ shined into your heart? Have you seen the sin that is there? If so, confess your sin. Ask God to forgive you, and receive the light from heaven.

TO MEMORIZE:

Those who do what is right come to the light so others can see that they are doing what God wants.

JOHN 3:21

BY RAELENE E. PHILLIPS

October 22

LISTEN TO THE WARNING

Read Acts 1:6-11.

Dark clouds rolled overhead as the Martin family drove home from church. "Jesus is coming in the clouds," five-year-old Mark said. "Is He coming today?"

"He could," Mom answered.

"I think preachers just say that to scare people into living right," fifteen-year-old Emily said.

"Emily!" Mom was shocked.

Just then came the wail of a siren. The wind began to blow fiercely.

"A tornado!" Emily cried above the noise.

"Keep calm," Dad said.

"Maybe Jesus is coming!" Mark said.

"Don't say that!" Emily cried. "Hurry, Dad!"

"Calm down, Emily," Dad said as he turned the car in to the driveway. Hail began to hit the ground as the Martins ran for the storm cellar in their backyard. Next door Mr. Carson stood on his porch, watching the clouds.

BE READY FOR CHRIST'S RETURN.

"Better come to the cellar with us, Mr. Carson," Mom called.

Mr. Carson laughed. "No thanks," he said. "They blow that tornado siren every time a little cloud comes up." As the cellar door closed behind the Martins, a loud roar filled the air.

Half an hour later Dad left the cellar to see what had happened. He came back looking sad. "It was a tornado. Mr. Carson's house is gone. Mr. Carson is on his way to the hospital," said Dad.

Emily looked scared. Mom said, "You don't need to be foolish like Mr. Carson. Do you see now why preachers sound the warning? Jesus might not come today the way the tornado did. But He is coming, and we need to be ready."

HOW ABOUT YOU?

Everywhere there are signs to warn us that Jesus is coming soon. It will be a wonderful day for those who are ready, but a day of sadness for those who are not. Don't be foolish and ignore the warnings.

TO MEMORIZE:

A prudent person foresees danger and takes precautions.
The simpleton goes blindly on and suffers the consequences.
PROVERBS 22:3

BY BARBARA J. WESTBERG

October 23
REMODELING TIME

Read James 1:2-4, 9-12.

The storm howled as Mr. Gordon stuffed an old towel under the door. "That should keep the water from leaking in," he said.

"I wish it wasn't raining," sighed Anne. "I wanted to go shopping."

"And I wanted to go down to the video arcade," scowled her brother, Timothy.

"Well," said Mom, "at least the storm is keeping us together as a family for an evening." At that moment there was a flash of lightning, followed by a sharp cracking sound. An instant later, an earsplitting crash!

Everyone hurried to the kitchen. They saw a tree branch poking through a big hole in the ceiling. Water was pouring over everything. "Let's run to the neighbor's house," Dad said.

Soon the family was huddled in the Taylors' living room. Mrs. Taylor fixed them some hot chocolate. "What a terrible night," Anne moaned.

"Don't feel bad," Dad said. "No one was hurt, and we have insurance." He grinned at Mom. "And we'll get the kitchen remodeled!"

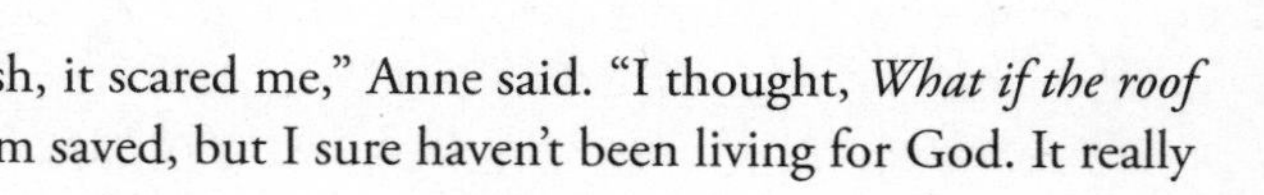

Mom smiled back. She said, "You know, I think God sometimes lets troubles come so He can do some remodeling on us."

"When I heard that crash, it scared me," Anne said. "I thought, *What if the roof caves in and I die?* I know I'm saved, but I sure haven't been living for God. It really makes you think."

"Yeah," Tim agreed. "I think I'll appreciate our family more. It even sounds good now to spend a quiet evening home together."

HOW ABOUT YOU?

Are you going through a rough time right now? Trust God! He can work, even in situations that seem tragic to you, to remodel your life into something better than ever. Use this time to rethink your values, your habits, and your goals in the light of God's Word.

TO MEMORIZE:

Let patience have its perfect work, that you may be perfect and complete, lacking nothing.

JAMES 1:4, NKJV

BY SHERRY L. KUYT

October 24

DARK GLASSES

Read 1 Corinthians 13:9-12.

Kevin watched as his little brother, Grant, wearing dark glasses, pedaled his big wheel down the driveway. It was getting dark, but Grant always wore sunglasses, night or day.

Then it happened. *Crash! Bang!* Grant plowed into a skateboard. Kevin went to help. "If you'd take off those sunglasses, you could see where you're going," he scolded.

Grant answered, "I need 'em to be a motorcycle driver!" Kevin gave up and left for his afternoon club meeting at church.

The lesson that day was about heaven. "Can you imagine never getting sick and never feeling sad?" asked Mr. Potts. "In heaven there will be no sadness or pain. And no one will ever sin—or even want to do anything that's wrong.

"We can't know exactly what heaven is like," said Mr. Potts, "although God has given some clues in the Bible. It's as if we're wearing dark glasses now. We can see just enough to show us how wonderful heaven will be. Some great day we'll actually experience it."

HEAVEN IS WONDERFUL.

Kevin thought about Grant wearing dark glasses, barely able to see the driveway in the dusk. *It'll be great to see heaven without dark glasses,* Kevin thought. *I'm looking forward to that!*

HOW ABOUT YOU?

Have you wondered what heaven will be like? There are many wrong ideas about it. One is that everyone will float on a cloud and do nothing but play a harp. The Bible doesn't say that, but God does tell us some of the good things that are in store for those who have believed in His Son, Jesus. There will be only good—no bad. Heaven is beautiful in every way, and we'll be happy all the time.

TO MEMORIZE:

Now we see things imperfectly, like puzzling reflections in a mirror, but then we will see everything with perfect clarity. All that I know now is partial and incomplete, but then I will know everything completely, just as God now knows me completely.

1 CORINTHIANS 13:12

BY CAROLYN E. YOST

October 25

PART OF THE FURNITURE

Read Psalm 19:12-14.

"I am not a slob!" Becky shouted at her brother, Talbot.

"Yes, you are," replied Talbot. "Everywhere you go, you leave things messy!"

Just then Mom walked in. "Now, Talbot, let's not be name-calling!" she said. Then she added, "I'll admit, Becky, your housekeeping habits do leave something to be desired. Have you looked at your room lately?"

"Of course I've looked at it, I sleep there," said Becky with a pout. "Sure, it's a little messy, but it's not that terrible. You two just like to pick on me." With that, she stormed into her bedroom and slammed the door.

Why did Talbot call me a slob? she thought. *I can keep things neat when I want to!* Suddenly she stopped and looked closely around her room. Half-done homework papers lay scattered across the floor. Clothes—both clean and dirty—were piled in one corner. Crumbs covered the carpet, and her bedspread was all wadded up.

Then Becky laughed out loud. On her desk she saw a plate with a dried-out bologna sandwich! *I must have brought that in here last week when I was studying and forgot about it,* Becky thought. *It was there so long that I didn't even notice it anymore—it was just like part of the furniture.* She threw the plate into the trash and started to pick up some papers. It was time to do some cleaning.

CLEAN YOUR LIFE.

HOW ABOUT YOU?

Have you taken a good look at yourself lately? Sometimes lives, as well as rooms, need cleaning. Perhaps there are some sins in your life that have been there so long you've gotten used to them. They've become part of the furniture. You may need to ask someone else to point out the messy spots. Do some housecleaning today.

TO MEMORIZE:

How can I know all the sins lurking in my heart?
Cleanse me from these hidden faults.
PSALM 19:12

BY SHERRY L. KUYT

October 26

THE SCRAWL

Read Romans 14:7-12.

"Mom, look at this!" called Brad from his bedroom. He had moved his furniture around. And when he moved the dresser, he saw ugly crayon marks on the wall behind it.

"Tricia must have done it!" Brad said as his mother walked in. "It looks terrible!"

Mom smiled. "Those marks were made long before your little sister was born."

"Then who did it?" asked Brad.

"You did!" Mom answered. "You were about two years old when you came into the kitchen and tugged my skirt. I followed you in here, and this is what I found. I tried to wash the marks off, but they wouldn't budge. So I moved the dresser in front of them."

"Did I get a time-out?" asked Brad.

"Of course!" replied Mom. "I had warned you several times about staying out of the drawer where the crayons were kept. Yet you happily showed me what you had done."

SIN BRINGS SHAME.

Brad looked at the scrawl and laughed. "Some art-work!" he said. "It's funny how things seem different when you get older."

"I wonder how many other things in life are like that," said his mother. "Probably quite a few. When I was a girl, I did a lot of things just to make myself seem older or more important. Now I wish I could go back and undo those foolish things, but I can't. You still have your life ahead of you, Brad. Be careful not to do things you'll be ashamed of later."

HOW ABOUT YOU?

Do you live for today, doing whatever seems like the most fun at the moment? If you live in sin, you'll regret it someday—at the Judgment, if not before. Obey God's Word and serve Him. Then you'll look back on your life with gladness, not with shame!

TO MEMORIZE:

And what was the result? You are now ashamed of the things you used to do, things that end in eternal doom.

ROMANS 6:21

BY SHERRY L. KUYT

October 27

A REAL MAN

Read John 11:32-36.

As Kyle turned his bike in to the driveway, he skidded on some gravel and scraped his elbow. "It doesn't hurt," he said as Mom bandaged it. Kyle wouldn't admit that his arm hurt quite a bit.

"Come on," said Mom. "Let's see if the TV has any news about that fire." As they watched, they saw Kyle's father, a firefighter, climbing a ladder to help a man escape the burning house. "Did you see that?" asked Kyle. "Dad is brave. He's a real man!"

When his father arrived home Kyle began, "Hey, Dad, we saw you on TV!" But his father just slumped down in a chair and started to cry. Kyle couldn't believe it!

"What's wrong, dear?" asked Kyle's mother.

Dad wiped his eyes. "The man we rescued died in the hospital. I feel so bad for his wife."

Kyle grew quiet and went to his room. Later his father came in and asked, "Are you all right?"

Kyle mumbled, "I thought that men never—well, I never thought you would."

REAL MEN HAVE FEELINGS.

Dad smiled. "You thought men never cried, right?" Kyle nodded, and his father continued. "I don't cry a lot, but I wouldn't make a good firefighter—or a good Christian—if I didn't care about people. Jesus cried when His friend Lazarus died. You don't think He was a sissy, do you?"

"No," Kyle replied. "He was brave enough to go to the cross and die for us. I guess I have a lot to learn about being a real man, don't I?"

HOW ABOUT YOU?

Do you think that men should hide their feelings to prove how brave they are? Jesus didn't hide His feelings, but He was no weakling either. He did many difficult things through the power of God. You can do the same, whether you're a young man or a young woman.

TO MEMORIZE:

Then Jesus wept. The people who were standing nearby said, "See how much he loved him!"

JOHN 11:35-36

BY SHERRY L. KUYT

Who Serves Whom?

I tell you the truth, when you did it to one of the least of these my brothers and sisters, you were doing it to me!
MATTHEW 25:40

What if we treated all people as though we were serving Jesus?

Write about the last time you helped someone who was lonely or in need of something. Describe that person's situation and what you did to help.

Now write about a time when you needed help. Who was there for you? Describe that person's actions.

What if we kept our minds and hearts focused on serving Christ with every interaction we have with others?

October 28

NOT WORTHLESS

Read Psalm 71:9-18.

In Andrea's town the newspaper carriers checked up on the senior citizens on their routes. Andrea did not like the time it took, especially with Mrs. Deaton. This old lady talked and talked while Andrea wanted to play.

One day Mrs. Deaton got out an old photo album. "Who are these people?" Andrea asked, pointing to a picture of four girls sitting on a log.

"They're my children," said Mrs. Deaton.

"Why don't they visit you or help take care of you?" Andrea asked.

"They all died of smallpox," Mrs. Deaton explained. "Then it was just George and me until he died." Andrea felt bad when she heard that. "Now don't fret," Mrs. Deaton added. "The Lord gives, and the Lord takes away, but He never leaves! He's been with me all these years."

One day not long after that, Mrs. Deaton didn't come to the door even though Andrea pounded loudly. Looking through a window, Andrea saw Mrs. Deaton with her head on the table. Just then Mrs. Deaton sat up. Seeing Andrea at the window, she hurried to the door.

LEARN FROM OLDER CHRISTIANS.

"Land sakes, child," she said with a smile. "I was so busy praying for the missionaries from my church I didn't even hear you."

Later Andrea told her mother, "I thought Mrs. Deaton was a silly old lady, but I was wrong. I've learned a lot from her. She really knows what it means to trust God and live for Him! If I live to be as old as she is, I hope I'll be just like her."

HOW ABOUT YOU?

How do you feel about older people? Do you respect them? Do you spend time with them and listen to what they have to say? You'll find that older Christians can teach valuable lessons from the experiences they've faced.

TO MEMORIZE:

Now that I am old and gray, do not abandon me, O God.
Let me proclaim your power to this new generation,
your mighty miracles to all who come after me.
PSALM 71:18

BY JAN L. HANSEN

October 29

THAT'S RIDICULOUS

Read 1 John 4:7-11.

It was the most ridiculous thing Shelly had ever heard! "Let your brothers and sisters know you love them," Shelly's Sunday school teacher had said. "And don't just tell them—show them too." Well, obviously Mrs. Johnson didn't know Todd, Shelly's brother. He was a pain!

When Shelly got home, Moppet, her dog, looked up from his basket. As Shelly sat down to pet the dog, Todd walked through the kitchen. Moppet jumped from his basket and followed Todd outside. Shelly glared at him. "Hey," she complained, "you belong to me."

That evening Shelly saw her brother watching TV by himself. She realized that Todd didn't have many friends. Shelly never talked to Todd much either, except to fight with him.

As Shelly thought about it, she remembered how she had felt when Moppet chose to follow Todd instead of her. It had made her feel sad and angry. *Is that how Todd feels?* she thought. *Sad and lonely and sometimes angry?* She thought of Mrs. Johnson's words. She did love Todd, even though she didn't always get along with him.

SHOW LOVE TO YOUR FAMILY.

Shelly got a soda, took it to the living room, and handed it to her brother. He looked up in surprise. "Todd," she said as she sat down next to him, "I . . . I just want you to know that I . . . I love you."

Todd gave her a funny look. "At least one person does," he mumbled.

It wasn't much, but it was a start.

HOW ABOUT YOU?

Do your brothers or sisters know you care about them? Sometimes it's harder to get along with family members than with anyone else, but it's important that you do so. Ask the Lord to help you be a good testimony at home.

TO MEMORIZE:

[God] has given us this command: Anyone who loves God must also love their brothers and sisters.

1 JOHN 4:21, NIV

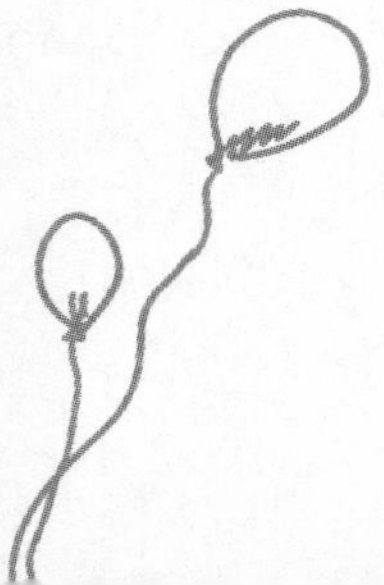

BY LENORA MCWHORTEN

October 30

WRAP IT RIGHT!

Read Titus 2:7-14.

Claudia welcomed her friends to her birthday party. But she had to be first in every game. She grabbed the biggest piece of cake. And as her guests ate ice cream she said, "Hurry! I want to open my gifts." After she tore open the packages, Claudia said, "I guess that's all."

"Wait!" cried Claudia's little sister, Kim. "You forgot mine. I wrapped it myself!" She held out a crumpled package. When Claudia tore open the wrapping, she found a beautiful little radio. "Mommy said I could use the money Grandma gave me," Kim said with a smile.

After everyone had left, Claudia said to her mother, "I got some neat presents—especially this radio from Kim. The wrapping was so messy, I never thought there could be anything nice inside." Then she added, "I gave everyone one of the tracts we got in Sunday school!"

Mom said, "I don't know if they will want to read them, because of the sloppy way you wrapped them."

WITNESS WITH WORDS AND ACTIONS.

"I didn't wrap them," said Claudia.

"I'm talking about your poor manners," said Mom. "You see, our lives show what Jesus really means to us. If people see that we are greedy, selfish, and unthankful, they're not likely to take our message very seriously."

Claudia knew she had been a poor example of a Christian. "I'll call the kids and apologize," she said. "Kim's messy present taught me a good lesson!"

HOW ABOUT YOU?

Do you try to witness to your unsaved friends? You should! But remember—the way you live will determine how seriously they take your message. The gospel has power to change lives and bring people to heaven. So be sure to wrap it right!

TO MEMORIZE:

[They] must show themselves to be entirely trustworthy and good. Then they will make the teaching about God our Savior attractive in every way.

TITUS 2:10

BY SHERRY L. KUYT

October 31

A HOME FOR CARYN

Read John 14:1-6.

Caryn gazed longingly at the miniature castle in the Chicago museum. How she wished she had a miniature house of her own! But she knew it would be expensive, so she'd have to get along with a cardboard box as she had in the past.

Caryn's birthday was a couple of months later, but she didn't even dare to hope for a dollhouse. She expected she'd get something useful just as she had other years. Sure enough, in her package there was a blouse and skirt.

"Now, close your eyes until I say you may open them," said Dad. The "birthday person" always had to do that while the cake was brought in. But this time when Dad finally said, "You may open your eyes," there stood a beautiful house with tiny rooms to furnish.

"Dad! I love it!" Caryn squealed.

Dad's eyes beamed with pleasure. "I'm sure I had as much fun building the house as you'll have decorating it. And all the time I was working on it, I thought about the wonderful home Jesus is making for those who believe in Him," added Dad. "If you think this is beautiful, just wait till you see what He's preparing."

HEAVEN IS THE BEST HOME.

"And best of all, Jesus Himself will be there," added Mom. Caryn smiled and nodded.

HOW ABOUT YOU?

Do you enjoy the home God has provided for you here? Do you like to decorate miniature houses? That's great, but think about the fact that Jesus is preparing a far more wonderful place for those who love Him. There will be no crying, sadness, or sickness in that perfect place. If you're a Christian, you can look forward to your home in heaven.

TO MEMORIZE:

There is more than enough room in my Father's home. If this were not so, would I have told you that I am going to prepare a place for you?

JOHN 14:2

BY CAROLYN E. YOST

November 1

INSIDE THE SHELL

Read Matthew 23:23-28.

"Half of these nuts aren't any good," said Cate, who was cracking nuts for the dessert her mother was making. "They're black inside."

"Use the good ones," advised Karl.

Cate told her brother, "You can't tell which ones are good. They all look fine on the outside."

"I can tell," insisted Karl. "This one's good." Cate cracked it open. Sure enough, it was good. Karl chose another one. Cate cracked it open. No, it was dried up and black. Karl handed her another nut. It, too, was no good.

"You can't tell any better than I can," Cate said, cracking one Karl had turned down. It was good.

"Let's choose every other one," suggested Karl. "Let's see who can find the most good ones." Soon the job was done.

As the family ate dessert that evening, Cate told Dad about the trouble with the nuts. "They sound like some people I know," said Dad.

Karl asked, "You know some nutty people?"

BE CLEAN INSIDE.

Dad smiled. "I know some people who look good on the outside, but I'm not sure what we'd see on the inside," he explained. "Jesus said the scribes and Pharisees were like that. They appeared to be good but really were hypocrites."

"I wonder how many people are like that today," added Mom. "We can't tell for sure who has accepted Jesus as Savior. Only God knows. He sees through the 'shell' and knows what everyone is like on the inside."

Cate nodded. "We can't fool God, can we?"

HOW ABOUT YOU?

Are you fooling people? Do you go to church, say your memory verses, and look good to others? Your parents and teacher may think you're a Christian, but have you truly trusted Jesus as Savior? If you haven't done so, accept Him today. Be clean and whole inside as well as outside.

TO MEMORIZE:

Outwardly you look like righteous people, but inwardly your hearts are filled with hypocrisy and lawlessness.

MATTHEW 23:28

BY HAZEL W. MARETT

November 2

A TRIP TO JEWEL CAVE

Read John 3:16-21.

The Carr family was on vacation, and one of the places they visited was Jewel Cave. Ryan was excited about being in a cave. He listened carefully as Peter, their tour guide, led them down the narrow paths. He really liked the different rock formations and was interested in hearing about the people who first explored the cave.

"Now," Peter said, as they stopped in a small opening, "I'm going to turn off the lights so you can see what it means to be truly in the dark." Peter was certainly right about it being dark. Ryan couldn't see a thing! He could not even see his fingers, though he put them right in front of his face. It was darker than night. At night Ryan could at least see shadows.

Peter made a joke about leaving the people in the darkness while he went on a coffee break. Everyone laughed, but it made Ryan think. He knew the Bible described people who didn't know Jesus as Savior as being lost in darkness. Now that he was in the dark, he realized that it was a scary place to be.

JESUS IS THE LIGHT OF THE WORLD.

Of course, Peter was just joking about leaving the tour group in the dark cave, but Ryan knew the Lord wasn't joking when He talked about the darkness of sin. Ryan remembered, too, that Jesus spoke of being the Light of the World, and he was thankful he had asked Jesus to be his Savior.

HOW ABOUT YOU?

Are you still in darkness—the darkness of sin? Jesus is called the Light of the World, and He is willing to take away the darkness from those who trust in Him. Ask Him to do that today!

TO MEMORIZE:

Jesus spoke to the people once more and said, "I am the light of the world. If you follow me, you won't have to walk in darkness, because you will have the light that leads to life."

JOHN 8:12

BY LENORA MCWHORTEN

November 3

LIKE THE TREE

Read 2 Timothy 2:19-22.

"Mom," called Jackson, "Dad and I are going for a hike."

"All right," said Mom. "Have fun."

So off they went, just the two "men" of the family. Jackson, his two younger sisters, and their parents were spending a weekend by Lake Michigan, and Jackson loved those hikes with his dad. Today he had an important question.

"Can people tell just by looking at you that you're a Christian?" he asked. "My Sunday school teacher said that people look at our lives."

"Good question," said Dad. "See that sand dune with all the trees growing on it? Does any one tree catch your eye?"

"Hmmm," said Jackson as he looked at the trees. "Oh, the one growing sideways on the slope stands out."

Dad nodded. "You picked out that tree because it was different. When people see what you do, they should see that you're different."

"Different in what ways?" asked Jackson.

BE DIFFERENT FOR JESUS.

Dad answered, "Maybe you hear kids using bad language. Or maybe someone asks you to go to an R-rated movie. God doesn't want you to do those things. He wants you to be different."

"Oh, I get it!" exclaimed Jackson. "If I don't do things that are wrong, people will notice."

"That's right. But even if everyone doesn't notice, remember that you're pleasing God. And that's most important."

HOW ABOUT YOU?

Can people tell that you're a Christian by looking at the things you do? They can't if they see cheating, bad language, disobedience, or lying. Instead, let them see honesty, kindness, love, and patience. Let them see that you are different for Jesus.

TO MEMORIZE:

Therefore, come out from among unbelievers, and separate yourselves from them, says the LORD.

2 CORINTHIANS 6:17

BY DEBORAH S. MARETT

Simply Have It

What does the LORD your God require of you? He requires only that you fear the LORD your God, and live in a way that pleases him, and love him and serve him with all your heart and soul.

DEUTERONOMY 10:12

Keeping the faith may not always feel easy, but God makes sure it's simple to understand. It's respecting Him and His laws. It's loving and serving Him with everything you have. Simply have faith.

These people from the Bible help teach the lessons and show the value of faith in God.

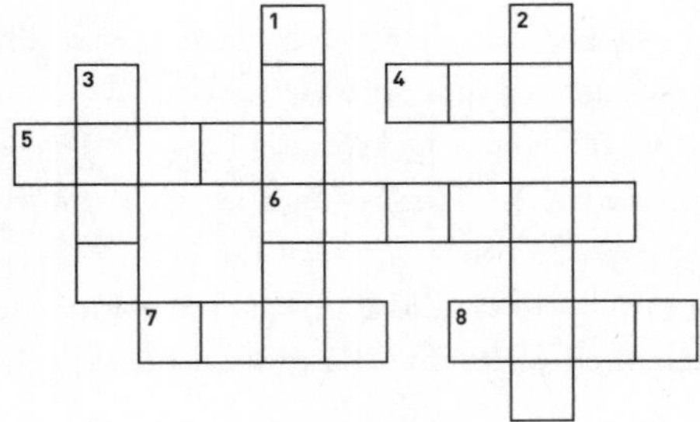

ACROSS

4. His whole life fell apart, but he kept the faith.
5. Through his faith, he led the Israelites as God instructed.
6. Elisha followed in this faithful prophet's footsteps.
7. This relative of Mary baptized Jesus in the Jordan River.
8. Once known as Saul, he became a Christian, then spent his life spreading the Good News.

DOWN

1. Neither his brothers' betrayal nor injustice changed the faith of this young man.
2. This biblical father followed the Lord and was saved for his faith, not his works.
3. The father of Shem, Ham, and Japheth who did everything God commanded him to do.

ANSWER KEY

ACROSS: 4. Job; 5. Moses; 6. Elijah; 7. John; 8. Paul

DOWN: 1. Joseph; 2. Abraham; 3. Noah

November 4

PRICELESS TREASURE

Read Matthew 6:19-21, 24.

Luis scowled as he raked leaves. "I was gonna collect aluminum cans today to make money for a new skateboard," he muttered to himself. "Instead, here I am, doing stupid yard work." It was the first Saturday at their new home, and Mom needed help.

Just then Luis noticed a large hole by a tree. "Look, Mom," he called. "This would be a good place to hide stuff."

Mom walked over to look. "Maybe there's a sack of stolen money inside," she whispered teasingly. She poked her rake into the hole, and they heard a scraping sound as the rake hit a metal object.

"Something *is* hidden in there!" cried Luis. Sticking his hand inside the hole, he pulled out a small box. Eagerly, Luis opened the old box and looked inside. Then he let out a disappointed groan. The "treasure" was a handful of stones, a rusty pocketknife, and a mildewed book of children's poems.

"Somebody must have treasured these things but then forgotten about them," said Mom. "I hope whoever did it stored treasures in heaven, too! Those are the best treasures, you know, and they can never be ruined or stolen."

HEAVENLY TREASURE IS PRICELESS.

Luis thought about the skateboard he wanted so much. As he looked at the rusty pocketknife, he realized that all material things are bound to wear out or break down. Somehow, a skateboard didn't seem quite so important anymore.

HOW ABOUT YOU?

Is there something you want very much? Maybe it's a phone or something one of your friends has. Earthly treasures don't last, but serving Christ brings treasure you will never lose. It's more priceless than all the possessions in the world.

TO MEMORIZE:

Store your treasures in heaven, where moths and rust cannot destroy, and thieves do not break in and steal. Wherever your treasure is, there the desires of your heart will also be.

MATTHEW 6:20-21

BY BRENDA DECKER

November 5

A DIFFERENT POINT OF VIEW

Read Isaiah 55:8-9.

Alexa sat curled up on the sofa with Whiskers purring on her lap. "Whiskers, things will never be the same," she told the cat. "We're moving, and I'll never see my friends again."

"Whiskers, you're not going to like moving." Alexa was surprised to hear Dad's voice behind her. "As far as you know, this apartment is all there is to the world," added Dad as he sat down on the sofa. "You're going to be scared when we put you in the pet carrier and put it on the plane. Maybe we should leave you here."

"But, Dad," protested Alexa, "you said that Whiskers will be able to climb trees at our new house. She'll do lots of things she's never done before. She might not like moving, but she'll like it after she gets there."

"I guess you're right," said Dad. "Since you're not a cat, you see things from a different point of view than Whiskers does. And Alexa, God sees your future from a different point of view than you do. He knows you'll hurt for a while, but He also sees past that to the wonderful things He has waiting for you in our new home. If you let Him, He'll help you get over the hurt so you can enjoy that wonderful future."

TRUST GOD'S PLAN.

Alexa sniffed as she stroked the cat. "Well, Whiskers, maybe there's a different world out there for both of us," she said. "We might even find a tree to climb together." Alexa smiled as she gave the cat a squeeze.

HOW ABOUT YOU?

Is there something in your life that is so hard you feel you'll never get over it? God doesn't let you see into the future, but He sees what's there. You must live by faith, trusting Him to use even the hard things to work for good in your life.

TO MEMORIZE:

We live by believing and not by seeing.

2 CORINTHIANS 5:7

BY KATHERINE R. ADAMS

November 6

KEEP KNOCKING

Read Luke 18:1-8.

As Max crawled into bed, his mind was made up. He was going to stop praying for Uncle Carl and spend his prayer time on someone for whom it would do more good. Uncle Carl was a hopeless case.

When Max came home from the park the next afternoon, Mom asked him to run over to Gramp Nelson's house. "He has fresh squash for us," she said.

Quick as a wink, Max was on his bicycle. He knocked loudly on Gramp Nelson's door. No answer. He knocked again, louder. Still no answer. "Must not be home," he mumbled as he jumped on his bike and pedaled home.

As Max came into the kitchen, Mom hung up the phone. "That was Gramp Nelson. He was on the patio, and by the time he got to the door, you had left. He wants you to come back."

"Oh no!" Max plopped down on the couch. "Let me catch my breath first."

Mom picked up the mail. "Here's a letter from Uncle Carl," she said. A smile spread over her face. "Listen to this. 'I am so unhappy. I'm going to have to change my lifestyle. Keep praying for me.'" She folded the letter. "Sometimes we're tempted to quit praying just before the answer comes," she added.

KEEP ON PRAYING.

Max felt guilty as he remembered last night's decision. Then he nodded. "Just like I quit knocking before Gramp got to the door," he said. "I'll go back and keep knocking until I get an answer." As he left, he made up his mind to pray for Uncle Carl again too.

HOW ABOUT YOU?

Have you been praying for something or someone for a long time? Are you about ready to give up? Don't! Keep knocking. The answer is on the way.

TO MEMORIZE:

Keep on asking, and you will receive what you ask for. Keep on seeking, and you will find. Keep on knocking, and the door will be opened to you.

MATTHEW 7:7

BY BARBARA J. WESTBERG

November 7

A SLOW START

Read Psalm 119:89-96.

For weeks Alyce had promised to take daily walks with her grandfather. Finally she began doing it and really enjoyed the walks. "I should have begun doing this a long time ago," she said as they walked together one day. "It was hard getting started, but now I see what I've been missing!"

"I know what you mean," answered her grandfather. "That's just the way I used to be about reading my Bible."

Alyce stopped. "You've read your Bible every day as long as you've lived with us!"

"That's true." Grandfather smiled. "But I had a hard time getting myself to do it every day even though I've always believed I should read it. One day someone said that if I'd just get started, it would soon become as natural as breathing."

Alyce knew what her grandfather was trying to tell her. She planned to read her Bible and had even started once, but soon she forgot all about it. She told her grandfather about that.

READ YOUR BIBLE FAITHFULLY.

"Did you try to see how many chapters you could read at one time?" he asked. "Or did you read a few verses at a time to see what you could get out of it?" Alyce admitted that she had tried to keep up with her brother.

"A slow start is best," Grandfather suggested. "It's like walking. You don't walk three miles the first day. You start slowly, do it regularly, and add the miles gradually."

HOW ABOUT YOU?

Have you found it hard to spend time each day reading the Bible? When you read, do you simply try to get through as fast as you can? God's Word should be read slowly and carefully so it can help you learn how to live as a Christian. Make God's Word a natural part of your life.

TO MEMORIZE:

Come, descendants of Jacob, let us walk in the light of the LORD!

ISAIAH 2:5

BY RUTH I. JAY

November 8

WATCH YOUR OPPONENT

Read 1 Peter 5:6-9.

Eight-year-old Mitchell was excited as he put an *X* on a corner spot of the tic-tac-toe game. He laughed because on the next move he could win against his big sister, Mari, in two ways. But his laughter stopped suddenly as Mari marked an *O* and went on to draw a line through three *O*s in a row! She had won again!

"I hate you!" he shrieked as he threw his pencil across the room and stomped out. A little later Mom found him lying on his bed.

"Mari told me what happened," she said. "You lost two things—the game and your temper. And you lost both of them because you didn't watch your opponent."

Mitchell sat up straight and looked at her, a question in his eyes. "That's right," she said. "Mari was your opponent in the game, but you were so concerned about how you would win that you forgot to think about how she would play. You also have another opponent, a more serious one. The Bible says that the devil is our enemy, or opponent. You weren't watching out for him when you lost your temper."

Mitchell nodded sadly. "I guess not," he said. Then he brightened. "But Jesus will forgive me, won't He? I'll ask Him, and Mari, too. And I'll ask God to help me not to do it again."

RESIST SATAN. 

HOW ABOUT YOU?

Do you sometimes forget to watch out for Satan? He loves to see you lose your temper. He's happy when you cheat. It pleases him if you disobey your mom or dad. He likes to hear you gossip. Whenever you sin, Satan is glad. But you don't have to lose to him. Resist him, and God will give you victory.

TO MEMORIZE:

Humble yourselves before God. Resist the devil, and he will flee from you.

JAMES 4:7

BY HAZEL W. MARETT

November 9

THE CROOKED ARROW

Read Psalm 127.

Scott shuffled along as he and his father went out to practice using their new bow and arrows. He was angry because he had been grounded for going to a friend's house without telling his parents where he was going.

Dad shot first. His arrow completely missed the target. Scott didn't try to hide his snickers. "Okay," Dad said, "let's see you do better!"

Scott took careful aim. He gave his father a superior smile as he hit the bottom of the target. After several more tries, both of them could hit the target most of the time. Then Dad saw a bent arrow. "I wonder what happened to this one," he said. "Why don't you try it to see what happens."

Scott tried it. The crooked arrow flew in a crazy arc and got lost in a tangle of prickly blackberry bushes. "I'm not going after that one!" exclaimed Scott.

"We'll leave it," agreed Dad. "Crooked arrows aren't any good. That's why I don't want you to be one."

THANK GOD FOR CORRECTION.

"What are you talking about?" Scott asked.

"Well," said Dad, "in Psalm 127 God says that children are like arrows in the hand of a warrior. God expects parents to keep the arrows straight. When we send you off on your own, you must be able to hit the target by living a life that pleases God. If we don't straighten you out when you're young, you may land in thorny situations."

As they finished collecting the arrows, Scott began to feel almost glad about being disciplined. After all, Dad was just obeying God. And Scott did not want to grow up crooked.

HOW ABOUT YOU?

Do you learn from your parents when they discipline you? God has given them the tremendously important job of raising you properly. They need to straighten you out when you start down the crooked path of sin.

TO MEMORIZE:

A youngster's heart is filled with foolishness, but physical discipline will drive it far away.

PROVERBS 22:15

BY ELLEN C. ORR

November 10

I MEAN IT

Read Psalm 12:1-4.

"Something funny happened in Nature Club today," Katy told her mother as she set the table for supper. "Amy Brown came over to me like we were best friends! I hardly know her at all. Anyway, she told me how nice I looked in my green sweater and asked if it was new."

"Really?" asked Mom. "You've had that sweater a long time, and you wear it a lot."

"I know," said Katy. "Then Amy went on to say how much she admired my math grades. I really started wondering what was up when she told me how she always likes to be with me!"

"She must have been in a good mood today," Mom commented.

"Well, after she got done telling me all those things, she went over to another girl and gave her the same treatment!" said Katy.

Mom looked thoughtful. "Maybe she's trying to make some new friends."

"You're right," laughed Katy, "and she wanted them in a hurry. I figured it out after the club meeting started. We were electing officers, and Amy was one of the three nominated for president. She thought she could get our votes by giving us compliments. I had already decided Natasha would be the best president, and I guess most of the other kids agreed, because Natasha won. After that Amy ignored me."

GIVE HONEST COMPLIMENTS.

Mom said, "It's sad when someone tries to control others through flattery. Even the Bible says that flattering people is wrong."

"I'm going to be sure that I really mean what I'm saying when I give someone a compliment," declared Katy.

HOW ABOUT YOU?

Have you ever given a compliment because you wanted someone to do something for you? Insincere compliments are called flattery, but actually they are lies. God's Word refers to flattery a number of times, but never favorably. It's nice to give a compliment only if you really mean it.

TO MEMORIZE:

To flatter friends is to lay a trap for their feet.

PROVERBS 29:5

BY LENORA MCWHORTEN

He Is Faithful

If we confess our sins to him, he is faithful and just to forgive us our sins and to cleanse us from all wickedness.

1 JOHN 1:9

God is faithful to us. He is always watching, always listening, with His plans for us in motion. God had plans for Jonah, too. When Jonah realized his mistakes, he looked to God and prayed. And even though the faithful disobey, God welcomes them back with open arms.

Help Jonah get to the city of Nineveh.

SEE ANSWER IN BACK

November 11

IT'S NOT FAIR

Read Acts 16:22-31.

"I didn't make the basketball team, Dad." Joseph slumped into a chair as he came in from school. "I'm not bragging, but I do play basketball well."

"Yes, you do, Son," agreed Dad, "but there were only two openings on the team. Who was it that the coach chose?"

"Aiden—we all expected that. He is good! But Randy got the other opening. In the tryouts, I made more baskets than he did, and I dribbled the ball longer. But his dad is a teacher at school, and I think that's why he made it," Joseph said.

Dad sighed. "I suppose that's possible. You could talk to the coach," he suggested. "But be careful not to say things you can't prove. And, Joseph, you must learn that life isn't always fair. You must also learn to have a Christlike attitude no matter what happens."

"Aw, Dad," Joseph whined.

"Think of Paul and Silas. It wasn't fair that they were thrown in jail for preaching about the Lord," continued Dad, "and yet they sang! They didn't let unfair actions get them down."

GROW THROUGH UNFAIR SITUATIONS.

"I know this is a hard experience, but you can learn something from it. Ask the Lord to show you what to do. You'll come out of it a stronger and more mature Christian."

Joseph sighed. He knew his dad was right. Being upset wouldn't do any good. He would ask the Lord to help him turn a bad experience into a growing one.

HOW ABOUT YOU?

Are you ever treated unfairly? It happens to everyone. The next time you're faced with an unfair situation that you can't change, remember Paul and Silas—instead of complaining, they sang! God used them through that experience, and he can also use you. Maintain a good attitude. Grow through what has happened.

TO MEMORIZE:

He is the Rock; his deeds are perfect. Everything he does is just and fair. He is a faithful God who does no wrong; how just and upright he is!
DEUTERONOMY 32:4

BY LENORA MCWHORTEN

November 12

FIRE IS HOT

Read Hebrews 11:1-4.

The twins, Jared and Jenna, were spending the weekend with their grandparents. As they sat by a fire, popping corn with an old-fashioned, long-handled basket, Jenna told her grandparents what they had been discussing in the Christian school they attended. "Mrs. Wilson says that a person needs faith to live in this world as well as to become a Christian. She says that almost everything we do takes faith."

"Yeah." Jared nodded. "Sounds kind of silly to me." He shook the corn popper vigorously. As the kernels finished popping, he pulled the basket from the fire. "Where's the pot holder?" he asked.

"What makes you think you need that?" asked Grandpa.

"Grandpa!" said Jared. "Fire is hot."

"Perhaps," said Grandpa. "At least fire always has been hot. But if you don't have faith that what was true in the past is still true, you might as well grab hold of that basket and open it up. Of course, if you do have faith, maybe you'd like this pot holder."

HAVE FAITH IN GOD.

Jared laughed. "I have faith," he declared, taking the pot holder. "I guess Mrs. Wilson's right. We do need faith for lots of things."

Grandpa nodded. "Seeing that we exercise faith in the ordinary things we do should help us to see what it means to have faith in God. It's simply believing that what He says is true—even though we may not understand it."

HOW ABOUT YOU?

Do you have faith? Do you ride in a bus or a plane or even a car without checking out the driver? That takes faith—a belief that those people will get you where you want to go. You'll find that you have faith in many other people too. Then certainly you can have faith in God. Others can make errors, but not God.

TO MEMORIZE:

It is impossible to please God without faith.

HEBREWS 11:6

BY GERI WALCOTT

November 13

OH, BOY!

Read Isaiah 55:8-11.

"Oh, boy! It's a boy, isn't it?" Leo was jumping up and down while his grandmother talked to Leo's father, who was at the hospital.

Grandma hung up the phone. "You have a beautiful baby sister named Melissa," she said.

"No!" said Leo. "I've been praying for a brother. It's not fair. Cory got a baby brother, and he didn't even pray."

Grandma sat down in the chair by the coffee table. "I got out the album that has your baby pictures in it," she said. "You sure were cute."

"That was a long time ago. I'm in school now," said Leo proudly.

"I remember how happy your mom and dad were when they were expecting you," Grandma told him. "When people asked if they wanted a girl or boy, they said that either would be okay."

Leo picked an apple from the basket of fruit. "I'm sure they were glad I was a boy."

"They were pleased, but I was disappointed. I wanted a granddaughter," confessed Grandma.

"Grandma!" Leo was shocked. "Don't you like me?"

"Oh yes," Grandma assured him, "but I already had five grandsons. I thought it would be nice to have a girl in the family." She gave Leo a hug. "But now I love you very much. You'll love your sister, too. Thank God for her."

"Grandma, I still don't think it was fair of you to wish I were a girl," Leo said, pouting.

Grandma's eyes twinkled. "Less fair than for you to wish your sister were a boy?" she asked.

Leo looked surprised. "When can Melissa come home?" he asked eagerly.

HOW ABOUT YOU?

Do you blame God if He doesn't answer your prayers your way? Do you ask for things to satisfy your own selfish desires, or do you ask for God's will to be done? He has a purpose for everything.

TO MEMORIZE:

Be thankful in all circumstances, for this is God's will for you who belong to Christ Jesus.

1 THESSALONIANS 5:18

BY RUTH MCQUILKIN

November 14

GET SMART

Read Deuteronomy 10:12-13, 17-21.

"I'm going to climb the fence around the power station's transformer," Jason announced.

Michael's eyes widened. "Don't do it, Jason. Dad says it's dangerous. Why do you think the electric company put up that high fence?"

"To keep out scaredy-cats like you," mocked Jason. "Have a good time playing with the girls."

I'd better stop him, Michael thought as he watched Jason leave. He jumped to his feet and ran toward the house, thinking, *I'll tell Mom*.

As soon as Michael's mother heard about it, she called the electric company. Minutes later they heard sirens. "Stay here," Mom ordered as she headed for the street.

When Mom returned, she gave Michael a teary smile. "Jason touched a high voltage wire just as the emergency squad arrived. He has some bad burns, but he'll be okay."

FEAR GOD.

"Jason said he wasn't afraid of anything," Michael told his mother.

Mom sighed. "It's good to fear some things," she said. "For instance, the Bible says that fearing the Lord is the beginning of wisdom."

"Does that mean we're supposed to be afraid of God?" asked Michael.

"We are to fear God in the sense that we respect and obey Him," answered Mom.

"Like I respect and obey you and Dad?" Michael asked.

Mom nodded. "That shows wisdom. If you're smart, you fear many things, and it keeps you out of a lot of trouble."

HOW ABOUT YOU?

Are you afraid of God? If you're a Christian, He's your heavenly Father. He loves you, but you do need to respect and obey Him. Do that, and you don't need to be afraid.

TO MEMORIZE:

Fear of the LORD is the foundation of true wisdom. All who obey his commandments will grow in wisdom.

PSALM 111:10

BY BARBARA J. WESTBERG

November 15

PERSECUTED—OR PUSHY?

Read 2 Peter 1:5-9.

Jordan was a Christian—and she let everybody at school know about it. But the things she did and said often made others angry. When Kelsey sent a text in class, Jordan told the teacher. And when a few girls tried to be friendly and invite her to their party, Jordan just looked shocked and said loudly, "Of course not! I'm a Christian!"

One day she walked home with Tina. "Nobody likes me," groaned Jordan, "and it's all because I'm a Christian!"

"I'm a Christian too," said Tina, "and I have a lot of friends. I've even been able to help some of them learn to trust Jesus as their Savior!"

Jordan complained, "I witness like the Bible says, but nobody lets me talk about Jesus."

"Maybe it's your attitude," Tina said. "Kids think you act like you're better than they are."

"But I am," replied Jordan. "I don't smoke, cheat, or tell dirty stories. You don't either!"

BE A LOVING WITNESS.

"Well, that's true," Tina smiled. "But I'm still not perfect. And if I didn't know Jesus, I'd be just like the others—or worse. Don't forget, Jordan, God loves them as much as He loves us. He wants them to be in His family too."

"But how can I witness to them?" asked Jordan.

"Try being friendly," Tina said. "After all, Jesus was known as a friend of sinners. Don't always be putting kids down. Let them know you care about them and God does too. They'll be more willing to listen to you then."

HOW ABOUT YOU?

Have you suffered for being a Christian? Be sure your attitude is right. Don't be afraid to witness for Christ, but do it out of love, not pride. Check to see if the qualities listed in today's Scripture can be seen in your witness. Don't be pushy.

TO MEMORIZE:

Remember, it is better to suffer for doing good, if that is what God wants, than to suffer for doing wrong!

1 PETER 3:17

BY SHERRY L. KUYT

November 16

NO LAUGHING MATTER

Read John 12:37-43.

Tim scuffed the toe of his shoe in the playground dirt. He didn't think the words some of the boys were saying were funny. He knew the words did not honor God. But he was afraid the other boys wouldn't let him play with them anymore if he walked away. So Tim stood in the small circle of boys, laughing at the words.

That night, as usual, Tim read his Bible before going to bed. He read from John 12, "They loved human praise more than the praise of God." Tim understood then that he had wanted praise from the other boys on the playground more than praise from God. He whispered, "Dear God, I'm sorry for laughing at words and jokes I knew were wrong. Help me to walk away the next time others are talking like that."

A few days later the same boys stood together in a corner of the playground. The tallest boy began to use bad language. Everyone laughed—except Tim. He turned and began to walk away. "What's the matter, Tim?" someone jeered.

SEEK GOD'S PRAISE.

Tim continued to walk away. He heard footsteps behind him, turned, and saw Roberto walking along with him. "I don't like that kind of language either," said Roberto.

"Do you collect baseball cards?" asked Tim.

"I sure do," answered Roberto, pulling some out of his pocket. That was just the beginning of a new friendship. Tim found that he was much happier than when he was trying to make the other boys like him. He learned that when he pleased God, he also pleased himself.

HOW ABOUT YOU?

Do you care more about what the kids at school will say than about what God will say? Make sure that the words of today's verse can never be said about you!

TO MEMORIZE:

They loved human praise more than the praise of God.

JOHN 12:43

BY CAROLYN E. YOST

November 17

THE NEW FRIEND

Read Philippians 2:1-4.

Paul noticed a boy sitting by himself in the school cafeteria. *He's new here, and he must be lonely,* thought Paul, remembering how he had felt last year when he was new.

Paul sat down across from the new boy. "Hi," he said. "I'm Paul. What's your name?"

"My name is Kim," said the boy.

"Where are you from?" asked Peter.

"South Korea," answered Kim.

As they walked to class together a little later, Paul invited Kim to come home with him after school. Kim looked pleased.

Hanging out with Kim turned out to be more fun than Paul expected. The boys played darts, marbles, and video games.

When Kim invited Paul over to meet his family, Paul went. He ate Korean food and learned to eat with chopsticks. He also learned about Korea. The boys became good friends.

KINDNESS COMES BACK TO YOU.

"I'm so glad I got to know Kim," Paul told his father one day. "I feel like I've had a trip to Korea every time I visit his home."

"Those who refresh others will themselves be refreshed," quoted Dad with a smile.

"What does that mean?" asked Paul.

"It's from the Bible, and it means that your actions often work like a boomerang—they come back to you," replied Dad. "When you are kind to others, you are blessed yourself."

HOW ABOUT YOU?

Kindness always pays, even if the person to whom you are kind should fail to respond in gratitude. God sees all, and He will repay you. He works things out so that if you are kind to someone, you will not only make that person happy but you will become happy yourself!

TO MEMORIZE:

The generous will prosper; those who refresh others will themselves be refreshed.
PROVERBS 11:25

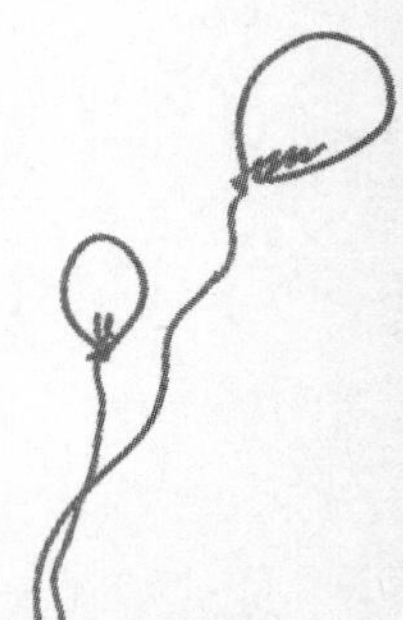

BY MATILDA H. NORDTVEDT

Things Not Seen

Now faith is the substance of things hoped for,
the evidence of things not seen.
HEBREWS 11:1, NKJV

Faith is a confident hope, as solid as evidence. We can't always see the hand of God guiding our footsteps. As the disciple Paul wrote, "We walk by faith, not by sight" (2 Corinthians 5:7, NKJV). Our certain faith is the solid ground under our feet. Our sure faith *is* the evidence.

Circle the words that mean "evidence."

```
E I F O J A E V I D E N C E A
T U J X T C D K A D D B Z G T
H D J M O O O H Q Z O V W G T
N Y Q N T N C G M U R H I J E
Q E Y T E F U H S S I Z T Y S
X V N E S I M C Z O W A N C T
K A S S T R E P S W H E E R A
R L L T I M N T A L D S S Z T
W I S A M A T Z S O B V S W I
V D A M O T A D R H I I H V O
B A O E N I T E C V B Y N F N
X T Y N Y O I D J M S Q H R V
G I E T M N O W A P F P E C D
N O G U T G N W D B F A F U T
R N D O M W L M Y O L Z T Y Q
```

attestation
confirmation
documentation
evidence
testament
testimony
validation
witness

SEE ANSWER IN BACK

November 18

SPIRITUAL CHECKUP

Read 1 John 2:3-10.

As Kevin entered the waiting room, the office nurse smiled at him. "Your father's almost done for the day, Kevin," she said.

Soon Kevin and his father were in their car, headed for home. "Dad, how can you tell if a patient is sick?" Kevin asked.

"Well," said Dad, "when a patient comes in for an exam, I first ask if he or she has any complaints. I also check height, weight, blood pressure, and heartbeat. I listen to the lungs, and I look at the ears, eyes, nose, and throat. If I suspect any illness, I sometimes take a blood sample or order some other tests."

"That sounds simple enough," said Kevin. "So why do some people skip their checkups?"

His father replied, "They don't realize that if they would have an examination regularly, many illnesses could be prevented." Then he added, "An even more important checkup is a spiritual one. And that's one we can give ourselves."

"How do we do that?" asked Kevin.

EXAMINE YOUR CHRISTIAN LIFE.

"By examining the vital signs of our Christian life," said Dad. "First, we need to think about our prayer and Scripture-reading habits. Do we do those exercises every day? What about church? How often do we attend? Then we must look at our attitudes toward other people. Perhaps we need to let God be a surgeon and remove our bad thoughts. We also need to ask ourselves what work we've been doing for the Lord to stay healthy."

"That doesn't sound too hard," said Kevin. "I think I'll give myself a spiritual checkup today."

HOW ABOUT YOU?

When was the last time you gave yourself a spiritual checkup? You'd be surprised by how often a simple lapse in Bible reading, prayer, or church attendance can lead to big problems. God doesn't want your Christian life to be an unstable, unhappy experience. Be sure to take regular checkups!

TO MEMORIZE:

You should examine yourself before eating the bread and drinking the cup.

1 CORINTHIANS 11:28

BY SHERRY L. KUYT

November 19

ACCIDENTALLY GOOD?

Read Philippians 2:5-9.

"Look, Dad!" Javier exclaimed one afternoon. "Sonny's playing dead, just like I taught him."

Dad laughed. "I think he's just resting," he said. "Let's go for a walk and teach him to heel."

The dog plodded along willingly at first. Then he began to strain at the leash. Javier scolded and tugged, but the dog didn't pay any attention. Suddenly Sonny turned and ran in the direction Javier had been pulling. "He's minding me now!" Javier called.

Then Sonny came to a trash can and stopped to sniff. Javier couldn't get him to budge.

"I don't get it," moaned Javier. "Sometimes Sonny minds me, and sometimes he doesn't."

Dad remarked, "Sometimes he just happens to want the same thing you do."

OBEY GOD ALWAYS.

"You mean he's accidentally good?" asked Javier.

"You could say that." Dad showed Javier how to direct the dog, giving the leash a firm jerk when Sonny went the wrong way.

"You know, people often behave the way Sonny did," observed Dad. "When they're in a good mood, they are kind. When they feel like it, they go to church. When they feel generous, they give money or time. But that's not really obeying God. The true test of obedience is how we act when we don't feel like obeying."

"I get it," Javier replied as he jerked the leash. "I'll try to remember that. I don't want to be just accidentally good."

HOW ABOUT YOU?

Do you think it's enough to obey God's commandments when you feel like it? That's not obeying. It's doing what you want to do. You need to follow Jesus' example. He became a servant and "humbled himself in obedience . . . and died a criminal's death on a cross" (Philippians 2:8). You need to obey God no matter how you feel or what it might cost you.

TO MEMORIZE:

Then Jesus said to his disciples, "If any of you wants to be my follower, you must turn from your selfish ways, take up your cross, and follow me."

MATTHEW 16:24

BY SHERRY L. KUYT

November 20

TOO MANY MICHAELS

Read Psalm 8.

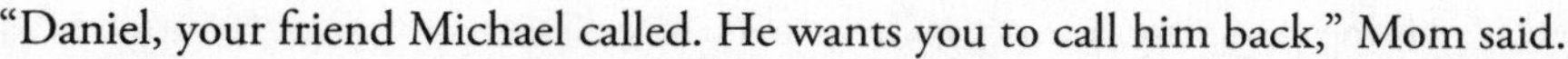

"Daniel, your friend Michael called. He wants you to call him back," Mom said.

Daniel went to call his friend. There was no answer. Then he remembered that Michael was out of town. "Was it Michael Burke?" he asked.

"Oh, no, it was Michael White," said Mom.

Just then Daniel's older sister came into the room, smiling. "I'm going out with Michael!"

Daniel and Mom burst out laughing. "Which Michael?" they asked together.

That night Daniel looked at his list of prayer requests. One name on it was that of a boy at church who needed surgery for a serious heart condition. "Dear Lord, please bless Michael," Daniel began. Then he paused. "You know, the one who needs heart surgery."

Suddenly, Daniel thought about how many Michaels there were in the world. There must be many Daniels, Jessicas, and Sarahs, too. All of a sudden Daniel felt small and unimportant.

GOD KNOWS YOU.

A few days later Mom said, "Michael's mom called today. Michael had his surgery today, and he's doing fine," she told Daniel. "Guess what? There are three other Michaels there! But don't worry—Michael's mother is the head nurse on that floor. Believe me, she knows which Michael belongs to her!"

When Daniel prayed for his friend that night, he knew he didn't have to remind God which Michael was being prayed for, or which Daniel was doing the asking. Just as a mother knows her son, God knows each of His children.

HOW ABOUT YOU?

Do you think God ever gets tired of caring for so many people? Do you ever wonder if He is too busy to hear your requests, fears, or problems? Don't worry! God knows each of His children, and each one is special to Him.

TO MEMORIZE:

Now, O Jacob, listen to the LORD who created you. O Israel, the one who formed you says, "Do not be afraid, for I have ransomed you. I have called you by name; you are mine."

ISAIAH 43:1

BY CATHERINE RUNYON

November 21

GRANDMA'S ATTIC (PART 1)

Read 2 Timothy 1:6-12.

Jill was helping her aunt clean out Grandma's attic. Everything in it reminded her aunt of a story. Now Aunt Sarah was reading a letter, holding it up to the light from the small window. "Who's the letter from, Aunt Sarah?"

Aunt Sarah folded the letter and put it back into the yellowed envelope. "When we were children, we all loved this lady, Mrs. Alexander, who went to our church. Her husband came to church once in a while, but he was unfriendly."

"What was the letter about?" asked Jill.

"Mrs. Alexander went away for a long time," said Aunt Sarah. "We thought she was on a trip, but this letter explains what really happened. She had left her husband. In the letter she is thanking Mother (your grandma) for praying for her and for encouraging her to continue living the Christian life even though it was hard for her." Aunt Sarah smiled and shook her head. "Your grandma never told us. She just went to the woman who was suffering and helped her get victory in her life."

GOD WILL REWARD HIS CHILDREN.

"I'm glad that letter wasn't thrown away," Jill said. "Otherwise you wouldn't know how Grandma helped that lady."

Aunt Sarah smiled. "It's nice to know. But it wouldn't have mattered if I'd never found out," she said. "Jesus knows. He's the keeper of all the good deeds and loving words of His children, and He'll reward them someday."

HOW ABOUT YOU?

Are you doing and saying things that will build rewards for you in heaven? Do you wonder if anyone notices when you're kind, helpful, and loving? You can be sure that God does. It doesn't matter if anyone else knows. God will reward you for what is done for Him.

TO MEMORIZE:

I know the one in whom I trust, and I am sure that he is able to guard what I have entrusted to him until the day of his return.

2 TIMOTHY 1:12

BY CATHERINE RUNYON

November 22

GRANDMA'S ATTIC (PART 2)

Read Psalm 1:1-3.

As Jill and her aunt cleaned Grandma's attic, Aunt Sarah found a box of high school souvenirs. She went through them, telling Jill about each one. Aunt Sarah held up a long piece of yarn. "This is the yarn I wrapped around Tom's ring so I could wear it. We went steady for a month! I haven't thought of him in years."

"Don't you forget anything, Aunt Sarah? Everything you see reminds you of something! Your head must be stuffed fuller than this attic."

"Well, I've heard that people never really forget anything," said Aunt Sarah. "It's in the brain, but it may take something like a souvenir to bring it into the part of our mind where we can recall it." She stretched and said, "I'm getting tired and thirsty. Let's take a break."

They went to the kitchen and found some lemonade. As they sipped it, Aunt Sarah asked, "Jill, what do you have in your attic?" Jill started thinking about the attic at her home, but Aunt Sarah leaned forward and tapped her on the head. "What I mean is, what do you have stored away up here?" she said. "Are there plenty of Bible verses in your 'storage area'?"

MEMORIZE GOD'S WORD.

"I try to learn as much as I can," Jill said.

"Once memories are in place, things we see or hear can bring them back," said Aunt Sarah. "It's the same with Scripture. When you've memorized God's Word, He can use people and events to bring it to mind as you need it. That's one way the Holy Spirit helps you each day."

HOW ABOUT YOU?

Have you ever seen or heard something that reminded you of a verse you knew? By memorizing God's Word and associating it with everyday things, you make it part of your life. As you become older, it will come back to you when you need it.

TO MEMORIZE:

They delight in the law of the LORD, meditating on it day and night.

PSALM 1:2

BY CATHERINE RUNYON

November 23
GROW, GROW, GROW

Read Luke 2:42-52.

"Will you measure me, Danielle?" Jeff asked his older sister.

"I just measured you yesterday," protested Danielle. At his pleading look, she gave in. "Well, all right. Stand straight."

"Have I grown any?" Jeff asked anxiously.

"Nope, you're still the same height," said Danielle. Jeff looked puzzled.

In Sunday school the next day, Jeff really didn't want to sing one of the songs. He joined in, but the words seemed to stick in his throat. "Read your Bible, pray every day . . . and you'll grow, grow, grow," went the words of the song. *It's not true,* thought Jeff. *I've read my Bible every day, but I haven't grown at all.* He was tempted to quit reading, but what if the other verse of the song was true? It went, "Neglect your Bible, forget to pray . . . and you'll shrink, shrink, shrink."

That afternoon Jeff and his parents visited his great-grandmother at the nursing home. "Jeff, you're growing to be more like your father every day," Grandma Owens said. "You talk like him."

CHECK YOUR SPIRITUAL GROWTH.

Jeff thought about that on the way home. Maybe there were more ways to grow than just getting taller. His great-grandma had said he was growing to be more like his father. Maybe the words in the song meant growing in another way. He decided to ask his parents. Mom answered, "Reading the Bible and praying makes a person grow more like Jesus."

Jeff thought, *This week I'll measure myself in a different way. I'll see if I've grown to be more like Jesus.*

HOW ABOUT YOU?

How much have you grown this year? It's fun to get measured and see how much you've grown physically, but have you checked to see if you've grown in your Christian life?

TO MEMORIZE:

We will speak the truth in love, growing in every way more and more like Christ, who is the head of his body, the church.

EPHESIANS 4:15

BY CAROLYN E. YOST

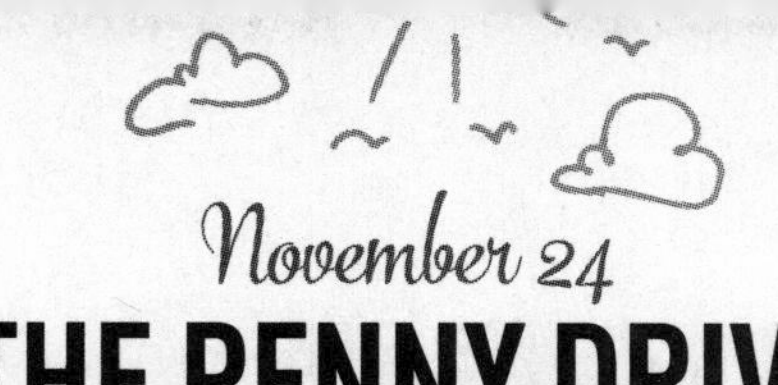

November 24

THE PENNY DRIVE

Read 1 Corinthians 1:26-31.

"Listen to this," said Jody's mother as she read a newspaper. "This article says, 'Nothing can be purchased for a penny. The nickel should be the smallest coin.' What do you think?"

"I agree," said Dad. "I have a jar of pennies on my dresser. I dump them in there because I don't like to carry a lot of change."

Just then Todd came into the house after his youth meeting at church. "Guess what!" he said. "We're going to have a penny drive to get money for our missionaries. The money will help pay for sending their stuff to Europe. We can only bring pennies! Will you help me? There's a prize for bringing the most!"

Mom laughed. "The person who wrote that article didn't know about missionaries," she said. "Sure, we'll all help."

The family dug pennies out of the sofa and from underneath the beds. Dad contributed the jar of pennies from his dresser. They all cleaned out pockets and purses.

"We have $31.68," said Todd on Sunday.

LOOK FOR GOD'S VALUES.

"Pennies seem worthless by themselves," observed Jody, "but they add up in a hurry."

Dad nodded. "God often takes something for which the world has no use and turns it into something valuable. We changed the way we think about pennies. There may be other areas where we need to change the way we think."

"That's especially true when it comes to people," said Mom. "We often fail to recognize that all people are of great value to God—and that we should value them too."

HOW ABOUT YOU?

Have you ever taken an object that someone threw away and made it into something useful? Or bought something no one else wanted because it was just right for you? Perhaps you know a person who doesn't seem very valuable to other people. Learn to see value in all kinds of people as God does.

TO MEMORIZE:

The very hairs on your head are all numbered.

MATTHEW 10:30

BY CATHERINE RUNYON

Let It Grow

Count it all joy when you fall into various trials, knowing that the testing of your faith produces patience. But let patience have its perfect work, that you may be perfect and complete, lacking nothing.

JAMES 1:2-4, NKJV

What if patience was the key to feeling strength in your faith?

Describe a time when your faith felt tested. What happened?

Write about how your patience felt at the beginning of this event.

Explain how this test changed your patience levels—with others and yourself.

What if we looked at temptation as a way to gain patience?

November 25

THE BROKEN THUMB

Read 1 Corinthians 12:12-22.

Shelly was the youth group secretary, but she had broken her thumb. "Could you take notes for me this afternoon?" Shelly asked Shawn as the student leaders met one Sunday.

"Sure," said Shawn.

As ideas were discussed, Doug, their president, offered a suggestion. "How about planning a summer missions trip and giving everyone something to do—you know, get everyone involved?"

"Sounds like a good idea," said their leader, Mr. Craig. "As a matter of fact, for the next few weeks we'll be studying the church, which the Bible often refers to as the body of Christ."

"What about kids who can't do anything?" asked Shelly. "Let's face it, there are some kids who don't seem to have anything to offer."

"Shelly," replied Mr. Craig, "how important is your thumb?"

"My thumb?" asked Shelly. "Well, last week I might have said I could live without it. But now that it's broken, I see how much I really need it. What does that have to do with our missions trip?"

DO YOUR PART.

"The Bible says that's how it is with His body, the church," explained Mr. Craig. "Each member is important for the total body to function properly."

"Oh, I see what you mean," said Shelly. She looked at her thumb. "I guess we can find something for everybody to do," she said with a grin.

HOW ABOUT YOU?

Each Christian is an important member of the body of Christ, the church. Can you show concern for others? Make visitors feel welcome? Give your time, talents, or money? Organize things or make encouraging cards to give to others? Do your part.

TO MEMORIZE:

All of you together are Christ's body, and each of you is a part of it.

1 CORINTHIANS 12:27

BY DEANA ROGERS

November 26

LET ME SLEEP

Read Ezekiel 3:16-21.

"Be quiet, Daisy," murmured Ellen sleepily as she burrowed deeper into her bed. The barking continued, but Ellen ignored it. Suddenly, a furry pooch landed on the bed beside her, barking furiously. Ellen pushed the dog away. "Quiet!" she commanded again.

Daisy ran down the hall toward Ellen's parents' room. Then *thump!* She was back again, pouncing on Ellen and barking loudly. Ellen sat up, very annoyed. "Lie down and be still!" she said. Instead, the dog ran out the door, barking and looking to see if Ellen was following.

Ellen sniffed the air. What was that smell? It was smoke! She leaped from her bed and ran into the hall, where her parents were just coming from their room. Soon they were all out in the yard, waiting for the fire trucks.

The next morning Ellen read about the fire on the local news's website. "Dog Saves Home and Family," the headline read. She hugged Daisy. "Sorry I got mad at you," she apologized. "I'm glad you kept trying to wake me up."

KEEP WITNESSING.

Mom looked over at Ellen. "Sometimes it's good to be awakened, isn't it?" she said thoughtfully. "That will be a good thing for you to keep in mind when you see your friend Alicia again."

"Alicia?" asked Ellen. "What do you mean?"

"Yesterday you said you weren't going to try to witness to Alicia anymore because it seems to annoy her. In a way she's saying, 'Let me sleep.' But she needs to wake up to her need for Jesus," explained Mom. "Daisy loved you enough to keep after you even when you didn't like it. So don't give up on Alicia."

HOW ABOUT YOU?

Are you afraid to witness to your friends because they might be annoyed or angry? Don't give up witnessing to them.

TO MEMORIZE:

Don't be afraid of suffering for the Lord. Work at telling others the Good News, and fully carry out the ministry God has given you.

2 TIMOTHY 4:5

BY HAZEL W. MARETT

November 27

THE FREE TICKETS

Read Romans 3:22-28.

As Sheranda and Kayla walked toward the gym, Sheranda asked, "Kayla, do you expect to be in heaven someday?"

"Oh, sure," replied Kayla. "I try to be good."

"But no one is good enough," said Sheranda.

"Well, I'm sure I stand a lot better chance of getting in than a murderer does," insisted Kayla, as they arrived at the gym. "Here we are. Got your money ready?"

"Money?" asked Sheranda. "My brother's on the team. I thought I could get in free."

"I doubt it," replied Kayla. "I brought a dollar."

At the ticket office, the girls found that they did need to pay, and tickets cost two dollars each. "Oh no! What are we going to do now?" moaned Kayla. "I really want to see this game!"

"Kayla, this is like what I told you about getting in to heaven," said Sheranda. "You had a dollar, and I had nothing. Which one of us is getting in to the gym?"

TRUST JESUS, NOT YOUR GOODNESS.

"Well, neither," answered Kayla. But before they could finish the discussion they turned to see Sheranda's father standing there.

"Oh, Daddy, I'm so glad to see you!" exclaimed Sheranda. "We don't have enough money to buy our tickets."

"I'll pay for them," answered her father.

The girls sat down in the bleachers just in time to see the teams take their places on the court. "You know, Kayla," said Sheranda, "we both got here because my father paid for the tickets. That's like what Jesus did for us. He paid the price to buy our tickets for heaven."

HOW ABOUT YOU?

Do you expect to get in to heaven because you're better than others are? That's not the way it works. Be sure you're not so proud of your "dollar"—your own goodness—that you refuse Christ's "free ticket."

TO MEMORIZE:

We are made right with God through faith and not by obeying the law.

ROMANS 3:28

BY MARY ROSE PEARSON

November 28

WHOLEHEARTED WORSHIP

Read Psalm 111:1-10.

"Praise the Lord," sang Erin as she wrote a note inviting Bethany over for the afternoon.

Although Erin continued to sing, bowed her head during prayer, and sat quietly during the sermon, her mind was planning what she and Bethany could do together. She knew she should be paying attention to the service but thought, *The Lord will understand. He knows I'm excited about Bethany coming.*

Bethany did go home with Erin. After dinner she noticed a book on Erin's dresser. "Have you finished this? Could I borrow it?"

"Sure," agreed Erin. Bethany sat down and began to leaf through the book. Although she murmured replies to what Erin said, she was soon so interested in the book that she didn't care about doing anything with Erin. "I really want to read this. You understand, don't you?" said Bethany. Erin felt hurt and disappointed.

WORSHIP WITH YOUR WHOLE HEART.

That evening Erin again went to church with her family. Once more she had Bethany on her mind. *She said she wanted to be my friend, but she didn't want to do anything with me,* Erin thought. As she thought about the day, she again felt some guilt for not paying attention to the worship service. *Oh well. I'm upset about Bethany,* she thought. *The Lord understands.* Then she remembered Bethany's words, "You understand, don't you?"

The Lord must feel as disappointed with me as I felt with Bethany, thought Erin.

Erin began singing praises with the others. This time she put her whole heart into it.

HOW ABOUT YOU?

Do you worship God in church? Or do you write notes and whisper to friends? Remember that the Lord wants more than your presence in the church service. He wants your wholehearted worship.

TO MEMORIZE:

These people honor me with their lips, but their hearts are far from me.

MATTHEW 15:8

BY KATHERINE R. ADAMS

November 29

THE OLDER GENERATION

Read Psalm 71:17-22.

"We'll meet here at the church Saturday afternoon and go together," Mrs. Kendall announced. "Class dismissed."

As soon as the children were out the door, Mark groaned, "Who wants to go to the nursing home? What have I got in common with those old folks?"

Adam shrugged. "Not much! But we've got to go, or Mrs. Kendall will be disappointed."

Coming up behind them, Natalie added, "Mrs. Kendall is the best Sunday school teacher we have ever had. But visiting a nursing home is a dumb idea!"

Adam shrugged again. "Maybe we won't stay long."

The next Saturday afternoon, eight fifth graders met at the church. "After we sing and read Scripture, go around and introduce yourselves," Mrs. Kendall instructed.

"What will we say to them?" Natalie asked.

Mrs. Kendall smiled. "You probably won't have to say much. Your main job will be listening."

LISTEN TO YOUR ELDERS.

Two hours later the boys and girls again piled into Mrs. Kendall's van. "That Mr. Wilson is sharp. He used to be the mayor," Mark said. "He offered to help me with my paper on the history of our town."

"Did you know that Mr. Rowland was once the foreman of the Flying W Ranch?" asked Adam. "He told me how the Lord helped him in a blizzard."

"And Mrs. Baker is going to teach me how to crochet," Natalie said. "Next time we come, I need to bring . . ." Natalie paused, then continued, "We are coming again, aren't we, Mrs. Kendall?"

Mrs. Kendall smiled. "I'll leave that decision to you. Everyone who wants to come again say 'aye.'" A chorus of "ayes" filled the air.

HOW ABOUT YOU?

Have you shunned older people because you didn't know how to talk to them? Many senior citizens need someone to listen to them. And you need to hear what they have to say.

TO MEMORIZE:

Let each generation tell its children of your mighty acts.

PSALM 145:4

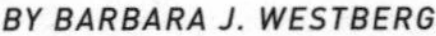

BY BARBARA J. WESTBERG

November 30

POWER FAILURE

Read Isaiah 59:1-4.

"Daddy!" wailed Shana. "My flashlight won't work! I just put in new batteries, but it still doesn't light."

"Let me have a look," replied Dad. He removed the batteries. "I think I see the problem, Shana." Shana peered more closely at the batteries in Dad's hand. "Here on the end of one battery—the place where it must contact, or touch—is a piece of clear plastic," continued Dad. "See? You didn't peel away all the packaging, and that ruined the contact."

Dad removed the plastic and wiped the contact points clean. Then he replaced the batteries in their proper position. "Now try it," he said, handing the flashlight to Shana. She flicked the switch, and the light shone brightly. Shana smiled happily as she thanked Dad for fixing the flashlight.

"You know, Shana," said Dad, "your flashlight is going to make a good illustration for the church school lesson I'm teaching this week. Just as that piece of plastic came between the batteries and stopped their power, sin in our lives comes between us and God's power to work in us. It ruins our fellowship with God. When His power is cut off, we can't shine for Him."

SHINE TODAY FOR JESUS.

Shana nodded. "Sin and plastic can sure cause big power failures, can't they?"

HOW ABOUT YOU?

Are you shining brightly for Jesus every day? Or is there sin in your life that hinders God's power? Such things as lying, cheating, swearing, stealing, gossip, jealousy, selfishness, and disobedience are sins that spoil your fellowship with God. Confess your sin to Him, and let God's power light up your life. Be sure there's no sin between you and the Lord.

TO MEMORIZE:

It's your sins that have cut you off from God. Because of your sins, he has turned away and will not listen anymore.

ISAIAH 59:2

BY LOIS A. TEUFEL

December 1

A GOOD, GOOD SAMARITAN

Read Luke 10:30-37.

Maryann was feeling uncomfortable. Last week at Sunday school someone had suggested they organize a "Good Samaritan Club." To become a member, a person had to do something special for someone else. Now it was report time, but Maryann had no report.

James was the first to tell what he had done. "On my way home from school an old man was trying to shovel snow. I did it for him."

Then it was Chandra's turn. "Our neighbor is in the hospital. She doesn't have any relatives in this area, so I went to visit her."

Mrs. Peters nodded at both James and Chandra. "I would say they deserve to become members of the Good Samaritan Club, wouldn't you?" Everyone agreed.

"Maryann, do you have a report?" Mrs. Peters asked.

Maryann shook her head. "I couldn't go anyplace. My mother was sick in bed all week."

Mrs. Peters said, "Oh, I'm so sorry. Who took care of your brother and made meals?"

HELP AT HOME. 

"I did," Maryann said. "I just made sandwiches and salads and things like that."

Mrs. Peters asked, "Did you stack the dishes?"

"Oh, no," Maryann replied. "I put them in the dishwasher. It didn't take long."

Mrs. Peters looked around. "All in favor of making Maryann a member of the Good Samaritan Club, raise your hand." Each one raised his or her hand. "The things you did, Maryann, were every bit as important as those done by the others," added Mrs. Peters. "You helped in the hardest place of all—home."

HOW ABOUT YOU?

Is it more fun to help a neighbor or a friend than to help at home? Both kinds of help are needed. Think of ways you can be a good Samaritan at home. There are many ways to help. Will you do it?

TO MEMORIZE:

I tell you the truth, when you did it to one of the least of these my brothers and sisters, you were doing it to me!

MATTHEW 25:40

BY RUTH I. JAY

Go In Peace

*I have told you all this so that you may have peace in me.
Here on earth you will have many trials and sorrows. But take heart,
because I have overcome the world.*

JOHN 16:33

When the rest of the world seems to be going crazy, we can rest easy in the words of Christ Jesus. He tells us to be of good cheer. He wants us to relax, knowing He's already won our battles for us. We can live in true peace, found in His gift of everlasting life.

Use this code to decipher the missing words below.

▼	●	★	♠	♦	✚	✣	♥	✦	♣	✪	✖	■
a	b	c	d	e	f	g	h	i	j	k	l	m

☆	✿	❑	◗	✔	➾	☎	✐	▲	➔	❖	☞	◓
n	o	p	q	r	s	t	u	v	w	x	y	z

And the ❑ ♦ ▼ ★ ♦   ✿ ✚   ✣ ✿ ♠ ,
_ _ _ _ _   _ _   _ _ _ ,

which surpasses all ✐ ☆ ♠ ♦ ✔ ➾ ☎ ▼ ☆ ♠ ✦ ☆ ✣ ,
_ _ _ _ _ _ _ _ _ _ _ _ _ ,

will ✣ ✐ ▼ ✔ ♠   ☞ ✿ ✐ ✔   ♥ ♦ ▼ ✔ ☎ ➾
_ _ _ _ _   _ _ _ _   _ _ _ _ _ _

and ■ ✦ ☆ ♠ ➾
_ _ _ _ _

through ★ ♥ ✔ ✦ ➾ ☎   ♣ ♦ ➾ ✐ ➾ .
_ _ _ _ _ _   _ _ _ _ _ .

PHILIPPIANS 4:7, NKJV

ANSWER KEY
peace of God; understanding; guard your hearts; minds; Christ Jesus

December 2

A MIGHTY WEAPON

Read Psalm 119:97-104.

Ruben and Ruby Marie went to visit Grandpa, who was known for quoting Scripture. "How do you remember so much?" Ruben asked. "Ruby Marie and I learn a lot of verses for Bible club, but it's hard to remember them all."

Grandpa smiled. "Do you know your phone number?" he asked. "And what about your locker combination or your address?"

Ruben said, "Sure! They're easy 'cuz I use them a lot."

"Well," replied Grandpa, "it's like that with the Word of God. We remember what's important to us—and what we use a lot." He sniffed the air. "Hey," he continued, "if my sniffer is still working, I smell fresh bread!"

Ruby Marie nodded. "Mama sent this loaf."

"That was kind of her," said Grandpa. He set the bread on the table, next to the lamp. "It looks good there, don't you think?" he asked.

"But Grandpa," said Ruben, "if you just let it sit there, it won't do you any good."

"What should I do with it?" Grandpa asked.

"Why, eat it, of course," Ruby Marie replied.

Grandpa smiled. "You're right! We need bread each day for our bodies, and we need the Word of God each day for our souls. Bread doesn't do any good on the table, and God's Word doesn't do any good on the bookshelf! We need to taste it by reading it and digest it by memorizing it. We need to get it into our hearts so it can work in our lives." He picked up the loaf. "I'm going to enjoy this bread, and I hope you keep on learning your verses."

READ GOD'S WORD.

HOW ABOUT YOU?

Where is your spiritual "bread"? Are you letting it just lie on the table, or are you "eating" it?

TO MEMORIZE:

People do not live by bread alone, but by every word that comes from the mouth of God.

MATTHEW 4:4

BY JAN L. HANSEN

December 3

WHAT'S IN A NAME?

Read Acts 9:36-42.

Nia and her mother were on their way to the shopping mall. "Oh, Mom. Alexis has a baby sister named Tracy, and she's so cute! Mom, how do people choose names for their babies?"

"Well," answered Mom, "some babies are named for a family member or another person the parents like. And sometimes a name is chosen because of its meaning."

Nia was surprised. "Names have meanings?"

"Some do," said Mom. "I have a book that tells the meaning of many names."

That evening Nia found the book and looked up the names of her friends. Father pointed out, "The Bible says, 'A good name is to be chosen rather than great riches, loving favor rather than silver and gold.'" (Proverbs 22:1, NKJV).

"But we don't choose our names," said Nia.

Dad answered, "No matter what we are named, we can have a good name."

Then Mom said, "The Bible tells the story of Dorcas, who did sewing for poor people. Her name meant 'gazelle.' But do you think people thought of a gazelle when they saw her?"

HONOR GOD'S NAME.

"No," said Nia slowly, "they probably thought of all the nice things Dorcas did for them. Oh! I get it! A good name is like a good reputation—what you're known for."

"That's right," said Dad. "And since you have accepted Jesus as Savior, you also have Christ's name—Christian. God wants you to live in a way that honors that name."

"If I do that, I'll always keep my good name!" exclaimed Nia.

HOW ABOUT YOU?

Do you have the name Christian? You do if you've asked Jesus to be your Savior. Each day ask Him to help you do everything in a way that honors Him, and then you will truly have a good name.

TO MEMORIZE:

Whatever you do or say, do it as a representative of the Lord Jesus, giving thanks through him to God the Father.

COLOSSIANS 3:17

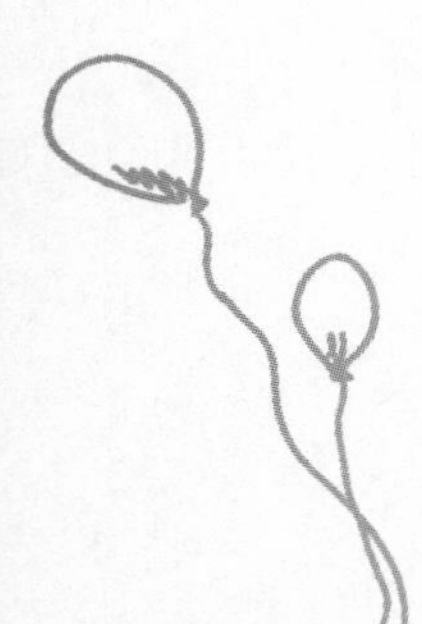

BY AGNES LIVEZEY

December 4

ALL THINGS GREAT AND SMALL

Read Psalm 100.

"I pray today," announced little Cody as the family sat around the breakfast table. Dad smiled at his young son, and they all bowed their heads. "Thank you, God, for Krispy Flakes an' milk an' juice an' toast," said Cody. He paused and peeked to see what else was on the table. "An' jam," he added. "Amen."

After breakfast everyone began doing weekend chores. When it was time for lunch, Mom had everyone gather around the dining room table. "We'll pray," she said. "Then you can sit and relax while your father and I fix burgers and get the rest of the food ready."

"I pray," said Cody again. Once more they all bowed their heads. "Thank you for . . ." Cody paused as he looked at the table, which had no food on it yet. "For plates an' knives an' forks an' spoons an' cups an' napkins an' salt. Amen."

Jessie and Suzanne giggled. But Mom said to Cody, "I'm glad you thanked God for all those things," she said. "We often forget them."

GIVE THANKS FOR EVERYTHING.

"That's right," agreed Dad as he got up. "Now, you've all been extra busy, so your mom and I will get the food. But you can think of other things we should remember to thank the Lord for but rarely do. You go first, Jessie."

"Uh . . ." murmured Jessie, "we should be thankful for our grill."

"Good," said Dad. "Suzanne?"

Suzanne was ready. "For pepper—Cody forgot that."

"And for the table," said Jessie.

"And chairs."

"And for a little child to teach us," added Mom with a smile.

HOW ABOUT YOU?

Are you really thankful for everything? Look around you. How many things can you find that you never thank the Lord for? Take a few moments to thank Him right now.

TO MEMORIZE:

It is good to give thanks to the LORD, to sing praises to the Most High.

PSALM 92:1

BY HAZEL W. MARETT

December 5

REFINED SILVER

Read Job 23:10-14.

Martin didn't understand why his mother had to be in the accident. Why did God let it happen?

One day during hospital visiting hours Mom seemed to sense Martin's feelings. She said, "Don't be angry. I believe God is refining me to make me more like Jesus. I was so busy that I was drifting away from a close walk with the Lord. Now that I'm lying here flat on my back, I have to look up to God." Martin nodded.

Later that week Martin's class took a field trip to a silver-refining plant. The refining process used chemicals and all sorts of complex equipment. At the end of the tour they saw a simple, old furnace. Their guide explained that they kept this furnace to remind themselves of how far the silver industry had come. "Years ago silver refiners heated the ore in furnaces like this, cooled it, and reheated it," he said. "It was a long process before the silver became pure."

"How did they know when it was pure?" one of the children asked.

LET GOD REFINE YOU.

The guide smiled. "We're told that when the refiner could see a clear reflection of himself in the silver, he knew his job was done."

That evening Martin thought about what Mom had said. Perhaps Jesus had let her suffer from the accident because Jesus knew that in the end she would better reflect His love.

HOW ABOUT YOU?

Do you ever wonder why people have to suffer? Sometimes God allows a tragic thing to happen because He knows it will make us more like Him. Don't rebel when God works to make you pure. Just as purified silver shows a clear reflection of the refiner, so your life should show a clear reflection of Jesus.

TO MEMORIZE:

He knows where I am going. And when he tests me, I will come out as pure as gold.

JOB 23:10

BY RAELENE E. PHILLIPS

December 6

PILOT IN CONTROL

Read Psalm 121.

Jenna clasped her hands together as the plane taxied down the runway. She had always wanted to fly, and here she was—flying with her brother, Devon, to visit their grandmother. But now she was nervous.

After they were airborne, Jenna didn't relax at all. "Do the engines sound funny?" she asked. "Should we be flying so high? What if there's another plane in the clouds? Won't we crash?"

"The pilot and copilot know what they're doing," Devon finally said. "You don't need to take over for them, okay? Now relax so we can enjoy our trip."

"Okay," said Jenna, but she was very glad when they were finally back on solid ground.

"Did you have a good flight?" asked Grandma.

Devon nodded. "I did. But Jenna was nervous as a cat. I told her she should trust the pilot and copilot and not try to take over for them. Then you tried to relax, didn't you?" She nodded.

TRUST GOD WITH YOUR LIFE.

Grandma put an arm around Jenna's shoulders. "I'm afraid we all forget to trust our Pilot from time to time."

Jenna looked at Grandma in surprise. "Are you afraid of flying too, Grandma?"

Grandma smiled. "Not really," she said. "I was thinking of how we sometimes fail to trust the Pilot of our lives. Do you know who that is?"

Jenna nodded. "God," she said.

"Yes," said Grandma. "You know, of course, that you couldn't have taken over the flight because it would have meant disaster. We need to let God keep control of our life, too—it's foolish for us to try to take over."

HOW ABOUT YOU?

Are you enjoying your trip through life? Or do you fret about things over which you have no control? Trust God. Think about how much He loves you, and remember that He knows what is best for you.

TO MEMORIZE:

You will keep in perfect peace all who trust in you, whose thoughts are fixed on you!

ISAIAH 26:3

BY HAZEL W. MARETT

December 7

UNDERGROUND RAILROAD

Read John 8:32-36.

As Karina and her family decorated the house for Christmas, she told them what she had been learning in school about the Underground Railroad. "If I had been living then," she said, "I would have helped lots of slaves escape."

"Are you sure?" asked Mom. "Being a part of the Underground Railroad was very dangerous. Some people were put in jail or even killed for what they did."

Karina thought about that for a minute. "I still would have done it."

As Dad put up a wreath he said, "There are slaves today that you can help to set free."

"Not around here," said Karina.

"What are people called before they accept Christ as Savior?" asked Dad.

"Sinners," Karina replied promptly.

"Exactly," said Dad, "and sin is a cruel master that enslaves people. Only Christ can set them free. I'm thankful that it isn't necessary for us to work undercover to help them, but workers are needed. You can help people escape by telling them what baby Jesus grew up to do."

HELP FREE PEOPLE FROM SIN.

"Like how He died on the cross and came back to life?" asked Karina. "Kids might make fun of me if I did that."

"Yes, they might," agreed Mom, bringing in some ornaments for the tree. "But you must keep at it if you want to help the slaves of sin escape to freedom in Christ. You're an important part of God's railroad—His system for moving slaves of sin into the freedom He offers."

HOW ABOUT YOU?

Are you trying to help point the slaves of sin to freedom in Christ? Or are you afraid someone will make fun of you? Be a part of God's railroad—help free the slaves. Tell someone about Christ today.

TO MEMORIZE:

The power of the life-giving Spirit has freed you
from the power of sin that leads to death.
ROMANS 8:2

BY JEAN A. BURNS

December 8

DANGER!

Read Ephesians 6:10-13.

Juan glanced uneasily at the danger signs posted around the old mine shaft. "Come on," urged his older brother, Jose, as he climbed over the fence and dropped down inside.

"We're supposed to be gathering wood for the fire," protested Juan.

Jose shrugged and walked away. Then a horrible crashing sound filled Juan's ears as Jose disappeared. "Where are you?" cried Juan.

"Down here," came the muffled reply.

"Hang on," called Juan. "I'll go get Dad." He ran to the site of the winter church retreat where the men were setting up camp. As soon as Juan saw the tents he shouted, "Help! Jose's trapped in an old mine!"

The rest of the evening was a blur to Juan. He dimly remembered Pastor Jake calling for help on his ham radio, the wait for the rangers to come in the helicopter, and the wait for his father to return with news from the hospital. How Juan wished he and Jose had obeyed the instructions to stay within sight of camp! How he wished they had paid attention to the danger signs!

SIN IS DANGEROUS.

When Dad returned, Juan was relieved to hear that Jose would be all right. He told his father how sorry he was that he had disobeyed.

Dad nodded. "What did the signs at the mine say?"

"They said, 'Danger. Keep out!'"

"When you and Jose didn't obey, you had to pay the consequences," said Dad. "God's Word also says, 'Danger. Keep out of sin.' It's not worded that way, but God warns that our sins will catch up with us. When you're faced with temptation, run away! And ask God to help you."

HOW ABOUT YOU?

Do you think you can disobey, cheat, or lie—just once—and it won't matter? Do you think no one will find out? God already knows, and very often other people find out too. Sin is dangerous and has serious consequences. You can't escape forever.

TO MEMORIZE:

Plant the good seeds of righteousness, and you will harvest a crop of love.

HOSEA 10:12

BY JEAN A. BURNS

Faith in Action: My Devotional Journey

God saved you by his grace when you believed. And you can't take credit for this; it is a gift from God.
EPHESIANS 2:8

This winter, keep a record of when you witness your faith in action. Specifically focus on God's grace as it relates to the activity themes for this season (peace, salvation, and love). Or make a note when you apply your devotional studies in everyday life. This way, you can see your faith in action! (Note: If you'll be completing your year of reading *The One Year Classic Family Devotions* this month, be sure to return to it and record your faith in action in January and February.)

God's grace was revealed to me . . .

DECEMBER: PEACE

WHEN ______________________________

____

WHERE ______________________________

____

HOW ______________________________

____

MORE ______________________________

____

____

JANUARY: SALVATION

WHEN ______________________________

____

WHERE ______________________________

____

HOW ______________________________

____

MORE ______________________________

____

____

FEBRUARY: LOVE

WHEN ______________________________

____

WHERE ______________________________

____

HOW ______________________________

____

MORE ______________________________

____

____

December 9

WIND WISDOM

Read John 3:1-8.

"Look at the wind!" shouted Jade. "Trees are swaying, and branches are breaking off."

"Wow! I've never seen such a strong wind!" said Oliver.

Dad joined them at the window. "You can't really see wind," he reminded them. "You only see what it does."

"Like making that garbage can roll down the street," remarked Jade.

Dad said, "Jesus compared the blowing of the wind to becoming a Christian. We can't see wind. And we can't see Jesus entering a person's life because His Spirit is what comes in."

Oliver looked at his sister. "That's why Jade has a button nose and freckles just like before she invited Jesus into her heart at camp last July."

Dad smiled. "We see what the wind does, though," he said, "and we see what Jesus does. When He comes into a person's life, He changes that person. A Christian wants to please the Lord and be obedient."

JESUS CHANGES YOU.

Jade nodded. "I still do bad things, but I try not to," she said. "When I do, I feel awful, and I ask Jesus to forgive me."

"And I've noticed that you don't get as mad when I tease you," admitted Oliver.

Jade slipped her hand into her father's. "I'm glad the wind doesn't always blow this hard," she said. "But I'm glad Jesus is always in my heart. Even though I can't see Him, I know He's always there to help me live as I should."

HOW ABOUT YOU?

Does your life show that you are a Christian? Has there been any change since you invited Jesus to come in? If you haven't invited Him in, talk to a Christian adult about doing it. Then ask God to help you live in such a way that those around you will see what He is doing for you.

TO MEMORIZE:

Anyone who belongs to Christ has become a new person.
The old life is gone; a new life has begun!
2 CORINTHIANS 5:17

BY MATILDA H. NORDTVEDT

December 10

UNDER THE SURFACE

Read Mark 12:28-33.

"I hate having to be nice to Joy," said Erica. "She's never nice to me."

"Well, it's a church party, so you have to do it," replied Amy. "Just pretend."

Mom looked at her daughters in the rearview mirror. "Why should you pretend to like someone just because you're at a church party?"

"It's the Christian thing to do," said Amy.

"Hmmm," said Mom, tapping her finger on the steering wheel. "Do you remember trying to paint over the old paint on your old desk?"

"Sure," said Amy. "Dad made me sand it first."

"Right," said Mom. "And why was that?"

"He said if I didn't, the new paint would chip off and the old paint would show through."

"Pretending to like someone is like painting over old paint," said Mom. "The old feelings are still under the surface, and sooner or later they'll show through."

"So should we just not bother to be nice to Joy?" asked Erica.

LEARN TO LOVE OTHERS. 

Mom shook her head. "Amy didn't just not paint the old desk," she said. "She sanded and got rid of the rough spots. You need to get rid of the rough feelings, too."

"But how?" asked Erica.

"A good place to start is with prayer," said Mom. "It's hard to dislike someone you're praying for. Let's ask the Lord to help you love Joy as He does, okay?" The girls nodded and bowed their heads.

As they got out of the car, they saw Joy right away. "Should we go over to her?" asked Amy.

"Yes," said Erica. "Let's go."

HOW ABOUT YOU?

Do you ever just pretend to like someone? Why not ask God to teach you to love somebody you find it difficult to love like He loves that person? Ask Him to fill your heart with His love.

TO MEMORIZE:

This is my commandment: Love each other
in the same way I have loved you.
JOHN 15:12

BY GAIL L. JENNER

December 11

THE TV RECIPE

Read 2 Timothy 2:19-22.

"Mom, can I watch *Blazing Guns*?" Samuel asked. "Almost all my friends are gonna watch it. Even my history teacher says it's worth seeing because of its accurate historical setting."

"How about helping me bake a cake, and we'll talk about it," said Mom, taking a box of cake mix from the cupboard. She poured the chocolate mix into a bowl and read the directions on the box. "Let's see—eggs, oil, water, what else? Oh yes, Samuel, please go to the basement and get a handful of dirt I keep for repotting houseplants. I'll add it to the other ingredients."

Samuel laughed. "Very funny, Mom. The box doesn't say, 'Add one cup of dirt.'"

"No," said Mom as she plugged in the mixer, "but it would make the cake bigger. And all the good things would still be there."

"But the dirt would ruin the cake," Samuel said. "It might even make me sick!"

"That's true, Samuel," agreed Mom. "So you'd be very unhappy if I ruined your favorite cake?" Samuel nodded.

WATCH WHAT GOES INTO YOUR HEART.

"I'm sure God feels that way about your heart," said Mom as she turned the mixer on low. "The program you want to watch may have some fine things about it, but from the ads I've seen, I'm afraid it also has a lot of cursing and violence. Those ingredients don't belong in your heart any more than dirt belongs in cake."

Samuel sighed. "I guess I need to find a show that doesn't call for dirt," he said.

HOW ABOUT YOU?

What ingredients go into the programs you watch? Are they good for your heart? Are they pleasing to God? Be choosy. Your mind needs pure ingredients to produce good thoughts.

TO MEMORIZE:

Fix your thoughts on what is true, and honorable, and right, and pure, and lovely, and admirable. Think about things that are excellent and worthy of praise.

PHILIPPIANS 4:8

BY DAWN E. MALONEY

December 12

HIDING PLACE

Read Psalm 143:7-12.

Tim curled up under the desk in his room. It was his special hiding place. He always came here when he felt sad. Today he felt bad because he'd missed a shot in his basketball game, and several kids had yelled at him.

Then he heard Mom calling, "Tim! Grandpa's here." Tim scrambled out.

He and Grandpa sat down in the family room to visit—just the two of them. "Where were you just now?" Grandpa asked.

"I was feeling bad about a ball game. So I went to my special hiding place," Tim said, knowing Grandpa would never tell anyone.

"Say, that's a good idea," said Grandpa. "I had a hiding place of my own when I was a boy. It was in the hayloft of the barn." Grandpa's face beamed as he added, "I still have a hiding place."

Tim looked surprised. "You do?" He wondered where Grandpa would hide out.

Grandpa nodded. "Get your Bible," he said, "and I'll give you a clue as to where I go."

When Tim returned, Grandpa said, "Look up Psalm 143:9, and you'll find the answer."

They read it together: "Rescue me from my enemies, LORD; I run to you to hide me."

"That's right," said Grandpa. "I go to God when I'm sad. When I'm alone, talking to Him, I'm in the best hiding place of all."

"Next time I'm sad, I'm going to go to the same hiding place you do, Grandpa," Tim said. "I can do that in my other secret hiding place."

HOW ABOUT YOU?

Are you sometimes sad? Do you take your problems and sadness to God? He wants to hear about anything that's bothering you—trouble with schoolwork, disappointments with friends, or problems in your family. The next time you need help, go and hide in a quiet place and talk to God!

TO MEMORIZE:

Rescue me from my enemies, LORD; I run to you to hide me.

PSALM 143:9

BY CAROLYN E. YOST

December 13

A VERY SPECIAL SERVANT

Read Romans 6:16-23.

At school, Amber kept thinking about the Scripture Dad had read that morning. It was about being a servant of God. She knew Dad was a servant of God. He was a preacher. Uncle Rob and Aunt Clarice were His servants too. They were missionaries. But how could she, a ten-year-old girl, serve the Lord? Just then she heard Mrs. Powell saying, "Who will stay in during recess and help me with the bulletin board?" Amber had planned to play in the snow with Kim, but she raised her hand. At lunchtime, she helped Emma study her spelling.

When Amber came home from school Mom said, "Oh, I'm so glad you're here. Amy is running a high fever. I need you to watch the boys while I take her to the doctor's office." Amber nodded and entertained her little brothers while Mom was gone. Later she set the table and put a casserole into the oven. After dinner Amber washed the dishes. Then she rocked the baby while her mom put the boys to bed.

After the toys were picked up and all was quiet, Amber asked, "Mom, how can I serve God? Daddy's a preacher. Uncle Rob and Aunt Clarice are missionaries. You're the church organist. But what can I do to serve Jesus?"

SERVE GOD BY SERVING OTHERS.

Mom hugged her daughter. "Oh, Amber, you are serving Him!" she exclaimed. "We serve God by serving others. Every day, as you help me around the house and take care of your little brothers and baby sister, and as you help other people, you're serving God."

Amber was amazed. "That's serving God?"

Mom nodded. "It certainly is. You're a very special servant of Jesus Christ."

HOW ABOUT YOU?

Do you want to serve the Lord? Then serve or help others. When you serve them, you're serving Him. Make up your mind to do something special today for someone else.

TO MEMORIZE:

You have been called to live in freedom, my brothers and sisters. But don't use your freedom to satisfy your sinful nature. Instead, use your freedom to serve one another in love.

GALATIANS 5:13

BY BARBARA J. WESTBERG

December 14

NAIL HOLES

Read James 3:2-10.

Brad started toward the family room. "VAROOM!" sang out his little brother, Kevin, as he charged through the room, crashing into Brad.

"Watch where you're going, you moron," yelled Brad.

"You know that you are not to call people names," Dad said sternly.

Brad sighed. "I'll apologize." But just then the phone rang, and Brad picked it up. "Hello? Oh, hi, Jason. Yeah, I heard the rumor about Mrs. Simpson. Can you believe we have an alcoholic for a teacher? Did you notice how she stumbled over her words in class? Oh, Dad wants me for something. Talk to you later."

"You're going to call Jason back and apologize for that gossip I just heard," said Dad. "Did you know that Mrs. Simpson's husband is sick?" he asked. "She has to stay up nights caring for him. No wonder she's tired in class."

"Oh, I didn't know that. I'll call Jason after I apologize to Kevin."

"First come with me to my shop," said Dad. He picked up a hammer and some nails. "I want you to pound these nails about halfway into this board."

THINK, THEN SPEAK.

Brad obeyed with a puzzled look. "Now what?"

"Pull the nails out." Brad did so. "Brad, your words lately have been as sharp as these nails. They've been cutting and hurting. Saying you're sorry is fine. But look at this board. What do you see?"

"The nail holes," said Brad.

"Exactly," said Dad. "You can apologize and be forgiven, but you can never take back all the harm you've caused."

Brad picked up the board. "I get your point, Dad. I'll try to be more careful with my words."

HOW ABOUT YOU?

Do you carelessly say things that hurt the feelings or reputations of others? An apology can bring forgiveness, but it can never erase all the harm. Ask the Lord to help you.

TO MEMORIZE:

I am determined not to sin in what I say.

PSALM 17:3

BY MARY ROSE PEARSON

December 15
LIKE JINX

Read Ephesians 6:1-3.

Sara overheard her mother telling Dad that Sara had failed to clean out her closet. "I even gave her a box to put the outgrown clothes into," said Mom.

Sara went outside and sat on her swing. Her collie, Jinx, came over to her, but Sara ignored her pet. She thought of all the things she did do right. She made her bed before school. She set the table for dinner each afternoon and dried the dishes her mother washed each evening. She would clean that closet later. Why did it have to be done right now?

Soon Dad was sitting on the other swing. "Sara, you need to clean your closet," he said.

"I'm going to do it," replied Sara. "I wanted to see that special on TV first."

Dad picked up a stick and threw it. "Get it, Jinx," he said. The dog was off at a gallop to retrieve the stick. Dad turned his attention back to Sara. "Now that is quick obedience. Jinx didn't say, 'I'll do it when I get around to it.' He just obeyed." After a pause, Dad added, "A truck collecting clothing for needy people stopped here today, Sara. None of your outgrown clothes got put on it, because you didn't obey your mother."

OBEY PARENTS.

Now Sara felt bad. "Why didn't Mom tell me the truck was coming?" she asked. "I would've cleaned the closet right away if I'd known."

"We want you to be willing to obey us without always asking for reasons," said Dad quietly.

HOW ABOUT YOU?

When your parents tell you to do something, do you put it off? Do you demand reasons? Or do you try to argue that you will do it later when you've nothing else to do? The only true obedience is *immediate* obedience.

TO MEMORIZE:

Children, obey your parents because you belong to the Lord, for this is the right thing to do.
EPHESIANS 6:1

BY RAELENE E. PHILLIPS

Be a Peacemaker

God blesses those who work for peace, for they will be called the children of God.

MATTHEW 5:9

Words of peace fill the lives of believers. "Let there be peace." "Peace like a river." "Peace on earth." As you prepare to celebrate Christ's birth, show those around you that you are a peacemaker. You can find powerful advice and memory verses about peace in the Bible.

Draw lines to match one sentence half to the other. Hints are shown in column 2 in case you need to use your Bible for help.

I am leaving you with a gift . . .

Let the peace that comes from Christ . . .

Those who use the sword . . .

May the Lord of peace himself give you . . .

If someone slaps you on one cheek . . .

Peace be with you. As the Father . . .

You will keep in perfect peace . . .

In peace I will lie down and sleep . . .

. . . all who trust in you. (Isaiah 26:3)

. . . for you alone, O LORD, will keep me safe. (Psalm 4:8)

. . . his peace at all times and in every situation. (2 Thessalonians 3:16)

. . . has sent me, so I am sending you." (John 20:21)

. . . peace of mind and heart. (John 14:27)

. . . offer the other cheek also. (Luke 6:29)

. . . rule in your hearts. (Colossians 3:15)

. . . will die by the sword. (Matthew 26:52)

ANSWER KEY

John 14:27; Colossians 3:15; Matthew 26:52; 2 Thessalonians 3:16; Luke 6:29; John 20:21; Isaiah 26:3; Psalm 4:8

December 16

THE RIGHT KEY

Read John 3:14-18.

"Josh, would you open the trunk, please?" asked Mom. She pulled the keys from the ignition and kept one, handing the others to him.

Josh grabbed the ring and ran around to the trunk, eagerly shoving in a key. The lock wouldn't budge. He fumbled with the jangling ring and selected another key. It wouldn't even go in. Frustrated, he yelled, "Mom! Which one?"

Mom took the key ring from him. "It was the one I was holding," she said. "You bolted out of the car before I could tell you." She held out a short silver key.

Sheepishly, Josh slid the key in and unlocked the trunk. He returned the ring with a grin. "I guess there's only one that will work, huh?"

Mom smiled as she gave him a grocery bag. "Yes, and do you know what? There are still many people who don't use the right key."

"What do you mean?" Josh asked.

"God gave His Son, Jesus, so that we may have eternal life. But instead of using that key to salvation, many people try their own way, even if they have heard of the right way." She turned to Josh and dangled the key ring in front of him. "Do you remember how you felt when you tried to use the wrong ones?"

JESUS IS THE KEY TO LIFE.

Josh nodded. "I thought for sure they'd work. They all looked like they would."

"Other people think the same thing about heaven," said Mom. "They try different keys, like going to church or trying to be good. But Jesus is the only way to heaven."

HOW ABOUT YOU?

Are you trying to get to heaven by being good, going to church, or giving money? Those are things God wants you to do, but they can't save you. You can enter heaven only through Christ.

TO MEMORIZE:

Jesus told him, "I am the way, the truth, and the life. No one can come to the Father except through me."

JOHN 14:6

BY JEAN A. BURNS

December 17

ATTIC ADVENTURE

Read Psalm 33:4-12.

"Come on, Cassidy," called Hunter. "Mom says we can play up in the attic."

"Cool!" exclaimed Cassidy. "I love to wear those old clothes and big hats."

Hunter and Cassidy climbed the steep steps to the attic of the old family home. Soon they were trying on clothes their grandparents and parents had saved through the years.

They trooped down the stairs, where they found Mom and Dad in the kitchen. "I wore those old saddle shoes when I was a teenager," said Mom as she observed Cassidy, "and that hat belonged to my grandmother. Hunter's old-fashioned tie is simply charming with that shirt!"

"These styles were fads once," commented Dad. "Everyone wanted them."

Mom nodded. "When it comes to styles, people always seem to want the latest thing," she said. "That's okay unless clothes become the most important thing in our lives."

"Yes," agreed Dad, "or unless we copy some of the sinful activities of the world just as we copy the latest fads."

GOD'S WAYS DON'T CHANGE.

"Is sinning a fad?" asked Cassidy.

"Not exactly," replied Dad, "but sometimes wrong activities are very popular. People in the world change as far as the things they like to do, but God's principles never change. As Christians we need to be careful that we measure the 'in' activities against what God teaches."

"I get it," said Hunter. "Like right now, many people think that if it feels good, it's okay. But that's not what God tells us."

"You got it!" said Dad.

HOW ABOUT YOU?

When kids around you use bad words, are you tempted to do the same? If a friend tells a lie, do you find yourself telling the same lie? Don't try to be like others when they sin. Styles of clothing and behavior may change, but God's ways never change.

TO MEMORIZE:

The LORD's plans stand firm forever; his intentions can never be shaken.

PSALM 33:11

BY GERI WALCOTT

December 18

WORN-OUT WELCOME

Read Job 16:1-7.

"Hey, Holly, want to hang out today?" asked Karen.

Holly hesitated. "Well, I don't know. I have a lot to do."

"Aw, come on," begged Karen. "What do you have to do? I could help you."

Holly shook her head. "Not really. I have to practice the piano."

"I could just come in and listen," persisted Karen.

"Karen," said Holly, "we were together last night after school and Monday night too. I like spending time with you, but I am busy."

"Well, okay," agreed Karen glumly.

Holly breathed a sigh of relief as she walked up the steps to the house. She found her mother in the kitchen starting supper. "Karen wanted to hang out again today, but I told her I had a lot of things to do. I hope she's not mad."

"Why would she be mad?" asked Mom. "You've been spending most afternoons with her lately."

DON'T BECOME A PEST.

"I know," sighed Holly. "I'm glad she's my friend, but sometimes I like being alone. I like to read and draw and write in my journal."

Mom nodded. "Did you know there's a verse in the Bible about this?"

"What verse?" asked Holly in surprise.

"Proverbs 25:17 says, 'Don't visit your neighbors too often, or you will wear out your welcome,'" quoted Mom. "See, Holly, the Lord who created friendship understands your problem. Friends do need to give each other time to develop different interests."

"Thanks, Mom!" exclaimed Holly. "I feel better about it now! I wish Karen could understand that verse too."

HOW ABOUT YOU?

Do you spend lots of time with only one friend? Reach out to other people and make new friends too. Spend time alone and do a creative project or read a book.

TO MEMORIZE:

Don't visit your neighbors too often, or you will wear out your welcome.

PROVERBS 25:17

BY LENORA MCWHORTEN

December 19

THE LYING CEREAL BOX

Read Proverbs 12:17-22.

"Can I get the prize out?" Gina asked Dad eagerly, pointing to the back of her cereal box. The picture showed colored candy pouring out of a package.

Dad shook the box. He reached in and brought out the prize—a small, sample-size package of candy. He tossed it to Gina.

When Gina tore open the package a little later, she poured out the candy. She counted every piece—only six. She counted the pieces in the picture on the cereal box. There were 100 pieces. "I thought I would get as much candy as there was in the picture," she told Dad.

"The people who make the cereal wanted you to think that so you'd buy the cereal," explained Dad. "They deceived you."

Gina frowned. "What does *deceive* mean?"

"Leading someone to believe something that isn't true," explained Dad.

That afternoon Gina's friend Ashley came to play. Gina had recently begun taking piano lessons, so she showed Ashley what she had been learning. "I'll be your student," said Ashley. They pretended that Gina was the teacher.

DON'T DECEIVE.

Soon Gina's friend Beth came to the door. "Do you want to play?" Beth asked.

Gina didn't want to play. "We're having a piano lesson," she said.

After Beth left, Dad asked, "Did you tell Beth the truth?"

Gina shrugged. "I didn't lie about it," she said.

"Do you think you deceived her?" persisted Dad.

"Yes," Gina answered. Then she hurried to the front door. "Come back, Beth," she called. "You can be in on our piano lesson too."

HOW ABOUT YOU?

Do you ever deceive someone by giving the wrong idea? Do you give your parents the impression you're one place when you're actually somewhere else? Do you get out of doing something by making excuses that aren't quite accurate? You can lie in ways other than *saying* something that isn't true.

TO MEMORIZE:

Do not steal. Do not deceive or cheat one another.

LEVITICUS 19:11

BY KATHERINE R. ADAMS

December 20

MARY'S PART

Read Luke 1:26-33, 46-49.

Shelly waited to hear the teacher call her name. She knew she was the perfect one to take the part of Mary, the mother of Jesus. No one could memorize the lines as well as she could. And her mother was the best seamstress in the church. She could have the best costume.

"Julie," said Mr. Roberts, "I think you would be a good Mary."

Shelly gasped! Julie missed church half the time, and she stammered. *What kind of Mary would she be?* Shelly thought to herself. *Who wants to be in a dumb old play, anyway!* When Mr. Roberts offered her another part, she made excuses and refused to be in the program.

Shelly sat in the front row the night of the program. She wanted to see how embarrassed Mr. Roberts would be for making such a foolish choice! Shelly watched Julie walk up front wearing a very drab outfit.

Slowly Julie began reciting from Luke. "For he . . . took notice of . . . his lowly . . . servant girl. . . ."

BE A HUMBLE SERVANT.

Lowly, grumbled Shelly to herself. That sure fits Julie. Then suddenly it struck her that Mr. Roberts was right! Julie was a good Mary! Julie was humble and stood in awe before God like Mary did—a servant willing to obey and carry out His commands. Shelly knew she would have exalted herself, but Julie brought glory to Jesus.

While the program continued, Shelly quietly asked God to forgive her proud spirit and make her His humble servant.

HOW ABOUT YOU?

Do you think you're better than some people? Do you think you're more talented? Do you think you should always be the one chosen to play special music, answer the questions, or lead in prayer because you do it best? Jesus wants obedient servants who will help others and bring glory to Him.

TO MEMORIZE:

Whoever wants to be first among you must become your slave.

MATTHEW 20:27

BY JAN L. HANSEN

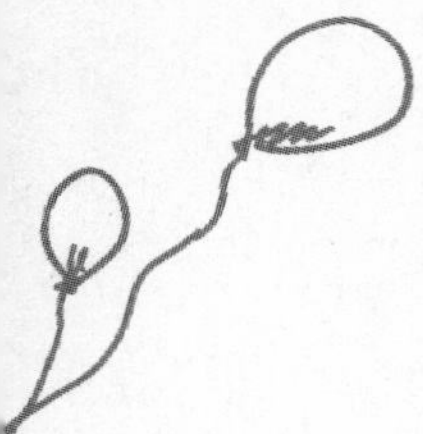

December 21

SILVER DOLLAR

Read 1 Corinthians 3:11-15.

"Sorry—maybe next time." Jolene hung up the phone and said to Mom, "The junior choir is giving a Christmas program at the nursing home today. Mrs. Wilson wants me to play the piano, but I have shopping to do."

"Couldn't you play and still have time to shop?" Mom asked. "Playing would be a real service to the Lord."

"No, Mom!" Jolene put on her jacket and went to the mall with a friend and her friend's mother.

When she came back home later, Jolene not only had two gifts, but a stuffed dog for herself. She giggled. "This is Orville. He cost only a dollar. I didn't have any money left, so I used the silver dollar Aunt Jo sent me."

Mom was shocked. "I thought you knew that coin was worth more than a dollar!"

"Well, yeah," Jolene admitted.

The following Saturday Jolene and her mother passed a coin shop and saw several silver dollars, each worth a lot of money. Jolene said, "Now I wish I still had my coin."

SPEND YOUR LIFE WISELY.

"It's spent, and you may as well forget it," answered Mom. "The day you spent your dollar was the same day you refused to play at the nursing home. You know, honey, your life is like a coin—you can spend your time any way you want to, but you can spend it only once. You need to make sure you spend it wisely."

Jolene nodded. "I didn't spend either my dollar or my time wisely that day, did I? I'm going to rename Orville. I'll call him Silver Dollar, and he'll remind me that I need to be careful how I spend my money and my time."

HOW ABOUT YOU?

Are you buying the most you can with your life? Are you using opportunities to work for the Lord? The things you do for yourself are soon gone. What you do for the Lord will be rewarded.

TO MEMORIZE:

If the work survives, that builder will receive a reward.

1 CORINTHIANS 3:14

BY HAZEL W. MARETT

December 22

FOOTPRINTS IN THE SNOW

Read 1 Timothy 4:12-16.

"I've got bad news for you," announced Mom one morning. Her eyes were twinkling. "I was listening to the radio, and they're canceling school for the day. The roads are all blocked."

"Oh, cool!" squealed Rachel. "Now we can play in the snow. Come on, Derek!" But after breakfast, it started to storm even harder, and the children had to stay in the house.

The next morning there was still no school, although the blizzard had stopped. Soon Rachel and Derek were making snow angels, jumping in the drifts, and having a snowball fight. Then they decided to go to an empty lot, where several children were playing in the snowdrifts.

"Rachel! I play too," they heard shortly after arriving at the lot.

"Oh no!" groaned Rachel. There was Nicole, their neighbor, who was only three. "She must have followed us. We'll have to take her back home." When they arrived at Nicole's home, they found her mother looking for her.

BE A GOOD EXAMPLE.

Nicole's mother sighed. "How did you know your friends were in the empty lot, Nicole?" she asked.

"I stepped in their steps in the snow," Nicole said, giggling.

That night Derek and Rachel told their parents about Nicole following them. Dad said, "You know, Christians are also to be *examples* that others can follow. Nicole followed your footsteps in the snow, but others will follow your footsteps as Christians."

"I get it," Derek said.

"Me, too," nodded Rachel. "I'm going to try to be a good example."

HOW ABOUT YOU?

What kind of an example are you setting for others to follow? If you're always late or if you tell lies, someone will notice. If you're helpful and always tell the truth, someone will notice that, too. Ask God to help you set the right example.

TO MEMORIZE:

And you yourself must be an example to them
by doing good works of every kind.
TITUS 2:7

BY BARBARA J. WESTBERG

Peace of God

Then you will experience God's peace, which exceeds anything we can understand. His peace will guard your hearts and minds as you live in Christ Jesus.

PHILIPPIANS 4:7

We don't have to understand peace to have it. One of the many beauties and benefits found in Christ is His peace. It's always there for us, in the midst of any situation. All we have to do is keep Him in our minds and hearts.

Unscramble the words that mean "peace."

cardco ______________________________

mitay ______________________________

malc ______________________________

nodorcc ______________________________

yamhorn ______________________________

tique ______________________________

yestiner ______________________________

iblastyit ______________________________

liquatynirt ______________________________

ANSWER KEY

accord; amity; calm; concord; harmony; quiet; serenity; stability; tranquility

December 23

NOT FOR SALE

Read Acts 8:14-23.

Cammie came to the Village Bible Church shortly before Christmas. She had just moved to the area, and attending church was a new experience for her. She couldn't understand the lessons very well. But her teacher's love for her drew her back each week.

One Sunday Miss Weaver asked Cammie if she could get some evergreen branches for the class Christmas party. Miss Weaver said, "We just need a few small branches to decorate the tables."

Eager to please her teacher, Cammie agreed to get the branches. But some places that sold Christmas trees didn't have any branches at all, and others would give her branches only if she bought a tree.

Walking home from school one day, Cammie saw a pile of evergreen boughs at a Christmas tree lot. She had an idea. Instead of asking for free branches, she would buy some. *They shouldn't cost much,* she thought. Cammie ran home to get some money, but when she offered it to the owner for the boughs, he said, "They're not for sale." Disappointed, Cammie started to walk away. The man called her back quickly. "Young lady, they're free. Help yourself." Cammie eagerly took all she could carry.

SALVATION IS A GIFT.

Later, while decorating the tables, Cammie told Miss Weaver about her experiences. "That's a good illustration of salvation," Miss Weaver said. "Some people tell us we can buy our salvation by doing good deeds. But the Bible says salvation is a gift. We can't earn it or buy it. It's not for sale. We can only receive salvation by accepting Jesus as Savior."

"Now I understand it," Cammie said softly.

HOW ABOUT YOU?

Are you trying to buy your salvation by being good, going to church, or getting baptized? It won't work! Salvation is a gift from God.

TO MEMORIZE:

God saved you by his grace when you believed. And you can't take credit for this; it is a gift from God.

EPHESIANS 2:8

BY JAN L. HANSEN

December 24

AN IMPORTANT DAY

Read Matthew 2:1-3, 7-11.

Christopher woke with excitement. "It's an important day, Mom," he announced as he came into the kitchen.

Mom looked up from pouring juice. "It is?" she asked. "Why is that?"

"Oh, Mom, you know!" Christopher said. "It's Christmas Eve!" The Benson family followed the Swedish tradition of opening their gifts to each other on Christmas Eve.

Throughout the day Christopher made many trips to the Christmas tree to look at the presents. Finally, when the evening meal was over, the family gathered to open the presents. Christopher was happy to get a movie, a sweater, a book, candy, and what he wanted most of all—a baseball mitt! Already he was dreaming of summer and . . .

But Dad was talking. "Let's read about the gifts the wise men brought to Jesus," Dad said. After reading the story he added, "We've given each other gifts to show our love, and we have a gift for Jesus, too." He picked up a box. "As you know, this box contains our Christmas offering money. Now I'd like you to think about giving Jesus what He wants most—yourself."

GIVE YOURSELF TO JESUS.

Christopher knew he had never given himself to Jesus. A few minutes after he had gone to bed, he jumped up and ran back to the family room. "I want to give myself to Jesus," he told his parents.

After he prayed he said, "Today is the day I asked Jesus to save me from my sins. That's even more important than opening all the presents!"

HOW ABOUT YOU?

Have you remembered a gift for Jesus this Christmas? If you haven't done so already, won't you make this the most important day in your life? Give Jesus your heart and life.

TO MEMORIZE:

They entered the house and saw the child with his mother, Mary, and they bowed down and worshiped him. Then they opened their treasure chests and gave him gifts of gold, frankincense, and myrrh.

MATTHEW 2:11

BY HAZEL W. MARETT

December 25

THE MISSING TURKEY

Read John 1:1-4, 9, 14; Luke 2:15-17.

Jamie's aunt and uncle, who weren't Christians, were coming for Christmas dinner. Jamie and her parents had prayed that somehow, this Christmas, God would help them witness to Aunt Ellen and Uncle Joe. When they arrived, Uncle Joe held out presents. "Merry Christmas, Jamie! See what Santa Claus brought!"

"We almost didn't come," said Aunt Ellen. "Joe stayed late at the office party last night and came home even more drunk than usual." She winked at her husband, but Jamie felt sad. Was this what Christmas meant to her aunt and uncle?

At dinnertime the table was loaded with delicious food. After Dad gave thanks, Jamie took helpings of several different things. Now all she needed was a drumstick. She looked around the table. "Where's the turkey?" she asked.

Startled, Mom stared at the table. "The turkey!" she cried. She ran to the kitchen and returned shortly with a large platter of meat. "The main part of the meal, and I forgot all about it!"

DON'T FORGET CHRIST.

Jamie giggled. "I guess we had so much other good stuff that we just didn't miss it at first," she said.

After dinner Uncle Joe stretched. "Now that was a good meal," he declared. "I'm glad someone remembered the turkey! It wouldn't have been the same without it."

Dad nodded. "This dinner without the turkey would have been like Christmas without Christ," he said. "Many people think they can enjoy Christmas without knowing Christ Himself. It's true that they may have some good times, but they're missing the best part."

Uncle Joe and Aunt Ellen looked at each other, then settled back to listen as Dad began to read the Christmas story from the Bible.

HOW ABOUT YOU?

Are you missing the meat of Christmas? Have you gotten so involved in the fun things to do that you've forgotten all about Jesus?

TO MEMORIZE:

[Christ] existed before anything else, and he holds all creation together.

COLOSSIANS 1:17

BY SHERRY L. KUYT

December 26

NO RETURNS

Read Hebrews 12:14-17.

Katie twirled in front of the department store mirror, admiring the blue dress she had found on the clearance rack. *It's too short, but Mom can fix that,* she thought. *I can return it if I change my mind.* She had decided to use her Christmas money to buy a dress.

When Katie brought the dress home, Mom pointed out that there wasn't a wide enough hem to lengthen it. Besides that, there was a stain on the sleeve. "I'd better take it back," Katie said. But when she went back the next day, the salesclerk pointed to a large sign on the wall: No Refunds on Clearance Merchandise.

Katie pouted. "I didn't see that sign before."

"I'm sorry," said the clerk, "but that's the store's policy, and I can't change it."

Katie trudged home and told her mother about it. "I'm sorry, honey," said Mom. "Maybe we can cut off the sleeves and turn it into a short-sleeved shirt."

Katie frowned. "I guess so, but I wish I could just take it back."

SIN HAS LASTING CONSEQUENCES.

"I do too," agreed Mom. "But there's a lesson here. Foolish decisions often carry lasting consequences, and no amount of wishing can turn back the clock. Sometimes people make foolish decisions about whether or not to obey God. It's so important to ask Jesus to help you make right decisions."

HOW ABOUT YOU?

Do you ask God to help you make the right decision whenever you're tempted to be unkind, lie, or cheat? You can come to Christ for forgiveness after you've sinned, but you may never be able to undo the consequences. Ask God to help you obey Him in all things. He will help you do so.

TO MEMORIZE:

Don't be misled—you cannot mock the justice of God.
You will always harvest what you plant.
GALATIANS 6:7

BY SHERRY L. KUYT

December 27

A LITTLE SCRATCH

Read 1 Corinthians 5:6-8.

"The time is 6:21 p.m.," announced Tim as he looked at his new digital watch.

"Well, thanks for keeping us informed," said his sister, Maddie, as she answered the phone. "For you, Tim," she said.

After he hung up, Mom asked, "Did I hear you tell Shawn you can't play ball tonight? I thought you and your friends were going to the gym for a while."

"Yeah, well, Shawn is such a klutz," said Tim, looking at his watch. "The time is now—"

"Don't change the subject," said Dad. "You lied to Shawn, didn't you?"

"Oh, Dad, it was such a little thing," protested Tim. "I mean it's no big deal—just a little lie." But Mom and Dad explained to Tim that God didn't see it that way. Although he refused to admit they were right, he agreed to call Shawn back and invite him to join him at the gym. "No answer," he said a few minutes later. "Well, at least I tried." He put on his jacket.

LITTLE SINS MATTER.

When Tim returned home, he wasn't quite so happy. "What's the problem?" asked Dad.

"I fell," replied Tim, holding out his arm. Across the face of the watch, Dad saw a small scratch.

"Oh, that's too bad," sympathized Dad. "But at least it's just a little scratch."

"Yeah," said Tim, "but it goes right across the numbers."

"A little scratch messes up a new watch," Mom said, "and a little sin messes up one's testimony for the Lord."

Tim knew what she meant. "You're right," he admitted.

HOW ABOUT YOU?

Have you told a little lie? Been a little unkind? Do you think a little sin doesn't matter? It does. Confess even the "small" sins and ask the Lord to help you overcome them.

TO MEMORIZE:

The person who keeps all of the laws except one is as guilty as the person who has broken all of God's laws.

JAMES 2:10

BY HAZEL W. MARETT

December 28

WEAR THE LABEL

Read Matthew 7:15-20.

The youth pastor had just gotten married, and Josh was in charge of planning a party for him and his wife. Josh decided on a food shower. "Everybody bring a couple cans of food," he told the youth group, "but exchange the label on each can with a different label."

The group thought it would be a good joke to pull on their youth pastor and his wife. Josh laughed and said, "I'd like to be a little bird looking in when they try to fix a meal with the food from our cans!"

On the night of the party each one presented Pastor Loren and his wife with one or more cans of food. Some had labels, others had none. Amid much laughter, Pastor Loren thanked the kids for their kindness. "You've reminded me of something," he said after the group had settled down. "Each of us wears a label too. If we're born again, our label is Christian. But some Christians are afraid or ashamed to wear that label. People may believe one thing, but their actions show something else. They're not ready to stand up for what they really believe."

LET CHRIST BE SEEN IN YOU.

Josh thought about Pastor Loren's message. It seemed to describe him. He knew he was a Christian, but he wasn't sure that his actions always labeled him as one. In fact, he was afraid that sometimes he wore one label and sometimes another. No wonder the kids at school didn't know where he stood.

When Pastor Loren closed the evening's activities with prayer, Josh bowed his head and asked God to help him let everyone know exactly what he believed.

HOW ABOUT YOU?

Can your friends tell by your label—your words and actions—that you belong to Christ? Or are you a question mark to those who see you? Stand up for what you believe!

TO MEMORIZE:

Never be ashamed to tell others about our Lord.

2 TIMOTHY 1:8

BY RUTH I. JAY

December 29

THE POTTERY LESSON

Read Jeremiah 18:1-6.

Jasmine and several friends watched as her mother poured a liquid into a mold. The girls wanted to see how something so runny could become a hard vase. Then Mom brought out a piece that had been molded a few days ago.

"Is that one done?" asked one of the girls.

"Oh, no," replied Jasmine's mother. "Now that it's dry enough to handle, I will rub, clean, and scrape it. Then I'll put it into the fire."

The girls watched again as Jasmine's mother worked on the pottery. With a knife she scraped away the extra clay. With sandpaper she smoothed the pottery. Finally she rubbed it with a soft sponge.

"What a lot of work!" Jasmine said.

"I'm just beginning," Mom answered. "After it has been in the fire, I'll add a colorful glaze. Then I'll put it into the fire again. It's the same way that God works on us. He scrapes off bad habits, smoothing us out to become more like Him. Then He makes us beautiful and shiny by putting us through fire."

LET GOD MOLD YOU.

"But I don't want to be put through all that," remarked one girl.

"It's important to ask God to make us willing to let Him work on us," said Jasmine's mother. "He wants to take away bad habits, sinful thoughts, angry words, and stubborn attitudes so our lives will shine for Jesus!"

HOW ABOUT YOU?

Has God been scraping off your bad habits and sinful deeds? Has He disciplined you when you lie, cheat, or talk back? Has He taught you patience through illness or through not getting something you really want? Are you willing to be whatever God creates you to be? He wants to help you serve Him!

TO MEMORIZE:

When a potter makes jars out of clay, doesn't he have a right to use the same lump of clay to make one jar for decoration and another to throw garbage into?

ROMANS 9:21

BY RUTH I. JAY

Turn to Peace

For a Child is born to us . . . and he will be called: Wonderful Counselor, Mighty God, Everlasting Father, Prince of Peace.
ISAIAH 9:6

What if we acted like it was Christmas all year long? People just celebrated Christ's birth. Offices and schools closed for the holiday. People gathered with those they hold most dear. And all hearts and thoughts turned to peace.

Describe how peaceful your life was or wasn't during this year's Christmas season.

What can you do for yourself next year to ensure your own sense of peace at Christmas?

How can you help the people you live with foster a sense of peace?

What if we focused on making this kind of peace year round?

December 30

FIRST IN EVERYTHING

Read Colossians 1:16-19.

Keyshawn was upset! He had been waiting all week to watch his favorite TV show. Last time it had ended at a very exciting place with the words "To be continued." But now the words "Special Bulletin" had come on the screen. An announcer said, "All regular programming is preempted tonight by a message from our president on the economy."

Keyshawn whined. "I don't want to hear the president. I don't even know what economy is."

"I'm sorry," said Mom, "but the networks think this speech is important. Now let me listen." Keyshawn was quiet, but he wasn't happy.

At Sunday school Mr. Wilson had the kids read Colossians 1:16-19. When they got to verse 18, Chase asked Mr. Wilson what it means that Christ "is first in everything." As he often did, Mr. Wilson asked if anyone could help with the meaning of those words.

PUT JESUS FIRST.

Keyshawn raised his hand. "On TV this week they put the president on in place of my favorite show. Mom said it was because what he had to say was important. Does being 'first in everything' mean Jesus is more important than anyone else?"

"That's right, Keyshawn," said Mr. Wilson. "This verse means that Christ should have first place over everything else in our lives. He is even more important than the president!" Then Mr. Wilson said, "Let's tell God we want Him to have first place in our lives, shall we?"

HOW ABOUT YOU?

Does Christ have first place in your life, or is He crowded out by other things like hobbies, sports, TV, or friends? Let Him be more important to you than anything or anyone else. You shouldn't let anything keep you from making Jesus number one in your life!

TO MEMORIZE:

Christ is also the head of the church, which is his body. He is the beginning, supreme over all who rise from the dead. So he is first in everything.

COLOSSIANS 1:18

BY RAELENE E. PHILLIPS

December 31

RESOLUTIONS

Read Psalm 61:1-8.

Every year Jack cleaned out his desk on New Year's Eve. Usually he found lots of good stuff that he had forgotten about. His desktop was soon piled high with old school papers, the birthday card he had gotten from his sister, empty pop cans, and even a five-dollar bill. Jack was reading a list of New Year's resolutions when he was interrupted by a knock on his bedroom door. "May I come in?" It was Dad.

"Sure, if you don't mind a mess," answered Jack. "I was just reading the resolutions I made last year and didn't keep. Here's one that says, 'Keep desk clean!'"

Dad grinned as he sat down on the bed. "What else did you write?"

"'Read Bible every day,'" read Jack. "I tried to do that, Dad, but I usually got busy or forgot about it. Maybe I'll skip making New Year's resolutions. That way I won't break them."

"When your mom and I were first married, we made a list of goals," Dad said. "But it wasn't until we turned that goal list into a prayer list that we saw progress."

SUCCEED IN GOD'S STRENGTH.

"So you think I should pray about my New Year's resolutions?" Jack asked.

"You can either quit making resolutions or you can ask God to help you," said Dad.

"This year, I'll talk to the Lord about my goals," Jack said.

HOW ABOUT YOU?

Have you decided over and over again to read your Bible every day, or to tell someone about the Lord? Have you been determined to get your homework done every night and then forgotten about it by the middle of the semester? Commit your plans to God. Ask Him for the courage and strength to succeed.

TO MEMORIZE:

Commit your actions to the LORD, and your plans will succeed.

PROVERBS 16:3

BY DEANA ROGERS

ANSWERS

JUST YOU WAIT

JANUARY 15

GOD HAS PREPARED

JANUARY 29

NEW PLACES

MARCH 18

STAND YOUR GROUND

MARCH 25

C R H F K F E O R D M L C M E
D H V R Y F N L A X L I D M R
I H E A Q V M K M L Z T P B S
I E Q A D H M T G B Q T O R G
R I W O T D G H L U Z E L D R
V H A H J I I F C L S R L M A
R A T B H V N C N L U I U P F
E O N Y U K Z G T Y P N T G F
J G X D D S T Y Y I F G I V I
N F D Q A X E X E N O X O J T
R P J P H L B T O G G N N A I
I A G Y D S I P Q V L Y I N G
Y Z H J T M N S T E A L I N G
A A X K S C G Q M B B X Z X R
X Y Q R T Z J G K C M Y E Y D

YOU ARE CALLED

MAY 13

SPREAD THE LIGHT

MAY 20

Y K B A G K J V H D F M G L T
E Y V B B X C O N G O I S Q R
E Y D N X T Y X Z R E C X C G
V P C J U S K Y C K I R T O K
D Y H Q Q X G H A V V O I R S
C K I W A R G E N T I N A T G
Y P L N I Q K E O M A E K D R
O X E A B S W D S F N S S L U
W E X S O U T H A F R I C A S
E J R R D U E C M Q P A B A S
I H I E P Z X I O I R W R Q I
P W P C I T B U A W N I A Z A
G T Y L S X C H O T S D Z K C
C I E G L P Z T D Y N N I E M
J B S J E A Z B Q K C Z L A T

STICK CLOSE

JULY 14

BETTER THAN ONE

JULY 21

```
F C O M R A D E X S A H R C K
L H S G S C O M P A D R E C N
P U K O X L H H D I H R U K V
C M F I V N U N T V D R K F A
H W M G H R E X H Y J T J C W
R F K T Y I Z D S P X N M B J
X F P J R G G M Y A A C U A J
T R F F A R A M I G O L S B Q
S B U D D Y U R L I N S K N R
M D M M G K J P V E X L E F F
C E T U C O N F I D A N T Z H
L E G V T M Y D W R R P E E Z
K P G C A J E J X S Z C E W G
B S B T C M Z D H T K X R Z P
E P O C C R O N Y O B Q K C R
```

PRAISE THE LORD

SEPTEMBER 16

SET A REMINDER

SEPTEMBER 23

```
T Z U S R E J L F P D G B Z P
T A T P Q O X C K C P H U T Q
S B E S F F T E C P H A H P P
T N F J F H X L A E R I P O D
P F Z J G O Q E S J X L L X S
T L Y E N N O B L E J T D P B
D R Q T E O P R M C X Y O Q E
B I F E D R V A A J G Z H L V
B R G Q L X W T D M Y K M Q Y
X X Y N F E P E Z T K D A M D
Z K M H I K G D Y S Z T G X Z
A R J I D F U P D F D N N I K
G L O R I F Y M J U R Z I U N
Y R J G E L E V A T E O F T H
L P Q E T U Q L G I J I Y T K
```

HE IS FAITHFUL

NOVEMBER 11

THINGS NOT SEEN

NOVEMBER 18

```
E I F O J A E V I D E N C E A
T U J X T C D K A D D B Z G T
H D J M O O O H Q Z O V W G T
N Y Q N T N C G M U R H I J E
Q E Y T E F U H S S I Z T Y S
X V N E S I M C Z O W A N C T
K A S S T R E P S W H E E R A
R L L T I M N T A L D S S Z T
W I S A M A T Z S O B V S W I
V D A M O T A D R H I I H V O
B A O E N I T E C V B Y N F N
X T Y N Y O I D J M S Q H R V
G I E T M N O W A P F P E C D
N O G U T G N W D B F A F U T
R N D O M W L M Y O L Z T Y Q
```